W9-BFH-776

You Are Your Father's Daughter

The Nurture Every Daughter Needs
—The Longing When It's Lost

Dr. Earl R. Henslin

Spirit of Hope Publishing
Irvine, California

You Are Your Father's Daughter
The Nurture Every, Daughter Needs
—The Longing When It's Lost

Copyright © 1994, 2000 by Dr. Earl R. Henslin
Published by *Spirit of Hope Publishing*

International Standard Book Number 1-929753-01-2

Written by Earl R. Henslin, Psy.D.
Edited by Chelese Guthrie Palmer
Cover & Book Designed by Charles Schnur
Cover Photo by Denise Fountain

Printed in the United States of America

ALL RIGHTS RESERVED
No part of this publication may be reproduced, stored in a retrieval system, or transmit-
ted in any form or by any means—electronic, mechanical, photocopying, recording, or
otherwise—without prior written permission, except for brief quotations in critical
reviews or articles.

Scripture quotations marked NIV are taken from the HOLY BIBLE, NEW INTERNA-
TIONAL VERSION®, NIV®. Copyright © 1973, 1978, 1984 by International Bible
Society. Used by permission of Zondervan Publishing House. All rights reserved.

The Twelve Steps are reprinted with permission of Alcoholics Anonymous World
Services, Inc. Permission to reprint and adapt the Twelve Steps does not mean that AA
has reviewed or approved the contents of this publication, nor that AA agrees with the
views expressed herein. AA is a program of recovery for alcoholism only—use of the
Twelve Steps in connection with programs which are patterned after AA, but which
address other problems, does not imply otherwise.

The names of persons and certain details of case histories described in this book have
been changed to protect the author's clients. In certain cases, composite case histories
have been constructed from actual cases.

NOTE: This book is designed to provide information on the subject matter covered. It is
provided with the understanding that the publisher and author are not engaged in
rendering individualized professional services. These processes and questions are
intended for group or individual study, and are not designed to be a substitute for one-to-
one professional therapy when such help is necessary.

For information:
Spirit of Hope Publishing
PO Box 53642
Irvine, CA 92619-3642
Phone (949) 733-1486 ❦ Fax (949) 733-9812

DEDICATION

For Rachel, Amy, and Jill

Rachel, I respect and admire the young woman you are. I appreciate your honesty and directness with me. I admire the passion you have for life, and your adventuresome spirit. God has already used you so deeply in so many lives. May your life continue to be such a blessing and example of his love, power, and strength. Your sensitivity and creativity is far beyond what mine was at your age.

Amy, you are a precious and godly young woman. I do so admire your perceptiveness and ability to ask such penetrating questions. Such a talented young woman you are! You are so gifted academically, musically, and athletically. May you always guard carefully the sensitive and perceptive spirit that you have so tuned into the Lord. I so admire and respect your faith.

Jill, what a delight you are! Such a happy and joyful spirit. Your very being seems to radiate the life and passion of the heart of Christ. You are so bright and perceptive. You notice everything and take such delight in every bit of God's creation. I am so proud of you!

To each of you, I am sorry for the times I have failed you, for the times when I have not been there for you. May our heavenly Father guard, keep, and bless you. He has given each of you many gifts and abilities. May he provide you with a strong community of women with whom you can grow and flourish.

I love you,
Dad

PUBLISHER'S PREFACE
for the Revised Edition

The revised edition of *Your Are Your Father's Daughter* has a number of significant improvements. The entire text of the book was revised to improve the readability of the material. The author, Dr. Earl R. Henslin, wanted the book to be accessible to more readers.

At the end of each chapter, Dr. Henslin has added a section titled *A Closer Look*. It is an opportunity for readers to focus on the key ideas and principles developed in the chapter. At the chapter's end there is also an opportunity for *Personal Reflection.* Dr. Henslin has provided questions that will help readers apply the material to their lives.

In the revised editon, Dr. Henslin has added an appendix to provide more information and resources for readers who would like to further pursue this topic or expand their journey toward recovery. The appendix begins with *A Word on Brain Chemistry.* This insightful addition helps readers understand that some problems exist because of inbalances within the neurobiology of a person's brain. Therapy and counseling may prove ineffective for some until they receive appropriate medical treatment.

Suggestions for Group Study and Support provides practical insight about organizing and conducting a small group meeting. Dr. Henslin answers some common questions and concerns about a small group. He has provided a *Suggested Meeting Format*, and added an important section titled *Guidelines for Sharing* to keep the meetings safe and nurturing.

An appendix for *Recovery Resources* is also included. It lists a number of organizations and groups that provide twelve-step recovery support for a number of problems. A *Suggested Reading List* offers written resources and recommended reading for specific needs.

May these pages provide you a pathway toward healing or improving your own father-daughter relationships. May you begin a new journey toward recovery, wholeness, and hope. And may you understand that your healing journey is never a solitary road. Your constant companion is also your Creator—the perfect Father.

The Publisher

CONTENTS

CHAPTER 1

❧❧

The Gift of a Father

The Nurture Every Daughter Needs

Long ago, a mighty empire stretched from the banks of Pakistan's Indus River to the seacoast nations of the Mediterranean. It dominated civilization from India to eastern Greece. It extended from the Aral and Caspian seas in the North to the deserts of North Africa. Unsurpassed in greatness and wealth, this massive empire was known as the Persian Empire, and Xerxes was its king.

To celebrate his reign, King Xerxes hosted a party unlike any other. For six months, noblemen, princes, military leaders, and officials of the empire joined in lavish celebration. The king displayed his power and wealth—the splendor of his kingdom. The festive capstone was a week-long banquet. The bar was open from morning till night, and every man drank his fill of wine.

On the seventh day, the king was full of wine, yet unsatisfied. He wanted something more—he wanted his queen. Vashti's beauty was renown, and the king wanted to show off. She was one more prize to display—one more sign of the king's glory.

Queen Vashti wanted no part of the king's exhibition. She had been around her drunken husband and his princes before. She would not parade before the drunken assembly—she would not submit to the humiliation. Drunks do not affirm or encourage beautiful women. They gawk, act out their lust, and think only of themselves. So Vashti refused the king's command.

What a furor her refusal raised! The king became enraged. He brought together the seven wisest and highest ranking noblemen of his empire. He asked for their counsel and advice. The men were disturbed that Queen Vashti had expressed her feelings. They feared that women throughout the empire would follow her example. "This very day the Persian and Median women of the nobility who have heard about the queen's conduct will respond to all the king's nobles in the same way," they cautioned. "There will be no end of disrespect and discord."

A public divorce was the advised course of action. They would make an example of Queen Vashti. All women of the empire would learn from her pain. "Let the king give her royal position to someone else who is better than she," they advised. "Then when the king's edict is proclaimed throughout all his vast realm, all the women will respect their husbands, from the least to the greatest."

The king followed through with the plan. His anger was quenched, his nobles were pleased, and Vashti was forever banished from his presence. The message went throughout the land. Women were warned to listen to their husbands—or else![1]

The old Persian Empire was not an easy or safe place for women to live. A woman's outward beauty was a source of pleasure for men. Her inner person was insignificant. This is the world into which Esther was born.

Death took Esther's parents. An orphan girl had little chance of survival. Like Ruth and Naomi, Esther was without property or protection. Ruth had grain fields to glean—Esther had but one advantage. She was beautiful—even in childhood. But her asset was also a threat. Harems abounded, and Esther's beauty put her at great risk. Still another fact threatened her survival: she was a Jew.

Esther did survive. God gave her a gift that made all the difference in her life. God gave her Mordecai, a cousin who took her into his family. The Bible says, "Mordecai had taken her as his own daughter when her father and mother died."[2]

What a powerful statement! What a word of hope! For Esther, it meant protection and provision—a family and a future. Mordecai reached out to Esther and brought her under his care and covering. He saved her from all the cruel possibilities that awaited her. He became her protector, her tutor, her mentor and guide. Mordecai became her dad.

Circumstances have changed. Women today are better off, but

they are also still at risk. On the surface, women appear to have self-sufficiency and legal protection—things unavailable to Esther. But below the surface and beyond the light of public scrutiny, women face the same injustice that Esther feared.

One out of four women alive today will experience sexual assault in her lifetime. Despite the sexual revolution, women are objectified more than ever. This is evident in advertising, television programming, and contemporary art and literature. Many male/female relationships still lack the respect, dignity, and maturity that women need. A formal complaint or a lawsuit for sexual harassment has become a woman's painful recourse. Women today still need a loving father just as Esther did.

The Need for a Father

It is normal to need a father. Male and female both need a dad. It's how God wired us. Every human being wants to feel the presence of a loving father. It's natural to long for this close connection. We hunger for a father's support, understanding, and comfort. God made us with this hunger for a father—it's important. We see evidence of this throughout scripture.

The story of Jacob and Esau is a classic struggle for a father's approval.[3] Jacob used extreme and deceptive measures to gain Isaac's blessing. Esau was a broken man when he realized that his father's blessing had been stolen from him.

This hunger for a father is seen in Joseph, one of Jacob's sons. Jealousy moved his brothers to cruel mistreatment. Joseph was ripped from home and family. Still, he prospered in his slavery and became second in authority to Egypt's pharaoh. He had all the power and wealth any person could want, still he longed to see his father's face.

Joseph's brothers came to Egypt for help. They did not recognize the man who controlled their fate. Joseph went to great lengths to break through his family's denial and ensure the safety he needed to reveal his identity. But when Joseph's oldest brother Judah spoke of their father's love for his sons, Joseph's pain spilled out. His loud cries broke beyond his walls and found their way to the Pharaoh's household!

The murder of Abel was due to hunger for the heavenly Father's acceptance.[5] Abel's offering of fatty meat from the firstborn of his flock received the favor and acceptance of his heavenly Father. Cain's offering of the fruit of the land did not. Cain responded to the rejection with rage not repentance. God told Cain how to bring an acceptable offering, but Cain could not rise above his anger and resentment. To quiet his pain, he killed his brother, who had been accepted by the Father.

The need to feel the presence and love of a father is foundational. A son needs the emotional and spiritual touch of his father's life. The men's movement taught us how to build and value an emotional bridge between father and son. And experience has taught us how the absence of this bridge leaves a man deeply wounded. A man, without this connection to his father, has an emptiness in his soul that longs to be filled. This hunger impacts every area of a man's life. Less is said about daughters, but women carry a similar wound.

The truth is that every human soul—both female and male— has space that needs to be filled through a deep relationship with a father. This is also true of the relationship with a mother, of course, but it is not our primary focus here.

The need for a father cannot be denied. Babies recognize the difference between their fathers and mothers by the time they are two or three months old. This is especially true of girls, who become attached to their fathers earlier than boys. Although both boys and girls attach to their mothers before they attach to their fathers, all babies need their fathers just as much as their mothers by the time they are eight months old.[6]

In the depths of her soul, a daughter truly needs her father. She needs him from infancy through adulthood. No matter what her age, she needs to feel that she is precious to him. She needs to feel his love, protection, encouragement, and sacrifice for her.

A daughter longs for her father's approval and affirmation. She seeks that recognition for every part of her life: her abilities, interests, accomplishments, and inner feelings. I have not met a woman, of any age, who does not want to hear her father say, "I'm proud of you." Nor have I met a woman who did not hunger for her father to put his arms around her and comfort her when she's hurting.

This fatherly connection and nurturing is not available to many daughters. Most fathers are not in touch with their own emotional and spiritual needs. For that reason, they find it hard to relate to the needs of others—especially a daughter. Many men have never learned how to give physical expression to their inner feelings of love and affection. Daughters are wounded when this important bond is weak or non-existent. Women carry that wound through all of life.

The hunger to heal that wound is strong. It often dictates the course of a daughter's life. It dictates how she views herself in the professional world and how she functions with men in the work-place. It dictates her intimate relationships with men, whether or not she will marry, the kind of man she will marry, and the course of her marriage. It dictates how she handles adversity in life, her response to failure, her pursuits of opportunities, her tendencies toward fear and worry, and her strength amid the physical and emotional threats of life in a dangerous culture.

An unhealed wound is a source of ever-present pain. And this father-wound is at the core of a woman's identity and personhood. Women seek a number of ways to ease the discomfort. It may be over-achievement, under-achievement, eating disorders, drug and alcohol abuse, sexual addictions, and codependency. Women also develop unrealistic expectations for the relationships that they have with men. A woman might fantasize about a knight in shining ar-mor with a red Mercedes. He would be all-loving, all-caring, and able to rescue her from all her problems. She may have such a deep longing to be touched or held by a man that she seeks physical closeness with male authority figures. All of these responses, and more, come out of the heart of a wounded little girl. They are acts of a daughter who still seeks the love, affirmation, and approval that she never received from her father.

The Gift of the Father

Esther was fortunate. Mordecai took her into his family and raised her as his own daughter. Mordecai was a wise man. The conflict and cruelty he endured, as a Jew in captivity, taught him the ways of their world. He was not naive about the ever-present danger in which they lived. He gave Esther physical protection and care, but he knew she needed more. He played a very special role in her life, a role that every father can and needs to play.

Let's see how the story of Mordecai, King Xerxes, and Esther progresses: After a while, King Xerxes missed Queen Vashti. His servants and close officials were concerned. In a miserable fit, the king might remember who had suggested Vashti's banishment! So they proposed a search for a suitable replacement.

"Let a search be made for beautiful young virgins for the king," they suggested. "Let the king appoint commissioners in every province of his realm to bring all these beautiful girls into the harem at the citadel of Susa . . . . Then let the girl who pleases the king be queen instead of Vashti."

The king liked the idea. Soon the proclamation was heard throughout empire. This was serious business! No one dared to stand in the way of King Xerxes. "When the king's order and edict had been proclaimed, many girls were brought to the citadel of Susa. . . . Esther also was taken to the king's palace and entrusted to Hegai, who had charge of the harem."

Esther was taken out of Mordecai's household, but she was not beyond his influence. "Esther had not revealed her nationality and family background, because Mordecai had forbidden her to do so. Every day he walked back and forth near the courtyard of the harem to find out how Esther was and what was happening to her."[7]

Mordecai had a father's heart! I admire his actions in response to Esther's new situation. She was taken into King Xerxes' harem, and Mordecai stationed himself in the courtyard. Mordecai's love for Esther moved him to teach her how to survive in a dangerous culture. He had built a spiritual and emotional bridge to Esther's heart. Because of that connection, Mordecai was able to warn and advise her about the danger of disclosing her identity. That bridge also enabled Esther to trust Mordecai's wisdom and heed his counsel.

Esther was, at times, out of Mordecai's sight and protection, but she was never out of his mind or prayers. Day after day, he walked back and forth in the courtyard. He watched and waited for news. He inquired about her welfare and her needs. Mordecai didn't wait for her to cry out in need. He was involved, informed, available, and ready to offer whatever he had to give.

Mordecai shows us what it means to be a father to a daughter. Few women today will ever experience the gift that Esther received from this man. Instead of fathers who impart wisdom, we see fathers who inflict wounds. Instead of fathers who create safety, we see fathers who cause suffering. Instead of fathers who admonish the foolish, we see fathers who abandon the family.

A father like Mordecai is a life-long gift to a daughter. That kind of support and affirmation prepares a daughter for the development of her full potential in all areas of life. Psychologist Charles Scull describes in today's terms what the gift of the father means to a daughter:

> A father is the first and often the longest connection a daughter will have with a man. The father-daughter bond (or lack of bond) shapes her future relationships . . . and influences how she moves out in the world.
>
> If he encourages her efforts to achieve, inspires her budding self-confidence, and teaches her competency skills, she will more easily develop an authentic self-esteem. If he discourages her efforts, undermines her self-confidence, shames her body, or discounts her personal opinions, her self-esteem will be marred, and it may take many years for her to learn to believe in herself.[8]

A father builds an emotional bridge to his daughter by learning how to be sensitive to his daughter's heart and being interested in what is important to her. Unfortunately, many fathers don't realize that it is important to pay attention to their daughters' interests. They may not know anything about their daughters' interests—much less take the effort to learn about them, encourage them, or participate in them.

Some well-meaning fathers try to correct or improve their daughters' efforts. They become critical rather than concerned. They fuel a competitive spirit rather than foster caring support. They note their daughters' accomplishments rather than recognize their daughters' affection. A daughter's interests come from deep within her heart. A father who does not recognize this will miss the opportunity to know and celebrate his daughter's life. And he will enlarge the wound she carries.

Fathers define masculinity for their daughters. A father's words, behaviors, and attitudes model manhood. A daughter learns something about all men from one man—her father. An abusive, manipulative, or controlling father may lead his daughter to feel that all men are supposed to be that way. A doting father, who spoils and pampers his daughter, may lead her to expect that "princess" treatment from all men. A needy or demanding father, who expects a daughter to take care of him, may cause her to see her role in life as a caretaker of men. In any of these cases, the daughter may grow up with unrealistic expectations of men and/or a distorted view of her place in the world of men. These misconceptions hinder her ability to survive and prosper.

The view of masculinity that a father projects influences how a daughter views God. The bridge a father builds to a daughter is physical, emotional, and spiritual. The health and strength of this connection plays a formative role in her spiritual life. In his relationship with his daughter, an earthly father mirrors the attributes of God the Father. He gives his daughter her first glimpse of her image and understanding of the heavenly Father.

Without an emotional bridge from her father, a daughter may not trust what he teaches her about life and about God. The wound and weakness in their relationship diminishes the power of his words. A daughter, who does not feel safe with her earthly father, may find it difficult to open her heart to her heavenly Father.

A strong emotional and spiritual bond between a father and his daughter provides a sense of security. A father's close and consistent connection serves to remind a daughter that God the Father is never far away. So the emotionally involved and present father offers an unfailing "God on earth" type of assurance during the best and worst of times. The sure presence of the earthly father and the heavenly Father establish a platform of security from which a daughter can venture into new territory and take risks.

The Difficulty of a Father

God's intended role for a father is a sobering responsibility. Most men are unprepared for the role. Some men grew up with the idea that "provider" was the primary job description of a father. A good father worked long and hard to meet his family's material needs. He went to the kids' games or performances when he could. He was firm, not fierce in his physical discipline. He made sure the kids went to church. Basics like these were considered to be the attributes of a good father.

Today life is different. The meaning of fatherhood has broadened. A father's job description is greater than we had assumed. Fathers are expected to meet not only financial needs, but emotional and spiritual needs as well. Fathers are confronted by expectations that seem foreign to them. Fathers are expected to be emotionally connected to their wives and children. They are expected to recover from their own dysfunctional family backgrounds. They are expected to deal with their own woundedness, codependency, and addictions. And they are expected to do this with the support of other men.

In addition to these expectations, men are told to exercise daily, improve their minds, participate in Bible studies, pray, read and memorize scripture, and more! The old job description for a father was much easier than the new one. The responsibilities, expectations, and necessities of a father's life can be overwhelming. Men cannot hope to accomplish this on their own. They need the empowerment of the Holy Spirit and the support of other men. It will not be easy; still the father's job description must change. Today's sons and daughters need all the spiritual and emotional tools a father can give. They need every advantage to survive and thrive in a complex and dangerous world.

A father's greatest hindrance is his own emotional and spiritual need. He cannot connect to his children unless he is connected. The emotional and spiritual bridge established by his father determines his ability to connect with his children. Masculine emotion is learned primarily through relationship with the father.

A man, who missed the opportunity to connect and learn from his father, is not without hope. Healing begins as a man faces the pain and grief of his lost or ineffective relationship with his father. This emotional and spiritual process helps a father respond to his children on that same level. That is why I am such a strong advocate of recovery and healing for the father-wound in men. A father, who is in touch with his own woundedness, is able to relate to his daughter with sensitivity, compassion, and truth.

I have two older children and two younger children. I dearly love each of my children, yet I have a deeper and more intimate connection with the two younger ones. The difference is in me and in the maturity of my own recovery time. My recovery experience has enabled me to respond to my children on emotional and spiritual levels unavailable to me before.

My youngest daughter used to explode with excitement when Dad came home. The jingle of my keys in the front door sent her flying down the hall. Like the Town Crier she would yell, "Daddy's home!" I hugged, and she snuggled. With her head buried into my chest, she would say, "Daddy! My Daddy!" She would hold me tight and wait for me to respond. And I could respond and meet the need in her heart to be loved by her father. I can experience and respond to that connection between us more each day. Every day that I face and deal with my own recovery needs is a day of growth and greater emotional and spiritual sensitivity.

Even with the help of personal recovery, it is no easy thing to father a daughter. The world of the daughter is different from the world of boys. Fathers know boys—it's familiar territory. Girls are a puzzle. Fathers prefer boys to girls by a four to one margin. Some men experience grief at the birth of a daughter rather than a son.[9] Other men feel confusion. Many men are at a loss to know what to do with a girl. The helplessness grows as the girl ages, and the move into adolescence is the most difficult time.

A father's confusion and lack of knowledge wounds his daughter. Families with sons are less likely to divorce than families with daughters.[10] Even with the family intact, a daughter may sense her father's discomfort or distance. The daughter assumes that she is in some way defective and unworthy of her father's attention and heart. Still, the daughter's need for an emotional and spiritual connection with her father is just as great as the son's need.

To make matters more difficult, men have few models of how a father can build an emotional bond with his daughter. This father-daughter connection is not common in our culture. My own father is now discovering the importance of this emotional connection. He admitted to my sister, "When you were growing up, I did not know how to relate to women." This is true of many men in my father's generation—and they were models for my generation.

As I became aware of these needs in myself, I shared my insights with my oldest daughter. I admitted to her that this father-daughter stuff was new to me. She said, "Well, Dad, you do a pretty good job anyway. You have your days, but you do a good job." That's the best a father can do. Take one step at a time—one day at a time, and discover the truth about his own emotional and spiritual life. And he can allow that discovery to open his heart to his daughter who needs him.

The Insufficiency of a Father

No father can be everything. The role God has ordained for fathers is not an easy one. It can be overwhelming. But God does not intend a father to be anything more than a father. A father can only meet the relational needs that a daughter has for a father. He cannot do what the mother needs to do. He cannot do what grandparents need to do. He cannot do what aunts and uncles need to do. He cannot do what the spiritual and professional mentors in his daughter's life need to do. He cannot do everything. No individual man or woman can meet every need a daughter has as she grows from infancy through adulthood.

For example, a father teaches his daughter a little bit of what it means to be feminine. But it is the mother who plays the vital role in the development of a daughter's feminine identity. A daughter also needs female and male mentors on her journey through adult life. These mentors offer the daughter strength and perspective that she could not gain from her father or her mother alone. A daughter always needs strong, supportive relationships with other women— friends to help her carry life's burdens.

The father has a unique role among all the other relationships in a daughter's life. He cannot be everything, but he can be a constant. He can be there no matter what turns his daughter's life takes. He can be available to listen to her heart and take an interest in her world. He can be alongside her as she discovers how to function in the world. He can acknowledge her unique blend of needs, interests, and abilities. He can keep his eyes open and prepare her to face potential pitfalls in her life and relationships. And he can be there to offer support and assurance when she reaches out to him.

This focus on the father's role does not minimize the role of the mother. A daughter needs a mother with spiritual strength, emotional connection, and active interest in the needs of her daughter's heart. A daughter is most blessed if she has a mother and a father who love the Lord, love each other, and are committed to a spiritual journey of healing here on earth. Both mother and father have a vital contribution to make to a daughter's life. It is especially important for fathers to realize that they can be a gift to their daughters in the same way that Mordecai was a gift to Esther.

⊚ A Closer Look

In my writing I use a number of terms that may be unfamiliar to some readers. I also put my own spin on some common terms. In this revision edition, I have added a section titled *A Closer Look* at the end of each chapter. It is not a glossary, but an aid to help readers understand and focus on key principles developed in the book. *A Closer Look* contains terms, concepts, and ideas that I do not want anyone to miss.

The strength of my personal experience comes from three important influences in my life. Like a strong rope with intertwined cords, three significant elements combine in my life. The first of those three cords is my personal, Christian faith and my confidence in the Bible as God's standard for life. The second is my professional education and clinical experience as a counselor. The third cord is my own personal recovery journey with the Twelve Steps which includes the support I have found within the recovery community. The combination of these influences affects my use of language and my understanding of the terms chosen for *A Closer Look*. But more importantly, these three influences enrich my life and increase my ability to help others.

Abuse—A simple understanding of abuse is the violation of a boundary. A controlling or manipulative parent or spouse causes abuse. Rage, volume, and physical intimidation may cause abuse. Disrespectful and demeaning language is abusive. Inappropriate touching or sexual contact with a child is abuse. Inappropriate emotional dependence upon a child is abusive. Unrealistic expectations placed upon a child can cause abuse. And of course, neglect of a child's needs is abusive.

Codependency—Care-taking, people pleasing, and unhealthy servitude or loyalty can be codependent behaviors. Codependency is an addiction to others, and it can take many forms. Some codependents help and "do" for others so that they can feel good about themselves. Their sense of self-worth comes from the value that others place upon them. They might work long hours and sacrifice themselves all for recognition or praise from the boss or the "biggies". Others enmesh themselves in the lives of others through controlling, fixing, or enabling. They mistake dependence and neediness for love and commitment. Codependents live their lives through the experience of others. But it takes it toll. Codependents are often resentful, angry, tired, and worn. They are the martyrs. Their thankless efforts never scratch their deepest itch—all the concern for others leaves them bankrupt, empty, and ill.

Recovery—Recovery is the journey toward healing that begins when we recognize that our lives are broken and beyond our ability to mend. The form that recovery takes will vary according to the individual—twelve steps, psycho-therapy, spiritual experience, mind and body, etc. In some cases, recovery begins in our late thirties and forties because unconscious physical and psychological processes urge us to seek health and a greater well-being. Our well-practiced coping strategies don't work as they once did. The pain of destructive relationships or lifestyle patterns intensifies and cries out for resolution. The physical impact of internal pain and tension begins to appear through illness or disease. Psychological and spiritual decay leads to physical breakdown. When the physical signs appear, we have a choice to make. We can continue in our denial and ignore the signs, or we can face the difficulties head on. In some cases, we are forced to make that choice—physical conditions threaten our life. The move toward spiritual and emotional healing, moves us toward physical healing as well. And the journey toward healing brings out our core self. The recovery process uncovers the true person inside. It releases gifts and unique potential.

*The Father-daughter Connection (*or *"Bridge"* or *"Bond")*—An emotional and spiritual connection between a father and his daughter is a bond of feelings, values, and truth. A connected father is emotionally available to his daughter—in touch with his feelings, and open and responsive to hers. A connected father can express the affection he feels and the value he places on his daughter. A connected father is in touch with reality about himself and his daughter. This connection also offers an unfailing "God on earth" type of spiritual assurance and security during the best and worst of times. The sure connection and presence of the earthly father teaches the sure presence and availability of the heavenly Father. It establishes a platform of security from which a daughter can venture into new territory and take risks.

The Father-daughter Wound—Daughters are wounded when the important bond between father and daughter is weak or non-existent. A father's absence, abandonment, or abuse are often to blame. Women carry that wound through all of life.

◆◆◆ *Personal Reflection*

1. In what ways is your father-daughter relationship different from the one that Mordecai and Esther shared?
●◇

2. What specific elements of Mordecai and Esther's father-daughter relationship would you most desire for yourself?
●◇

3. Through your life, when or where have you felt the deepest need for a father?
●◇

4. How have you sought to meet the needs that have not been met through your relationship with your father?
●◇

5. Take a few moments to honestly evaluate your relationship with your father. What comes to mind? Specifically thank God for the times your father has been a gift to you. If you have never known your father, thank God that he is the perfect Father.
●◇

NOTES:

CHAPTER 2

❧❧❧

Wounded by the Father

The Pain of Imperfection

The following are words from wounded hearts:

"I know my father loved me. He worked hard and provided everything for us. I am so thankful for that. Yet he could never say he loved me. He could never just put his arm around me and let me know that I was important to him. He would come home from work anxious and irritable, and I knew that I needed to stay far away from him. When he relaxed after a couple of drinks, things were calmer, but it was often the calm before the storm. I never told my dad a thing about me. He never asked."

❧

"My father was a successful, powerful businessman who was respected by everyone at church. My tears, fears, and worries were insignificant to him. And my mom was just overwhelmed by his strength. When I got pregnant at age seventeen, I was nothing but an embarrassment to him. He said I needed to get married and be a mother. He said he would never pay a penny to send me to college. I felt so much pain from the pregnancy that I gave up and married even though I knew it was the wrong thing to do. So I've been a single parent for years, and I don't want anything to do with men. To this day my father will not talk to me. I try real hard, but I will never please him. I can't please God either. Deep inside, I'm afraid that God doesn't really love me."

❧

"My father was an alcoholic and molested me when I was six years old. He managed to hide all of his secret sins from his coworkers and from the church. I had sex with the first boy I dated. Even today I cannot say, 'NO!' I am married, but I have no boundaries with men. I am sexually addicted and have had one affair after another. How can God love someone like me?"

&

"My dad was a pastor. A child in a minister's family quickly learns that there is a different set of rules for the pastor's kids. I was always well behaved, obedient, and nice, but how I hated being an example to others. I could never be real. I couldn't worry. I couldn't be afraid. I couldn't let anybody know how horribly insecure I felt. When a Sunday school teacher touched me where he shouldn't, I felt so bad. I felt like I had failed my father. But he didn't even notice that I wasn't the same person anymore. He had time for others, but he didn't have time for me. Now my relationship with my husband is filled with conflict, and I know why. I expected him to take the place of my father, which is more than any husband can give."[1]

These words pour from the hearts of daughters—wounded daughters. They demonstrate the importance of an emotionally connected relationship between father and daughter. The pain these women carry in their hearts is obvious. The hunger they feel for a father is at the core of their being.

Many women have been denied an emotional and spiritual connection in their relationship with their fathers. The wounds that result are similar to those described above. And women bear the burden of these wounds for a lifetime. I believe it is time to recognize the impact of the father-daughter relationship. It is time to take whatever steps are necessary to heal the wounds of that imperfect relationship.

The women I help in psychotherapy are also my teachers. Their scars, brokenness, and heartache have taught me to understand the magnitude of this problem. The impact of the father-daughter wound affects a woman's personal development and every aspect of her life. Psychology has focused on the mother's role in a daughter's psychological and spiritual development. The father's role has been discounted and diminished. But my work has shown that the father plays a significant role in his daughter's development. A woman's view of herself is often dictated by men. Men influence how she views her potential, capabilities, identity, and spirituality. And her father is the most powerful of those male influences.

Every area of an adult woman's life is affected by the relationship she had, and continues to have, with her father. Past wounds can cause pain in the present. Many women do not understand what they missed or what they suffered. Many fathers do not understand what they neglected or the harm they inflicted.

Nothing—no amount of money or gifts—can replace the emotional and spiritual connection a father must have with his daughter. God can help us heal, forgive, and grow beyond past mistakes. Still, a woman has a place in her heart for her father. It may be wounded, wanting, or whole, but it is real, and it impacts her life today.

My own eyes and heart were opened by *You Are Your Father's Daughter.* I was instructed, inspired, and encouraged. It's rare to find a counselor who strives to search God's Word in such a compassionate way. Dr. Hendlin finds our Lord's hope for daughters who take healing steps in the relationship with their fathers. Fathers discover new ways to build deep bonds with adult daughters, and they learn the vital importance of their role with daughters still little girls and teenagers.

You Are Your Father's Daughter will benefit every daughter and father who reads it. Both will find the tools to connect or reconnect lines of communication and love. Sometimes reconnection is impossible, but wounds heal and hearts mend. Our Father in heaven is full of love and unlimited in healing grace.

Charles Stanley

Foreword by
Dr. Charles Stanley

Every area of an adult woman's life is affected by the relationship she had, and continues to have, with her father. Past wounds can cause pain in the present. Many women do not understand what they missed or what they suffered. Many fathers do not understand what they neglected or the harm they inflicted.

Nothing—no amount of money or gifts—can replace the emotional and spiritual connection a father must have with his daughter. God can help us heal, forgive, and grow beyond past mistakes. Still, a woman has a place in her heart for her father. It may be wounded, wanting, or whole, but it is real, and it impacts her life today.

My own eyes and heart were opened by *You are Your Father's Daughter*. I was instructed, inspired, and encouraged. It's rare to find a counselor who strives to search God's Word in such a compassionate way. Dr. Henslin finds our Lord's hope for daughters who take healing steps in the relationship with their fathers. Fathers discover new ways to build deep bonds with adult daughters, and they learn the vital importance of their role with daughters still little girls and teenagers.

You Are Your Father's Daughter will benefit every daughter and father who reads it. Both will find the tools to connect or reconnect lines of communication and love. Sometimes reconnection is impossible, but wounds heal and hearts mend. Our Father in heaven is full of love and unlimited in healing grace.

Charles Stanley

Loss of the Father

A highly functional family has a father who willingly seeks out the daughter and builds an emotional and spiritual bridge to her. Most families function far below that level. The typical father hasn't experienced his own emotional life well enough to recognize or respond to his daughter's emotional needs. So, no bridge is built to his daughter. As a result, the daughter suffers a loss in the depth of her soul. It is a persistent ache that is beyond her ability to cure— a profound sadness deeper than she can reach.

How is the father-daughter connection lost? What prevents the construction of the emotional bridge between father and daughter? A number of factors put this connection at risk. Consider the following examples:

Work—Employment outside the home takes a father away. The hours they spend at home and awake are few. And a father who is physically present may not be emotionally or spiritually present. It is the emotional and spiritual presence and connection with his daughter that touches the need of her heart.

Divorce—The break-up of a marriage means that a father may only see his daughter every other weekend. In some cases he may drop out of her life completely. Abandonment is a bitter wound to a daughter.

Death—A fatal illness or accidental death may steal a father from a daughter. The younger the daughter, the wider the wound left in her heart. The physical protection and the security she needed to feel from her father are lost. The deeper, masculine voice of nurture is silenced. A mother can comfort, but she cannot fill the emptiness a father leaves in a daughter's heart.

Addictions—An addicted father is connected to his drug of choice, not his daughter. His addiction displace relationships. No matter what the addiction—food, work, sex, drugs, or alcohol—it is the addiction, not the daughter, that commands the attention of the father's heart. The daughter of an addicted man has been emotionally and spiritually abandoned.

Pain—Physical and emotional pain can isolate a father. Chronic illness, unresolved issues, personal struggles, and emotional wounds can absorb the energy a man would otherwise give to his daughter. He may come across as cold, defensive, or harsh. He is unable to recognize his daughter's pain because he works so hard to avoid his own discomfort.

Control—Manipulation, domination, and control rob any free exchange in a father-daughter connection. A controlling father may shatter the bridge to his daughter's heart in a variety of ways. His need to control who she is blinds him to her true identity. His need to control her thinking forces her to withdraw. His need to control her behavior limits her opportunities for learning. His need to control her faith hinders her personal search for God. Through control (rather than guidance and correction), a father may violate or deny a daughter's intellect, spirituality, integrity, physical ability, or sexuality. He may also limit her ability to own her own feelings as valid emotions.

Abuse—Any abuse (physical, emotional, or sexual violation) by a father causes immeasurable loss and suffering to a daughter. An abusive father cannot build a bridge to his daughter's heart. He has destroyed the very foundation on which the bridge is built. He has enlarged her emptiness and the distance that separates them. He has unleashed a terror that resists all comfort for a very long time.

The daughter may not be able to identify the nature or source of her loss. She may feel a vague sense that something is wrong with her or that she lacks something. She's not pretty enough, athletic enough, thin enough, smart enough, sexy enough, or successful enough. So she may strive for these things, or seek the opposite. All to gain her father's attention. All in the hope that she might gain acceptance, approval, and—ultimately—his emotional involvement.

The daughter's effort is futile—certain to fail. A daughter is powerless to make an emotional connection with her father. To be legitimate and satisfying, the father must initiate that connection. Without the father's effort to connect, the daughter cannot heal or fill the emptiness in her heart. Still, the daughter will try. Mindless mistakes, painful patterns, and toxic entanglements will be repeated over and over. No effort, no self-improvement can quench the longing in her heart and meet the need she can't define.

A woman will search for a father in many other places. She may seek to fill that void through her work, her marriage, or her relationships with authority figures. She may fall into a variety of addictions, or even become lost in church activities. But no one and no thing can fill the void left by her birth father. All her attempts to do so will only lead to greater pain and increase the toxic impact of her mistaken behaviors.

Impact of the Father-wound:
Appearance—Her Perception

At an early age, a daughter needs to be acknowledged and appreciated by her father. My youngest daughter needed me to acknowledge her physical appearance at the age of two. While she would dress or have her hair combed, her eyes reached out for my recognition. I would say, "Oh, my! How beautiful you look today!" or "What a lovely dress!" She would beam and glow and bask in her father's praise. Once, her only adornment—other than the diaper— was one of Mom's necklaces. She paraded before me and waited for my response. Of course, I was awe-struck, and I told her so. But the necklace and pageantry weren't my focus. I was captured by the sparkle in her eyes and the gift of her love for me.

A daughter needs this kind of affirmation from her father. An involved father, who expresses his love and emotion, affirms his daughter's personal identity and nurtures her self-confidence. He gives her an important sense of pride and confidence and enables her to stand strong in a world that threatens her uniqueness. A daughter needs this kind of involvement from her father to handle the pressures of our "Barbie Doll Culture". Our society has an obsession with large bustlines and perfectly toned, thin bodies. It places no value on the heart and soul of a person—appearance and image are everything. So it takes a secure young woman to stand up to the media image of the idealized woman.

Many fathers fail to realize the affirmation their daughters need. Daughters watch their fathers. They look for affirmations for their physical appearance, and they watch their father's attitudes toward women. A little girl notices what kind of woman draws her father's eyes. If the father turns his head to look after attractive women, his daughter may develop an extreme body obsession. Her view of herself and her required appearance may become distorted. She may strive to be thin, glamorous, or sexy. It's not for other men to notice—it's for her father. That's the recognition she needs.

A daughter takes note of a lustful or sexually addicted father. His visual fantasies or verbal remarks do not escape her eyes and ears—they sink deep in her heart. She knows that she is becoming a woman. And she knows that her father treats women as objects or playthings. She may work doubly hard to please men by her appearance, or she may protect herself from men by being unattractive.

Far too many daughters have looked for a tool in the garage or for a pencil in their father's desk, and discovered his stash of pornography instead. The daughter concludes that this is the kind of woman her father desires. She assumes that this is what men want her to be. This wound in the daughter's soul may never be acknowledged, but it will impact her life on a daily basis. A lifetime struggle with her appearance and weight may result. Feelings of inadequacy and efforts to fit the image may torment her. And the impressions and attitudes that a daughter assumes will impact her relationship with all men—including the man she marries. Her ability to instill a sense of personal value and a healthy body image to her own daughter will be affected. No woman can communicate a healthy body image to her daughter without an acceptance of her own body—as it is.

Impact of the Father-wound:
Physical Strength—Her Perception

The father has a key role in affirmation of his daughter's physical strength. Daughters hunger for this recognition. They like to wrestle on the floor with their fathers—just as sons do. They like to hike, swim, climb trees, and ride bikes. And they delight in doing these activities with their fathers.

The wise father affirms and encourages his daughter's physical strength and ability as she grows up. He has many opportunities to recognize and praise her strength: her first steps, the tree or jungle gym, the bike, the ball-toss, and other backyard adventures. The opportunities grow as the daughter matures. Water sports, hikes, winter activities, tennis, trail bikes, and more.

My daughter Rachel and I have enjoyed biking together. When she was nine years old, we completed a twenty-five-mile ride on a tandem. At the end, she put her arm around me and declared, "We really did that, Daddy! All twenty-five miles!" A commemorative T-shirt for completion was her reward. She wore it with pride. And she relished the opportunity to tell her friends and neighbors—including adults—that she had completed a twenty-five-mile ride. They were amazed that a nine-year-old girl had ridden that far.

Rachel grew in confidence because of her adventure with me. She received the important message that she is physically capable and strong. My presence and participation in her discovery affirmed the reality of her accomplishment. Just as a piano's sounding board gives voices to the strings, a father's recognition gives validation to a daughter's physical achievements.

Impact of the Father-wound: Physical Affection—Her Need

A daughter needs to experience appropriate physical closeness with her father. A father's playful antics and good-natured horseplay with his daughter cause her to feel special to him. When he holds and comforts her after an injury or accident, she feels safe and loved. When he gives his teenage daughter a congratulatory pat on the shoulder, she feels confident and encouraged. Expressions of physical closeness strengthen a daughter's confidence, self-assurance, and identity.

The *safe* man in a daughter's life should be her father. From him, she learns about appropriate physical boundaries in her relationships with men. But many fathers fail to provide the safety or the proper standard. A father, for example, may violate his daughter's physical and sexual boundaries. This sends a confused and distorted message to the daughter. She is left with feelings of shame that devastate her self-confidence.

On the other hand, there are fathers who physically withdraw from their daughters. They may refuse an appropriate touch or hug. They are overly fearful of violating her physical boundary. This, too, wounds a daughter. Either extreme—physical abuse or the absence of all physical touch—leaves the daughter with no experience of physical closeness with men. She has no standard by which to discern appropriate physical touch. This wound in the relationship with the father impacts the daughter's sexuality. She is confused and tends toward extremes being over-sexualized or under-sexualized.

Some women, who have not received appropriate physical affection and comfort from their fathers, have a deep skin-hunger. It is an aching desire to be held or comforted by a man. This skin-hunger is powerful and very confusing. It often plays a role in sex-love addiction as well as in sexual dysfunction. Women with this craving for physical touch long for the comfort of closeness to another warm body. The need to be held feels essential to their survival. Their desire for physical comfort is so strong that they become involved in relationships with men just to be held. They are surprised when the relationship becomes sexual. And these women are powerless to stop the man's progression from physical closeness to sex. Or, they may feel detached and uninvolved—as if they have no choice about what happens to them sexually.

Impact of the Father-wound:
Role in Life—Her Perception

The way in which a father relates to his daughter affects how she views her role in life—her fit in the world around her. The dynamics of the father-daughter relationship models and tests the daughter's ability to relate to men. So the father-daughter relationship has a long-term impact on every aspect of her life. In the best cases, the dynamics of the relationship serve the daughter well. In other cases, it may have devastating results.

Psychologists have identified seven distinct types of father-daughter relationships. Note that the way in which a father relates to his daughter results from his own woundedness and pain.[2]

Princess Daughter—Some fathers pamper their daughters. They provide every material desire their daughters have. This may result from the father's own insecurity and fear. The need to feel loved may compel him to buy his daughter's love. Or, the material expressions may substitute for the emotional and spiritual connection that is difficult for him to give. Material things are the only way he knows how to give. Other fathers offer material things to atone for what they cannot give because of addictions or misplaced priorities. Work, substance abuse, social relationships, or whatever take the fathers away. The material offerings make up for what they cannot give in person.

A daughter with this kind of father grows up with a *princess mentality*. She goes through life expecting all men to pamper her. In personal relationships, she measures her importance according to the gifts she is given. The more expensive the gift, the more loved she feels. In the workplace, she often considers herself better than others. She expects special treatment and privileges beyond those that are given to her coworkers. This affects her spirituality. If all goes well, God is good and loves her. During difficult times, she doubts God's goodness, love, or even his existence. And the princess mentality follows her into any marriage.

Many fathers feel relieved when a princess daughter marries and moves out of the home. The man who marries a princess runs into incredible expectations. He has no clue about what's in store for him. All he sees is a good-looking woman, well dressed with a fancy car. He doesn't realize that his wife will feel betrayed and unloved if he doesn't provide the gifts and material expressions.

Angry Daughter—A father, who has been wounded by women, will reflect that hurt in his relationship with his daughter. He may demand affection and care from her in a way that violates her role as his daughter. This is a type of emotional incest. Or, the father may control and overpower his daughter to cover up his pain.

This father-daughter dynamic produces an angry woman. The daughter feels frustrated or violated by her father's attempts to express or mask his pain at her expense. Anger is her defense. It is the wall she puts up between herself and others whenever she feels threatened or unsafe. She may have difficulty discerning between friend and foe. So closeness or vulnerability frighten her. Anger defines and motives this woman. It is her way to prove competence and worth.

The father-daughter wound that produces an angry woman also distorts her relationship with the heavenly Father. It is evident in her strong rejection of God the Father. It is hard for her to see God as loving and compassionate. He is angry and judgmental to her.

In the workplace, her anger is an ever-ready weapon. She is poised to attack any man who threatens her or gets too close. And the man who marries an angry woman lives in a minefield. Any wrong step may lead to an angry outburst of resentment or pent-up rage. All the husband can do is duck. Only the crazy man is foolish enough to rage back. But if that happens, the scene is set for a mutually destructive relationship.

Amazon Daughter—The father, who makes promises and fails to keep them, also creates an angry daughter. The broken promises may have resulted in lost activities for the daughter or the father's absence at important events in her life. The break may have been in the inherent commitments of the father-daughter relationship such as the promise of physical, sexual, and emotional safety. This break results in severe anger. And if it has occurred through abuse or incest, it will ignite rage. Explosive rage, at the slightest provocation, is one sign of an abusive relationship in the past.

Abuse—particularly sexual abuse—in the father-daughter relationship, may move an angry daughter to go a step further. She becomes what can be called an *amazon woman*. This woman is angry, but she has added skill to her anger. She is not content to just get mad. She acts upon her anger and finds ways to destroy her opponent at his own game. This woman is a survivor. Extreme competition is her game—*win at any cost* is her motto.

The amazon daughter can be cold, ruthless, and calculating. These skills can be necessary for survival, but she uses them to a destructive extreme. She may be a successful entrepreneur, but she doesn't know how to be interdependent. She has encased and hardened herself and has no need for men. The thought of being dependent upon anyone is frightening. In a marriage, she often makes more money than her husband does. In the workplace, the amazon daughter meets every conflict with a drawn sword. Someone is usually cut—rarely is it her. She has the potential to succeed against all odds. Still, she cannot overcome the feelings of loneliness and isolation.

The M*A*S*H character Major Margaret Hoolihan fits this type of daughter. In one episode, she berates another nurse for crying at the death of a wounded soldier. Hoolihan has no tolerance for a nurse who displays emotion on the job. She wants the offending nurse transferred to another unit. The other nurses rally in support of the nurse who cried. The other nurses have a bond and an ability to share their feelings with one another—both joys and sorrows. Hoolihan is excluded from their camaraderie. Then Margaret overhears that the camp's stray dog was hit and killed. It was a dog she had befriended and fed. The news broke her heart, softened her armor, and opened a door for her to relate to the others. Margaret apologizes to the nurses, and they open their arms to her. She is accepted as a warrior with a compassionate heart.

Victim Daughter—Abuse in the father-daughter relationship can cause some women to internalize a message that they are insignificant and have no rights. They may not believe they have a right to own their feelings or bodies. They allow themselves to be dominated, controlled, and abused. They are powerless to set boundaries and protect themselves from abusive relationships. They relive their suffering over and over at the hands of abusive men.

In the workplace, victim daughters may over-achieve or under-achieve. Their behavior cannot compensate for what they feel inside—defective and inadequate. Powerful shame issues are at work beneath the surface. These women are at high risk for addiction or codependency. Their relationship with God is tentative and performance-oriented. God will not punish them if they do right. But God is not personal and near. He cannot fill their emptiness—he cannot ease their pain. We know, of course, that God can heal and help. But God's proper place in the victim daughter's heart has been displaced by fear and distrust.

Mother-Earth Daughter—A father, who is not available for either the daughter or the mother, may cause the daughter to become a kind of parental caretaker. Both the father and mother may project helplessness or neediness. The daughter is expected to heal their wounds and meet their needs. At an early age, the daughter exists to meet the needs of the parents. And they are unavailable to meet her needs. This is a type of emotional incest. The daughter has had no childhood. She internalizes the message that it is wrong for her to have needs. To feel needy is to feel bad.

The mother-earth daughter learns to be nice and kind. She is a caretaker and first-class codependent. She is the glue that holds everything together. Companies and churches love her. She sacrifices her life to do whatever impossible tasks she is given. She earns approval by being there for others who need her. But she believes that she is unworthy of love or care from others.

The mother-earth daughter carries tremendous pain inside. She has denied her own needs and sacrificed her dreams to juggle the needs of others. But no one knows her pain. She has lost touch with the root of her pain. If she were able to identify those deep needs, she would dismiss them. Her feelings are unimportant, her needs don't matter, and her suffering should remain unspoken. So she carries her pain alone.

Yearning Daughter—A father, who lacks confidence in his ability to relate to his daughter, may cause her to yearn for affection and love. He is unable to play with or show tenderness to girls. He doesn't know what it means to show love to a daughter. So the father feels insecure and keeps her at arm's length. He builds an emotional wall between himself and his daughter. She can't be allowed too close—she can't be allowed to see his insecurities.

The daughter of a distant father feels his coldness and distance, but she may not be aware of why it happens. It is an implied rejection by her father, and it settles deep in her soul. Like a snake in the grass, it defies capture or understanding. It is unfinished business that pulls at the soul. As she grows, she yearns for closeness with her father. But it is always beyond reach.

The yearning daughter may have poor boundaries with others—especially men. She is easily overwhelmed and tends to function at extremes. She may let others take advantage of her, or she may keep others at a distance where they can't hurt her. She may appear self-confident and poised, or insecure and fearful. Her strong yearning for affection and physical closeness may weaken her sexual boundaries. Or she may be sexually detached and cold to protect herself.

In marriage, she is a mystery to her husband. Her emotional disposition is a coin toss. She may indicate that it is safe to approach, but when he moves toward her, insecurity grips her and she slips away. Her husband is confused and is likely to respond in ways that will further wound her. It is a painful situation for both husband and wife.

In the workplace, the yearning daughter rides an emotional roller coaster. She may doubt the praise that is given to her, or she may accept it and then feel tremendous rejection at the slightest hint of negative feedback. The yearning daughter longs for security in all of her relationships.

She also hungers for a secure relationship with God. But she can't trust God's stability and faithfulness. It is difficult for her to reach out to God with any confidence. She lives on a roller coaster. Gross fears or great thrills propel her through the ups and downs of her daily experience. She has little or no control, and she doesn't believe that God does either.

Companion Daughter—Some men assume a Pygmalion-type role in fatherhood. Pygmalion was a character in Roman mythology. His hatred for women kept him from marriage but caused him to create a statue of the perfect woman. He fell in love with his own stone image of feminine beauty, but it wasn't real. So he prayed to Venus, and she gave the statue life.

To a father like this, the daughter becomes his way to create the perfect woman. She will prove to the world that he is a great person. His love, care, and support have a selfish end. His daughter must make him look good. He is not motivated by her best interests. So he may not be able to support or affirm his daughter in her pursuits that do not benefit his image. He may even withdraw his love and support if his daughter embarrasses or displeases him. This father's personal worth and value rises and falls with his daughter's performance.

This type of father devastates a daughter's self-esteem. She believes that she is nothing without her father's approval. She is a perfectionist and codependent. She must perform to the highest standards or face her utter worthlessness.

The companion daughter cannot say "no" to her father's needs, and she cannot grow up. The father needs her emotional sustenance, and he keeps her bound to himself. She will be unable to care for her own needs in life and unable to have an emotionally intimate relationship with her husband. She will be unavailable to all but her father. Her only hope is to be released by her father. He must release her into adult life—he must let her go.

Not all father-daughter relationships fall into these categories. Several aspects of these relationship dynamics may be at work. Relationships are never static. The father-daughter dynamics may change over time. And good changes occur when a father or daughter takes steps toward recovery. These relationship dynamics illustrate the impact a father has on his daughter. He can impact her self-perception, her place in the world, her work, her relationships with men, and her marriage.

As a father, I am thankful that my daughters and I have a heavenly Father. We rely on God for help and strength. His presence heals the wounds that we suffer. Relationships with earthly fathers will always be imperfect because we are marred by sin and its effect. But our heavenly Father has none of our weakness or sin. He is perfect in his love and goodness toward us. The Bibles says, *"Every good and perfect gift is from above, coming down from the Father of the heavenly lights, who does not change like shifting shadows."*[3]

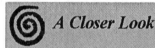

A Closer Look

Fear—Fear is a gift from God. Without it we would walk into traffic or place ourselves in danger. But fear often becomes our first response to anything new. We meet change with fear because we feel threatened by so many things. Fear creates a physical response that begins with the release of adrenaline and ends up with the whole body on alert. This alerted state often leads to persistent and unwanted tension and can develop into stress related illness.

Heart—When I use the word *heart*, I am referring to an emotional and spiritual place within each person. It is the seat of a person's emotions, affections, and personal reality—their true self. It is where we are honest with ourselves—our heart of hearts. People often say, "In my heart, I know that . . . . " What they mean is that in that truest place within themselves—where personal honesty and certainty exists—they know their own personal reality about what they feel, what they value, and what they believe as true.

The first two usages of the word *heart* in the Bible are quite interesting to me. They appear in the book of Genesis chapter six just before the great flood. And they are used together—just one verse apart. Verse five:

"The LORD saw how great man's wickedness on the earth had become, and that every inclination of the thoughts of his heart was only evil all the time." Verse six: *"The LORD was grieved that he had made man on the earth, and his heart was filled with pain."* Scripture refers to the same place (the heart) within man and within God. But each was filled with a different content. Man's heart was filled with evil—evil emotions, evil affections, and evil or corrupt reality. God's heart was filled with pain—painful emotions about the state of man, painful affections about God's relationship to man, and painful reality about what must happen to man.

I write about a father-daughter connection that builds a bridge between two hearts. It is a connection and disclosure of emotions, affections, and reality—truth. It is a father who expresses his feelings, reveals his values, and speaks his truth. But what if the father or another person's heart is filled with evil, deception, wicked affections, misplaced values, cruel emotions? For this, scripture warns: *"Above all else, guard your heart, for it is the wellspring of life."*[4] And how do we guard our hearts? Boundaries.

One more important reason to understand and guard the heart is *hope.* Hope enters through the heart—the heart is hope's door. The Apostle Paul prayed for the folks he had nurtured in faith. Among his prayer requests for the Ephesian church was this function of the heart. He said, *"I pray also that the eyes of your heart may be enlightened in order that you may know the hope to which he has called you . . . ."*[5] So when a father nurtures his daughter's heart through an emotional and spiritual connection, he enables her to see and grasp hope. When a daughter's heart is unattended or wounded, she is kept from hope's light. Her heart can easily grow dark—hopeless.

Soul—In the chapter, I refer to the soul as place where a daughter can experience profound injury from the father-wound. The soul is often described as a person's mind, will, and emotions. In many ways, it is like the heart. In fact, the Old Testament scriptures often speaks of the heart and soul as if they are inter-changeable. But the key distinction that makes the soul truly important and different is the component of human will—our volition and choice. The part of a daughter that chooses—decides her own way—can be wounded and warped. Abuse that penetrates the soul can bend it toward the will of another and a loss of freedom results. A daughter whose soul is wounded and overpowered will actually choose to continue in troubled and toxic relationships—not because she wants to, but because the part of her that chooses freely (her soul) has been bent and broken. It is bondage and imprisonment of the heart. The Apostle Paul said it this way: *"For I have the desire to do what is good, but I cannot carry it out. For what I do is not the good I want to do; no, the evil I do not want to do—this I keep on doing.*"[5]

Spirituality—In twelve-step programs, spirituality is defined as being in proper relationship to the truth. That truth begins in God, as we know God in Christ and in the Bible. But there is also a truth about ourselves with which we must come into proper relationship. It is the truth that denial and other "figs leaves" have hidden from us. We say in recovery that "you are as sick as your secrets." It is true. Spiritual people are freed by the truth that they uncover and embrace.

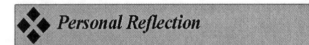

Personal Reflection

1. Which wounds in your life today have resulted from your relationship with your father?

2. If you could encourage your father to initiate an emotional connection with you, what would that connection be like?

3. How has your relationship with your father impacted your self-image?

4. What losses in your relationship with your father have been most difficult or painful for you?

5. Which of the seven father-daughter relationships describe you and your father?

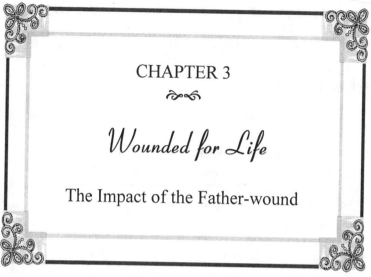

CHAPTER 3

ॐ

Wounded for Life

The Impact of the Father-wound

he true/false statements that follow identify the attitudes and messages that women face every day, throughout life. Some messages shame. Others insult or belittle. And some discourage and demean women. These messages come from family, church, the workplace, or our culture in general. Add your own observations to this list!

T / F   The way a woman dresses determines a man's sexual response toward her.

T / F   Eve is responsible for Adam's bite out of the forbidden fruit in the Garden of Eden.

T / F   A man's sexual needs are primary, and a woman's sexual needs are secondary.

T / F   Men are always right.

T / F   According to God's Word, women are to be submissive to men in all things. They are not to have any thoughts, feelings, or opinions of their own.

T / F   If a woman wants to get a man's attention, she has to have a perfect body, just the right clothes, and a beautiful face.

T / F   Women do not have business and administrative abilities. That is why they should stay at home—out of church, business, and government.

T / F   The words feminine and strength do not belong together.

T / F   Men become sex addicts, have affairs, or sexually abuse children because their wives are not sexual enough.

T / F   Women should control family finances only when they are single parents or widows.

T / F   It is never right for a woman to say no to her husband's sexual advances.

T / F   Delilah is responsible for Samson losing his hair, strength, and eyesight.

T / F   If a woman would only meet her husband's needs better, he would not be emotionally, physically, or spiritually abusive.

T / F   Women are not as capable as men are when it comes to planning military strategy or fighting in combat.

T / F   Physically strong women usually aren't very attractive.

T / F   Men think that women who are physically attractive are more intelligent than those who are unattractive.

T / F   With all those female hormones at work, you never know what a woman is going to do next, and you can't trust what she says about her feelings.

These statements illustrate the false and destructive messages that women encounter. They distort a woman's view of herself and her value before God. A woman, who has a weak or nonexistent emotional bridge to her father, is easily devastated by these cultural influences. She cannot shield herself from the insult these messages add to her injury.

Impact of the Culture-wound:
Sex and Shame

Sex sells. The media can super-impose a sexual element upon any product it advertises. But two messages about women accompany the marketing appeal. The first message is that women are supposed to be sexy. The second message is that women are successful to the degree that they are sexy. Little girls must have industrial-strength boundaries to stand up against these messages.

These messages do not end with advertising. Television programs deepen the wound in a woman's sexual identity. What was once considered R-rated programming a few decades ago is now regular fare on television. Every day, children are exposed to sexual abuse, pre-martial sex, and extramarital affairs. For twenty-four hours a day, anyone who turns on the television will view the message that it is normal for two people to meet, kiss, and have sex.

The Christian culture has also inflicted its share of wounds on a woman's sexual identity. Many Christian women were taught to consider their sexuality as shameful rather than sacred. Pregnancy for young unmarried women was a shameful episode. Some were sent away to avoid embarrassment for the family. Some had to make public confessions before the whole congregation. Others were concealed and carried away for abortions. All wanted to escape the judgment and shame inflicted by the church. The sense that anything sexual was sinful seeped into the Christian consciousness. These distorted messages also tainted a woman's sexual experience within her marriage.

The misguided application of certain Christian doctrines has also wounded women. Eve's first bite, Bathsheba's compliance, Delilah's seduction, and Jezebel's idolatry—all these caricatures of a woman's weakness, lay an inordinate responsibility for the world's sins on women. The teaching that a wife should submit to her husband at all costs—even if he is abusive—has inflicted deep wounds on women young and old. These wounds bring physical and spiritual destruction to women who lack emotional and spiritual connection with a loving father.

Women also suffer from messages that invalidate their feelings or inhibit them from acting upon their feelings. A young woman, who reaches adolescence, may be attracted to a young man, but she can't openly express her interest. Rather than ask him out on a date, she has to play the game of attracting his attention. If she can hold his interest, he may ask her out. This doesn't encourage openness and honesty in her relationships with men.

Women who express strong feelings are often mocked or criticized. Women who cry are written off as too emotional—or worse, unstable. Women who express anger get a special designation from the men around them. Women can have their feelings dismissed as invalid if they are close to their premenstrual time. Feelings may be somewhat magnified during the woman's premenstrual time, but it doesn't discount the truthfulness or legitimacy of her feelings. A daughter, whose father depreciates her feelings, finds it hard to own her feelings and stand up to destructive cultural views.

The destructive cultural messages that bombard women will deepen the father-daughter wound. They will impact every wounded area of her life. But a strong emotional and spiritual bond between a father and daughter will galvanize and protect a woman against these messages. An unbreakable bond to her father's heart gives a woman the resources to fulfill her potential.

Impact of the Father-wound:
Her Marriage

A daughter may use romantic relationships to fulfill the unmet emotional need left by her father. She is not conscious of her reasons, and so the relationships are primed for disaster. Her expectations for the man that she marries will be very high. The deeper her father-wound, the more unrealistic her expectations will be. And the man will fall right into it.

The man who marries a woman with a deep father-wound feels needed and important. No doubt, he has his own wound. This magnifies the problem. The progress and development of many male/female relationships is predictable:

The wounded daughter begins to date a man. She thinks she has found Mr. Wonderful. The little girl inside does cartwheels and cheers. She thinks, *This guy is going to love me all the time. He's going to care for me all the time. He will always be there for me.*

Two problems are at work in this relationship. First, the woman wants what she missed from her father. That is not what romance and marriage are about. Second, the man is wounded too. The little boy inside thinks, *All right! This woman will love and hold and care for me all the time. She thinks I'm wonderful, that I do great things. She will always affirm and adore me.*

What develops between this man and woman is a toxic state of love and romance. No amount of premarital counseling can address the real issues in the relationship. The couple needs a month in detoxification to withdraw from each other. Once the toxic expectations, unrealistic romance, and self-serving adoration are cleansed, the couple can see each other as they really are. Divorces would be cut in half if premarital counseling included a period of romance-detox!

Many marriages are based on a shaky foundation of woundedness. The man and woman each live under the burden of unmet needs. The real man and woman—who lie beneath their need—are difficult to find. The little girl and the little boy inside have taken center stage. They act upon the hope that they have found somebody who can love them as no one ever has before. Then, twenty-four hours, six months, or five years into the marriage, things begin to fall apart.

The husband's wounds—his neediness—may have kept him from his true feelings for years. The only emotions he really feels are sex, anger, and rejection. When his wife no longer matches his image of the all-magical woman he expected, he feels rejected and he withdraws from her. Then the woman realizes that her husband isn't the all-loving, Mr. Wonderful. He isn't what she hoped for—what she expected him to be. She becomes angry, depressed, and resentful.

The spark that ignites the woman's disillusionment is not in the marriage. It is in her need for connection with her father. A husband can complement a woman's emotional and spiritual connection with her father, but he cannot provide it. The daughter's need for her father must be worked out through her relationship with her father, not her husband.

Every husband and wife enters into marriage with some emotional needs, woundedness and hurt. Marriage can meet only some of those needs. The woman, who has a solid relationship with her father, has the best resource available to her. She will be better equipped to handle the rigorous ups and downs of marriage and family life.

A woman, who has a strong bridge to her father's heart, has more to give to her husband. The strength of her father's love supports her and lightens the burdens that she and her husband each carry. This doesn't mean that the father is involved in the marriage. Rather, his relationship with his daughter and his faithful presence in her life have given her the wisdom, strength, and support she needs to handle life. His daughter does not stand alone. She stands with her father's presence behind her.

The existence of father-wounds can affect a daughter's marriage relationship in hurtful ways. The father-wound that has been deepened by abuse, brings anger into the marriage. A little girl who is abused by her father can't express her anger toward him. She would invite more abuse. So she carries that unspent anger into her adult life. She marries. Then, one day, an issue arises between her and her husband. Something—his tone of voice, a particular phrase, a look, a hand gesture—recalls her abusive father and triggers the anger within her. Boom!

The explosion changes the landscape—her perception of reality. Now, the woman is sure that her husband is the most inconsiderate man in the world. She can't imagine why she married him. Her husband is the biggest jerk in history.

Her husband may have said or done something insensitive, but the trigger and the trouble was within his wife—the wounded daughter. The husband's action unleashed the anger she had stored up against her father. So the husband receives all of the anger his wife has ever had toward her father. The damage to the marriage is devastating. It is not possible for this kind of anger and affection to exist at the same time. The woman cannot make a distinction in her feelings. She cannot separate her father from her husband.

Another type of woman may deal with her pain and fear through codependent behavior. She loves, cares for, and serves everyone in her family. She is self-sufficient and does everything on her own. She may go to extremes to gain her husband's approval. And she may stay with an abusive husband—ever hopeful that things will change (just as she did when she was a little girl). It may take a long time for her to wake up to reality. She resists the scary emotions inside and denies the self-destructive behaviors.

Impact of the Father-wound on a Woman's Marriage

When the hunger for father is unmet . . .

Adult Self

Adult Self

. . . both relate to one another according to the unconscious feelings and unmet needs of the inner child.

Inner Child

Inner Child

Anger
Shame
Pain
Fear of Rejection

Sometimes the weakness in a father-daughter relationship becomes evident through the father and son-in-law relationship. A father may be wounded by his great need for a son. He may abandon his daughter when she marries and bring the new man into the family. The father and his son-in-law may share interests and enjoy each other's company. This is fine and even healthy, within limits. But sometimes a father and son-in-law become almost inseparable. This will wound a daughter who did not have the benefit of a close relationship with her father. Some women fear the future of their marriage and they worry that they will lose both father and husband.

In other situations, a father may control and dominate his daughter's life. He is unable to let go and allow his adult daughter to develop her own marriage relationship. The father may compete against his son-in-law for his daughter's attention. An expensive gift for his daughter may be his way to counter the threat he feels by his son-in-law's financial success. Or the father may point out his son-in-law's faults to his daughter.

There are times when a father should express his concern about events or developments in his daughter's marriage, but he must leave the decision-making and consequences in his daughter's hands. Adult daughters are responsible to God to make and work through their own choices in life. A father who wants to maintain a relationship with his adult daughter will love her even when he doesn't approve of her choices.

Impact of a Strong Father-Daughter Bridge on a Woman's Marriage

When the father has established an emotional and spiritual bond . . .

Adult Self

Adult Self

. . . both relate to one another with acceptance, the ability to give and receive love, the ability to support one another, and a desire for God's potential to be fulfilled in one another.

Inner Child

Inner Child

Confidence
Self-esteem
Feels Father's Heart
Has & Respects Boundaries

Impact of the Father-wound: Other Relationships

An unmarried, adult daughter can also lack an emotional connection with her father. Alicia, for example, is in her thirties but has never married. Both of her parents worked full time. She grew up in day care. Her parents took her out of bed in the morning, still in her pajamas, and dropped her off at day care. The day care provider had many other children to care for. As she was able, Alicia had to dress herself and prepare her own breakfast cereal. No one kept her company as she dressed or ate breakfast. "For as long as I can remember," Alicia says, "I've taken care of myself."

Not surprisingly, Alicia has never had a strong emotional bond with either parent. Loneliness and a sense of being lost haunts her adult life. She is uncertain about where she belongs and finds it hard to stay in a relationship. She is in her second long-term relationship, but she cannot bring herself to make a commitment to marry. She's a tough survivor—it's the only game she knows. Without a strong emotional connection with her parents, especially her father, Alicia doesn't know how to get beyond surviving.

Consider the damage caused when a father has an affair. A daughter is shot in the heart when she learns of "another woman" in her father's life. She assumes that the other woman is more important to her father than his own wife and children. The daughter personalizes the situation. And it is more painful if the father appears to be happy and wants to spend all his time with the other woman. The daughter who already lacks an emotional connection with her father will be heart-broken.

An affair, that progresses to divorce and marriage to the other woman, prolongs and magnifies the daughter's suffering. It is common for a father to become more emotionally involved with his new wife's children than he ever was with his own. The daughter may see her father play with his new wife's children. His enthusiasm may be greater than when he played with her. Whatever his level of connection to his new wife's children, his daughter will see this loving man care for his new children, but not for her.

A daughter may grow to overcome the obstacles of a divorced and remarried father. She may even develop an involved relationship with her father. But her mother is still a factor. Her mother may be jealous of her daughter's ongoing relationship with the father. She may seek to undermine the father-daughter relationship through criticism of the father. Or she may chide the daughter for wanting to have a relationship with him. This confuses and splinters a daughter's affection and loyalty.

More complexity is added if the daughter's mother remarries. A stepfather can become the target of the daughter's unresolved anger and resentment toward her birth father. The stepfather may be a nice guy, but he receives a continual "on again, off again" treatment from the daughter.

I once knew a man in this situation. He was generous to his
step-daughter—both with finances and emotional support. He was
an involved parent as she grew. He paid for her college, gave her
cars, provided money to shop, and more. Still, he was not appreciated. Into her twenties, she remained at home, irresponsible, immature, and unflinching in her anger and resentment toward her
stepfather. He realized one day that she had never grown up. So
long as he was the designated problem, she was out of touch with
her deeper pain and frozen in time, unable to move on.

Impact of the Father-wound:
Her Workplace

Large numbers of women doubt their potential, settle for low pay,
and remain in low-level positions. They may run the companies
and have skills that match any executive, yet they get none of the
credit or recognition. This is a common effect of the father-wound
in the workplace.

Don't misunderstand. There is nothing inherently wrong with
these jobs. The issue is not the position, but how a woman views
herself in her job. Many women feel inadequate, yet they are highly
skilled and extremely capable. As a result, they lack the confidence needed to take risks and improve their situation. They don't
believe they have what it takes to gain further education, advantage, recognition, or rewards.

Julia is a good example. She grew up in a home where the father ruled with an iron fist. He also served up large doses of guilt
and shame. Her husband was also controlling. His addictions abused
the family, and brought about emotional, spiritual, and financial
bankruptcy. Julia divorced later in life and needed a job. She would
have settled for simple clerical position, but I encouraged her to
aim higher.

"Julia," I said, "I've seen you administrate a women's ministry
and orchestrate retreats for a large church. You have raised children, managed a household, and supervised a Sunday school training program. You have the skills necessary to manage a small company. Don't limit yourself to a clerical job."

Julia still wasn't sure of her abilities. She started part-time as a secretary at a college. She worked her recovery program and grew in confidence. When a position for coordinator of campus activities became available, she applied. The job was hers. She scheduled classes, seminars, and other activities for the whole college. Soon the director of a large camp noticed her abilities. He offered her a job as camp activity coordinator. Now, she works at the camp, lives in a great house, and has a good salary with benefits.

It is sad when a woman has all the brain power, gifts, and abilities she needs, but she feels inadequate to reach for her God-given potential. The picture is very different when a woman has an emotional connection with her father. That connection provides confidence and enables a woman to take risks and step into new areas of growth. The father's encouragement and support of his daughter during her growth is no small thing.

How does a father nurture this confidence in his daughter? The process starts while his daughter is still a little girl. It starts when he helps her learn new things. It happens when he praises her accomplishments. It builds when he lets her know that he is confident of her abilities. It deepens as he encourages her to pursue new areas of interest.

This is a role the father plays throughout his daughter's life. It does not end when she leaves home. It is important that a father remain active in his adult daughter's life. He needs to continue to encourage her and at the same time respect her independence. It is helpful for him to know what his daughter does and how she views her work. Then, when she dreams about a future goal, he can provide some perspective and input. His confident support can encourage her to take chances and reach for her dreams.

On the other hand, an abusive father will magnify a woman's lack of confidence. This lack of confidence may or may not be obvious. Some women believe they are inadequate and seem to live their lives proving it. Other women use their deep sense of inadequacy to over-achieve. They are driven to perform far beyond what is expected. They are successful in meeting their goals, but unable to receive pleasure or satisfaction in their accomplishments. Their achievement is born more from fear of failure than from a desire to succeed. They got A's to keep from getting F's in school. Those fears are powerful, and able to spawn addictive work patterns. No amount of work or financial security will fill the emptiness her father has left in her heart.

A woman, who lacks the assurance of her father's love and confidence, is vulnerable to work-related addictions and/or codependency. The cover and apparent competency of over-achievement does not lessen the potential for problems. The corporate reality is that over-achievement is rewarded—even encouraged. When the woman's need and the corporate greed combine, a toxic work situation is born.

For instance, a woman may work long and hard to prove her worth to her father or father figures in the workplace. Excessive effort earns her promotions and success. She hopes to stave off her foreboding fears of failure. Sometimes her work will be noticed and rewarded. But if she is addicted to her work, no amount of thanks or praise or recognition will comfort her. It may even drive her to work harder.

A codependent woman, who is compelled to please and enable others, may produce sixty hours a week, month after month, year after year, and never advance in position. The financial rewards and the promotions go to others. The company has increased productivity and higher profits. Still, the codependent woman is left with nothing except lost years, a worn body, and bitter resentments.

High achievement and self-sacrifice will never heal the wound in the daughter's heart. Instead, a toxic work situation will exact a high price from its victim. She will pay the price in the poor health and chronic illness that result from stress. She will suffer emotional and psychological damage, and may need psychotherapy. She will risk the relationships she has with husband, children, friends, and other family members. The energy she should have for her marriage and her children has been spent at work—unnecessarily. If she is not married, she will see romance as beyond her reach—a fairy tale for others, the fortunate.

Oh, the gift of a father! These things—the lost opportunities and the misery—are not theories in a book. These are the every day experiences of daughters who were robbed of the nurture that only their father could give. The inner confidence and personal strength that a loving father provides is a priceless gift.

Impact of the Father-wound:
Her Spirituality

A little girl absorbs her father's spirituality. She learns about God the Father through her relationship with her earthly father. Thus the emotional, physical, and spiritual wounds she suffers in her relationship with her father have a direct impact on her connection with God. Those wounds leave distortions about her heavenly Father. Her spiritual health and the state of her soul will depend upon her willingness to process and move beyond these distortions.

Ellen's father, for example, was a quiet, passive man. A good Christian, he worked hard to provide food and shelter for his family. He did not, however, build a strong emotional and spiritual bridge to Ellen's heart. He was distant and disconnected. He was unaware of the damage caused by his wife's depression. Ellen filled in the void he left. She became a mother to her own mother.

Self-reliance characterized Ellen's adult life. She viewed God through the distorted example of her father. God was neglectful and passive. She didn't—she couldn't—rely on him. She was able to handle her own problems. There was nothing she couldn't work out on her own. God had more important people to listen to and care for than her.

Ellen wrote out a description of God, and it surprised her. She didn't believe God was strong or involved enough to take care of her problems. Like her earthly father, God was not powerful, present, or practical. Then she realized that this distortion of God was about her father. Once that was known, she was free to begin a new journey of spiritual healing.

Ellen's experience is only one way a daughter might open her heart to re-discover the heavenly Father. A father, who faces and deals with his addictions or codependency, can lead the way for his daughter to find spiritual healing. With recovery, the father will be able to connect with his daughter on an emotional and spiritual level. She will, in turn, gain a greater ability to connect with her heavenly Father.

Will, an older friend, had this experience with his daughter. Will began his recovery when his daughter was an adult. He soon realized the impact his addictions had on her childhood. He began to build an emotional and spiritual bridge to her through the direct expression of his feelings. He also listened to her feelings without judgment or shame. In time, she felt safe in her relationship with him. A new level of trust was established.

Will tried to share the Christian message of salvation with his daughter when she was younger. She would not accept it. But on the basis of their new relationship, Will was able to introduce his daughter to her heavenly Father. This time she heard something that she had been unable to hear before. The new relationship with her earthly father helped her trust the reality of a relationship with her heavenly Father.

A father's response to the day-to-day events of life makes a positive or negative impact on his daughter's spirituality. He must recognize his potential to spiritually nurture his daughter. And a father must take advantage of the opportunities that arise daily.

I was able to share a significant, spiritual event with my daughter Rachel when my great aunt Lenora died. Lenora was a spiritual matriarch of my family and a powerful prayer warrior. She had prayed for me every day since I was fourteen years old. Every time my family visited Minnesota, I made sure my children spent time with her. My last visit with Lenora took place in a hospital. She was ninety-five years old and ready to leave us. It was a visit I shared with Rachel.

I knew the visit would be difficult. The strong and stately woman was now thin and frail. The hiss of oxygen was the only sound. Her arms were exposed. Rachel's eyes found the IV tubes, white tape, bruises, and patient ID bracelet. We wanted to say good-bye, but the time for conversations had passed. So we prayed. I lifted her limp hand and held it. I thanked God for Lenora's life, and for the way she had represented his love and grace. I thanked him for her Christian example as a committed and strong woman of God. Tears filled my eyes and ran down my face. I thanked God for the faithful prayers that she offered for my family and me. And then I asked God to bless her journey home and welcome her with joy.

Rachel and I walked back to the car with no words along the way. Once in the car, we cried. The thoughts that came were memories—her words, her prayers, her legacy, and loss. A place was empty now and a prayer warrior gone. I wonder aloud, "Who will take her place? God seems to raise up such a women of prayer in every generation." I looked to Rachel and said, "Who knows?

Maybe you. You've got a kind spirit and you've got her God in your heart."

It was a tough yet important day for us. My daughter had the chance to see my grief and share it. She helped me to say good-bye, to honor, and to show respect to a beloved woman of God. It was an emotional time—a spiritual time. It was a brief opportunity as Lenora was on the last pages of the last chapter of a long life. Rachel and I were there—together. We let go of Lenora and grew closer to one another. I said farewell to one woman of God, but helped build strength into another. The emotional and spiritual bond between my daughter and myself grew in depth that day. And Rachel grew ever closer to her full potential as a woman of God.

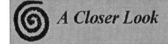

A Closer Look

Resentment—Resentment is a major roadblock to recovery that must be removed. Resentment is the bitterness and anger we feel toward those whom we perceive as threats to our security or well-being or those who have caused us harm. If not removed, our resentments act as anchors and hinder our progress and growth.

Survivor—This term can mean a number of different things. In a sense anyone who has experienced abuse in their childhood—and lived through it—is a survivor. But a survivor is also a character trait. In the midst of our powerlessness as children, we learned to take control, develop survival skills, create coping mechanisms. We learned to survive. But those survival skills were developed with "child logic," and now we are forty years old still living life like a four-year-old.

Still another kind of survivor is one who faces death and survives when others did not. We might think of a car accident or a war survivor. But some women, who have experienced abortion, consider themselves survivors. Many felt that circumstances (their unplanned pregnancy) brought them to a life or death decision. They faced the battle, but only one came out alive—they did. Another one—another person—was sacrificed so they might live. And now, they feel like the survivor of an accident, a war. They experience guilt, shame, regret, remorse, loneliness, and every color of pain. But they believe that they must not allow this part of themselves to be known. They work very hard to keep the secret, but the survivor secret gnaws within them and cries to be told. This kind of survivor needs the support, love, and acceptance of others who have experienced this same pain and found healing, forgiveness, and restoration.

Distorted Image of God—As I noted in the chapter, a daughter absorbs her father's spirituality. She learns about God the Father through her relationship with her earthly father. Thus the emotional, physical, and spiritual wounds she suffers in her relationship with her father have a direct impact on her connection with God. Those wounds leave distortions about her heavenly Father. Her spiritual health and the state of her soul will depend upon her willingness to process and move beyond these distortions.

How do we heal our image of God? A book, *Divine or Distorted? God As We Understand God*, was written for this need. In it, author and pastoral counselor Jerry Seiden says:

> *"You thought I was altogether like you!"* These are God's words, found in Psalm 50:21, when he spoke to the injustice and delusion of the day. Think of it: a God who is just like us. No thanks!
>
> That's backward. We don't want a God who is like us. We want to be like God.
>
> An important distinction emerged between the God of Israel and the gods of the ancient world. Few ancient peoples wanted to be like their gods. Godliness was no virtue. Remember how capricious, immature, and cruel the Greek gods of Olympus were? Or what of the Roman's gods? Worse yet, would anyone want to be like Molech, the god of the Ammonites, who demanded that children be sacrificed by fire? To be godly would be cruel, unfeeling, and immoral.
>
> However, the opposite was true in Israel. God was good. And he wanted his people to be like him. He said again and again, *"Be holy for I, the Lord your God, am holy!"* So in Psalm 50, God points out a grave mistake: the assumption that God is like us.[1]

Toxic State of Love and Romance and **Romance-detox**—Being "in romantic love" can alter a person's brain chemistry and profoundly affect one's ability to reason and think objectively. The old saying "love is blind" is medically accuate. The intoxication caused by romantic-love is a true toxic state and can actually be seen in a SPECT scan of a person's brain.

For love to be genuine and lasting, a couple needs to move beyond the physiological effects of romantic-love and base their relationship upon their true experience together. Otherwise, toxic expectations, unrealistic romance, and self-serving adoration will cloud the truth. Time and physical separation can both provide romance-detox. But if a couple intends to marry, it is important that they seek pre-marital counseling. A knowledgeable and experienced counselor or minister will provide a foundation for communication and reality testing to discover the truth and dispel unrealistic expectations.

Personal Reflection

1. How has contemporary culture affected the way you see yourself as a woman?
◆

2. How has Christian culture affected the way you see yourself?
◆

3. What "baggage" have you carried into your marriage and other relationships because of your relationship with your father?
◆

4. What issues do you face in your workplace because of your relationship with your father?
◆

5. In what ways has your father affected your image and understanding of God? What distortions? What positive attributes?
◆

NOTES:

CHAPTER 4

ॐ∼ॐ

Healthy Boundaries

The Father's Role in Boundary Development

Esther was one among many young women who came to the citadel of Susa in response to King Xerxes' proclamation. The young women began preparation to enter the king's harem. They were put under the care of Hegai, the king's eunuch. Esther caught his eye from the start. He saw to it that she received the best food, the finest beauty treatments, and the most luxurious accommodations in the harem. Hegai even hand-picked seven maids from the king's palace to serve her. And so Esther began a full year of preparation and grooming before her moment with the king.

All the young women received twelve months of beauty treatments. Six months of treatment with oil of myrrh was followed by six months of treatment with perfumes and cosmetics. When the preparation was complete, each young woman would be taken to the king. She would enter the palace in the evening and would be given anything she wanted to take to the palace. In the morning, she would be returned to the harem and housed in the area reserved for the king's concubines. She would never again see the king, unless he requested her by name.

Esther's time of preparation drew to an end. Everyone who had seen or worked with her was impressed. Hegai notified Esther that her moment was at hand. He asked her what she would take to the palace. She said that she would only take what Hegai advised, and followed his instructions exactly. It worked. King Xerxes was impressed with Esther. She won his favor and approval more than any other virgin did. He set a royal crown on her head and made her queen in place of Vashti.

What a celebration followed! King Xerxes was so pleased with his new queen that he proclaimed a royal holiday throughout his empire. In Esther's honor, he gave generous gifts and conducted a great banquet for all of his noblemen. Esther was in the spotlight. She was the pride of the Persian Empire. Still, Esther kept her family background and nationality a secret. She continued to follow Mordecai's instructions as she had done since the day he adopted her.[1]

Esther had made it! Imagine what it was like for her, a captive Jewish orphan, to be catapulted into this lifestyle. She was among the rich and famous. She lived in luxury—everyday a beauty spa. She was fed the finest foods. She was pampered with beauty treatments and adorned with the finest cosmetics. The best of the Persian Empire belonged to Esther.

Life in the king's harem could sweep a young woman off her feet. Esther could have become absorbed and obsessed in her new life. She could have tossed away her family and forgotten the training she had received at home. Her personal identity and boundaries could have collapsed under the pressure of her new life. She could have conformed to all her new standards and trusted in her external beauty. She could have lost herself and become what the others wanted. But no—not Esther. She continued to maintain her boundaries and follow Mordecai's instructions.

It was no accident that Esther was able to stand strong in her new role as King Xerxes' queen. Her character and strength were the result of her relationship with Mordecai. Mordecai had both loved and trained his daughter well. She had solid, strong boundaries that enabled her to thrive in the midst of unpredictable and risky circumstances. Daughters today need the same nurture and support from their fathers. Fathers like Mordecai give their daughters the tools and training they need to establish boundaries and form their unique identities.

What Are Boundaries?

Boundaries are the beliefs and feelings that serve as barriers to anything that might harm a person. They are essential to ensure the inner safety of every human being. They are like invisible fences that provide spiritual, emotional, and physical protection.

One way to illustrate boundaries is to imagine a medieval castle. A tall and strong wall that provides protection from enemies surrounds it. Within the walls, the castle community is safe. Families grow, children play, people conduct business, and civic events take place in the courtyard without fear of attack. Sentries on top of the walls watch what happens inside and outside the castle. They question those who want to come inside the castle walls to conduct business. They deny admittance to anyone who could bring harm. The wall and the watchful sentries are a formidable obstacle to any attack. Boundaries operate in the same way.

Boundaries establish a safe atmosphere that enables us to live, learn, and survive in an unsafe world. They enable us to know when we are at risk, and they give us the ability to take steps to protect ourselves. Boundaries help us define areas of personal responsibility and enable us to refuse responsibilities that belong to others. They keep toxic feelings and information out, and they provide the separation needed for healing to occur when we have been wounded. In short, boundaries help us develop and realize the full potential God has intended for us.

Boundaries play an essential role in the physical, emotional, and spiritual development of our lives. We are aware of the boundary of our visible, physical bodies, but we are often less aware of our invisible boundaries. We cannot see the invisible boundaries, but we can certainly feel them. The following exercise will help you feel an invisible physical boundary.

Stand up and ask a friend or family member to walk toward you. As the person approaches, you will at some point begin to feel uncomfortable. That point of discomfort represents your invisible physical boundary with that person. The boundary may be a few inches or several feet away from you. If your boundaries are severely damaged, you may feel uncomfortable while the person is still on the other side of the room. On the other extreme, you may allow the person to walk right into you!

We also have emotional and spiritual boundaries. They are just as real as our physical boundaries. Feelings of fear, anger, or shame are the points of discomfort that indicate when a spiritual or emotional boundary is crossed. If our boundaries are damaged, we may be too afraid to stand up for ourselves. We may be unable to express our feelings when another person is angry or abusive toward us. If our boundaries are intact, however, we will be able to stand up for ourselves in such situations.

The Father's Role in Nurturing Boundaries

God created us to need physical, emotional, and spiritual boundaries. They are an essential part of our humanity. But no one is born with boundaries. They are something we must learn.

We learn about boundaries very early in life. Learning begins in our interaction with parents, then siblings, and extended family. Both parents play a significant role in the development of a daughter's boundaries. Her success and safety in life will depend upon the accomplishment of this parental task.

During infancy, parents provide complete protection and safety for their children. But children grow and move beyond a parent's reach. Therefore, parents must teach their children how to set their own boundaries. These boundaries will follow and protect the children throughout life. The following are some of the boundaries that parents must help their children establish:

Safe Limits—Set firm limits and intervene if children move into areas that could be harmful or potentially destructive. This type of boundary is especially important during adolescence, but not popular with the adolescent child.

No Shame—Take steps to stop shameful or abusive behavior that others may inflict. The others may include anyone from family members to teachers.

Personal Privacy—Respect a child's privacy needs. Everyone has a need for private space, private things, private time, and private affections/attachments.

Moral Protection—Protect against pornography and other inappropriate sexual messages that may appear on television or in books and magazines.

Spiritual Respect—Respect the manner in which children connect with God. Faith in God and love for God are personal steps in a child's spiritual journey. Spirituality can be directed, not dictated.

Relational Responsibility—Instruct children about appropriate responsibilities in various relationships. Describe what role a child plays in the family, and how it differs from the role of an adult.

Appropriate Behavior—Define appropriate behavior in a variety of situations. Begin with life at home and then life at school, church, play, and in public settings.

Personal Modesty—Teach children that no one needs to touch their bodies or private areas, and that it is okay to say "no" when physical closeness makes them feel uncomfortable.

Parents should model good boundaries, teach about boundaries, and maintain emotional involvement in their daughter's life. Both the mother and father empower a daughter. They empower her with understanding about the world around her. They empower her with a sense of confidence in her unique identity. And they empower her with the courage to venture out into the world and to make her way in it.

Most of us recognize that the mother plays a significant role in this process. We have, however, underestimated the father's role. The daughter whose boundaries are nurtured by both the mother and father is fortunate indeed. The mother can model or instruct about a particular boundary, but it helps when the father conveys the same message. The father's input has a rock-solid quality that is invaluable. A daughter, who has an emotional and spiritual connection to both of her parents, never stands alone. And if she receives teaching from both of them, she stands on very solid ground.

Esther received this kind of love and training from Mordecai. He strongly affirmed Esther's value and identity. He also taught her about some of the boundaries she would need to set if she were to survive in their world. He taught her that there were dangerous people in the world. He warned her not to consider the world a safe place. He advised her to protect herself, keep her precious identity to herself, and watch out for those who would harm her. There is no substitute for this kind of love and nurture from a father.

A father, who maintains good boundaries with his daughter, models a safe relationship. He is able to express his love for her in appropriate ways. He can show both his affection and respect for her personal identity. The skills he models will equip her for both relationships and survival. She will be prepared for her peers, teachers, pastors, physicians, and authority figures of all types. She will understand what appropriate, safe behavior is.

Without a father's nurture and instruction, a daughter is put at great risk. The ups and downs of daily life become unnecessarily painful and destructive. The lessons learned in family relationships set the course and attitude for many of her adult relationships. The spiritual, emotional, and physical boundaries that parents set in place create the opportunity for a daughter to learn, express creativity, and grow. Boundaries, that affirm, nurture, and respect who she is, help her identity grow with her. They also help her maintain a strong grip on her identity through all the ups and downs of her experience. That includes the self-confidence to own and express her feelings in her relationships with others. But if her boundaries are violated or damaged during early childhood, the castle of her life will have crumbled walls, absent watchmen, and enemies in the courtyard.

The Problem with Boundaries

The violation of a child's boundaries leads to many difficulties. The most important problem is the inability to set new boundaries— by the parents or the child. The problem will grow worse in adolescence and continue well into adult life.

Boundary violations are experiences, events, or patterns that wound a child. Boundary violations come in countless ways. The following are some common ones:

Rage—Directing rage or excessive anger at a child.

Insensitivity—Ignoring or scorning a child's feelings.

Inappropriate Conduct—Touching a child sexually, making inappropriate sexual comments, or viewing pornography with a child.

Emotional Incest—Turning to the child, rather than to the spouse, for emotional support.

Physical Abuse—Physically abusing a child, including excessive corporal punishment or neglect.

A boundary violation is an experience of abuse for the inner child. It wounds her very soul. It lowers her self-esteem and leaves her with feelings of shame, anxiety, and fear.

Every boundary violation is a learning experience for the child. A lesson that will stick with her throughout life and impact every area of her life. She learns that the world is a scary place. She receives a conflicting message and fails to learn how or where to set appropriate boundaries. She loses confidence in her identity and her ability to express her needs and desires. And this lack of confidence will lead to boundary failure later in life.

Many of these boundary violations come at the hand of parents, grandparents, teachers, church leaders, and other authority figures. The ones who should nurture a girl's boundaries, not destroy them. The violations may be as subtle as a shaming look or a glare of disapproval. They may be as violent as a beating or forced sexual activity. The child is traumatized—no matter how the violation occurs or how insignificant it may seem. A child may not be un-aware that a boundary is supposed to exist. Still, she feels the wound deep inside when it is violated. That wound impacts every aspect of her being.

What does it mean to nurture boundaries? How easily does boundary violation occur? For the answers, consider the following common areas of boundary violations:

Nurturing Relationships vs. Covert Incest

The primary relationship in the family exists between husband and wife. God designed the family to operate in this way. The troubled family begins to fail in the marriage relationship first. The spiritual and emotional bond that should exist between husband and wife can shift to a relationship between child and parent. This is called covert incest. It is perhaps the most common form of emotional and sexual abuse today. It shatters the child's boundaries.

Kenneth Adams describes the devastating impact of covert incest:

> "Covert incest occurs when a child becomes the object of a parent's affection, love, passion, and preoccupation. The parent, motivated by the loneliness and emptiness created by a chronically troubled marriage or relationship, makes the child a surrogate partner. The boundary between caring and incestuous love is crossed when the relationship with the child exists to meet the needs of the parent rather than those of the child. As the deterioration in the marriage progresses, the dependency on the child grows and the opposite-sex parent's response to the child becomes increasingly characterized by desperation, jealousy, and a disregard for personal boundaries. The child becomes an object to be manipulated and used so the parent can avoid the pain and reality of a troubled marriage.
>
> The child feels used and trapped, the same feelings overt incest victims experience. Attempts at play, autonomy, and friendship render the child guilt-ridden and lonely, never able to feel okay about his or her needs. Over time, the child becomes preoccupied with the parent's needs and feels protective and concerned. A psychological marriage between parent and child results. The child becomes the parent's surrogate spouse.
>
> . . . An important difference between overt and covert incest is that, while the overt victim feels abused, the covert victim feels idealized and privileged. Yet underneath the thin mask of feeling special and privileged rests the same trauma of the overt victim: rage, anger, shame, and guilt . . . . The adult covert incest victim remains stuck in a pattern of living aimed at keeping the special relationships going with the opposite-sex parent. It is a pattern of always trying to please Mommy or Daddy.[2]

Covert incest destroys a part of the daughter's childhood. Before her time, she is forced out of a child's world and into an adult role. Her boundaries are not nurtured and her rights are not noted. She begins to live life through the eyes of her parent.

Sue, for example, remembers being like a wife to her father since she was six years old. Her family had a high profile in the church, but they hid a dreadful secret: Sue's mother was an alcoholic. Ever since she can remember, Sue's father depended on her to keep up the family image. He would tell her what to do and would praise her for her help. Sue and her father did special things together. They would have a good time, but he would talk about his loneliness. He criticized his wife and told Sue what a lousy mother she had. Sue's mother increasingly resented the relationship her husband and daughter shared.

By the time Sue reached adolescence, her mother's rage was out of control—due in part to the disease of alcoholism and to the relationship between her daughter and husband. For years Sue's father had treated her as if she were his wife. As Sue developed into a young woman, her father's touch became sexual rather than paternal. His hands wandered during hugs and brushed against her breasts. He even did this in her mother's presence. An angry attack on Sue would be triggered. Sue's mother would rage, and Sue's father would do nothing to stop it.

At her first chance, Sue left home and married. But she wasn't happy in her marriage. Her energy was consumed in anger and resentment for her passive husband. Sue felt that her husband did nothing. She handled the family finances. She initiated and conducted any discussion of family problems. She decided about where and when to eat. She was the one who initiated sex. Sue married a man who needed her to take care of him. She had married a man just like her father.

Emotional incest also occurs between mothers and daughters as well. Deb, for example, was the daughter of a traveling salesman. Her mother struggled with depression and rage. And she used tantrums to get her way. Depression could put her mother in bed and keep her there for days.

By the time Deb reached her early teens, her mother was unable to manage the household. One day her father took her aside and said, "We have to be really careful of your mother now. She isn't doing well. She is really fragile. I need you to take care of her." Deb did as she was told. She took care of her mother and her younger brothers and sisters. *Mom is sick*, she thought. *Dad wants me to take care of her. He will be really happy with me if I do a good job. God will be pleased with me, too, because I honor my parents when I take care of my mother.*

This internal message compelled Deb to take care of her mother for thirty years! In her mid-forties, she realized that her father had abdicated his responsibility to care for his wife. He had pushed it off upon his daughter. And Deb knew that none of her care-taking had earned her father's love. No amount of care for her mother could bring love from her father. Her heart was broken and years were lost.

It is one thing to help out and take care of a parent when there is illness or a crisis in the family. But parents need to ensure that the household returns to normal as soon as possible. In this case, Deb's father took away her childhood when he gave her the responsibility of care for her mother. He elevated Deb to a special status in the family, but it was not for her benefit. For his own convenience, Deb's father ignored and violated her boundaries. And he stole from her the carefree innocence of childhood.

Covert incest occurs in other ways as well. In families where the father is absent, addicted, or emotionally detached, the mother-daughter relationship may become too close. In this situation, the mother and daughter may share everything. The daughter becomes an equal with her mother and loses her childhood. This is more likely if the marriage is experiencing difficulty. It is easy for the mother to share her hurts and disappointments about the marriage. A child should not be put in a position to take on the troubles of a marriage. This is a terrible violation of the child's boundaries. Marriages will always have troubles. It is the parents' responsibility to deal with those problems with God's help. The children ought to never bear the hurts of their parents.

God intended parents to be available to meet the needs of their children. Covert incest switches the roles. The parents no longer exist to meet the children's needs—the children exist to meet the parents' needs. That is a destructive boundary violation.

We see a beautiful illustration of appropriate parent-child boundaries in Esther's story: *"Every day he [Mordecai] walked back and forth near the courtyard of the harem to find out how Esther was and what was happening to her."*[3] Mordecai was there for his daughter every day! He was not there for his own benefit, to see what he could gain by hanging out with the rich and famous. He was there to meet Esther's needs. He was concerned about her welfare and wanted to make sure she was safe. That is the kind of nurturing relationship that God intends for fathers and daughters.

Symptoms of Covert Incest

The symptoms of covert incest are not difficult to recognize. Most of them apply to adult children as well as to younger children:

❑   The parent looks toward the child for emotional support that is not provided by the spouse.

- [ ] The child is the primary source of the parent's emotional support.

- [ ] The parent would rather spend time with the child than with the spouse.

- [ ] The parent shares angry, critical feelings with the child concerning the spouse.

- [ ] The parent's happiness rises and falls with the child's accomplishments.

- [ ] The parent becomes resentful or jealous of the child's happiness or accomplishments.

- [ ] The child is afraid or worried that the parent's marriage will fail unless he or she supports the parent(s).

- [ ] The child worries about what might happen if he or she isn't available to meet the parent's needs.

- [ ] The married child is closer and more emotionally supportive of his or her parent than his or her spouse.

- [ ] The child feels that he or she exists to meet the parent's needs, but since the parent does not reciprocate, the child feels used or manipulated.

- [ ] The parent provides emotional support and encouragement for the child, but not for the spouse.

Addiction vs. Availability

A father must be emotionally available to his daughter to meet the needs God intended him to meet. But a father, who deadens his pain through addiction, is numb to the feelings of his children. It is impossible to be addicted and emotionally available at the same time. So an addicted father cannot feel or even desire to respond to the needs of his daughter's heart. The type of addiction makes no difference. Workaholism, sexual addiction, eating disorders, or drugs—they all will wound his daughter.

Addiction leaves chronic tension and fear in its wake. As the father's addiction progresses, the tension and fear turn into terror. Many adult daughters of alcoholic fathers still remember the jolt of fear they felt whenever they heard their father come into the house. They never knew whether he would be sober or drunk, reasonable or enraged. Some have memories stained with images of fathers in the family room, with a pornographic movie or webpage, and masturbating. Some are afraid to ask the father for anything. They remember how his irritable mood combined with their request to cause an explosive "No!" It was too great a risk to ask him to fix a bike or play.

Others still feel terrified at night. They fear that he might soon be next to the bed to touch or rape. Some cringe at the sound of raised voices. Scary nights flood back in memories of fights between mom and dad. He would storm out of the house and seek solace at the office, with his lover, or in a bar. Still other daughters grow weary to meet their fathers' high standard. Legalistic and perfectionist fathers are never satisfied. Daughters seek a narrow way to the father's heart—a route that only an anorexic or bulimic daughter could walk.

All of these wounds, and many more, come from fathers who are not emotionally available to their daughters. These wounds leave a daughter with a damaged boundary system. The father is the first man a daughter learns to love. She naturally desires to be emotionally close to him—whether or not he is capable of closeness. The daughter of an addicted father learns by experience that men will be emotionally unavailable and unresponsive. This lesson follows her throughout life. It leads her to feel most comfortable in relationship with addicted men. It's all she knows.

Rage vs. Safety

Parental rage is a horrible experience for a child to endure. It sets off an uncontrollable fear response in the child. Adrenaline pumps and a natural "fight or flight" response is triggered. Small children learn that they cannot fight back. They are trapped in a state of fear. And their bodies bear the signs and the evidence for years.

Children learn to live with the chronic tension of fear. Later in life they pay the price. They are always on alert—always tense. Others look for the rewards in life. These daughters watch for the threat. Their necks and shoulder are tense. The energy that should metabolize food, restore cells, and fight disease is spent to maintain vigilance—to counter the threat. So they become victims of auto-immune diseases, panic attacks, headaches, chronic-fatigue, fibromyalgia, irritable bowel syndrome, colon problems, and a host of other stress-induced diseases.

A father who rages cannot nurture his daughter's unique potential. Instead, he squelches her uniqueness and feeds her codependency. A little girl who lives with rage learns to walk on eggshells. She pleases others to keep the peace. She denies herself to disarm any threat. Some Christian women rationalize a lifetime of self-denial, peacekeeping, and people pleasing as a proper theology. In fact, it's anything but trust in God. If it were trust in God, they would find rest. But it is self-will and human effort, and it will end in weariness, illness, and loss.

A raging father positions his daughter for emotional failure in her marriage. She is bound to be unhappy. She may marry a controlling, abusive man. Or she may marry a man who is "safe" but spineless and passive. By age forty, she may be tempted to take her husband for electro-convulsive therapy to see if she can jump start him into activity.

It is easy to point the finger of blame at a raging father, but the blame doesn't stop there. A passive, codependent mother wounds her daughter as well. A mother, who is unwilling or unable to stop a father's rage, reinforces the damage done by the rage. By doing nothing to protect her daughter, the passive mother communicates that it is normal to be abused. She implies that rage is a natural part of a relationship with a man.

Rage from the mother is just as devastating to a little girl as rage from the father. A daughter who suffers rage from her mother develops a distorted feminine self-concept. The daughter learns to handle anger in the same destructive way as her mother. She learns to deny her anger and pretend it doesn't exist. But denial will bring on feelings of shame and fear—even when she experiences justified and normal anger. She may deny her anger out of fear that it will become uncontrollable and explosive. But denial will not allow her to learn ways to measure or restrain her anger. She develops no middle ground, only extremes—rage or no response at all.

Many women have suffered deep wounds because their fathers did not stop their mothers' rage. An inactive father, who takes no steps to stop a mother's abusive rage, appears to approve of the abuse. Jennifer, for example, grew up with a raging mother and a codependent father. Her father was an effective minister in a growing church. Outside the home, the family had the perfect image of a peaceful, loving family. Behind closed doors, the mother ruled with rage.

Now an adult, Jennifer views God as a passive, ineffective force. She believes that everything that happens in her life rests on her shoulders alone. She goes to church, but her heart isn't in it. In fact, her heart isn't in much of anything. She learned to turn off her feelings in order to survive her mother's rage. Her father was a nice, loving man who would never harm his daughter. But his passive response to his wife's rage inflicted great harm on his daughter. She lives with that wound every day in her adult life.

Sexual Abuse vs. Physical Closeness

God has placed in each of us a need to be loved, comforted, and nurtured by a mother and a father. When a father holds his little girl, he meets a spiritual, emotional, and physical need deep within her. That physical closeness gives the daughter a sense of value and confidence in her identity. A natural outgrowth of a solid, valuable, personal identity is the ability to set boundaries. Thus a father's physical touch greatly influences his daughter's boundaries—to strengthen or wound them.

The greatest wound from a father's touch is the impact of sexual abuse. It violates and devastates a daughter's boundaries and destroys her soul. It literally separates the inner person. To survive this violation, the little girl dissociates or detaches from the situation and the feelings it brings. This survival skill of dissociation from her feelings continues into adulthood. She will have difficulty recognizing and responding to her feelings throughout life.

Sexual abuse is far more widespread than most of us realize. We easily recognize that rape is sexual abuse. But there are more subtle forms of sexual abuse. Consider the following behaviors that some fathers practice:

Verbal Disrespect—Denigrating treatment of women may include verbal comments about women's bodies or vulgar comments about a woman's body.

Visual Conduct—Visual behaviors may include staring at a woman's breasts or body, and directing other men to look at her.

Sexual Addiction—Addictive behaviors may include pornography, prostitution, extramarital affairs, and the purchase of certain kinds of clothing for the daughter to wear.

Inappropriate Contact—Improper contact may include touching or fondling various body parts or inappropriate kissing.

Boundary Violations—Disrespect for a daughter's boundaries may include disregard of her need for privacy, intrusion into the bathroom or bedroom when the daughter wants privacy, or bathing with the daughter.

Mistreatment of the Mother—To treat the mother as a sexual object rather than a person is abusive to a daughter.

Sexual Comments—It is abusive for a father to make comments about the daughter's body or her sexuality, including comments about the size of her breasts.

Sexual Jokes—Humor with inappropriate sexual content is abusive to a daughter—a damaging message is conveyed.

Inappropriate Disclosure—It is abusive for a father to talk to his daughter about his sexual relationship with his wife or other women.

Sexist Comments—For a father to adhere to and speak of any ideology or theology that shames or dominates women is abusive.

These forms of sexual abuse devastate a girl. They shatter her sense of self, distort her body image, damage her sexuality, and negate her personal boundaries. A girl who has been a victim of this abuse may experience memory gaps, post-traumatic stress syndrome, interpersonal relationship problems, codependency, and addictions. These forms of abuse send mixed messages to a daughter. They blur the lines between closeness, affection, and sex itself.

Other important men in a little girl's life can initiate these forms of abuse. Grandfathers, uncles, family friends, pastors, teachers, doctors, therapists, and others. These men function as father figures in a girl's life. In the girl's eyes, all male authority figures carry the impact of her father. So sexual abuse by any of the men listed above is wounding to a daughter.

One out of every four women will experience sexual assault in her lifetime. To protect his daughter from sexual abuse, a father must strengthen her personal boundaries. He does this first by honoring her boundaries himself. He respects her need for privacy, shows affection (e.g. hugs and kisses) appropriately, and models appropriate boundaries with other women.

A father, with good boundaries in place, has a basis from which he can teach his daughter. His model of behavior has already taught her that she has control over her body. From the age of three or four, his daughter needs to know the difference between a good touch and a bad touch. As she grows older, he strengthens her boundaries by teaching that she has a right to say "no" to any touch or hug that makes her feel uncomfortable. He teaches that if anyone touches her in a bad way—whether it be grandpa, the neighbor, a teacher, or a pastor—it is okay to run away, scream, or tell the whole world what happened. He affirms that there are no secrets, and that she is not responsible to protect any other person.

The father's role to respect and strengthen his daughter's sexual boundaries is very significant. All sexual boundary violations leave deep wounds that have life-long consequences. They render adult women helpless to face abusive men. They rob a woman of her ability to set the protective boundaries that an adult should be able to set. They strip her of the strength to stand against abusive treatment. And they hinder her ability to bring abuse to the attention of others who can share her pain and support her. The woman, without protective boundaries, feels just as abused and vulnerable as she did in childhood.

There is no way to overestimate the impact a father's sexual abuse has on his daughter. One sexual comment damages his daughter's boundaries. One inappropriate touch tears her soul. These wounds are felt deeply in her body, soul, and emotions. If she suffers these wounds, it takes a tremendous amount of work on her part to recover.

Impact of Sexual Abuse on an Adult Woman's Life

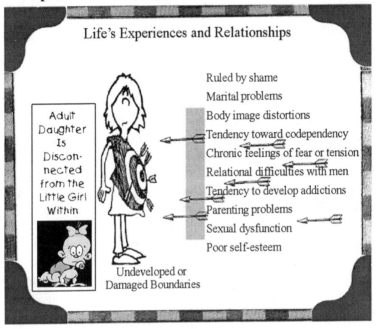

Life's Experiences and Relationships

Adult Daughter Is Disconnected from the Little Girl Within

Undeveloped or Damaged Boundaries

Ruled by shame

Marital problems

Body image distortions

Tendency toward codependency

Chronic feelings of fear or tension

Relational difficulties with men

Tendency to develop addictions

Parenting problems

Sexual dysfunction

Poor self-esteem

Disrespectful vs. Respectful Attitudes toward Women

Women need strong boundaries to withstand the onslaught of disrespectful and demeaning attitudes toward women. As Queen Vashti learned many years ago, a woman must be able to take steps to protect herself in a world that views women as second-class citizens. Again, the father's attitude and actions toward women either weaken or strengthen his daughter's ability to protect herself.

There are many ways in which a father can nurture his daughter's personal boundaries and feminine identity. His respect of women in general, and the treatment his wife as a valuable partner, affirms women. A father's appreciation of his daughter's intuition and recognition of her feminine qualities provide a foundation for a healthy pride in her feminine identity. When he considers her feelings, opinions, and perspectives to be valuable and important, he strengthens her self-confidence. When he encourages her to explore and develop the potential God has given her; she is better able to pursue her dreams. When a father develops this kind of foundational relationship with his daughter, he is able to teach her about survival in a world where not everyone values her as he does.

Many men do not respect or value women. They view women as second-class citizens. Women of strength threaten them. They care little for a woman's heart, but lust much after her body. They see women as sex objects. Men who view women in this way violate a woman's boundaries. A daughter who has such a man as a father is stunted from the start. She grows up with a damaged view of herself and her feminine nature. She is primed and pointed toward relationships with abusive men. Abuse, codependency, or anger will characterize those relationships.

Every woman will run into some men who are disrespectful of women. The daughter, whose father has honored her feminine character and instructed her to set boundaries to protect her value, will fare best. The daughter, who has an emotionally connected relationship with her father, will come to him with questions and will be open about the events in her life.

For example, she may talk to her father about mistreatment by a teacher at school. The father can listen to his daughter and validate her experience. He can help her separate the shame and social pressure. He can help her deal with authority figures without fear. He can affirm her need to be treated with respect and understanding. And if his daughter is not yet mature enough to set boundaries with authority figures, he can take appropriate action to set those boundaries for her.

The father, who cares about his daughter's safety in the world, will anticipate the risks she will face. He will prepare her to navigate through those difficult areas. Mordecai did this for Esther. He taught her that it was not safe to reveal her Jewish background. Fathers today do this when they teach their daughters that some men do not respect women. These fathers reinforce their daughters' right to set boundaries with those men.

"Do not expect men to have boundaries," one father taught his daughter. "No man has the right to talk to you or touch you in a way that is not respectful. In junior high school, if a boy tries to pinch you or pull on your bra, he is violating your boundaries. He is not treating you with respect. Tell him to stop it. If he persists, you can go ahead and kick him!"

It is not easy for daughters to stand up to the disrespect for women that is common in our culture. For example, one day, our family walked across a restaurant parking lot. I was with my wife and two youngest daughters. Our older children, Ben and Rachel, walked some distance behind us. A pickup truck with several guys in the back passed between us. They whistled and shouted something at Rachel. I didn't hear what they said, but I saw the look on Rachel's face.

When we had a minute to ourselves, I said, "Rachel, you looked shaken when that pickup went by. Was it something they said to you?" She nodded. I looked her in the eye and continued. "You are not what those men think you are. Their whistles and comments are about them, not you. How they view you has nothing to do with who you are. You are Rachel—nothing they say can change that."

A father's respect for his daughter and her identity strengthens her stand in a destructive world. A father builds up his daughter's boundaries by the way he loves her and in what he teaches her. He empowers her to live up to the potential God has given her. He is a blessing to her now and in years to come.

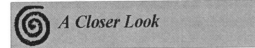 *A Closer Look*

Boundaries—Boundaries are the beliefs and feelings that serve as barriers to anything that might harm a person. They are essential to ensure the inner safety of every human being. They are like invisible fences that provide spiritual, emotional, and physical protection. In the chapter, I used the illustration of the medieval castle. The wall and the watchful sentries are a formidable obstacle to any attack. Boundaries enable us to know when we are at risk, and they give us the ability to take steps to protect ourselves. Boundaries help us define areas of personal responsibility and enable us to refuse responsibilities that belong to others. They keep toxic feelings and information out, and they provide the separation needed for healing to occur when we have been wounded.

Castle walls are made of stone. Fences are made of wire and wood.

But what material are used to build boundaries? We use truth. Truth will set us free and keep us safe. For example, when another person rages at us, we embrace the truth. We speak truth to ourselves and to others.

To myself I might think the following:

> *This person's rage is not about me. This unfortunate conduct is his problem. I am not responsible for it.*

> *I don't have to subject myself to this kind of abuse. I am free to remove myself from this situation.*

To the other person I might say the following:

> *I don't appreciate the way you are talking to me. If you want to discuss this or anything else with me, you must control your anger.*

> *I deserve to be treated with respect and spoken to in a reasonable manner.*

Denial—Denial is a key survival skill. We protect ourselves by not admitting that anything is wrong. We ignore the real problems by replacing them with a host of elaborate explanations, rationalizations, and distractions such as minimizing, blaming, excusing, generalizing, dodging, attacking, etc.

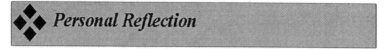

Personal Reflection

1. In what ways has your father modeled appropriate boundary lines? What has he done to encourage you to develop your own personal boundaries?

2. What could your father have done to be more helpful in establishing your boundaries?

3. Has your father ever violated your boundaries? How?
➥

4. Do you feel safe with and respected by your father?
➥

5. Evaluate the present condition of your boundaries. Consider strengths, weaknesses, damage, and deficiencies.
➥

NOTES:

CHAPTER 5

໑ຂຶໜ

Life in the Real World

The Father's Role in Facing Reality

To look at her, a person might think that Esther was the luckiest woman in the whole Persian Empire. She had the best life had to offer. She had riches, servants, beautiful clothes, prestige, and a king for a husband. Still, the Persian Empire was a dangerous place in which to live, even for the queen. Esther's father, Mordecai, was well aware of the dangers.

Mordecai did not abandon Esther once she became queen. He was in no hurry to return to his own life and interests. Instead, he remained as close to her as possible. Every day, at the king's gate, Mordecai sat, listened, waited, and watched for news about Esther. One day, he overheard two of the king's guards plan to assassinate King Xerxes! Mordecai informed Esther of the plot, and she warned the king. The report was investigated and the conspiracy foiled. The two guards were hanged, and the king's life was spared. The entire story was written in the official record of the king's reign.

Those two guards were not the only threat in the Persian Empire. Other evil awaited an opportunity to advance. A nobleman named Haman was hungry for honor and power. He was a highly regarded nobleman before King Xerxes. The royal officials at the king's gate were required to kneel before Haman. All of the officials obeyed except one Jew—Mordecai.

The other royal officials didn't like to kneel down before Haman, but Mordecai flatly refused. Day after day, they asked Mordecai why he did not obey the king's command. He told them that he was a Jew and that he would not bow before Haman, a man. No amount of persuasion would change Mordecai's mind. So the others went to Haman to see if he would tolerate Mordecai's behavior. He would not. In fact, he became enraged. He wanted to destroy, not only Mordecai, but every Jew in the Persian Empire!

Haman plotted to use King Xerxes' authority in his vengeful plan to destroy the Jews. "There is a certain people dispersed and scattered among the peoples in all the provinces of your kingdom," he said. "They have customs that are different from those of all other people. And they do not obey the king's laws. It is not in the king's best interest to tolerate them." Haman proposed a bargain with the king. If the king would issue a decree to destroy those people, Haman would donate 345 metric tons of silver to the king's treasury. The silver would pay the soldiers who would do this job.

The king was easily persuaded. He told Haman to do whatever he wanted to with the people. He also told him to keep the money! Soon the order to destroy the Jews went out from one end of the empire to the other.

King Xerxes and Haman partied and drank to celebrate the decree. The Jews mourned and prayed to counter the command. In every province, the Jews fasted, wept, and wailed. Many of them lay in sackcloth and ashes. Mordecai tore his clothes when he heard the news. He put on sackcloth and ashes. He walked and wailed and wept through the city. His cry was loud and bitter. He was not allowed to pass through the king's gate because of his mourning. So he sat down in the open square in front of the king's gate.[1]

Who would have guessed that this deadly danger was so close at hand? In the midst of plenty and prosperity for Esther, destruction was about to strike. Mordecai knew the ever-present dangers that lurked in the shadows. He told Esther to keep her ethnic origin to herself. She was wise to obey him. She told no one, not even her husband, that she was a Jew. Even the queen had to face the reality of a life-threatening challenge. How fortunate she was to have Mordecai's understanding love and wise training.

The Blessing of a Strong, Wise, and Feeling Father

We learn more about Mordecai as Esther's story progresses. His character, his convictions, his fatherly insight, and his personal strength take shape in the adversity. Look closely at the man who was a father to Esther.

Mordecai was wise. He sat at the king's gate among the royal officials. It is possible that he was an elder in the city. Others would have come to him for advice or to resolve disputes. But Mordecai had another reason for being at the king's gate—Esther. He wanted to be as close to her as possible. He wanted to hear about her welfare. He wanted to be available for messages she might send. He wanted to do whatever he could to keep her safe.

As circumstances turned out, Mordecai was in the right place at the right time. When he learned of the plot to kill King Xerxes, he took immediate action and warned Esther. His quick action saved them. If Xerxes had been killed, Esther would have been in a difficult and dangerous spot. She would have been killed, or at the least enslaved by those who strong-armed their way to power. Mordecai's wise act saved the lives of both the king and Esther.

Mordecai was a man of integrity and courage. He was not afraid to take risks and stand up for what he believed. Even when pressured by his peers, Mordecai didn't give in. He was not afraid to say that he was a Jew and would bow to worship no one but God. Mordecai left no doubt about the value he placed on his religious beliefs.

What a contrast between Mordecai and Haman! Mordecai stands out as a man of character and self-sacrifice. Haman stands out as a man of corruption and self-seeking. Honor bestowed on Haman went straight to his arrogant head. When he felt that he had been crossed, he was determined to destroy Mordecai. But more, his hatred moved him to seek the destruction of Mordecai's entire race. Haman was obsessed with a cause—to inflict pain on Mordecai. He was willing to give up great riches to carry out his evil plan. Haman's hateful revenge was so powerful that he sent out an edict to kill every Jew. An entire race of people would perish—the old, the innocent, the infant, the unsuspecting. Men and women, boys and girls—their lives taken, their property plundered. Haman's heart was hardened and evil. Once his holocaust was approved, he celebrated with a drink.

Faced with men like this, it is no wonder that Mordecai instructed Esther as he did. He knew the history of his people. He knew the danger that lay in wait to destroy his race. And he knew from his experience in the Persian Empire that the anger of one powerful man could lead to the death of many.

Life stopped for Mordecai when the news of Haman's holocaust reached him. He cried out, tore his clothes, he put on sackcloth and ashes—the signs of mourning. He publicly proclaimed the atrocity of what had been decreed.

Mordecai's actions provided spiritual and emotional leadership for the community. He didn't take one look at the edict and run for his life. He didn't organize a mass exodus. Instead, he went straight to the king's gate. There he pled with God, in full view of the king. He prayed for God to stop the great loss of innocent lives that had been decreed. Mordecai did exactly as God's Word encourages. He spilled out the anguish of his heart : *"Put on sackcloth, O priests, and mourn; wail, you who minister before the altar. Come, spend the night in sackcloth, you who minister before my God."*[2]

Fathers today can and should seek God in this same way. I know a man named Bob. He learned that his daughter had been sexually abused by a man in his church. Devastated, he went to the church leaders. He sought a biblical response to this violation of his daughter. But the church leaders refused to take action. They went on as if nothing had happened. Bob was dismayed at their denial. He reported the abuse to the police. He wanted the perpetrator to be held accountable by the legal system. He wanted recognition of the damage done to his daughter.

Bob set aside any concern for his standing in the eyes of the church leaders. He chose instead to stand by his daughter, to affirm her worth and value, and to ensure the future safety of other little girls in the church. This is the kind of father who has a tremendous impact on his daughter's life.

Mordecai was a positive influence on Esther. Throughout her life, he had touched her heart and gained her confidence. She was open and eager for his instruction. He modeled what it meant to live with personal integrity in society. Likewise, fathers today can develop the same kind of relationship with their daughters. And they can model values and behaviors for life in the real world.

Exposing the Fantasy

All of us—men and women alike—want to believe that life will be fair and hard work will be rewarded. Treat others well, and they will treat us well. Is it too good to be true? Trust others to respect us and protect our boundaries. Isn't that what we want? It's what we want, but not what we can expect.

Life isn't that way today, and it wasn't that way when Esther and Mordecai lived. In light of the harsh reality of the real world, a father must speak the truth about what he knows. He must break through the comfortable myths that his daughters and sons are tempted to believe. He must cast God's light on the illusions that offer an erroneous way of life to his children.

Robert Bly, the noted storyteller and poet, who sparked a men's movement, tells a story about a father. The man encourages his little girl to jump off the front steps into his arms. She is afraid, but he convinces her that she won't get hurt—he will catch her. Before her leap, she bites her bottom lip and shifts from one foot to another. She looks down and then out at her father. She jumps—arms and legs like a windmill flying. But she lands secure in his arms. He tells her to do it again. She does, and he catches her. The third time, she is eager to climb the steps. With no hesitation or fear, she jumps. He steps back. She falls. When she finds her senses and her father's eyes, he says, "The world is not your mother!"

This father's methods need a strong dose of compassion, still, there is truth in his message. It is easy for a daughter to think that the world is like her mother—a better place than it is. So her father gives her a great gift if he is available and willing to ground her in solid reality. As in the previous chapter, the process of teaching a daughter to deal with real life begins when the father nurtures the development of his daughter's boundaries. This process continues as the daughter matures. It increases in operation as the daughter ventures into the world outside the home.

The father, who operates in love, will not be afraid to expose his daughter to real life. He will help her face playground injustice in her earliest years. He will help her discern the truth in the midst of the troubles. He will help her grieve the painful loss of innocence that comes with knowledge. He will help her distinguish between her responsibilities and the responsibilities of others. He will help her cope with the good as well as the bad in life.

The emotionally connected father will continue in this helpful role throughout his daughter's life. Her needs and his involvement will rise and fall according to the seasons of life. But if he does his job well, his adult daughter will be equipped to face life in the real world. Most of the time, she will handle life confidently without his counsel and assistance. She will view her father as a resource, a wise counsel in the troublesome times. She will rely on her father for a reality check when she's lost or astray.

Mordecai confronted Esther with the reality of life in their world. Mordecai's spectacular demonstration of grief traveled like wildfire through the palace. Esther's maids and eunuchs brought her the news. She was troubled and confused. Her response was to send down a change of clothes for Mordecai to wear.

Esther's actions seemed to say, *Mordecai, get out of the sackcloth and ashes! I can't believe this! Do you realize that everyone in the palace is talking about the old Jew at the king's gate? A crazed fool dressed in ashes and rags. He howls and wails like a wounded beast. You tell me not to let my husband know who I am, and yet you put on a public display at the king's gate! This makes no sense!*

The change of clothes was a message from Esther. She wanted him to clam up, get back in his Brooks Brothers suit, and look the part. But Mordecai refused. Esther was forced to send Hathach, her most trusted eunuch.

Hathach met with Mordecai in the open square of the city in front of the king's gate. Mordecai told him everything that had happened, including the exact amount of money Haman had promised to pay into the royal treasury for the destruction of the Jews. He gave him a copy of the text of the edict for their annihilation. He also asked Hathach to explain the whole situation to Esther. And he told him to urge her to go into the king's presence to beg for mercy and plead with him for her people.[3]

What a turn of events! It was apparently too dangerous for Esther to speak directly with Mordecai. Everyone knew he was Jewish. So Esther sent Hathach to minimize the risk of association. But Esther's secret did not matter now. A greater harm was imminent. Mordecai made it clear that Esther needed to take a stand for her people. The interaction between Mordecai and Esther demonstrates the important role of a father in the life of his adult daughter.

By this time, Esther had been queen for several years. She was well aware of royal protocol. She now understood why Mordecai insisted that she conceal her Jewish heritage. So, at this point, her own experience led her to be alarmed by Mordecai's open display.

Mordecai met her concern with a full presentation of the facts. He could not keep his daughter safe in an evil world. And she could not survive with an illusion of safety. Her best chance for survival was strong action to match the reality of their circumstances. Mordecai knew that, despite her status as queen, Esther still needed the support and guidance of her father. This was especially true in a crisis. That's why Mordecai explained the situation to Hathach and stated the exact action Esther needed to take.

Wise fathers follow Mordecai's example. They are available to help their daughters face the difficult realities of life. We like to think of our country as a safe place, but our daughters still face life-and-death issues. Our society does not uphold biblical values. Sexual standards are set by the herd, not the Word. Sexual abstinence before marriage and monogamy in marriage are culturally obsolete. By today's standards of intimacy, sexual intercourse carries the same significance as holding hands and kissing did in the 1950s. Today's fantasy projects an illusion that this is the normal way to live. Truth's reality proclaims the facts: God's standards for sexual conduct have not changed, and it only takes one sexual encounter to contract the HIV virus.

Spiritual and physical death awaits those who follow the fantasy of today's culture. Well-maintained boundaries and prudent actions are necessary today. It takes an emotionally and spiritually strong young woman to see through the illusions and face the realities of life in a sexually addicted society.

Like Mordecai, fathers today need to confront the dangerous reality of life. They need to feel the pain, foresee the loss, and face the tragedy that is possible. They need to live out the convictions of their hearts in daily life. They need to demonstrate in word and deed the importance of God's truth. And they need to shatter the illusion, the fantasy, and the lie of this present day.

Fathers accomplish this with a full explanation of the facts. They share God's truth and note it's blessings and wisdom. They expose the lie and detail it's dangers and consequences. And fathers tell their daughters what they must do to remain safe.

A father's teaching is not limited to areas of sexual behavior. A father needs to help his daughter face reality in the workplace. Success in the business world is not easy today. Many young women think that hard work, done well, will lead to success. This, too, is a fantasy. The reality is that women are likely to face sexual harassment, dishonesty, emotional torment, abusive supervisors, and more. Success requires an astute learner—someone who understands the unwritten rules of her workplace. The wise woman knows how office politics work. She protects herself without being drawn in to their worldly ways.

Dave's daughter, Jennifer, needed his help to sort through issues on her first job. Jennifer was still in high school, but she worked part time at a fast food restaurant. Dave noticed that she talked often about an unfair supervisor. Her supervisor favored the young men, gave them better shifts, and rarely criticized them. On the other hand, he yelled at the young women on the job. After several weeks on the job, Jennifer began to have severe headaches—daily. Dave knew it was time to talk with his daughter.

"Jennifer," Dave began, "are you afraid to walk away from this job?"

Jennifer didn't answer at first. She stared into her lap. Her face trembled—tears brimmed and then broke down each cheek. "Daddy, you always said to never give up. I don't want to disappoint you."

"I mean—don't give up on yourself. This job is another story. You don't need that kind of abuse from a supervisor. And it doesn't help you to tolerate it. Let's think about what options you have."

"Well, I could quit," she answered.

"Yeah," he nodded. "Or you could confront the supervisor."

"I'm willing to try that, but I'm just one person."

"You could keep a record of the supervisor's behavior. Did you know that a well-kept journal is admissible evidence even in court?"

"No, I didn't know that." Jennifer answered and shook her head.

"Then you could pass it on to the manager at the corporate headquarters," Dave explained.

"I like that idea," Jennifer said. So she put the plan in action and got results. The manager immediately changed her to a different supervisor. And since there had been previous complaints about the first supervisor, he was placed on probation. Within a month, the first supervisor was fired, and Jennifer was given his job.

Jennifer learned valuable lessons through the experience. It was her father's involvement that made the lessons possible. He helped her face the reality of a difficult situation, and he taught her important survival skills.

A father should also expose the fantasy his daughter may have about marriage. Mary's father, a widower, did that for her. She was in her mid-twenties and had been living with her boyfriend, Bill. He was a yet-to-be-discovered musician, and she had been supporting him for most of their relationship. Bill wanted marriage, but she had declined. Mary's father was concerned that marriage would mean a difficult and painful future for his daughter. It would be a future that he could not share or help her with. Mary's father knew that his illness would take him from her. He asked to speak with her heart-to-heart.

"It's been tough for both of us, Mary. Life has been a blur since the first signs of your mom's illness. All those treatments—the false hopes. You didn't have any brothers or sisters to share it with. I know I wasn't much comfort to you. I was too busy looking for the next miracle treatment. And now you have this news about me."

Mary reached out her hand to comfort her father. "You'll be okay, Dad. You'll see."

"Mary, I know that Bill has been a comfort for you. I can imagine that you're grateful to him."

"I don't know what I would have done without him," Mary answered.

"He probably feels the same way about you."

"What do you mean?"

"Well, for three years, he helped you deal with your mother's illness and death. But you supported him through his unemployment."

"He's not unemployed. I mean, he's a musician. It's different than you think," Mary answered.

"Baby, I don't know how long I have left. I can't play games. Please let me tell you what I feel—what I fear." Mary's father reached out to her. His hands trembled—his voice cracked with emotion.

"Sure, Dad," Mary said. "Go on, I'm listening."

"I want to see you in a relationship built on love, not need. I want to see you married to a man who will treasure you and provide for you. I want you to feel secure—so those babies are a joy, not a burden. I don't want you to worry about how you'll provide for children. You should be free to give them your best. But Mary, I'm afraid that Bill can't give you any of this. And I think you fear that too. Otherwise, you would have married him by now."

Mary sat in silence. She studied the hands that she held. After a moment or two, she cleared the emotion from her throat and said, "You need hand lotion, Dad." She lifted moist eyes and found his. "But your hands have always been rough—as long as I can remember. Hard work, right?"

Her father had no words—tears spoke for him. Mary continued. "I used to cry when you left for work. Remember?" Her father nodded. "You used to say, 'I gotta go to work so I have money to buy you toys!' Well, that always worked. I'd send you off with a stern warning to hurry back. And you never failed. You always came back, and I never lacked for toys—or anything else. I'm glad that you're afraid for me—'cause I'm afraid too. I'm afraid to let go of these hands. I'm afraid there aren't any more like these."

"You're wrong, baby," her father said. "The manufacturer who made these hand is still in business. And he does custom work. Don't settle for less."

Several weeks later Mary ended her relationship with Bill. Not because her father shamed her, commanded her, or controlled her. Mary's father just spoke the truth, as he knew it, in love. He shared his feelings and fears. He opened up a place for Mary in his heart. Her fantasies and false illusions had no room in there. She alone was free to enter in and to relate and to respond.

A father must nurture and protect a daughter as she matures. It is difficult for an adult daughter to forget destructive fantasies and focus on reality. A father can help her accomplish this, but only if he has earned the right and established the connection. It requires more than a fragile thread of emotional contact. To handle the business of life, the bridge between father and daughter must be strong and solid. When the heavy loads and burdens of life come along, a daughter must be able to trust the connection to her father. His wisdom, love, and support must be constant and sure. His solid footing will expose the fantasies and ground his daughter in truth.

Grounding in Reality

The emotional and spiritual connection between Esther and Mordecai causes me to envision the Golden Gate Bridge. It is a strong and enduring structure. It can bear whatever weight the business of life brings. It can handle the strain of daily stress and the uncertain forces of shifting winds. Mordecai and Esther faced a spiritual and social storm of historical proportions. Millions of lives depended upon the strength of their relationship. Other relationships would have failed, but theirs stood strong—united and unyielding.

Mordecai asked Esther to place herself at risk for a greater good. She was hesitant, of course. What Mordecai asked could cost Esther her life! Esther knew the cost. She sent Hathach back to Mordecai with the following message:

> "All the king's officials and the people of the royal provinces know that for any man or woman who approaches the king in the inner court, without being summoned, the king has but one law: that he be put to death. The only exception to this is for the king to extend the gold scepter to him and spare his life. But thirty days have passed since I was called to go to the king."[4]

Esther was confused—things were changing so fast. Mordecai, whom she trusted to guide and protect her, seemed to have lost his senses. He always told her how to be safe. Now he instructed her to risk her life and approach the king! He always taught her to guard her identity. Now he told her to expose the truth about herself. He told her to tell the very man who had decreed the annihilation of her people!

Esther had strong feelings and opinions about these new instructions. Her message back seemed to say, *Get real!* She explained the perilous laws about entering the king's presence. Then, she added a bit of personal information about her current relationship with the king. He had not asked for her in over a month!

Mordecai sent back this answer:

> "Do not think that because you are in the king's house you alone of all the Jews will escape. For if you remain silent at this time, relief and deliverance for the Jews will arise from another place, but you and your father's family will perish. And who knows but that you have come to royal position for such a time as this?"[5]

Mordecai doesn't mince any words. He cuts through any false illusions Esther might have. He says, *Stop! Don't think for one minute that you became queen just because you have a pretty face. Remember who you are. You are a Jew, a child of the living God. It is He—not you, not your husband—who controls your destiny. It may be that God made you queen for this very occasion.* Wow! If Esther's head had been in the sand, this got it out. Mordecai gave her a strong dose of reality. He could not let her live in any false sense of security.

Daughters today need the same reality check. But is not an easy task for a father to accomplish. A father must learn how to relate to his daughter. He needs to understand her world and interact with her thoughts, feelings, and responses. One father, who has both a son and a daughter, expressed his frustration. "When I impose a consequence for my son's behavior, he gets mad. I can handle that— I understand anger. But when my daughter suffers some consequence, she cries! I feel like a jerk. It's hard for me to follow through when I feel like such a bad guy."

This father is right. It is not easy to follow through, stick with the consequences, and help a daughter face reality. But it is necessary. Fathers who don't know how to connect with their daughters and direct them toward reality often indulge them. A father who doesn't know how to give of himself will often give money instead. When this happens, the father is in danger of creating a princess who has few responsibilities and little knowledge of life in the real world.

There is no reality in this kind of father-daughter relationship. The father who gives material gifts in the place of personal connection creates a damaging illusion. His daughter will have to survive in the real world. As she ventures into that world, her false expectations will be shattered by the hard realities of life. She will have to learn these lessons alone. And she is sure to be confused about the illusions from home.

A father must teach his daughter the practical skills needed to make her way in the world. She needs to realize that a dollar only buys so much. She needs to budget and learn to live within her limits. She needs to pay her bills and live responsibly. She needs to develop work habits that make her an asset to her employer. She needs to know that credit is a temporary tool, not a way of life. She needs to face life as it is, not as she would like it to be. She needs to know that her actions have consequences that cannot be escaped. What she sows, she will reap. That's reality.

A father must direct his daughter toward spiritual reality as well. Mordecai helped Esther see her role in God's plan. He clarified the spiritual reality of God's relief for the Jews. He helped Esther see that she could be God's provision for the need. But Mordecai made it clear that his daughter needed to act and make herself available to God.

The spiritual reality that a father gives his daughter is necessary for her survival. It is more than spiritual comfort, personal insight, character growth, community service, etc. It is a personal connection with the Author of life—our individual lives. It is a wake up call to our ultimate accountability. It is our private link to the order of the universe—our God, who made the plan and wants to insert us into it. Mordecai modeled this connect with God for Esther. The very fact that he took over parenting for Esther shows his willing use in God's grand scheme.

At the time of crisis, Mordecai brought spiritual reality to Esther in the following ways:

God Is—He reminds Esther of who God is—the one in control and the one who loves his people—the Jews.

God Delivers—He assures Esther that God will deliver his people from the evil that oppresses them.

Stuff Happens—He does not deny that some of God's people may perish before deliverance comes.

You Choose—He states that God can use Esther, but the choice is hers to make.

Mordecai is gentle, but clear. He admits that there are risks, and it is natural to be afraid. He does not tell her what she must do. Instead, he points out the spiritual reality of God, who is at work in their behalf. He clarifies the choice that Esther must make. And he leaves the decision between her and God. She alone carries that responsibility.

This interaction was possible because Mordecai has modeled spiritual reality and made it a part of Esther's life. She is in a position to face the difficult realities of life and deal with them as an adult woman before God. This level of communication was possible because of the solid connection between father and daughter. The emotional relationship existed first. It enabled their open, straightforward communication. It helped them deal effectively with both the temporal and spiritual realities of their lives.

Open Communication

Many well-meaning fathers are unable to have the positive impact they would like to have on their daughter's lives. They lack the strong emotional and spiritual connection necessary to communicate with their daughters. Bob, for example, was concerned about his fifteen-year-old daughter, Nancy. She lost interest in her church youth group and became involved with a group of angry teens at school. Her dress, hairstyle, and demeanor changed to match her new friends.

Bob attended a men's Bible study that focused on ways for fathers to improve relationships with their children. He decided to take Nancy out for breakfast and share his concerns. As they ate, Bob shared his feelings about the changes in Nancy's life. He talked about his desire to see her draw closer to the Lord. He encouraged her to re-engage in the church youth group again.

Bob's talk with Nancy was more than he ever got from his father. God bless him for his effort. Still, it wasn't the emotional and spiritual connection they needed to support honest, two-way communication. Nancy became angry and accused her father of not trusting her. Later that night, she joined her friends and took an overdose of pills. She nearly died.

Bob was heartbroken and confused. He had tried his best. *Where did I go wrong?* He wondered. He felt like he did more harm than good. The fact is that Bob's relationship with Nancy was not strong enough to handle that level of communication. The necessary foundation did not exist.

Notice the contrast between Esther and Mordecai's interaction and that of Bob and Nancy. One daughter takes her father's advice seriously while the other daughter rebels. Both fathers cared. Both wanted to address tough issues. Yet only one father had a solid bridge over which he could travel to counsel his daughter and connect to her heart. Mordecai had a solid and wide Golden Gate Bridge of communication. Bob had a shaky, splintering thread that was not maintained. The span was far and the chasm deep. The waters below boiled with rage—the foam was fraught with danger.

Few fathers and daughters have the strong bridge of emotional connection that Esther and Mordecai had. Most daughters—adult or child—feel uneasy sharing their thoughts and feelings with their fathers. This hesitancy comes from being shamed or judged in the past. They found that to share feelings of anger, hurt, or fear was to invite shame, judgment, or advice.

A father who is not connected to his own feelings cannot be a safe or sympathetic listener for others. A daughter learns when and where it is safe or unsafe to share her feelings of anger, hurt, or fear. And it is only in a safe relationship that she can feel love, care, and respect. In safe father-daughter relationships, love and care can be shared and received. But in emotionally disconnected relationships, sharing is superficial—support impossible.

Fathers without an emotional connection to their daughters can only create the illusion of a relationship. It has a plastic quality to it. When things get intense and hot, the relationship may melt under the pressure. Under cold, difficult conditions the relationship may become brittle and break. Only when the relationship is strong enough to embrace difficult and painful feelings, is the deeper level of love possible. That is where real communication exists. Love does not seek control, it offers care.

The depth of communication between Esther and Mordecai blesses and amazes me. I admire their honesty and respect. Under the pressure of imminent death, Mordecai and Esther were direct and sincere in their communication with each other. Mordecai was patient to explain what he wanted Esther to do. And Esther was unafraid to express her fears and concerns. Mordecai was sympathetic to her feelings. He felt the turmoil and fear she faced. So he did not make light of her apprehension and concern. He did, however, remind her of the seriousness of their situation. He exposed her false sense of security: *"Do not think that because you are in the king's house you alone of all the Jews will escape. For if you remain silent . . . ."*

Fascinating things happen when this kind of communication takes place. When both father and daughter are vulnerable and honest, the emotional and spiritual bridge between them becomes stronger. The daughter is able to feel God's presence and guidance in her life. She becomes empowered to take the risks necessary in the real world.

Remember Bob and his daughter Nancy? Nancy was hospitalized following the pill overdose. The whole family began therapy. Bob began a recovery program for alcoholism. Nancy entered a treatment program for drug dependency. And Bob's wife began attending a twelve-step group for codependents. It took several years of hard work, but now father and daughter relate to each other on a new level. They communicate in a way that was impossible in the past. Bob gained sobriety and started to face his own issues. He became more responsive to the needs of his daughter's heart. For the first time, Nancy felt her father's love for her. When she became confident of her father's love, she was able to listen to the wisdom he had hidden in his heart for her. In time, her relationship with God the Father improved too. It was that relationship that empowered her to make her deepest changes.

Mordecai created a safe place for Esther to speak the truth about her feelings, fears, and opinions. In that safe place, Esther was free to discovered some important truths about herself as well. Mordecai's nurture and guidance allowed her to see the truth in his difficult message. She also discovered her place and responsibility in the crisis. She gained the courage, as a daughter of the living God, to risk her life for others. She was empowered to reach beyond herself and live up to her full potential in the real world.

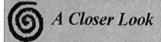

A Closer Look

Safety or *Safe Place*—The sense of safety that I speak of has several layers of meaning. Safety is physical, emotional, social, intellectual, and spiritual. A daughter feels safe when she feels secure, protected, provided for, listened to, unconditionally accepted, and valued for who she is. No genuine father-daughter connection can exist without safety. A father demonstrates safety for his daughter through his physical protection, gentle presence, and fatherly embrace or comfort. He offers safety in his provision of basic material needs. He provides safety through his emotional stability and sensitivity to his daughter's feelings. He extends safety when he allows his daughter to be herself. He displays safety when he respects his daughters ideas and opinions. He creates safety through his love, acceptance, listening, and honesty. He models ultimate safety through his faith in God. When a daughter feels safe, she can take risks, pursue her full potential, and stand securely in the world. Mordecai gave Esther this kind of safety. Even in grave danger, Esther felt secure enough to risk her life. She knew that God was her ultimate safety net.

For many women, this safety was not experienced in the home or in the father-daughter relationship. Therefore our churches, support groups, and supportive relationships must be safe places. In Appendix B, *Suggestions for Group Study and Support,* note the *Guidelines for Sharing.* Observance of these guidelines is one way that we can ensure safety in our small group meetings. The guidelines will promote safety in the church and in personal relationships as well.

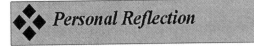

Personal Reflection

1. In what ways has your father given you protection and wisdom?

2. Desccribe a time when your father was transparent and vulnerable about his feelings for you. What affect did it have on you?

3. Describe a time when your father helped you deal with reality. How receptive are you to his instruction?

4. In what ways are you and your father able to share deep and difficult feelings with one another?

5. Take a few moments to thank God for His fatherly protection and wisdom.

◆

NOTES:

CHAPTER 6

❧✦❧

Feminine Strength

The Father's Role in Nurturing Strength

The people of Israel were often afflicted and oppressed during the period of the Judges. Neighboring nations, savage strongmen, and ruthless raiders would terrorize the Israelites. Their cries for a deliverer would ascend to God. Heaven heard and answered. God sent judges—heros, holy men, and once he sent a woman.

During one period of this violent time, Israel was tormented by King Jabin of Hazor, and Sisera, the commander of Jabin's army. There lived in Israel a prophetess named Deborah. She was a married woman, who lived in the hill country, but she was more than a country wife. God made her a judge of Israel! She sat under the Palm of Deborah, and all of Israel came to seek her judgment.

One day, Deborah received a message from the Lord for a man named Barak. Her message was not ordinary. God called Barak to lead a rebellion against Sisera and his army! Barak was hesitant to take on such a task. The strength of Sisera's army, with its nine hundred iron chariots, was well known and feared. Sisera had a reputation for cruelty. And Israel had suffered under his oppression for twenty years.

Barak feared Sisera, but he also feared God. To disobey the Word of the Lord could prove more troublesome. So Barak struck a deal with Deborah. He said, "If you go with me, I will go; but if you don't go with me, I won't go."

"Very well," she replied, "I will go with you. But because of the way you are going about this, the honor will not be yours, for the Lord will hand Sisera over to a woman." So Barak raised his army and led them into battle with Deborah in their midst.

Barak's army routed Sisera's troops, but Sisera himself escaped on foot. Sisera ran to the tent of Jael, a Kenite woman. The Kenites were friendly to King Jabin of Hazor. Sisera expected to find safe refuge. Jael invited him in, gave him milk to drink, and hid him under a rug in her tent.

The exhausted Sisera fell into a deep sleep. Jael picked up a tent peg and hammer, and she crept up to the commander. In an instant and deadly blow, she drove the peg through Sisera's head and into the ground! Soon Barak came by in search of Sisera. He asked Jael if she had seen him. She had more than a story to tell—she had a trophy to uncover.[1]

The Book of Proverbs closes with a character sketch of a woman who is noble and worth far more than rubies. Her husband has full confidence in her. She considers land and buys it, and out of her own earnings she plants a vineyard. She is strong in body and vigorous in work. She opens her arms to the poor and extends a helping hand to the needy. Clothed with strength and dignity, she has no fear of the future and can laugh at the days to come. She speaks with wisdom and is always ready to offer a kind word of instruction. A woman like this, who fears the Lord, is worthy to be praised.[2]

The deep, inner strength of biblical women is a rare topic for sermons. Still, the strength, power, and accomplishments of female Bible characters is worthy of consideration and study. The Bible can teach today's woman what it means to be godly, feminine, and strong. But God-given feminine strength and character is unrecognized and unknown because it is not taught.

When I speak to women's groups, I ask what feminine strength means to them. The common response is a blank and confused look. The words feminine and strength don't seem to go together, but they should.

Many biblical women exhibit undeniable feminine strength. Deborah was one who held great power and respect. Barak was afraid to go to war without this woman of God. And Jael must have been a woman of tremendous, inner strength. She was cool under pressure and fearless in the face of the enemy. She drew in

Sisera, held his confidence, and then single-handedly killed him.

The woman described in Proverbs 31 has the strength to manage a home, tend a family, direct a ministry, or even control a Fortune 500 company. And, she can do these things with tenderness, compassion, wisdom, and business savvy.

These biblical accounts of the depth and power of godly feminine strength can touch and teach the hearts and minds of women—and their fathers. The stories inspire women to renew their efforts to serve God in love. They fill women with a sense of awe. They stir women with a sense of pride in their heritage as women of God. They cause new reservoirs of feminine strength to rise up within women. And, I hope they will encourage fathers to nurture the strength of their daughters.

Most women don't feel the reality of their own value and strength, as they should. A secondary status in society has caused this under appreciation of feminine value and strength. Laws that protect and improve the status of women have been passed, but our culture is slow to change. And, in general, the world is still not a safe place for women.

The Christian culture should champion the value of women in the world. But in reality, the culture born from church often minimizes the worth of women. Any depreciation of women is not biblical. Jesus died for both male and female. In his great sacrifice of love, he demonstrated that every human being—female as well as male—is a priceless treasure.

It is hard for a woman to feel treasured by God when man has wounded her. She should feel strong, not shamed. She should feel loved, not less than. She should feel capable, not culpable. Proverbs 31 portrays what every woman is capable of—provided she is grounded in the Lord and given a solid identity and an unshakable, inner strength. This passage defines feminine strength and provides keys for its development.

> *A wife of noble character who can find?*
> *She is worth far more than rubies.*[3]

A woman, who feels her high worth, is capable of anything. She is a seedbed for miracles. A woman, who feels her innate worth as a child of the living God, has the ability to take risks. She can face new challenges with strength and bring them to fruition. She can go head-to-head with a Sam Walton or Dot.Com in business. She can provide a loving and secure environment for her family. She can sacrifice her own needs for those she loves and still find ways to care for herself. She can nurture her own spiritual and emotional growth. She can be confident in her creative work and take risks to expand her market. She can make a political stand on issues and serve in positions of leadership at any level.

The ultimate foundation for this feeling of feminine value and strength comes from God. But that foundation is laid through the involvement of a father who is emotionally and spiritually connected to his daughter. Few fathers realize the impact they have on their daughters.

The attitudes toward women that are displayed by the men in a family sink deep into a daughter's heart. They shape her opinion of herself. If her father, grandfathers, uncles, and others view women as weak and incapable, that is the image she will carry in her heart. If these men believe that women are to submit to men without exception, that becomes her standard. She will submit to all men— even to abusive men. On the other hand, if these important men demonstrate care and compassion for others, she will learn to feel the same. If her father is willing to take a stand, she will feel pride in his strength and realize that she can do the same. If her father develops his creativity and learns from mistakes, the stage is set for her to enjoy the challenges for creativity and learning.

In her book, *In God's Image*, Craig Ballard Millett writes about the types of women found in Scripture. One of those women is called "the father's daughter."[4] This woman is intelligent and has great inner strength. Millett describes her as a planner, achiever, and survivor who is not only capable, but also adaptable. The father's daughter will make herself successful in whatever she chooses to do. She is not a victim or enemy of her father. She is well equipped to thrive in a competitive, male-dominated world.

A good and loving father gives his daughter a sense of value beyond her physical appearance. He teaches that her value is not based on good looks, make-up and clothes, material possessions, houses, cars, her husband, social status, or titles. By word and deed and time invested, the father places value in her heart and soul. This investment, and the bond it builds between father and daughter, gives the daughter a taste of her worth and value before God.

> *Her husband has full confidence in her*
> *and lacks nothing of value.*
> *She brings him good, not harm,*
> *all the days of her life.*[5]

What a comment on marriage! The husband of this woman trusts her completely. He receives personal benefit as a result of that trust. *Deep trust yields great rewards.* A woman, with the freedom to discover and explore her gifts, abilities, and interests, will bring great worth to her relationship with her husband. He has the benefit of her support—which frees him to take risks. They both benefit from the assets that her freedom to discover and explore brings. Trust ensures their continued growth and maturity. And trust makes true partners in life.

The marital relationship is not simple. The kind of marriage described in Proverbs 31 does not happen automatically. In fact, a wife cannot "do good" toward her husband if she experienced physical or sexual abuse from her father. The same is true for those who grew up in alcoholic homes, or in homes with emotional abuse, shame, and control. An abused woman needs to recover from her own wounds before she can "do good" toward her husband. This is particularly true for the woman who suffered in an abusive relationship with her father.

Recovery is a necessity. A woman cannot see her husband as a safe person until she faces the hurts she received from her father. She must heal the wounded child within herself. Otherwise, any pain she feels from her husband will be interpreted through her experience of her past abuse. Emotionally she cannot feel the difference. Her husband and the men who have wounded her are all the same. Her husband then receives all the anger and shame of those past experiences. When this happens, a woman can bring no good to her husband.

It is difficult for any woman to face her wounds from the past. But it is particularly difficult when the memory of those wounds has been blocked out of conscious awareness. I counseled a woman who became fearful and tense whenever her husband reached toward her in bed. She was frustrated and had no idea why she responded in that way. We explored her childhood experiences in counseling. She connected with memories of sexual abuse by both her father and her grandfather. No wonder she cringed at her husband's touch! To the little girl within her, touch from a man—any man—was scary. She had to deal with what had happened before she could distinguish between the touch of her father, her grandfather, and her husband. A woman who works a strong recovery program becomes able to respond positively toward her husband for a lifetime.

Proverbs 31 also carries a message for husbands. The message is about the husband who trusts his wife from the depth of his heart. In Hebrew, the word heart is *leb*. It literally means "inner man" or "being." So this passage indicates that this woman's husband trusts her without reservation. He trusts her from the depths of his being.

Some men are afraid to trust their wives. Releasing their wives to be and do what they need to do in life is scary. This is particularly true when a woman starts to face her woundedness and begins the process of emotional and spiritual healing. Her husband may become fearful and suspicious at this time. He may find it difficult to deal with a strong woman. He may be more comfortable when he controls or dominates his wife. This prevents his ability to support, trust, and encourage her. It is a great loss for the woman, her husband, and family.

An emotionally healthy woman who has a solid identity in Jesus Christ overflows with inner strength. She brings great good to her husband and family.

She selects wool and flax
and works with eager hands.
She is like the merchant ships,
bringing her food from afar.
She gets up while it is still dark;
she provides food for her family
and portions for her servant girls.[6]

The woman described here must have had an awesome relationship with her heavenly Father, her earthly father, her grandfather, and her uncles! It is easy to sense her self-assurance and physical confidence. This woman knows who she is. She is connected with the physical world. She produces goods through the work of her hands. And her work is done with passion and enjoyment. The Hebrew word for eager is *chepets*. It literally means "to take delight" or "find pleasure." So this woman finds pleasure in creating garments of flax and wool.

Her passion and creativity overflows to other areas of life as well. She is competent in business and able to manage her household. She works with energy and purpose. She is not satisfied with a fast food mentality day after day. She samples the variety of life and enjoys it. She takes risks to discover the many delights God's world brings.

Unlike this woman, many women never create something tangible or accomplish a physical feat. Nor do they experience the joy and satisfaction that comes with it. They do not know what it means to delight in their work. A daughter benefits greatly when her father is active and involved in her physical efforts. Fathers are involved in the physical world, and they gain confidence and satisfaction from their accomplishments. They build fences, make furniture, paint houses, repair cars, compete in sports, scuba dive, plant trees, or ride bikes. Yet they often exclude their daughters from such physical activities. They do not consider these to be feminine activities, or wrongly assume that their daughters will not enjoy them. The truth is that daughters enjoy most of the activities that fathers enjoy.

A daughter gains much when she shares in her father's interests and experiences. Side by side with her father, she discovers how to use her mind and hands to build, repair, or create something new. Her self-confidence grows with each experience. She learns important survival skills and confidence in her physical ability through participation in her father's physical world. Activities in that world may include sporting activities, physical labor, or adventures in everyday life.

Cortney's father enjoyed the outdoors. Whenever possible, he grabbed his backpack and hiked into the mountains. It was his way to get away from it all. Cortney's father took her on short day hikes after she turned five-years-old. They explored the woods together or followed streams as far as they could. Along the way, they skipped rocks across the water, looked for tadpoles and minnows, or picked wild flowers. Cortney grew and so did their hikes. Her father lengthened the hikes and made them more strenuous. He taught her to pace herself and conserve her strength. He taught her the safe way to cross a rushing stream. He taught her about the plants and animals that inhabited the areas they explored.

Cortney and her father took an overnight hike into the mountains when she was ten-years-old. To hike for a day and camp out under the stars was a great treat. She came back full of tales and new experiences to share with her friends. Pictures of their trip made Cortney the center of attention in class. Even the boys envied her. She had the know-how and experience to hike and camp out in the mountains! The physical confidence that Cortney gained that weekend made a life-long impact on her.

Gabby's father, on the other hand, didn't spend much time in the mountains. His weekends were filled with construction projects at home. Ever since she can remember, Gabby was his constant companion and assistant. She handed him tools, carried wood, fetched supplies, held things in place, and offered an extra hand. She learned at an early age how to distinguish tools, measure materials, hammer nails, and tighten screws. By adolescence, she could used her dad's power tools. She built simple wood projects on her own. And she developed the skill to do it all well.

As Gabby and her father worked together, she learned many important lessons. She learned that a mistake is only a mistake, and when you make a mistake, you pick up and try again. When Gabby cut a piece of wood too short, her father would say, "It's only wood. We can start again with another piece. And I'm sure we will find a use for that piece on another project."

Gabby's father made a deep and lasting impact on her life. His influence followed her into adult life. Gabby is not afraid to tackle any remodeling project at home. In fact, her husband came home one day to find a hole in the wall. Gabby decided that was a good spot to put a door! She is also an excellent negotiator at work. She can find a way to negotiate even the stickiest disagreements. She has strong boundaries in all of her relationships, yet she is emotionally and spiritually involved with her husband and children. She is a strong woman, yet is vulnerable and tender. A woman who is able to maintain both strength and tenderness has a deep inner confidence. That confidence was nurtured in Gabby's life during the many hours she spent woodworking with her father.

The kind of physical confidence that Cortney and Gabby have is a gift that any father can give his daughter. Physical confidence enables a woman to take on a task, set a personal goal, and see things through to completion. It enables her to stand strong against

forces that would harm her. Building this kind of confidence requires a father who does more than give his daughter a credit card
to use at the mall. It requires a father who is willing to open the
door to his life and invite his daughter to participate in his world.

She considers a field and buys it;
out of her earnings she plants a vineyard.[7]

Look at the skills this woman has! She knows how to operate a
business, buy and sell, stay within a budget, negotiate deals, and
plan for the future. This is a woman of strength! She knows what
she wants and takes action to get it. I don't think she would allow
anyone to pay her less than what a man gets for the same work.

This astute businesswoman has confidence, business know-how,
plus vision. Notice that she did not buy a vineyard. She bought a
field and planted a vineyard. She saw a field that had potential, and
she made that potential happen. Notice that she did not take out a
loan for this venture. She used her earnings—perhaps from another business—to make it happen. As a young girl, she must have
had someone to look up to and learn from. I can picture her: She
was with her father on business. She stood in the background, listened to every word and watched every movement and facial expression as her father conducted his affairs.

Karen, my wife, received similar training from her father. She
grew up on a farm in central Minnesota. She watched her father
negotiate deals for farm equipment, cars, and supplies. She learned
how to hold out for the best deal possible. Her skills have served
us well through the years. When I was in graduate school we needed
to buy a new car. Our old Buick had 127,000 miles on it. It still had
a good engine, but annoying repairs were a financial burden. A car
dealer offered us $1,000 in trade, but we needed $2,000 for a down
payment on another car, so we had to sell the Buick ourselves.

We advertised the car in the paper, and the calls soon started.
Every caller asked for "the man of the house," but Karen handled
this deal. Her negotiating skills are far better than mine are. She
would not budge from the $2,000 mark. Callers said they were not
interested. Finally, a man, who owned three businesses and was
buying a fourth, came to see the car. His wife really liked the car,
so he offered Karen $1,500.

"No," Karen said. "We have to have $2,000."

The man countered with an offer for $1,800. I started to get excited. *Okay, we've got a deal,* I thought.

"No" Karen said. "We need $2,000."

"You know," the man answered, "it is customary for you to come down when I move up!"

"No. We need $2,000," was all that Karen would say.

The man left. I turned to Karen and said, "I would have taken the $1,800."

Karen reminded me that we needed $2,000 to purchase another car. At that point, I figured that we would have the Buick for a very, very long time. But I knew it was wise to let Karen handle the sale in the way she believed was best.

Two hours later, the man called and said he would buy the car for $2,000. He paid Karen with twenty $100 bills, and he praised her sales ability. Karen knew what she wanted, had strength of purpose, maintained firm boundaries, and did not waver from her goal. She gained this gift of strength from her father.

She sets about her work vigorously; her arms are strong for her tasks.[8]

Physical strength is an important aspect of feminine strength. The woman in Proverbs 31 is certainly strong. She takes special effort to have the strength necessary to face what life brings. Being a wife, mother, and entrepreneur requires physical strength. It also requires emotional well-being and spiritual wholeness. It is easy to forget that we are emotional, spiritual, and physical beings. We cannot afford to neglect one or more of these aspects of life.

Many women minimize the importance of their physical strength. Some women and their fathers do not see physical strength as feminine. So they ignore the development of physical strength. Strong women threaten some fathers. They have trouble encouraging the development of their daughters' strength. Other fathers don't take care of themselves physically. They set poor examples for their daughters. Yet physical strength is essential if women are to handle the stresses of school, work, marriage, and/or parenting. Furthermore, recent medical research indicates that regular aerobic activity and strength training can prevent certain degenerative diseases such as osteoporosis.

I was fortunate to grow up on a farm. I saw that mothers, grandmothers, aunts, and sisters were physically able to do almost any task that a man can do. Women were just as capable as men to milk cows, drive tractors, make hay, or tote feedbags. In fact, it often took both men and women to get the crop in on time. And both did chores in spite of blinding blizzards, bitter cold, or blistering heat. These experiences—early in my life—gave me a respect for the physical strength of women. I want to communicate that respect and appreciation of feminine strength to my daughters.

A daughter is very fortunate if her father approves and affirms the development of her physical strength. Consider some of the following ways that a father can do this:

Model Proper Care—A father, who cares for himself physically, communicates the message that physical strength is important.

Participate in Activities—A father, who participates in physical activities with his daughter, nurtures her confidence in her physical ability.

Affirm Her Strength—A father, who affirms his daughter's physical strength, fosters her acceptance of her body as it is. This is crucial in a culture that worships physical perfection.

Encourage Her Capability—A father, who encourages his daughter to take on new physical challenges or push beyond present limits, reveals her physical capability to withstand the stresses and pressures of life.

A woman is blessed to have a father who nurtures her physical strength and confidence. This aspect of her feminine strength will help her set boundaries and assert herself in the world.

> *She sees that her trading is profitable,*
> *and her lamp does not go out at night.*
> *She opens her arms to the poor*
> *and extends her hands to the needy.*
> *When it snows, she has no fear for her household;*
> *for all of them are clothed in scarlet.*
> *She makes coverings for her bed;*
> *she is clothed in fine linen and purple.*
> *Her husband is respected at the city gate,*
> *where he takes his seat among the elders of the land.*[9]

It is hard to imagine a more successful woman than the one described here! She has it all. She is successful in her work, and she feels good about her accomplishments. She ensures that her family and children have what they need, but her concern goes beyond her family. She is compassionate and generous to the poor. She has a husband who is an honorable and respected community leader. Both husband and wife are secure and successful in their individual accomplishments. They support one another, and one does not compete with or threaten the other.

Many women cannot enjoy the blessings of the success God brings into their lives. Instead, they are fearful of losing what they have gained. They feel that no amount of success will ever be enough. Other women learn at an early age that some men are threatened by a woman's success. So they minimize their accomplishments or hold back, and their full potential is never realized. This is true in some marriages where the wife is expected to support and encourage her husband's success. But the husband will not encourage his wife because her success threatens him.

The woman described in Proverbs 31 has a deep sense of satisfaction in her accomplishments. The *New American Standard Version* translates the passage this way, *"She senses that her gain is good."* A strong and emotionally secure woman is able to feel a healthy sense of pride and pleasure in her accomplishments. A spiritually secure woman is able to feel blessed by the prosperity God brings her.

This woman's feeling of confident satisfaction is not self-serving. A strong, well-grounded, successful woman can see beyond her personal world. She does not distance herself from the needs of others. She does not use her success to insulate her from the harsh realities of life. She feels the pain and needs of those who suffer. She reaches out to them in love and compassion. God designed feminine strength, and it is right and good and beautiful.

She is clothed with strength and dignity;
she can laugh at the days to come.
She speaks with wisdom,
and faithful instruction is on her tongue.[10]

What a tribute for the Scriptures to say that she is "clothed with strength and dignity." This woman, who lived thousands of years ago, did not mature into a woman of strength and dignity through psychotherapy! These qualities must have developed through her spirituality, her family, and her extended family relationships.

Perhaps her father took great delight and pride in her strength. Perhaps he was a sensitive man who affirmed what she felt in her heart. Perhaps a similarly strong mother, grandmother, or aunt mentored her. Whatever took place in her development, it produced a godly woman of strength who inspires and encourages women even today. The strength and dignity of this woman radiated through her appearance. A woman like this speaks with great wisdom and has much to offer her world.

I would like to know more about this woman's father. I'm sure that his example and teaching would be a great help to other fathers and myself. Although we know nothing about the father of the Proverbs 31 woman, we do know something about Esther's father, Mordecai. We know that Mordecai nurtured Esther's feminine strength. His example shows us how important this is in a woman's development.

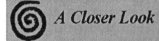 *A Closer Look*

Feminine Strength—One of the best definitions of feminine strength is in Proverbs 31. The woman described in Proverbs 31 has the strength to manage a home, tend a family, direct a ministry, or even control a Fortune 500 company. And, she can do these things with tenderness, compassion, wisdom, and business savvy. A woman, who feels her high worth, is capable of anything. She is a seed bed for miracles. A woman, who feels her innate worth as a child of the living God, has the ability to take risks. She can face new challenges with strength and bring them to fruition. She can provide a loving and secure environment for her family. She can sacrifice her own needs for those she loves and still find ways to care for herself. She can nurture her own spiritual and emotional growth. She can be confident in her creative work and take risks to expand her market. She can make a political stand on issues and serve in positions of leadership at any level. The ultimate foundation for this feeling of feminine value and strength comes from God. But that foundation is laid through the involvement of a father who is emotionally and spiritually connected to his daughter.

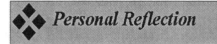
Personal Reflection

1. How would you describe your feminine strength? In what areas would you like to develop your feminine strength?

2. How has your father's view of women affected the woman you are today?

3. What strengths or abilities, weaknesses or limitations, do you attribute to your father's involvement in your life?

4. What aspects of strength in the Proverbs 31 woman inspire you to take risks in your own life? What risks and challenges are calling to you?

5. Take a few moments to thank God for the example of the godly woman in Proverbs 31. Ask him to build the same strength in you.

NOTES:

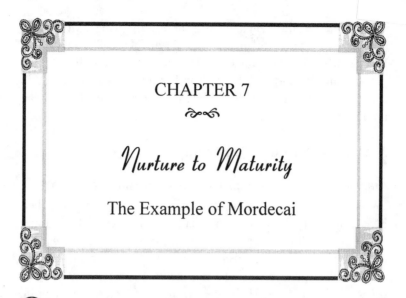

CHAPTER 7

Nurture to Maturity

The Example of Mordecai

Queen Esther was upset with Mordecai's public display of grief at the city gate. The cause for his distress troubled her more. And the dangerous stand he wanted her to take shook her to the core. She must have wondered, *Doesn't Mordecai know that his request could mean my immediate death?*

Esther's only hope of survival was in the hands of her unpredictable husband, King Xerxes. He would grant her admission into his presence, or order her death. Mordecai's grave request had torn the young queen's heart. She considered his words that God may have placed her in this royal position for this moment. She alone could ask relief and deliverance for her people. She thought about Mordecai's heavy heartache—his public pain. She recalled her Jewish identity—one of God's chosen people. A new resolve gripped her. She sent back this reply:

> "Go, gather together all the Jews who are in Susa, and fast for me. Do not eat or drink for three days, night or day. My maids and I will fast as you do. When this is done, I will go to the king, even though it is against the law. And if I perish, I perish."[1]

Esther kept her word. She fasted, prayed, and took action. Dressed in her royal robes, Esther walked into the inner court of the palace. She came face-to-face with King Xerxes.

What a powerful scene! What strength and conviction! Esther

walked into certain death to make an appeal for justice. Mordecai's actions had a powerful impact on his daughter. She knew that Mordecai's spirituality ran deep. He was not afraid to live out the emotion in his heart and the truth in his spirit. He modeled these things for Esther. It touched her heart and enabled her to walk the path before her.

A Model of Genuine Spirituality

Modeling is a key part of the father-daughter relationship. What a father models either builds up or destroys his daughter. For Esther, Mordecai modeled genuine spirituality. His actions left no doubt about his love for God and his concern for God's people. He modeled spiritual courage by his expression of grief for his people.

The honest expression of deep feelings is a gift that a father gives to his daughter. He conveys a powerful message when he shares his fears or worries. And he sets a godly example when he takes those concerns to his heavenly Father in prayer. His example of honesty and spirituality in the difficult times teaches his daughter to ask for help in her tough seasons of life. He helps her express her feelings to God. His worship, praise, thanks, and joyful celebration in God's house helps her connect with God in joy and thankfulness.

Christian fathers can fail to realize the impact their actions have on their daughters. Fathers consider spirituality to be acts of worship, Bible reading, and prayer. Father do not connect emotions and spirituality. But emotions are intertwined with every part of life. Spirituality and emotions cannot be separated.

Praise and affirmation of our daughter, conveys an unspoken spiritual message that God also delights in her. When we express anger toward our daughter, we convey a spiritual message that God may not be pleased with her. A fathers must be aware of the potential spiritual impact that his emotions have on his daughter. It is important that he shares the feelings of his heart; and yet, he guard the emotions that would harm his daughter.

A Test of Strength

Earlier, we saw how Mordecai broke through Esther's fantasy world and forced her to deal with reality. He also challenged her to move into new territory—to take risks. He encouraged bold action that would test what she was made of. Look again at what he said to her:

> *"Do not think that because you are in the king's house that you alone of all the Jews will escape. For if you remain silent at this time, relief and deliverance for the Jews will arise from another place, but you and your father's family will perish. And who knows but that you have come to royal position for such a time as this?"*[2]

Mordecai had nurtured a strong daughter. He trained her in a spiritual heritage. He taught her to set boundaries and protect herself. He helped her face life as it is—not as she wanted it to be. He had been unafraid to express deep, heartfelt emotion.

Now it was time for Esther to discover and test the depth of her feminine strength. This was not an easy transition for father and daughter. They faced a difficult issue. They experienced an honest struggle—one on one side of the issue, one on the other. During that struggle, Mordecai voiced strong words to Esther. Esther responded with strong emotion to Mordecai. Both had to hear the other's concerns. In the end, Esther, like a true leader—a queen who cares for her people—rose to the occasion. Notice her next communication to Mordecai:

> *"Go, gather together all the Jews who are in Susa, and fast for me. Do not eat or drink for three days, night or day. I and my maids will fast as you do. When this is done, I will go to the king, even though it is against the law. And if I perish, I perish. So Mordecai went away and carried out all of Esther's instructions."*[3]

Do you sense how strong Esther has become? She seizes her role as queen and acts on behalf of her people. She feels the spiritual, emotional, and physical reality of her position. She knows what happened to Queen Vashti. She knows what it means to stand up to the king. She knows what action she must take. She knows it could mean her death sentence. Her fear is great, yet Esther takes a bold step of courage. She is a woman of strength and valor. She accepts the difficult reality and is willing to sacrifice her life for her people.

Esther reveals her action plan to Mordecai. She gives him his marching orders. Mordecai recognizes Esther's strength—the trans-

formation of new leadership. He senses her growth—her independence and autonomy. She is no longer dependent on him. Esther is
an adult woman. Mordecai steps back from his role as father and
teacher. He moves into the role of father and supporter. In humility, he obeys his queen's command with no further discussion.

The Role of Support in Encouraging
Feminine Strength

I admire Esther's strength to face such a great a risk. She has a
deep conviction that this step of faith is the right thing to do. She
lived in a world where men are all-powerful. A woman's feelings,
ideas, and opinions mattered little. Still, she followed her father's
lead and took a great risk.

There is something important about the way in which Esther
assumes this risk. She does not do it alone. In this time of great
trial and trouble, Esther enlisted others for support. She did not
consider attempting the task on her own. She knew that it required
diligent fasting from all involved. She told (not asked) her father
to get the help of the whole community to fast on her behalf: *"Go,
gather together all the Jews who are in Susa, and fast for me."*

In this simple statement, the strength of the father-daughter bond
shines through. Esther knows that she can trust her father. She knows
that she can count on him for support. She knows that he will enlist
others to help her. Most importantly, Esther knows that she can
turn to God in times of trouble. Mordecai has taught her to pray,
and he will support her now through prayer.

The message here is clear: Strength does not mean being alone.
Strength means being vulnerable to our heavenly Father and his
people. Strength rises up when we share our needs, our pain, and
our concerns with God and his people. Yet in the church today, too
many women carry their heaviest burdens alone.

Norma, for example, suffers through a secret struggle with depression. Without provocation or warning, she can weep uncon-
trollably. She loves her husband and children, yet she often feels
like running away from them. She relies on lots of coffee to get
through the day. She is burdened with frequent thoughts of dying.
She is confused and afraid. *How can I be a Christian and have
these feelings?* she wonders. She is too embarrassed to talk to her

pastor—too afraid to see a therapist. She hasn't been to her family doctor in years. Even though she thinks she feels a lump in her breast, the fear paralyzes her. She cannot make the appointment. *I'm afraid of what the doctor will find,* she thinks. *I can't bear to know.* She wants help, but she does not know where to find it or how to ask for it.

Claudia also carries a secret burden. She does not understand her anger toward her husband. His lack of emotional involvement with her and the children irritates her. His lack of initiative at work has her at wits end. *If he only would care a little more,* she thinks, *maybe he could be a better provider for his family.* But there's more. His lack of spiritual leadership in the home embitters Claudia. Her anger is beginning to frighten her. She increasingly takes it out on the children. She doesn't feel she can talk to her friends about it. Even they make her angry.

Debbie, too, is angry. Not at her family. She is angry at God. She has a successful career, but at thirty-eight years of age there is still no man, at least no one she feels she could marry. She has had plenty of opportunities, but she is still a virgin. She does not see even one, single, godly man in her church. Sometimes she feels as if she should throw in the towel and compromise. *Maybe I should settle for less,* she thinks. *Maybe my view of a godly life is too lofty.* Debbie is respected at church. She is reaping the rewards of her hard work at the office. But she is unhappy and dissatisfied with church, work, and her lonely life.

The individual circumstances of these women vary, yet they have the same problem. They are trying to make it alone, without the support of others. It is tempting to remain silent and alone when we deal with deep, painful issues. It is tempting to silence and numb the real hurts and struggles inside. Some use food, prescription drugs, or a drink or two to make it through the day. Others binge and purge or starve. It is tempting to silence the rage of an abusive father—to push the memories deeper and deeper inside. It is tempting to silence the devastation of an alcoholic spouse by working overtime. But that silence can be deadly. The support and safety of others is needed to break the silence.

Esther was tempted to remain silent. She hoped that she would not fall victim to the coming devastation. Mordecai, however, could help her see the destruction that her passive response would bring.

Esther needed the support of her father and other people. Norma, Claudia, and Debbie also need the support of others. They need someone to break through their fantasy that life will be okay if they keep trying hard enough on their own. They each need someone to help them know that it is okay to ask for help. They each need someone to help them realize that their outer image needs an inner reality for a foundation. Norma needs to share her fears and hidden feelings with others. It will help her stop the self-medication with coffee and begin to deal with the roots of her depression. Claudia needs a safe group of women with whom to share her anger. Perhaps a Codependent's Anonymous or an Overcomers Outreach group can help her face reality. The support could direct her focus from her husband and her circumstances to her own recovery and positive action. Debbie needs a supportive group of Christian women. She needs others who recognize her struggle, who can grieve with her, who will see her through the lonely times, and who will affirm her values.

It is not easy for women to ask for support and help. Women often put the needs and feelings of others first. They think it is the Christian thing to do. Esther's proclamation for support is the proper and right action. Her godly example is an encouragement to make our needs known.

Esther's grand request indicates that she had a strong connection with her earthly father and a solid faith in her heavenly Father: *". . . fast for me. Do not eat or drink for three days, night or day. I and my maids will fast as you do."* This was no casual, "please say a quick prayer for me" type of request. Fasting for three days is serious business. Esther and the women closest to her were going to do it. The step was risky enough that Esther wanted the support of the entire religious community as well. At the end of the prescribed time, Esther felt enough faith in God, enough inner strength, and a strong enough resolve to take the risk. Well aware that she might fail and die, she accepted the challenge.

Feminine Strength Is Sufficient

The moment of truth came when Esther walked into King Xerxes' court and approached him face to face:

> *On the third day, Esther dressed in her royal robes and went to the king's hall. When the king saw her, he was pleased with her and held out to her the gold scepter that was in his hand. So Esther approached and touched the tip of the scepter. He then asked her what she wanted, but before she could answer, he offered her up to half of his kingdom—just for the asking!*[4]

Imagine how hard Esther's heart must have been beating! One moment she doesn't know if she will live or die, and the next she is offered half of the kingdom! This is no place for weak boundaries or faltering strength. But Esther—the adult woman and queen of her people—handles the situation beautifully. She approached the king with a wise and calculated plan. Clearly focused on her task, she ignored his offer of wealth and power. Esther simply asked the king if he and his top man, Haman, would have lunch with her.

King Xerxes eagerly agrees. A short time later they enjoyed the meal that Esther had prepared. During the meal, the king again asked her what she wants. He tells her that no matter what it is, she can have it. He even repeated his offer to give her half of the kingdom. But Esther did not waver. She was gracious but clever. She asked the king and Haman to join her again for lunch the next day:

> *"If the king regards me with favor and it pleases the king to grant my petition and fulfill my request, let the king and Haman come tomorrow to the banquet I will prepare for them. Then I will answer the king's question."*[5]

Of course, the king accepts her second invitation. How could he refuse? Esther knows exactly what she is doing. She is honoring the king, which we know delights him. And her refusal to reveal what's on her mind intrigues him. With his curiosity aroused, he will be eager to meet with her. Haman also is delighted. He returns home feeling very proud of himself.

The next twenty-four hours were eventful. Haman's hate for Mordecai reached its crescendo. At the suggestion of his wife and friends, he built a gallow on which to hang Mordecai. In high spirits the next morning, Haman went to the king to ask for Mordecai's execution. But before he spoke, the king asked for his advice.

During a sleepless night, King Xerxes read the official records. He noted how Mordecai has uncovered the plot on his life. He realized that Mordecai has never been honored for his great deed. The king is determined to honor him. Haman entered the court at that moment. The king asks him how a person who has done a great service to the king should be honored. Haman was sure that the king was referring to him. So he made the honor as regal as possible. To Haman's great dismay, Xerxes then asked him to personally bestow that honor on Mordecai.

Afterward, Haman rushed home. Humiliation and panic seize him. He and his friends bemoaned his fate—certain ruin. Then it was time for Esther's banquet. Escorts brought Haman back to the royal court. It was then that Esther dropped her bombshell:

> "If I have found favor with you, O king, and if it pleases your majesty, grant me my life—this is my petition. And spare my people—this is my request. For my people and I have been sold for destruction and slaughter and annihilation. If we had merely been sold as male and female slaves, I would have kept quiet, because no such distress would justify disturbing the king."
>
> King Xerxes asked Queen Esther, "Who is he? Where is the man who has dared to do such a thing?"
>
> Esther said, "The adversary and enemy is this vile Haman."[6]

Esther's statement so enraged the king that he had to leave the room. Haman was liquefied with terror. He clung to Esther begging for his life. At this point, we see Esther's great strength. Haman knew he was doomed. He begged for his life—his tears flooded Esther's lap. Esther was not moved. She felt no pity. She never considered that he had learned his lesson and would kill no more Jews. She never yielded to his plea for mercy. No! Esther did not rescue Haman or try to fix things. She let the consequences fall where they needed to fall.

Then things got worse for Haman. The king returned and saw Haman hanging on the queen. To the king, Haman appeared to be molesting Esther. His death sentence was sealed. He was hung on the gallows that he had prepared for Mordecai. The king gave Haman's wealth to Esther, and Haman's home to Mordecai. The king issued a new decree that allowed the Jews to kill anyone who might attack them. The celebration was great! All of God's people were delivered—saved.

I am moved by the magnitude of Esther's risk—her willing sacrifice. I am amazed by her courage and the strength of her appeal before this powerful and vengeful man. She physically stood alone against the treachery of Haman's plot. Spiritually and emotionally, she had legions of support behind her. She carried in her heart a lifetime of experiences with her earthly father. She carried in her soul the support of her people. She carried in her spirit the ever-present reality of her heavenly Father.

Mordecai and Esther show us the spiritual and emotional connection that a father and daughter can have. We see a father who seeks out his daughter, who teaches her about boundaries, who encourages her emotions, who models godly principles, and who demonstrates his absolute confidence in her. We also see a daughter, who before our eyes is transformed from a child to a queen—a woman of God. We see her grow into a woman of spiritual and feminine strength. We see her act with bold and unselfish courage. We see her seize the challenge, face the ultimate the risk, and stand victorious above all her enemies.

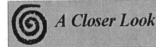 *A Closer Look*

Modeling—Values are imparted from one life to another. *Values are caught not taught.* Models are the living examples of character that impact another human being—for good or evil. The whole direction of a person's life is set by his or her values. We pay attention to what we value. Christian discipleship is an example of positive modeling and value impartation. Another positive example is the sponsorship one finds in twelve-step programs. But the most important modeling takes place in the home from parents to children. Like it or not, children look to their parents' behavior for the most important lessons of life. Words are not needed. Modeling imparts values through conduct, attitudes, behaviors, and beliefs.

Humility—Many in recovery misunderstand humility. It does not mean putting myself in second place and doing more for others. Humility does not mean saying *I'm sorry*. Humility is seeing myself as God sees me. It is putting myself in proper perspective in light of God's plan. The basic ingredient of all humility is a desire to seek and to do God's will.

Support—The support that heals and helps us is the support we get from others—individuals who share our problems, pains, and struggles. We cannot make it alone. It is tempting to remain silent when we deal with deep, painful issues. But that silence can be deadly. The support and safety of others is needed to break the silence and speak the truth about our lives. The support of others can direct our focus away from painful circumstances and onto recovery and positive action. We need a supportive group of others who recognize our struggles, who can grieve with us, who will see us through the lonely times, and who will affirm our values.

Prayer—Prayer is communication with God. It is most effective when it is honest and frequent. It is fitting to complain to God, to lament before God, to thank God, to share the details of our lives with God, to praise God, and to talk to God as we would talk to a trusted friend. Avoid "wish-list" prayers that ask God for something. Our best pursuit in prayer is to seek God's will for us, and to seek the power to carry out God's will.

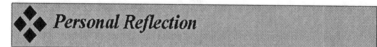

Personal Reflection

1. What characteristics has your father modeled for you?

2. What are the "difficult issues" you have faced with your father?

3. How willing and able are you to accept the support and assistance of others during life's hard times?

4. How has your father helped you develop the inner strength necessary to take risks, act courageously, and live independently?

5. Take a few moments to reflect on your feminine strength. In what ways has your inner strength been put to the test?

CHAPTER 8

❧

Face the Loss, Heal the Wounds

The Journey toward Health

My tears are trapped beneath the glaze,
    beneath my blurring eyes,
My muscles tense, to keep restraint,
    for fear the rage should rise.
My quivering tips betray the fear
    I tried so hard to hide.
I'm numb in helpless effort,
    to keep it all inside.

I feel the wet of tears that fall,
    the red of blood that bleeds.
Though others cannot see it,
    my wound is real to me.
Inflicting pain I find release,
    from torment deep within.
It doesn't seem to matter
    if they label it as sin.

The burn is warm, with sweet relief
    I feel the twinge of pain.
It's easier to keep the hurt,
    than give away the blame.
I spit back out that thing
    which brings a sense inside of comfort.
I don't deserve to soothe the pain.
    It seems so right to hurt.

Oh angry child inside of me,

you needn't bear the shame.
There is someone who understands,
    you know His precious name.
He sees the tears that never fall.
    He knows the rage inside.
He's felt the fear that torments you,
    the helplessness you hide.

Remember child, the promise:
    He's not like other men.
Jesus holds you safe inside.
    You won't be hurt again.
                Silent Rage, author anonymous[1]

Written by a bulimic, this poem symbolizes the pain that many women feel inside. The efforts to numb that pain take many forms. They range from anorexia to compulsive overeating, from alcoholism to compulsive service to others, from sexual addiction to codependency, from workaholism to controlling others, or from passivity to perfectionism.

The causes of the pain may vary as well. They may include abandonment, shame, physical abuse, verbal abuse, emotional distance, sexual violation, rage, and the like. Yet no matter how varied the circumstances surrounding the pain, two things are certain. Firstly, a significant portion of a woman's pain results from her broken or ineffective relationship with her father. Secondly, as the poem's author discovered, healing ultimately comes from God.

Beth, for example, has a good job and a loving husband. Still, she is crippled by fear. The fears have always been there—all her life. Her family was in church every time the doors opened. Yet her parents fought non-stop. Beth grew afraid of her father's anger. She learned not to ask him for anything. She was on edge all through childhood and always on alert. She began to relax after she married and moved out of her parents' home. But the relief was not perfect. A change in her husband's voice or an unexpected demand from her supervisor, and Beth is filled with panic. She struggles to function. She feels guilty and fearful—emotionally transported back in time to her angry father and chaotic home.

Mary was a young girl when her father died. Now, at age thirty-five, she is about eighty pounds overweight. "People at church make comments about my weight," she says. "They tell me that if I just give it over to the Lord, I'll be okay. But I'm not so sure. I've already tried everything. I've been to diet centers, weight-loss programs, Bible studies, and prayer groups. I can be 'good' with food for a while, but then I start feeling tense and worried. The only thing that makes me feel better is to eat. I just wish my father were still alive. I can't believe how much I miss him."

June, in her late forties, is still unsure of herself. She's like a timid, little girl. Her father was always home at 5:15, but he went straight to his workbench in the garage until it was time to eat. He would eat dinner with the family, then retreat to the garage until bedtime. June and her brothers had to deal with the rage of her alcoholic mother. "Dad always attempted to please Mom," she said. "He never stood up to her when she screamed at us for just being kids. I wish he would call me to ask how I'm doing. It would mean so much if he would just recognize me as an adult and want to talk with me."

Each of these stories has a common thread: a father who was not emotionally available to his daughter. Each of these women has a hole in her soul—a void that God designed the father to fill. As we have seen, that hole can be a painful wound—a deep longing, a gnawing hunger. A woman can search in many directions to fill that wound. Some women have sought fulfillment through relationships with the perfect man. Others have fallen victim to compulsive diseases (such as bulimia). Some have been entrapped by addictions that bring spiritual, emotional, and physical destruction. Others have pursued achievements, accomplishments, and affluence to fill the emptiness. And some have chosen to care for and please other people in the hope that someone in turn will care for them and soothe their pain.

In truth, there is only one way to heal the wound. Healing comes through a journey. The process begins at the point of loss—the broken relationship with the father. This journey requires a commitment to seek sobriety from those things that numb the pain. A woman must put aside whatever substance, activity, or person she has used to fill her emptiness. She will need her pain and her longing, for it will be her greatest guide.

The healing journey cannot be taken alone. Other women must come alongside to share the process and acknowledge the pain. The deep hurt inside longs for expression and it cries for comfort. But the hurt that has been hidden must be brought to God. Others can help, but God must heal. He is the perfect Father. This journey, the recovery process, is not short. It lasts a lifetime and yields rewards at every turn. The growth and the healing never ends. And every woman, needy or not, can benefit from this journey.

The Risk and the Reward

There comes a time in life when the journey toward healing becomes inescapable. During her twenties, a woman is preoccupied—driven to find her place in the world. By her mid-thirties, the course of her life takes shape. She begins to take stock of where she is. The idealism and illusions she had about work, life, and marriage have been replaced by stark reality. In her forties, a woman begins to realize her mortality—life isn't forever. She starts to consider the rest of her life: *How will I survive in the years to come? Will life always be this hard? Is there a better way?*

The woman in her late thirties and forties considers the state of her life on a conscious level. At that same time, unconscious physical and psychological processes urge her to seek health and a greater well-being. Her well-practiced coping strategies don't work as they once did. The pain of destructive relationships or lifestyle patterns intensifies and cries out for resolution. The physical impact of internal pain and tension begins to appear through illness or disease. There is no escape.

Psychological decay leads to physical breakdown. When the physical signs appear, a woman has a choice to make. She can continue in her denial and ignore the signs. Or she can face the difficulties head-on. In some cases, a woman is forced to make that choice—physical conditions may threaten her life. The good news is that a woman's move toward spiritual and emotional healing, moves her toward physical healing as well.

The journey toward healing brings out a woman's core self. A woman can live with a distorted view of herself. She sees herself in terms of particular roles rather than personal reality. A woman may be viewed as a wife, a mother, a teacher, an athlete, a waitress, a scholar, or a corporate executive. These are worthy roles and functions, but they do not represent the full scope of her person. A mother may also be a brilliant administrator. A corporate executive may be a creative and passionate artist. A waitress may be a powerful prayer warrior. The difficult task is to discover "the other woman"—the one behind the roles she plays. The recovery process uncovers the true person inside. It releases a woman's gifts and unique potential.

A woman who discovers her core self finds great delight in new creative, spiritual, or intellectual pursuits. I have seen women create businesses that reflect their personal interests and unique abilities. I know one woman who leads a Bible study. Her preparation matches the effort many pastors spend on a Sunday sermon. I have seen women go back to school and earn degrees. They were enabled to fulfill dreams that were given up for lost. Women in recovery function better in their established roles. And they are in a better position to fulfill their unique gifts.

Recovery brings relational blessings as well. A married woman who seeks emotional and spiritual healing finds that her relationship with her husband improves. Even if her husband is destructive, she is able to maintain strong boundaries that keep the relationship safe for herself and her children. A healthier, more emotionally developed mother can be available and intimate with her children. They are able to see a more complete picture of what it means to be feminine. Her sons will have a greater appreciation and respect for the feminine sex. And her daughters will be more likely to develop their full, feminine potential.

Change and healing are not without risk. These risks can be frightening. A husband may feel threatened by his wife's steps toward recovery. The change and growth in his wife will reveal who she really is inside. A husband may fear his wife's recovery and be apprehensive when he experiences her true identity for the first time. He may think, *She isn't the same person anymore.* Fear of abandonment or rejection may arise and that may spawn anger. He may try to sabotage her efforts toward healing.

In many years of counseling, I have yet to see anything but good come out of a solid journey into healing. In fact, I believe recovery work is necessary for a husband and wife to become "one flesh", intimate in the biblical definition of marriage.[2] We all live by the old rules—things learned in our family of origin. To leave our parents' way of doing things, we have to face the reality of our relationship with our parents, good and bad. When we examine and let go of our family dysfunction, we can see our spouse as the person he or she really is. If we do not leave our family dysfunction, we will view our spouse through the distortion of our wounds and live life as victims of our pain. We will also be doomed to repeat the mistakes that our parents made.

A woman who pursues a journey of healing will at times face difficult risks in other areas of life. Shirley, for instance made great progress in her recovery until she had to deal with a new supervisor at work. Shirley had been with the company for years and had earned a solid reputation as a good and trustworthy worker. When she had a question or problem, she was free to speak directly with the president of the company. Her new supervisor, however, operated through power, control, and fear. He told Shirley that she would no longer have direct access to the president. All her questions were to be discussed with him. If she did not respect his authority, he promised to make things very difficult for her.

Shirley's new supervisor did make things difficult. He blamed her for failures that were his problem, not hers. Shirley knew the failures would damage the company, but her supervisor had forbidden her to speak with anyone about it. She felt trapped. *How can I do my best for the company*, she wondered, *when my supervisor is so negative about me?* Shirley feared for her job.

I had worked with Shirley long enough to know that she had a rock-solid place in the company. It would take more than this newcomer to make things go sour for her. We worked to strengthen her boundaries with her supervisor. She learned to clearly express what she had done and what her supervisor had not done. She gathered the courage to politely, but firmly, state that she would not allow anyone to speak to her in a degrading manner. She announced that she would leave the room the next time it occurred. The first time she set boundaries like this, her supervisor exploded like Mt. Vesuvius! Shirley stood her ground and documented the incident. In time, she had a big, fat folder of documentation. I told her to reveal these happenings to the president of the company.

The president of the company respected Shirley. He was irate when he heard the news. He took immediate action and dealt with the supervisor. These were scary, unsettling times for Shirley. Her supervisor was furious. And in a short time, he was back to his old tricks. Shirley had to be strong and maintain the boundaries she had set. She had to face the fear of losing her job each time she stood up to her supervisor. She had to stay on her toes, document the truth, and go to the president at the right time. After a number of similar episodes, the supervisor's track record was clear to the president. The supervisor was fired.

Shirley was relieved when things turned out as they did. But no one can control how someone will respond to growth and change in another. There is always a risk that the disastrous results we fear may come about. In spite of these risks, the journey toward healing is worth the cost.

Pearl S. Buck said, "Those who do not know how to weep with their whole heart don't know how to laugh either." Healing the wounds of the past does bring whole-hearted weeping. But it also brings a new wholeness, fullness, and health to life. We experience these good changes physically, emotionally, and spiritually.

Consider what happened to Annette. When she was six years old, her father left her with her alcoholic mother. He took her younger sister to live with him. Annette watched her father, a wealthy doctor, remarry and develop a whole new life for himself and her sister. Meanwhile, Annette's life was a continuous nightmare. She weathered one crisis after another. Although she and her mother attended the same church throughout her childhood, they moved nineteen times in thirteen years. Annette's mother never had enough money to pay the bills. They lived in one place until they were evicted, or until the bill collectors caught up with them, and then moved on to another.

Annette always felt like a failure. She believed that something was wrong with her. *After all,* she would think, *if I had been good enough, Dad would have taken me to live with him, too.* Annette even felt responsible when her mother couldn't pay the bills. These wounds, in her relationship with her father and mother, devastated Annette's future choices in her relationships with men. Her first two husbands were angry, controlling, alcoholic men. They were both abusive. By the end of her second marriage Annette knew she needed help just to survive. That's when she began in counseling and embarked on an active recovery program.

Annette's journey of healing completely changed her life. She developed a spiritual connection with God that she had never experienced before. She viewed herself and men differently. Eventually she began dating a man in her church choir. Before they were married, Annette would come into my office glowing. She once said, "Earl, I feel like I'm sixteen! I go out with this man, and it's like I've never been on a date before. I've been married twice, but I feel like this is my first marriage!"

"That makes sense to me," I answered. "In a way, it is your first marriage. It is the first time you have consciously chosen to marry a man. In your first two marriages, you did nothing more than live out the pain of your relationship with your parents."

The Process of Recovery

Like Annette, many women (and men, too) spend their lives living out the pain of their wounded relationships with their parents. In an effort to maintain their own sanity, they often turn to behaviors and actions that lessen the pain they feel. These pain-numbing behaviors include codependency, toxic relationships, and a host of addictions—prescription drugs, sex, work, or alcohol.

These behaviors provide a very shaky foundation for living. They do nothing to build up the core self of the person. They do nothing to fortify the boundaries that protect the core self from harmful attack. They do nothing to heal the painful wounds. They only mask the pain that threatens to overwhelm the person. Eventually, codependent and addictive behaviors do one of two things: physically destroy the person, or fail to match her level of pain. In either case the result is the same—killing the pain is killing them.

In order to recover and heal from this damage, a woman needs to replace her shaky footing with a rock-solid foundation. This will enable her to heal from past wounds and establish appropriate boundaries. Her core self—the beautiful, unique individual God created—will be free to grow and impact the world around her. A solid foundation for living consists of three parts:

Spirituality—a conscious connection between the wounded inner child and God the Father.

Support—healing help from a twelve-step group, church community, or other support groups.

Sobriety—abstinence from addictions, codependency, toxic relationships, and other pain-numbing behaviors.

Woman in Recovery with a Solid Foundation

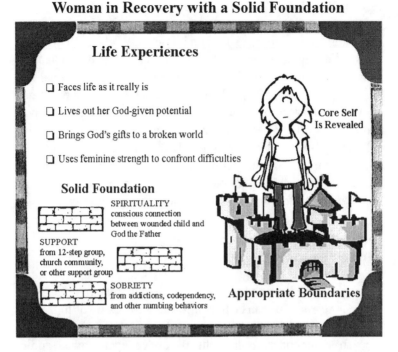

Life Experiences

❏ Faces life as it really is

❏ Lives out her God-given potential

❏ Brings God's gifts to a broken world

❏ Uses feminine strength to confront difficulties

Core Self Is Revealed

Solid Foundation

SPIRITUALITY
conscious connection
between wounded child and
God the Father

SUPPORT
from 12-step group,
church community,
or other support group

SOBRIETY
from addictions, codependency,
and other numbing behaviors

Appropriate Boundaries

All three elements are necessary for long-term healing and recovery to take place. To neglect any one of these foundational areas of recovery will hinder the healing process. We need sobriety so that we can feel the pain that is hidden in our hearts. Unless we feel our pain, we cannot identify or heal from the wounds that have hindered our growth. We need support because none of us have the personal resources and strength required to fight this battle on our own. The wisdom, encouragement, acceptance, and comfort of others keep us on track. They urge us to press on with the healing process and resist the temptation to give up and not fall short of what God has created us to be. We need a conscious connection with our wounded inner child and our loving Father so that we can feel what takes place inside our hearts. Insight and awareness of our wounds is insufficient to bring about change and growth. We need to feel the impact of our wounds in the core of our being.

It is no small thing to rebuild a solid foundation for living. Many of us have built our lives on the shaky footing of codependency or addiction. We want the quick fix, the easy solution, the magical cure. We envy those who receive instant deliverance through God's grace and healing.

The fact that there is no quick fix—recovery is hard work. That fact should not discourage us. God is concerned about all that happens in the depths of our hearts. He sent his Son to die so that our hearts could be healed. He cares about us all, the individual and the Christian community. I believe God wants us to support one another in all areas of life, as the early Christians did. This support is nothing short of a life-and-death matter. It's rock bottom, honest spirituality—all pretense is gone, all shame is gone, all blame is gone. God intends for his people to honestly seek him and support one another. This kind of mutual focus and support brings healing. It brings us to life—spiritually, emotionally, and physically.

Confronting the Feelings, Choosing Healing

The work of healing and recovery requires that we first feel what is in our hearts. This can be uncomfortable and cause us to feel out of control. We don't like that, so we deny our feelings and block them from our conscious thought. We use codependent and addictive behaviors to mask the unpleasant feelings. We learned to do this early in our childhood. Some of us are very successful at minimizing the impact of our feelings on a conscious level. But we ultimately cannot escape from our deepest feelings. They leave their mark on us no matter what we do.

The feelings we were exposed to, through our interaction with our parents and others, and the feelings we had in response interact with our central nervous system. This creates powerful emotions, called *affect states*. We physically feel these states. They include fear, anger, pain, and shame. They can cause an array of physical symptoms that include tightness in the stomach, clammy palms, perspiration, increased heart rate, changes in body temperature, shallow breathing, and light-headedness.

Affect states can be triggered by events as benign as a slight hand movement, a song, a change in tone of voice, a facial expression, or a particular choice of words that mimics or suggests a past, painful event. The association with the past triggers the emotions of the past. Immediately the affect state takes over and produces the physiological changes described above. An individual's natural response is to perform behaviors that restore a sense of comfort or calm. The tragedy is that codependency or compulsive, addictive behaviors are often the quick fixes that smooth or settled the feelings. As a result, many of us are not consciously aware of affect states until they impact us, or others, in a toxic way.

I have a personal example of the power of affect states on our lives. My grandfather was in his early thirties during The Great Depression years. Although he survived, he lived the rest of his life in unending fear of total economic disaster and personal failure. His fears impacted every member of my family. At times, the same fears my grandfather lived under gain a grip on me. When they do, I feel compelled to work longer and harder. I also eat more satisfying foods to keep the fear at bay. At those times, I need the support of others so that I can turn away from the urge to work and eat. It is not easy to release my fears to God and trust him to meet my needs.

My situation is not unique. Many adults carry feelings that were induced by members of their family of origin. One adult may experience panic attacks. Another may tend to be suspicious of people in general. Another may have trouble sleeping for fear of nighttime abuse. These are a few of the feelings that trigger affect states.

We often think of affect states as being negative or sinful. The truth is that these feelings are not an act of volition—not a choice of our will. We feel them whether we want to or not. We can never free ourselves from the reality of these feelings, but we can (and must) learn to recognize and confront them. We do not have to respond to them in destructive ways. That is why sobriety is essential to the healing process.

Impact of Family Learning on Our Feelings

Carried Feelings:	Affect State:	Gift:
Panic, Fear, Terror	FEAR	Wisdom & Protection
Rage, Depression	ANGER	Power & Energy
Hopelessness	PAIN	Growth
Worthlessness	SHAME	Humanness

It helps to realize that affect states are, by God's design, a part of our humanity. They are a gift from God and have an important function in our lives. Fear is a warning signal that cautions us to see if it is safe to proceed as planned. Anger is a source of strength that enables us to take firm action. Pain is a signal that we need healing and comfort. Shame is a reminder of our imperfect humanity. Each affect state can lead us toward further dysfunction and destruction or toward the gift of healing.

When we are in pain, for example, we have a choice to make. We can choose to ignore and numb our pain, or we can choose to feel our pain and draw closer to God for comfort and healing. Emotional pain can result from feelings of hopelessness. But the gift of God is that we can learn and grow as a result of the pain. It is not hopeless suffering, but a learning experience. This requires that we face our pain and hopelessness head-on.

The same is true of the other affect states. We can choose to live in debilitating fear, or we can discover God's gift of wisdom and gain the ability to set protective boundaries. We can direct anger inward in depression, we can direct anger outward in rage, or we can face anger and discover new strength and energy in pursuit of righteousness. We can feel shame and spiral deeper into feelings of worthlessness, or we can accept our humanity and discover the grace of making mistakes and making amends. To gain the benefit of the gift, we have to choose to face our feelings and turn away from the toxic expression of affect states.

Support for Recovery

As you can see, recovery is hard work. We cannot do it alone. We need the encouragement and support of others to maintain sobriety and face the deep feelings we harbor inside. Since we have been wounded through our relationships with others, we may seek healing in isolation—apart from anyone who could hurt us. Healing for the deep wounds of the heart and spirit, however, comes through relationships with others.

Remember the Bible story about the crippled man who waited by the pool of Bethesda for thirty-eight years? He never made it to the healing waters in time.[3] The man knew what he had to do to be healed. He was doing his best to be healed. Still, he could not succeed. He needed someone to wait beside him, pick him up, and carry him the last few steps into the pool. Without support from others, we, too, are like the crippled man. We may make it to a certain point in our recovery, but we are helpless to take the next step on our own. What has been impossible in the past can happen with the help of others.

Woman Without Recovery Has a Fragile Foundation

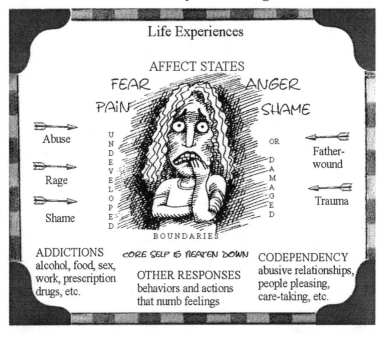

When Marla came to me for counseling, she suffered from severe depression and panic attacks. She also had a problem with food. She had been through a number of hospital programs for her depression and had established a familiar pattern. She would get a little better, begin to feel spiritually renewed, and assume that she was completely better. At that time, she would drop out of her support groups, discontinue counseling, stop taking medication, and begin a downward decline. She was highly motivated to get better, but she couldn't make a long-term change.

I explained to Marla that she had an eating disorder. The foods she ate intensified her depression and anxiety symptoms. I outlined a recovery program for her that included counseling, sobriety, and support. She wasn't convinced that this new approach would be any different from before. She grudgingly began to attend Overeaters Anonymous (OA). One day at a time, Marla learned to stay free of sugar and her favorite binge foods. She began to lose weight. By actively working the twelve steps, she renewed her relationship with the Lord. Then she began to remember the times her father had abused her.

This was an extremely difficult time for Marla. The urge to use food to numb those feelings was powerful. At times she was tempted to remain silent about her painful memories. But through OA, she obtained the resources to maintain sobriety from pain-numbing, depressive foods. She also became involved in a support group for survivors. So in the middle of the night, when the flashbacks of abuse would come, she was supported by women who held her, sobbed with her, and prayed for her. In time, she became aware of her heavenly Father's deep love for her. She experienced spiritual, emotional, and physical healing in a way she never imagined possible. She was able to let go of the painful memories of her earthly father and fully embrace her heavenly Father.

Did OA play a role in her recovery? Yes! Did her survivors group play a role? Yes! Did her pastor play a role? Yes! Did her therapist play a role? Yes! Did her family physician play a role? Yes! Did her church play a role? Yes! Could God have healed Marla without all of the above? Yes! Yet he chose to make his presence known to her through all of those people who supported her.

We cannot underestimate the role of adequate support in the healing process. It is particularly important for women who seek healing for wounds suffered in their relationships with their fathers. When a man deals with the wounds of the father-son relationship and is mentored by an older man, he establishes an emotional and spiritual connection with a father-like figure.[4] This relationship can bring about significant healing, particularly if there is little hope for the son to connect with the father. It is highly unusual, however, for a woman to have a mentoring or father-like relationship with an older man other than her father. When a woman's father is emotionally incapable of such a relationship, it is essential that she receive support from other women.

This is not to say that a woman cannot receive support from men. There can be times when male mentoring or support is helpful to nurture a woman's personal growth. For example, support may come from a professor who takes interest in a woman and delights in her growth of knowledge and wisdom. Mentoring may come from a male colleague who is able to guide a woman toward success in her career. Encouragement may come from a pastor who is able to communicate God's truth with deep feeling and passion. Support may also come through a compassionate family doctor.

I have seen my friend, Dr. Hawkins, put his arm around a woman who is distressed and talk to her. When he does this, he doesn't give just a quick squeeze. He gives a firm hug while he talks to the person. "God is going to be with you through this thing," he may say. "You're going to get past this difficult time." There is tremendous power and hope in that kind of male support, but a woman must have strong boundaries because there is risk in these relationships as well.

This is one reason why I am such a strong advocate of support groups. There can be no secrets when a woman is involved in a good support group. When she is able to share everything in her life, everyone in the group benefits. A man who has a supportive relationship with a woman (a physician, pastor, or therapist, for example) may violate her boundaries. When that happens, the man thinks he has control of the relationship. This allows some terribly destructive relationships to go on for a long time. But when a woman has accountability and support from other women, boundary violations and the secret behaviors that result have little chance of survival.

I have come to view support as an issue of health, an issue of the soul, and an issue of the mind. At times, God instantly heals people who have suffered life-long hurts and serious illnesses. But the greatest number of people must learn to draw on God's grace and the support and encouragement of others. In this way they can progress toward healing one day at a time.

Support is essential on a daily journey of recovery. Healing is hard work. We need someone with whom to share our deepest grief, our fears of failure, our worries about the future, our recent setbacks, our hopes and expectations, and our feelings of anger. A therapist alone cannot provide enough support for healing. Consultation with a pastor is not enough support. A visit to a physician is not sufficient. But daily, faithful support from others can work miracles in healing hurts and changing lives.

Alcoholics Anonymous is a seventy-year-old testimony to the

power of mutual support. Those who agree to share in honesty and vulnerability before one another and God can achieve long-term sobriety. Overcomer's Outreach, a network of church-based support groups, is a testimony to the fact that the church of today can bear the burdens of the hurting.

To bear one another's burdens was a normal part of life in the early Christian church. Material needs, spiritual needs, and emotional needs were met within the context of the Christian community. In more recent times, however, the church has focused on spiritual needs first and material needs second. The concept of meeting emotional needs has been all but ignored. As a result, God's people have suffered. But God is calling the church to return to the biblical mandate to bear one another's burdens. This implies that the emotional, spiritual, and material burdens weigh upon us.

Healing Connections

With a basis of sobriety and support, the feelings of the wounded girl inside will begin to surface. These feelings may rise up spontaneously without conscious effort. They may present themselves within the safety of a counseling relationship. They may be triggered by everyday events. They may also be awakened when a woman looks at photographs from her childhood, when she remembers family outings, or when she draws pictures of her childhood. A variety of memory and exploration activities can awaken the feelings. When those feelings arise, the adult woman has the opportunity to connect with that wounded child and deal with the old hurts inside.

Janice, for example, was a frustrated overachiever. A professional woman, she appeared to have everything she could want—a good paying, part-time job, a loving husband, two adorable children, no weight problems, and involvement in a great church. Yet she sought counseling because of depression and anxiety. No matter what she did for others or what she accomplished, Janice never felt that she did enough. She wasn't happy unless everyone around her was happy. But the tension of trying to please everyone took a heavy toll. Headaches had been a part of her daily life. Now they were unbearable, but her physician found nothing wrong with her.

Janice became involved in a twelve-step group for codependents and an Overcomer's Outreach group exclusively for women. Her group participation helped her realize that she wasn't alone—others had similar struggles. She felt safety with those who accepted her fully, and she was able to connect with the pain in her own heart. Tears flowed, and she remembered being a little girl and trying so hard to please her father. Nothing she did softened his criticism and judgment of her. Her father was now very supportive of her, yet she could not silence his negative, critical voice. Since her childhood, she had heard it over and over again inside her head. With the shame of that critical voice ringing in her ears, she was unable to set boundaries or know when to stop caring for others.

Connection with the feelings of the wounded child inside, enabled Janice, the adult, to direct the feelings of shame and pain back to her earthly father, where they belonged. She was able to share her deep feelings of shame with her support group. When shame is brought into the open, it loses its power. Set free from the controlling power of shame in her life, Janice began to set boundaries in her relationships. She no longer tried to do everything and please everyone. She was no longer robbed of the joy of her accomplishments. And she suffered fewer and fewer headaches. She began to grow into the person God had created her to be.

There is yet another connection that is very important in the recovery process. That is a connection with the heavenly Father. The process of spiritual healing, or growth in relationship with the heavenly Father, is where a woman finds ultimate healing for the father-wound.

For some women, the wounds in their relationship with their earthly fathers are so hurtful that they diminish the opportunity for relationship with God the Father. Some women find it difficult to read the Bible, listen to Christian music, or go to church. This is perhaps the greatest tragedy of the father-wound, because the heavenly Father is the perfect Father. He never shames. He always loves. He never rages. He always comforts. No matter how far away from him we may feel, he is much closer than we can ever imagine.

I have found that as a woman progresses in the healing process, her heart becomes more open to the loving touch of the heavenly Father. At times, when a woman connects with the painful feelings of her inner child, I will ask her to imagine Jesus standing beside her. I will have her ask Jesus to be her Daddy, to love and protect her in whatever pain she suffers. When that happens, nothing can stop the tears. A very deep and precious healing takes place in the heart of a woman when she connects, on a feeling level, with her loving, heavenly Father.

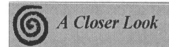 **A Closer Look**

Affect States—They include fear, anger, pain, and shame. They can cause an array of physical symptoms that include tightness in the stomach, clammy palms, perspiration, increased heart rate, changes in body temperature, shallow breathing, and light-headedness. Affect states can be triggered by events as benign as a slight hand movement, a song, a change in tone of voice, a facial expression, or a particular choice of words that mimics or suggests a past, painful event. The association with the past triggers the emotions of the past. Immediately the affect state takes over and produces the physiological changes described above. An individual's natural response is to do behaviors that restore a sense of comfort or calm. The tragedy is that codependency or compulsive, addictive behaviors are often the quick fixes that smooth or settled the feelings. As a result, many of us are not consciously aware of affect states until they impact us or others in a toxic way.

Sobriety—We experience sobriety when we put aside whatever substance, activity, or person we have used to fill the emptiness or numb the pain. In recovery, we discover that we need our pain. It is our greatest guide. We need sobriety from addictions, codependency, and other numbing behaviors so that we can feel the pain that is hidden in our hearts. Unless we feel our pain, we cannot identify or heal from the wounds that have hindered our growth. Sobriety is an essential element of recovery.

The Twelve-steps—The following are the Twelve Steps of Alcoholics Anonymous. The word "alcohol" in Step One can be replaced with other issues or drugs of choice. For example, one might put "We admitted we were powerless over our broken past . . . ."
1. We admitted we were powerless over alcohol—that our lives had become unmanageable.
2. Came to believe that a Power greater than ourselves could restore us to sanity.
3. Made a decision to turn our will and our lives over to the care of God as we understood Him.
4. Made a searching and fearless moral inventory of ourselves.

5. Admitted to God, to ourselves, and to another human being the exact nature of our wrongs.
6. Were entirely ready to have God remove all these defects of character.
7. Humbly asked Him to remove our shortcomings.
8. Made a list of all persons we had harmed, and became willing to make amends to them all.
9. Made direct amends to such people wherever possible, except when to do so would injure them or others.
10. Continued to take personal inventory and when we were wrong promptly admitted it.
11. Sought through prayer and meditation to improve our conscious contact with God as we understood Him, praying only for knowledge of His will for us and the power to carry that out.
12. Having had a spiritual awakening as the result of these steps, we tried to carry this message to alcoholics, and to practice these principles in all our affairs.

Reprinted with permission of Alcoholics Anonymous, World Services, Inc.

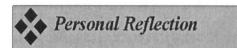
Personal Reflection

1. In what ways, healthy or unhealthy, have you dealt with the pain of your past?

2. At what point in your life did you feel compelled to start your journey toward healing? What factors and feelings helped you choose to heal?

3. If you have not yet begun this journey, what holds you back? What are your fears? What is your next step toward healing?

138

4. What are your support systems? How can you use those healing connections more effectively?
◆

5. God wants healing in your life. Pray that his loving presence will be real to you in the days ahead.
◆

NOTES:

CHAPTER 9

Forgiving Father

The Process of Restoration

For years Carol struggled with anxiety and depression. Her husband Jim was an alcoholic and sex addict, which made him a horror to live with. Still, he managed to keep his job and put up a good front. Carol helped him keep up the good front. She did everything for him. He never had to face the consequences of his actions. Carol made it work—no matter what. But the strain was about to break her. Something had to change.

Carol desperately needed support from others. She did not get it at church, and the struggles at home kept her from consistent participation in a support group. Carol was ashamed of the state of her marriage. That shame kept her from sharing her struggles with her friends or the women in her Bible study group. During a counseling session I said, "Carol, you cannot make changes in your life without some kind of support. Would you want your father to come to a session with you so he could understand what is happening in your life? I suspect that he would want to help you."

"Oh no," she replied. "I could never do that. He believes that you stick with a marriage no matter what. If he knew the truth, he would be so disappointed in me."

"Even so, I think it would be worth a try," I said. "If it doesn't work, it doesn't work. You have no support now, and given your situation he's the most likely source of support you have. You really have nothing to lose."

Several sessions later, Carol brought her father with her. The first time in a counselor's office can be a scary thing for a sixty-year-old man. He felt uncomfortable at first—guarded and on edge. I explained the importance for an emotional and spiritual bridge from a father to his daughter. He looked puzzled. I added, "This connection can be difficult for fathers. Most men didn't have a real connection with their own fathers. It's tough for some men to show their feelings and tell the truth about what's in their hearts."

Carol's father didn't answer, but a tear formed in the corner of his eye. His feelings had form too, but he couldn't let loose.

I continued, "Carol is going through a difficult time in her life right now. She needs a close relationship that she can count on. She needs you and the support you can offer her. She needs your understanding—not judgment. Life has been tough enough."

Carol's father dropped his guard and opened up to me. He leaned in and listened as I explained her situation. Then I asked Carol to tell her father what life with Jim was like. She told him about Jim's alcoholism and sexual addiction. She described Jim's rage toward her and the children. With tears, she recounted daily battles. She poured out her hurts and sorrows, her suffering and pain. The tears that filled her father's eyes began to course down his cheeks. Those same tears gave Carol strength, a new comfort. I could see her take it in. She knew that her father felt her pain. At that moment, the hurt was shared and divided. The burden lessened with every tear down her father's cheek.

Carol finished and her father began. "I'm sorry that you had to go through this. I'll do anything I can to help you. If you feel that you need to move out, I'll be there. I'll help you."

Months passed and Carol's father kept his word. He was a listening ear, an affirming voice, and a ready support. Carol was no longer alone. She had an emotional and spiritual ally in the battles she fought. She had the strength and support of her father.

The acceptance of her father gave Carol the courage to attend a support group. Her boundaries with her husband developed and grew stronger. At a point of crisis, she had the words, the wisdom, and the will power to tell her husband what he needed to do. She told him to get treatment or lose his wife and family.

Carol's courageous stand was a miraculous step for her. Her home church taught women to submit to their husbands without exception, without question. She was so ashamed of her failure to change her husband by her submission. Somewhere inside she knew the truth. No amount of submission or suffering would change her husband. But it would destroy her and harm the children if she continued in the situation.

Carol overcame her fear and spoke the truth about her marriage to her father. She found that when she reached out, her father reached back and responded with his heart. An emotional and spiritual bond between them began to be restored. Her father's love was demonstrated by the emotional connection he made. And his spiritual and physical support was evident when he walked with her through the difficult times. His love and concern released Carol from her shame and empowered her to continue healing.

It is the father's responsibility to build an emotional and spiritual bridge to his daughter. Reality, however, is that many fathers are unaware of this responsibility and their daughters' need. Even if they are aware of the need, most fathers have not experienced this kind of connection with their fathers. They have no idea how to connect with the heart of a daughter.

A daughter in recovery becomes connected with her feelings. She becomes aware of her desire and need for an emotional bond with her father. She will want to reach out to her father and establish that connection. It is best for the father to build this bridge, but, as Carol discovered, the daughter can initiate the process.

Reaching Out Toward Dad

Before an adult daughter can reach out to her father, she has to let go of her expectations for their relationship. She has to let go of the father she never had, as well as the father she may never have. If no emotional bond existed between them, it is not likely or wise for her to expect a serious talk with her father. It is even less likely that an immediate relationship will be kindled. The fact is no matter how pleasant or well intentioned her father may be, he may not be capable of the kind of relationship she wants. As there are risks in the recovery process, there are also risks in seeking to reestablish a connection with the father. It is not easy for a daughter to give up her expectation about reconnecting with her father. To reach out toward her father is something she needs to do regardless of the outcome.

This is not easy. I generally recommend that a daughter establish herself in a strong recovery program before she undertakes an emotional and spiritual connection with her father. A woman who seeks to connect with her father on a feeling level needs to have strong boundaries and ample support. This gives her strength to address the issues that stand between her and her father. Women that I have counseled often ask their whole recovery group to support them in prayer. They may even pray for her at the exact time she talks with her father.

With a foundation of recovery and support, a woman can connect with her father in a variety of ways. Some women, like Carol, ask their fathers to join them in counseling. Others write a letter to their fathers and then meet to talk about it. Still others write a letter and then read it to their fathers. They ask their fathers to refrain from comment until the whole letter is read.

Some daughters are fortunate. Their fathers immediately connect with what they say. But that is not the normal experience. In most cases, a father will be somewhat defensive. It is important for the daughter to realize why this happens. Without an emotional bond with his own father, a man is unaware that there is something missing in the relationship with his daughter. He is proud of her accomplishment. He gave her an education and a good start in life. Therefore, he has done a great job. *What else is there?* he wonders. It is difficult for him to understand why his daughter wants something more from him. It is not easy for any of us to face our shortcomings, especially when we have done the best we know how. So defensiveness or anger is a fairly normal response.

How does a daughter handle this kind of response? Strong boundaries are her first defense. Boundaries enable her to keep her father's comments from becoming personal. His response is about himself—not her. Boundaries remind the daughter that her father's lack of awareness or understanding is not her fault. It is not a problem she has to fix. Her father owns the problem, and it is his responsibility. She also needs to recognize that as lasting recovery and healing take place over time, genuine reconnection with her father will not happen in a day. Patience is required.

Reconnecting becomes far more difficult when the father is active in an addiction. Whatever his addiction—alcohol, drugs, work, food, sex, or religion—he alters his moods and masks his feeling. A daughter cannot connect to a numb father who is disconnected from his own feelings. She must realize that the addictions will affect the interaction between her and her father. As long as the addiction is in force, her father isn't fully capable of developing the relationship she desires. So she must be strong enough to sustain an extended "on again, off again" relationship. If this is the case, it is very important that she have strong support to keep her own recovery on track. Although it does not happen often, some daughters, in this situation, gain the support of other family members and participate in an intervention to motivate the father to seek sobriety.

Ongoing recovery is a significant part of the reconnecting process. As the daughter becomes healthier and stronger, it becomes more difficult for her father to maintain the status quo. He will have to change as his daughter changes. Sooner or later he will realize that change is a necessary part of a meaningful relationship with his daughter. If he doesn't change, loneliness is his option.

When a Daughter Has Been a Victim of Abuse

An abused daughter suffers a tremendous wound in her relationship with her father. This is true even when her father is not the perpetrator. Abuse from any source causes the daughter to feel unprotected. This wounds her relationship with her father. Abuse damages the father-daughter relationship in such a way that both father and daughter lose out. The abuser, in essence, becomes part of the relationship, standing between the father and daughter. In most cases, the father doesn't even know the abuse has happened. Yet he is the one who must deal with the damage of that abuse in his relationship with his daughter.

When a girl is abused by another man, she feels shame. Those feelings of shame seep into and affect all of her relationships. The wounded part of her may distance herself from her father because all men seem dangerous and scary. Or, the wounded part of her may overly enmesh with her father since she's hungry to know that he still loves her. Both responses lead to further damage in the relationship.

If the daughter withdraws, the father may not even notice the change. If he does notice, he may have no idea about how to reestablish an emotional bond. Without knowledge of the abuse, the father is at a loss. He cannot repair the bridge until he understands that it has been damaged. As time goes on, he and his daughter will grow further apart because of the third party's influence on the relationship.

If the daughter takes the other approach and pursues inappropriate intimacy with her father, the father-daughter relationship suffers damage in other ways. A daughter who takes this approach may be extremely needy and physical with her father, as if boundaries do not exist. She may want to be held all the time. She may hug and kiss her father inappropriately. A father who seeks to maintain appropriate boundaries wants no part of this. He may push his daughter away or avoid physical contact with her. This response adds further confusion and hurt to the relationship. It leaves the daughter with weak, underdeveloped boundaries that will fail under pressure.

In both scenarios, the father-daughter relationship usually becomes increasingly stressful, even bizarre. In order for the relationship to change, the truth concerning the abuse has to be made known. Yet it takes a tremendous amount of courage for a daughter to tell her father and mother what has happened to her. She does not know beforehand what her father's response will be. So support is essential for her to be able to reveal this dark secret. Women that I have counseled will often have their fathers come into my office. In the office they are not alone and they feel a sense of safety. It is easier to break the news of their abuse.

A father's response to the news of his daughter's abuse is often intense. Many times he will express strong emotion and weep. Or he may rage and express his intention to kill the one who abused his daughter. He may be overcome with guilt and shame because he was not able to protect his daughter. He may see the puzzle come together and understand why the relationship has been so confusing. These emotions and reactions are difficult for the father and his daughter. But it is a good thing that the father feels. His response helps the daughter know that what happened to her is real. It also helps her to know that her father has deep love and compassion for her.

A daughter who reveals a history of abuse faces significant risk in the process. Abuse results in damaged boundaries. When an abused daughter witnesses the pain her father feels, she will often feel responsible for his pain. She will be tempted to keep silent— spare him further hurt. This is why it is important for a daughter in this situation to have a solid recovery and adequate support. She needs strength to keep from assuming the burden of her father's discomfort. It is not her responsibility to lessen his pain. He has to find his own way through it.

Once the abuse has been exposed, the third party is known, but not eliminated. This knowledge opens the door for rebuilding the father-daughter relationship. The father and daughter who have dealt with the reality of abuse have already handled a difficult issue. If the father responds to his daughter's pain on a feeling level, the bond between them is already strengthened. They may make good progress in addressing the other issues in their relationship.

When a Father Is Not Safe

Of course, there are times when the perpetrator of abuse is not a third party, but is the woman's father. Even when a woman has been abused by her father, there is often a great hunger for an emotional and spiritual bond with him. She may want to establish such a connection with him. This is an extremely risky step to take. No woman should even consider this without "major league support."

To touch the feeling level of an abusive father is a monumental task. Difficult obstacles must be overcome. If the father is still active in his addictions, the daughter must cut through the addictions to connect with her father. If she gets through the addictions and has an interaction with her father, she will run into a solid wall of denial. A perpetrator has to have a tremendous amount of denial to commit abuse in the first place. Denial becomes more entrenched as time passes. In addition to her father's denial, the daughter also has to confront the denial of others in relationship to him.

This may include the denial of a codependent wife, siblings, family friends, and even his church. Often when there is abuse, strong denial, and active addiction, the father is disconnected from his feelings. He may even be a multiple personality. It is as if one part of him lives in California and another part lives in Ecuador!

Reconnecting with an Abusive Father

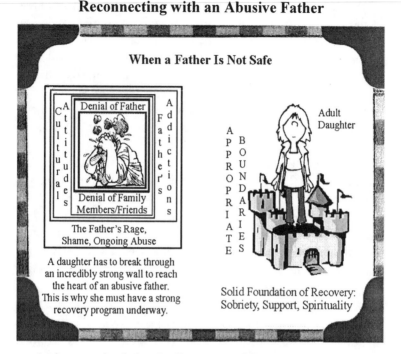

When a Father Is Not Safe

A daughter has to break through an incredibly strong wall to reach the heart of an abusive father. This is why she must have a strong recovery program underway.

Solid Foundation of Recovery: Sobriety, Support, Spirituality

As long as the father is disconnected from the feeling part of himself, he cannot connect with his daughter on a feeling level. All of these obstacles have to be broken down before the daughter can make the connection she desires. This is why an unshakable recovery program and strong support are absolutely necessary before a woman even considers reaching out to an abusive father.

It is also wise for a woman to involve a third person, such as a pastor or therapist. One important function of the third party is to assess whether or not the father is an emotional killer. An emotional killer is usually a person who has also been abused and is disconnected from his feelings. The emotional killer has no consistent reality in the relationship. A daughter may have a confrontation with her father, and he will admit the abuse. But the next day, or an hour later, he will absolutely deny it.

An emotional killer has industrial-strength denial! His denial is so powerful that he believes the abuse, which he may have admitted to previously, never happened. The possibility of connecting with a father who is an emotional killer is remote.

It is difficult for some people to realize that denial can be this powerful, but it is. Consider for a moment how our memory works. Most people can recall events that happened fifteen, twenty, or thirty years ago. They wonder if the events really happened just as they remember. Someone who experienced those events with another person can confirm the memory. The memory can become clearer and more real. A certain amount of uncertainty or fuzziness of memory is a fact of normal recall. A perpetrator of abuse is dealing with memories of sick, horrible, shame-filled, depraved events. It is easy to see how the mind moves toward denial or an inability to recall the event.

The workings of denial in the mind and the lack of feelings in an emotional killer demonstrate the great need for truth. Twelve-step groups offer that kind of rigorous honesty and a consistent reality. But it only results when a person makes a lifetime commitment to recovery with regular participation in twelve-step meetings. A person involved in twelve-step work knows that, left to his or her own devices, trouble will result and denial will return. Within the twelve-step support system, however, the person is able to expose the insanity of his or her own thinking—the deceit, lies, manipulation, and control. No condemnation or judgment will be offered. In an atmosphere of acceptance the person will be able to discover and deal with the truth. I do not imply that all those involved in twelve-step groups are emotional killers. But the kind of support and work that is necessary to help an alcoholic deal with reality, helps an emotional killer face the truth.

I explain this to show how unlikely it is for a daughter to connect with an abusive father, especially an emotional killer, who is not in recovery. In most cases, powerful outside forces must be at work to pressure an emotional killer to change. These might come through a dramatic spiritual experience or a family intervention. But even then it is up to the individual to sustain the recovery.

During almost thirty years of counseling, I have seen perhaps half a dozen instances in which a daughter connected with an abusive father. In each case, massive intervention was required. Even such intervention often is not sufficient to hold the person accountable. The only protection against an abusive father who will not remain in recovery is to have solid, impermeable boundaries.

Consider what typically happens when I counsel a teenager who has suffered abuse from her father. This illustrates the kind of intervention and external force required to bring about change in an emotional killer. Once the abuse is revealed, the legal and criminal justice system comes into play. The father can't easily brush off the forces that demand accountability. He faces arrest. He has to go to court. He faces emotional and physical separation from his family. His actions become public knowledge. He may be forced to undergo counseling. He may lose his job and even go to jail. A father in this position has no escape. He is usually motivated to do whatever he can to prove that he really is a good guy. When all of these forces are applied, there is a higher chance of a sustained recovery.

A daughter experiences real emptiness when her father is too sick for a relationship with her. Her best option is to continue with her own recovery and support. This is important so that her need for a father does not lead her into deception or denial. She must not be misled and believe that her father is less dangerous than he is. No one can replace a father. But other relationships, including a woman's relationship with God the Father, can help to fill her emptiness. Although a daughter's options for restoring a bond with an abusive father are very limited, she can continue to heal and forgive. She can continue to maintain strong boundaries with her father and prevent further abuse.

When It's Time to Forgive

There comes a time in a woman's healing journey when forgiveness is important. But even the mention of forgiveness for a father can produce a powerful emotional reaction. Forgiveness is never easy. In some cases it seems impossible. Yet forgiveness does have its place. Christian women have experienced unconditional forgiveness from God the Father. They also understand the mandate to forgive as they have been forgiven. Still, it is not easy.

Part of the problem is a misunderstanding of forgiveness. Some people think that forgiveness condones the harmful deed. Others view forgiveness as gift to the perpetrator and further punishment for the victim. Still others think of forgiveness as an open invitation for future abuse. Within some Christian circles, forgiveness becomes a vehicle of shame rather than the liberating force God intended it to be. All these views distort forgiveness.

Forgiveness is a divine gift. We have all wronged God and deserve to suffer the consequences of our sin. However, when we confess our sins to God, he promises to forgive those sins and to cleanse us from all unrighteousness.[1] God offers forgiveness freely because Christ paid the penalty for our sins through his sacrificial death on the cross. All that remains for us to do to receive God's forgiveness is to confess our sins.

We get into trouble when we apply the divine model for forgiveness to earthly relationships. There are consequences for sin. There are consequences when a wound is suffered. No one who has major surgery goes out and engages in three hours of aerobics the same day. He or she must allow the surgical wounds to heal. In a similar way, emotional and spiritual wounds require time to heal. Forgiveness is a part of the healing process—not a substitute for healing.

We are fortunate that Jesus paid the penalty for our sins. He opened the way for healing in our wounded relationship with our heavenly Father. Because of his gift, our humble confession and sincere faith restore us to God. The consequences of harm done in earthly relationships require more than forgiveness. God forgives sin, but the consequences of wrongs done must be faced. We must not demand forgiveness from those who have been wounded through a relationship. This only adds shame. And it is wrong to assume that healing will instantly follow forgiveness.

Forgiveness and healing of human relationships are related, but separate issues. To understand the difference between forgiveness and healing, consider the following common misconceptions about forgiveness:

Forgiveness = Trust
Forgiveness = No Consequences, No Boundaries
Forgiveness = No Behavior Change, No Mention of the Past

Misconception #1:
Forgiveness = Trust

The story about Leo the Lion illustrates this misconception. Leo was the star attraction of the circus. Every night his trainer would put him through his paces and end the act by shaking hands with

Leo. One night, however, Leo was a bit hungry, and grumpy too. At the end of the act his hunger turned to anger. He didn't shake the trainer's hand. Instead, he took a swipe at her arm. She was cut badly.

After the show, Leo said he was sorry, and the trainer forgave him. But the next night, the trainer didn't attempt to shake Leo's hand. "What's wrong with you?" Leo snarled. "I said I was sorry. Aren't you going to forgive me?"

"I have forgiven you," the trainer said. "I'm just not ready to shake your paw. I won't risk it until I'm sure your anger is in check."

Leo let out an angry roar and took another swipe at his trainer. This time, she was far enough away to avoid injury!

Many of us are like Leo. When we wrong others, we want forgiveness. We also want the relationship to be restored as soon as possible (which really means instantly). We are upset if trust isn't restored immediately following our apology.

Trust, however, is a result of time and experience, not a result of forgiveness. Trust grows out of the spiritual and emotional healing process. For some wounds, trust is restored rather quickly. For deeper wounds, the restoration of trust takes longer. A father who has wounded his daughter cannot expect the restoration of trust to occur on his timetable. The restoration of trust is in his daughter's hands—a fact that can be difficult for him to accept.

Although a father cannot control the rebuilding of trust, he can control his behavior. And, as Leo the Lion discovered, his behavior strongly influences his daughter's ability to trust him. A father, like the emotional killer who denies or minimizes the impact of his behavior and continues to engage in behavior that wounds his daughter, is not trustworthy. His daughter can forgive him so that her feelings of hurt, anger, fear, or resentment do not harm her. But she would be foolish to trust him. For her own protection, she must maintain strong boundaries with him.

Of course, not all fathers are stuck in denial. A father, who has discovered his own wounds and who understands how he has wounded his daughter, can make a commitment to his own healing and growth. Such a father is not perfect, but he will change. In time, his daughter can feel safe with him. She will realize that he is not the father he used to be. Her trust in him can grow as he grows.

Misconception #2:
Forgiveness = No Consequences, No Boundaries

A wound needs time to heal. Forgiveness promotes healing, but time is required. A wounded and vulnerable daughter may need to distance herself from her father. She is fragile and needs a season to rebuild trust. The daughter of an actively addicted or codependent father may need to set boundaries to protect herself (and perhaps her children) from the father. These consequences are not comfortable, but a necessary part of the healing process. The wise father, in this situation, will use the time to continue to grow spiritually and emotionally. He will prayerfully wait through his daughter's healing process.

Dorothy and her father experienced this situation. Dorothy's father was successful at work and a recognized leader at church. He was also a closet alcoholic. Her mother, a first-class codependent, denied that her husband even had a problem. Dorothy had been in recovery for some time. She had made good progress in healing from the hurt, anger, and shame of the double-standard household in which she grew up.

Dorothy had pulled away from her parents early in her recovery. One day she felt strong enough to approach her father. She wanted to talk to him about what had been happening in her life. When she was alone with her father, she said, "I haven't been by to see you and Mom for a long time. I think it's time you know why I withdrew from you. I'm afraid of you when you drink. I always have been—since I was a little girl. Somewhere along the line that fear turned to anger. I can forgive you for the past, and I ask you to forgive me for my anger. It was wrong for me to hold that against you for so long."

Dorothy's word struck deep in her father's heart. He looked down and searched for the word to answer her. He finally said, "I'm glad to know why you haven't come by. Thank you for forgiving me. Of course, I forgive you. Will you drop by again? Will you bring the kids? Can they spend a weekend with us soon?"

"I'd like to bring the kids, Dad, but . . . ." Now Dorothy looked down and searched for words.

"But what?" her dad asked.

"Well, I won't leave the kids. They can come, but only when

I'm here."

"What are you saying?" he shot back.

"I'm saying that I want to be here when my kids are with you," Dorothy answered. Her gaze was steady—her words strong. "If you are drinking or drunk when we arrive, we'll turn around and go home. And if you start drinking while we're here, we'll leave."

Her father stepped away. He struggled to find words, to fire back. "How can you say you that? I—I—I thought you claimed to be a Christian! You haven't forgiven me! You haven't forgotten anything! You're still holding it all against me!"

"Dad, I have forgiven you, but I haven't forgotten. You're not the same person when you drink. So if you choose to drink when the children and I are here, we will choose to leave."

When Dorothy left, her father was angry and her mother was in tears. Two months passed without contact with her parents. Then her mother called and asked if they could talk. Dorothy agreed. When they met, Dorothy asked her mother's forgiveness for the anger and resentment she had harbored against her.

Dorothy realized that her anger toward her parents had been a boundary to keep her safe. But her boundary of anger and resentment took a terrible toll on her. She had problems in her marriage, chronic headaches, and bouts with depression. Counseling and support groups taught Dorothy how to set boundaries without feeling angry. She learned that respect for personal boundaries is a characteristic of a healthy relationship. She learned that she could forgive her parents and still maintain protective boundaries. She could also set consequences for violations of those boundaries.

When Dorothy met with her mother, they talked about the family and her father's alcoholism. Her mother began to realize the role that her denial played in the problem. As a result of their conversation, Dorothy's mother began to attend Al-Anon meetings with her. In time, her mother's recovery from codependency enabled the family to do an intervention with her father. It led to his recovery from alcoholism.

An intervention involves setting firm boundaries that are backed by serious consequences. It is not an easy action to take. In this case, as in many others, setting firm boundaries with stiff consequences are a necessary part of healing family relationships.

The change in her parents' behavior brought new consequences to the family. Dorothy, her husband, and her children could at last enjoy the kind of relationship with her parents that they had long desired. Boundaries and consequences do not negate or diminish forgiveness. They create an environment that allows forgiveness and healing to take place.

Misconception #3: Forgiveness = No Behavior Change, No Mention of the Past

The word *forgiveness* is often used like a steamroller to cover up a multitude of issues. In practical terms, forgiveness often means, "Let's just go on from here as if this never happened. We're not going to talk about dirty laundry. What's in the past is in the past." There are two problems with this approach. The past is not dealt with. And there is no requirement for a change in behavior.

This is not true forgiveness. It is denial. Behavior must change for healing to occur. The past cannot be left unanswered.

Consider the dynamics of Elizabeth's relationship with her father, Bill, a work addict and an alcoholic. A dramatic change occurred when Elizabeth was twelve years old. Bill was arrested for driving under the influence of alcohol. While he sat in jail, he realized that his life was out of control. At that time, he asked Jesus to forgive him, and he made a commitment to change his life. When he was released from jail, his good friend who had shared Christ with him, steered him to a church that was supportive of recovery. He urged Bill to participate in Alcoholics Anonymous and Overcomers Outreach meetings. Bill grew in his faith and kept his commitment to sobriety. As he worked the twelve steps, he made amends to his wife and daughter.

Despite these changes, all was not well at home. When Elizabeth was fourteen years old, she started to express great anger and resentment toward her father. She had seen the change in her father and knew he was sincere. His effort to make amends made her feel worse. *What kind of a daughter am I?* she wondered. *I'm still so angry at my dad! He's so much better than he used to be. What's wrong with me?*

Bill was wise enough to connect her anger with his past alcoholism. He suggested that they see a counselor together. It helped.

Elizabeth learned to recognize and verbalize her feelings. She expressed her anger and disappointment at the times he had broken promises to her. Through many tears, she talked about her fears: the terror of drunken fights with her mother, the panic when he left the house in a rage and drove away fast, and the dread that he might never come home again.

"I'm so sorry," Bill said. Tears streamed down his face. "I never realized how deeply my actions had hurt you. I hope the day will come when you will be able to forgive me for what I have done." Bill offered no explanation, no excuses, and no defense. He simply acknowledged that he was guilty as charged.

Elizabeth released a flood of emotion. Years of sorrow poured out of her heart. She cried and sobbed and washed every gully clean with tears. I asked her if she would like her father to sit next to her and hold her.

"No" she answered. "I can't trust him yet."

"That's okay," Bill said. "When you're ready, I'll be here for you."

When Bill allowed Elizabeth to keep her distance, she immediately felt safer with him. She could feel that he respected her needs and her pain. "You can sit next to me if you would like," she added.

When Bill sat down near her, Elizabeth began to cry again. In time, she allowed him to hold and comfort her. In time, she was able to forgive him for past wounds. This emotional healing was possible because the wounds of the past were addressed and Bill's behavior had changed.

Repentance and Forgiveness in Healthy Relationships

The Bible has a great deal to say about relationships—between humanity and God, parents and children, husbands and wives, believers and believers, and believers and unbelievers. It also has much to say about repentance and forgiveness—for good reason. God knows that repentance and forgiveness play an ongoing role in all human relationships. So he gives us as much wisdom in these areas as possible. Notice what Jesus says about repentance and forgiveness:

So watch yourselves. If your brother sins, rebuke him, and if he repents, forgive him. If he sins against you seven times in a day, and seven times comes back to you and says, I repent, forgive him.[2]

Jesus warns us to be aware of what happens in our relationships. We are supposed to take appropriate action when we are wronged. This means several things:

Openness: If someone wrongs us, we are to bring it out in the open and talk about it. We are not to ignore it or sweep it under the rug.

Forgiveness: If the person repents, acknowledges the wrong, and has a change of heart and behavior, we must forgive the person.

Repeated Forgiveness: Even if the person repeats the same wrong, we are to forgive when repentance is offered.

Our relationships are important, and repentance and forgiveness are necessary ingredients of healthy relationships. When Peter asked Jesus if he should forgive his brother as many as seven times, Jesus answered, *"Not seven, but seventy-seven times."*[3]

We are thankful that God always forgives. But to ask the same high standard of ourselves is a tough row to hoe. It is impossible to forgive if we wrongly equate forgiveness with immediate trust, no consequences, no boundaries, no change in behavior, and no mention of the past. The misconceptions must be stripped away for forgiveness to feel possible and safe enough to risk.

When we forgive, we release the anger, resentment, fear, and worry we have attached to the wrongs committed against us. Forgiveness does not justify the wrong committed. It promotes healing in the heart of the person who has been wronged. Medical research links resentment and the inability to forgive to the development of serious illnesses in some people.[4] Robin Casarjian, a therapist who writes extensively about forgiveness, summarizes the healing aspect of forgiveness:

So often when people think about forgiveness they think about what it's going to do for someone else . . . . They say, "I'm not going to forgive them, after what they did," as if forgiving them would be doing the other person a favor. What they don't realize is that forgiveness is really an act of self-interest. We're doing ourselves a fa-

vor, because we become free to have a more peaceful life—we free
ourselves from being emotional victims of others.[5]

Forgiveness truly does bring freedom. The discovery of true
forgiveness within safe boundaries makes forgiveness possible. It
creates the environment for a person to learn how to change emotionally destructive behaviors. So even repeated forgiveness—seventy-seven times—does not seem beyond reach. We see that it is
possible to express our feelings, maintain boundaries, and forgive.
We can discuss the old wounds, open the door for repentance, clear
the slate of past wrongs, and make way for an ongoing relationship. We understand that it is possible to forgive while we grow
toward trust. We learn that it is possible to forgive without expos-
ing ourselves to further mistreatment. And our genuine forgiveness advances God's healing work in our lives.

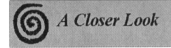 *A Closer Look*

Emotional Killer—This is a person who has also been abused and is disconnected from his feelings. The emotional killer has no consistent reality
in the relationship. A daughter may have a confrontation with her father
and he will admit the abuse. But the next day—or an hour later—he will
absolutely deny it. An emotional killer has industrial-strength denial! His
denial is so powerful that he believes the abuse, which he may have admitted to previously, never happened. A perpetrator of abuse is dealing
with memories of sick, horrible, shame-filled, depraved events. It is easy
to see how the mind moves toward denial—an inability to recall the event.

Forgiveness—Forgiveness is a decision, not an emotion. True forgiveness is accomplished only with God's help. God alone can give us the
grace, desire, and ability to release those who have hurt us. When we
forgive, we release the anger, resentment, fear, and worry we have attached to the wrongs committed against us. Forgiveness does not justifies
the wrong committed. It promotes healing in the heart of the person who
has been wronged.

Forgiveness for sin is a divine gift. We have all wronged God and
deserve to suffer the consequences of our sin. However, when we confess
our sins to God, he promises to forgive those sins and to cleanse us from
all unrighteousness. God offers forgiveness freely because Christ paid the
penalty for our sins through his sacrificial death on the cross. All that
remains for us to do to receive God's forgiveness is to confess our sins.

Wrongs—Wrongs are the behaviors, traits, and shortcomings that surface when we, through self-will, take action on our resentments and fears. They are often manifest in the harm we have done to others.

◆❖ *Personal Reflection*

1. Do you feel the need to initiate the bridge-building process with your father?
●◇

2. What risks are involved in reaching out to your father?
●◇

3. If you are unable to establish a relationship with your father, what positive steps can you take to fill the emptiness his absence leaves?
●◇

4. What is your response to the prospect of forgiving your father? Do you understand forgiveness as God sees it?
●◇

5. Thank God for the process and gift of forgiveness. Pray that he will help you understand what forgiveness means.
●◇

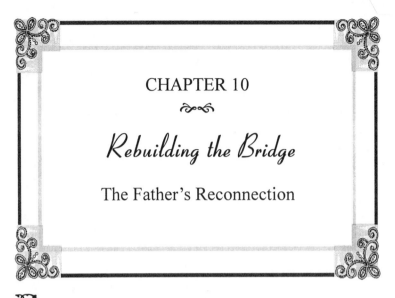

CHAPTER 10

෨ᤑ

Rebuilding the Bridge

The Father's Reconnection

D on had been an abusive husband and father. In time, he came to his senses and sought help. His healing from guilt and shame caused him to realize how much he had hurt his family. His children were now adults. The pain of their growing up years was evident in the problems of their adult lives.

Don's twenty-eight-year-old daughter, Ann, had a major spending problem. Ann's addictive pattern was obvious in her behavior. Don had noticed it for a long time, but he was powerless to do anything about it. Every time Ann ran out of money, she would call, and he would send her a check. Don's recovery deepened, and he recognized that his codependent giving enabled Ann to avoid her real issues. He was well connected to his feelings and understood the difference between material gifts to Ann and the gift of himself.

Don felt ready to take a bold step with his daughter. He met with her and asked forgiveness for his verbal and physical abuse during her childhood. His open admission of guilt and lack of defensiveness touched Ann. But she did not like what followed.

Don said, "Ann, I know that my past behavior hurt you. I can't change the past, but I can make a difference today. I'm concerned about your spending—I'm afraid it's out of control. And I've added to the problem. It was wrong of me to give you money. It only supported this destructive habit and prolonged your pain. I'm sorry.

To help you, I need to stop giving you money every time you ask for it. I still love you. I'm not abandoning you. I'm still here for you—more than ever. Let me know when you're ready for help with this problem. I'll stand by you as you work through these things, and I'll pay for six months of outpatient counseling."

"You're no better today than you were when I was a kid!" Ann barked. "Your apology means nothing to me!"

Don did not respond like he would have in the past. There was no anger in him. He knew beforehand that his action would not be easy for Ann. He knew that the withdrawal of the material connection he had with Ann would spur anger. It was a necessary risk. Before Don took this approach, he talked with me and with his support group about his plans. He made sure that his boundaries were strong. Ann's anger and accusations were about herself and her condition. He would not take them personally.

Ann called Don some months later. She was ready to talk. Ann admitted that she had a problem with alcohol and drugs. She was close to losing her job. And she asked Don to help her get better. He found a therapist for her, and he stood by her emotionally and financially as she began recovery. As a result of Don's actions, he and Ann share a strong emotional bond today. The emotional healing was more meaningful and real than the material connection could have ever been.

Don is a father who recognized his own pain later in life. He sought out a path toward healing and recovery. His wounds healed, his heart revived, and his sensitivity for others grew. He was able to see his daughter's wounds. He recognized the flawed relationship he had with her that was built on codependency and denial. He wanted a new relationship with her, one built on emotional integrity and trust. Like many fathers who have found healing in their lives, Don wanted to make amends. He wanted to turn past hurt into present healing.

The Right Starting Point

It would have been best if Don had built an emotional and spiritual bridge to Ann from the beginning of her life. But when she was young, he was not connected with his own pain or feelings. He was incapable of reaching out to her. Later, her addiction and his codependency made the task more difficult. Don's recovery helped him discover that it is never too late for a father to reach out—to build a bridge to his daughter's heart. The passage of time may make the task harder, but it is not impossible.

No matter what the daughter's age, a father who wants to connect with her must start with himself. The father's heart and feeling life is the foundation of the emotional bridge between father and daughter. A father cannot build a bridge to his daughter if he cannot feel what is in his heart.

A father, who has not connected with his feelings, might believe he has a bond with his daughter. He may believe that his hard work, material provisions, and gifts are an adequate connection. These are expressions of his love—not the experience of an emotional and spiritual bond with her. Without an emotional and spiritual connection, the relationship between father and daughter is primarily an illusion. It appears to be a strong bridge that can weather the storms of life. In reality, it is a paper-mache bridge that will crumble when put to the test.

On the other hand, a father who is connected with his feelings appreciates the weight of his responsibility. He realizes deep in his heart that God has given him a sacred role to nurture his daughter's heart. He realizes the impact that his feelings can have on his daughter. He realizes his imperfections, tendency toward error, and failure. The awesome role of a father may leave him feeling overwhelmed and powerless. Yet that is not where God leaves him.

As Jesus was dying on the cross, He prayed, "Father, forgive them, for they do not know what they are doing." Fathers today need to remember that prayer. It was directed to the people who crucified Jesus, but it reveals the eternal passion of Jesus' heart. He has unfailing compassion for those of us who do wrong when we don't have understanding of our actions. When we fathers do the best we know how for our daughters and still fall short, we can take comfort that God forgives.

As a father, I need that. I cringe when I think of the times I wounded my daughters with shame because I had not faced the shame in my heart. I ache when I consider the times I have wounded my daughters with anger because I was unaware of the anger hidden within me. God's forgiveness is my comfort, my encouragement and hope to move forward.

Does God's forgiveness take away my responsibility to do better? No! Do I have to humble myself and make amends to my daughters? Yes! Will it take time for my daughters and I to heal? Definitely! Am I harder on myself than I need to be? Probably! Am I forgiven? Absolutely!

I thank God for his forgiveness. It brings healing to my heart and my relationship with him. The strength of my relationship with God, my commitment to continued recovery and growth, and the support of other men make it possible for me to stay in touch with my feelings. These things allow me to deal with the contents of my heart and reach out to the hearts of my daughters.

Connecting with a Daughter's World

The route to a daughter's heart is through the things that are important to her and through shared discovery. It is, of course, easier for the father to bring the daughter into his world. And there is a place for that. But it does not establish the quality of bond that happens when a father shares in the experiences of her world. So we fathers have some learning to do.

In my own situation, I am drawn to physical activity. I feel good when I play basketball, ride a bike, hike into the mountains, or play racquetball. My son and I enjoy these activities together. It is one of the ways in which we connect. My oldest daughter enjoys some of these activities too. I participate in her world when I take her to a Lakers game or when I watch her play basketball.

But I have to connect with my grade school-age daughter in an entirely different way. To participate in the discovery of her world means smelling flowers, inspecting bugs, discussing cartoon characters, petting dogs, and fielding a thousand-and-one questions. The physical activities are less competitive and more intuitive. We might jump in puddles, do flips in the pool, or ride bikes in the neighborhood. This level of participation in a young daughter's world does not take a lot of ability—just willingness to share in what she enjoys.

It is important for me to remember that my daughter's world is just as important and valuable in God's eyes as my world is. When she senses my interest and involvement in what is valuable to her, the bond between us grows. And the deepest part of her being is nurtured. It's funny, but when I enter her world and share in life as she experiences it, I am nurtured, too. I slow down and rediscover an appreciation for the small delights in life.

The ways that a father can connect with his daughter change as she matures. And it is a challenge for a father to respond to his daughter according to her age and maturity. It is sad when he responds to his teenage daughter as if she were still six years old. A father needs to recognize his daughter's status as a young woman. He needs to realize that he cannot control her life or protect her from reality. She must grow, learn, and make her own choices.

Another way to connect with a daughter is simply to spend time with her. I occasionally would take Rachel with me on business trips—speaking events or retreats. During these times we had the opportunity to talk together without distractions. We established new friendships and enjoyed discovering a new part of the country. Rachel had the opportunity to learn more about what I do. I answered her questions about my work and profession. On these trips she also had the opportunity to escape the stresses of her life and spend quiet time alone. For any father, the challenge in this type of interaction, is to be emotionally present for his daughter during the time they share together.

A father can connect with a daughter through his genuine interest in activities that are meaningful to her. This might mean that a father would provide the opportunity for his daughter to explore a new area of interest. For example, a young daughter interested in business might need help with her first venture, like a lemonade stand. An older daughter might want help with trading stock online. A father should not superimpose his interests upon his daughter. Rather, he should be open to support her in whatever activity she is drawn to. Remember that play is a child's work.

The time a father spends nurturing his daughter's interests is time spent toward building her foundation for life. Whether the activities are spiritual, physical, creative, or intellectual, the key is for the father to encourage and support her. He must be careful to nurture her growth without becoming critical or manipulative.

In this way she gains a sense of his affirmation, caring, encouragement, and emotional support. It helps her develop the spiritual and emotional resources she needs to live her life and discover her full potential.

Connecting Requires Planning and Effort

We all have the same amount of time in a day. Yet there never seems to be enough time to accomplish all that is required of us. This makes our choices and priorities all the more significant. A father has to plan time to connect with his daughter. Without a plan, no amount of good intentions will matter. There is always a new crisis or deadline that will take center stage and steal away our few precious moments with our children.

Our best investment is the time we give to our daughters. We cannot afford to approach our time together casually. We need to plan ahead and coordinate our activities with those of our daughters. We need to take note of the busy seasons and ensure that time together is not neglected. We need to look for regular opportunities to connect with our daughters; breakfast before school, weekend rituals like Sunday brunch, or an evening meal together.

I know that all this planning is difficult. I have to plan retreats and speaking engagements a year in advance. Yet I want to be able to attend sporting events, school activities, and church programs that involve my four children. Sometimes our home calendar looks like a community bulletin board.

In every family, a father has to work hard to ensure that an emotional bond continues to develop as his daughter grows older. During adolescence, the daughter's life becomes increasingly centered outside the home. She is often less available to the father. So he must dedicate an increasing amount of effort to maintain their emotional and spiritual connection. The task becomes even more difficult when a family also faces the separation of divorce.

Connecting after Divorce

Divorce often reduces the contact between father and daughter. The daughter most often lives with her mother. Father and daughter may get together every weekend, every other weekend, or only two weeks out of the year. When a daughter has infrequent contact with her father, she usually learns one of two extremes: Do not expect anything from men; or always expect Disneyland.

Neither option nurtures the daughter. Neither promotes a sense of her own identity or a sense of her worth to her father, God, or anyone else. Neither challenges her to deal with life in a realistic way. Neither teaches her how to accept responsibility and establish appropriate boundaries. Neither builds up her feminine strength.

A daughter who has insufficient contact with her father feels abandoned. Her great hunger for a father may lead her to latch on to any guy who shows her attention. She wants to be with him all the time. She may also become very enmeshed with his family. The particular guy and his family are not the issue—the idea is belonging to a family.

On the other hand, there is the indulgent father who lavishes playtime, gifts, and extravagance on her. She becomes used to nothing but ice cream. Then she may expect other men to treat her royally. And she will become bored and depressed about ordinary living.

A father who is the custodial parent will have more time to spend with his daughter, but he has other concerns to guard against. He must realize that he cannot be everything for his daughter, and she cannot be everything for him. No matter how hard he tries, he cannot meet all of his daughter's needs. No matter how much she may want to help him, he cannot allow her to meet all of his needs. To parent effectively, he will need the support of others, both for himself and for his daughter.

A custodial father must not allow the bond between himself and his daughter to become emotional incest. It is appropriate for her to help maintain the household. It is not appropriate for her to carry the responsibility for these tasks. He should not allow her to take on the role of wife; caring for his clothes, preparing his meals, doing the shopping, and the like. The father who allows his daughter to become a surrogate wife will have to go through another divorce if he decides to remarry. This time he will have to divorce his daughter. She will understand this second divorce even less than the first.

Emotional incest is difficult to guard against because it is so frequently rewarded. The father may reward the daughter for her help. Relatives or family friends may say, "Oh, you are such a fine young woman because you take such good care of your dad! What would he do without you?" This kind of talk sounds nice, but it is destructive to the daughter.

A custodial father whose daughter has a limited relationship with her mother must ensure that his daughter has some kind of consistent relationship with older women. This mentoring relationship may be with a grandmother, aunt, family friend, or woman in the church. She must be a trustworthy woman who will commit to a consistent relationship with the daughter over a period of time. This relationship becomes essential as the daughter makes the transition from child to young woman. Fathers are not equipped to handle some aspects of this transition. The wise father will ensure that trustworthy women are available to mentor his daughter through this transition. These mentoring relationships will take some of the pressure off the father-daughter relationship. He will be freed to nurture his daughter in the way only he can.

Connecting with an Adult Daughter

Fathering does not end when a daughter graduates, moves out, or marries. I have yet to hear an adult woman say that her father calls her too much or is too supportive of her. No matter what her age, the little girl inside still desires affirmation, understanding, and nurturing from her father. She still wants to know that he is proud of the woman she has become. She still wants the opportunity to share some of her joys, sorrows, frustrations, fears, and worries with him. Because of this need, adult women are still wounded when their fathers are not emotionally responsive to them. They carry the hope that their fathers will some day respond differently.

Shortly after Debra miscarried, her father called. In tears, she told him what had happened. She reported that she was scheduled for a D and C. "Oh," her father said, "can I talk with Bob [her husband]?" Debra was crushed. Her father responded to her pain as if she had told him about a new roof on the house. On top of the loss of her baby, she was further grieved by her father's insensitivity. It added to her past pain—the wounds she had suffered through his lack of emotional responsiveness in the past. Debra felt like she was in a dark valley, weak and alone.

Even a father, who is capable of an emotional connection with his daughter, must realize that their relationship changes as she moves into adulthood. He cannot play by the old rules. He moves away from the role of setting limits and intervening in her life. In his new role, he listens, supports, and encourages her as an independent adult. He recognizes that his daughter has her own ideas, opinions, and feelings. He realizes that she will spend her lifetime growing, maturing, and making mistakes. Although he can no longer prevent her from making mistakes, he can support her in her recovery from them.

An adult daughter, who has a strong emotional and spiritual bond with her father, gains a tremendous sense of security that enables her to handle the risks of life. It may seem surprising, but the father has little to do to instill this sense of security. His faithful presence in her life is enough. The daughter knows she has someone to turn to in times of trouble. She has someone who can help her walk through the scary times.

A start-up business, a new job, a rough time in her marriage—whatever—she will navigate the waters with confidence. Her father believes in her and accepts her no matter what the outcome. This is a tremendous gift that empowers her to fulfill her potential. It is the kind of fathering that Mordecai gave to Esther.

Rebuilding the Bond

It is great when a father realizes what has been lost in his relationship with his daughter. Especially, if he seeks to make things right and establish an emotional and spiritual bond with her. Adult daughters with fathers like this have positive feelings about their relationship with their fathers. A daughter is strengthened and empowered when her father calls her at work, takes her to lunch, or offers to entertain the kids for a bit. His genuine interest in her world and in the person she has become is a shot of sunshine.

Tom is in his fifties and has been in recovery for several years. Connection with the wounds of his relationship with his father caused him to realize what he was missing with his adult daughter. He wanted his relationship with her to be better, and today it is. She welcomes the one or two telephone calls he makes to her office every week. They don't talk long. He asks about her work. He listens as she shares her feelings. For a few minutes every week, he connects with her world.

A father must be prepared. The process of reconnecting with an adult daughter is not a rose-lined path. He must be willing to initiate a relationship without expectations. He must accept the level of relationship that his daughter is willing and able to give. This may mean he will have to try, try, and try again. He must resist feelings of frustration or failure. His daughter may respond with anger, resentment, or coldness. A father who wants to connect with his daughter cannot give up after one or two, or even three tries.

Tom discovered this through firsthand experience. At first, his daughter seemed to enjoy his calls. Then after a few weeks, she became a bit cold. He wasn't sure what to do. He was tempted to give up. *Well, maybe she doesn't want to chat with the old man anymore,* he thought. *Maybe she doesn't want a relationship.* Tom was puzzled, and he asked me what to do.

I said, "Don't give up, Tom. This is an important time in your relationship with her. Why don't you ask her if she is upset about something? When she responds, listen carefully. It's possible that a past hurt in her relationship with you has popped up. Just be careful not to take what she says personally. Remember that it's the wounded little girl inside who feels the hurt and shares the pain. You disappointed that little girl many times in the past. She wanted to capture your attention many times. Eventually she gave up. The emotional bridge between you and your daughter has been down for a long time. She isn't sure she can trust you. She doesn't have a history of experience to convince her that you will be there for her. She doesn't know—not yet—that you really have changed. It is a big risk for her to trust you now."

Tom talked to his daughter. She was upset with him. He worked two jobs while she was growing up. She did not feel as if she had a father at all. "Who do you think you are?" she asked. "Why come into my life now? It's a little late, isn't it?"

The words were hard for Tom to hear. He knew they came from the wounds in his daughter's heart. He answered, "I'm sorry I wasn't there for you when you were younger. I want you to know that I'm here now. If you really don't want me to call you, I'll understand— I'll respect that. You let me know what you want me to do."

There was a long silence. Tom's daughter said nothing. When she spoke, her voice was changed—the anger gone. "It's okay for you to call me. Maybe we can have lunch sometime soon."

Tom was consistent in his search for a relationship with his adult daughter. That was a major factor in her acceptance of the relationship. When a woman realizes that her father is real, not just playing a hide-and-seek game, the relationship changes dramatically. When the father simply says, "I'm sorry," he has said something his daughter needs to hear. Of course, this doesn't mean that everything in the relationship gets instantly better. It does create an emotional closeness necessary to talk safely about issues and feelings. Father and daughter then have a foundation on which to build a relationship.

Reconnecting Following Abuse

It can be especially difficult for a father in recovery to reconnect with an adult daughter if he has ever abused her physically, sexually, or emotionally. In practical terms, a father who has abused his daughter has lost the "right" to have a relationship with her. If he is serious about establishing an emotional and spiritual bond with her, he must learn to respect her boundaries and conditions for the relationship.

Abuse creates intense feelings of terror. For any hope of restoration, the daughter must perceive the relationship to be safe. In a safe relationship, the father will respect his daughter's fears and will take her feelings seriously. A father who is safe will make amends to his daughter. This may include asking for forgiveness as well as paying for counseling for her. A father who is safe will recognize that healing and forgiveness are on the daughter's timetable, not his own. He will recognize that she may need to define when, where, and how their relationship will be conducted. These emotional, spiritual, and physical boundaries allow a measure of safety that enables the daughter to heal. They create an environment that allows forgiveness and restoration to take place.

There are times when fathers need to set boundaries. An adult daughter may hold onto her hurt and bring it up over and over again. If this happens, the father doesn't have to be punished repeatedly for past offenses. He can say, "I have said that I'm sorry for what happened. I wish I could make it up to you, but I can't. I can only be the best father I know how to be today. It isn't right for me to be beat up over and over again for something in the past, for which I am sorry. Since this particular issue keeps coming up, perhaps we should see a pastor or a therapist together so we can work through it."

No father can maintain this level of safety for his daughter and for himself unless he has a solid commitment to his own recovery. Reconnecting after such a deep wound is not easy. The relationship can be volatile—great hope one moment and crushing defeat the next. So a father who attempts to build an emotional bond needs to remain sober from all his addictions. He must have adequate support so that he does not emotionally withdraw when the going gets tough. He needs ongoing recovery to remain on track and to keep working toward an improved relationship. Finally, his ongoing recovery shows his daughter his genuine repentance. It shows that he is serious about being a safe father. The past may have been painful. But the father must maintain a feeling connection with his own heart. This makes it possible for him, at last, to touch his daughter's heart.

A Closer Look

Amends—Within the context of the Twelve Steps, the idea of amends is broadly defined as "repairing the damage of the past." Amends can be as simple as an apology or as complex as restitution for physical or financial liability as a result of a harm done. The best amends are the true and lasting changes in character.

Personal Reflection

1. Think about your growing up years. What factors limited the growth of a strong emotional bond between you and your father? In what ways are those factors different today? In what ways is your relationship with your father different today?

2. What would you like your relationship with your father to be? How realistic are your expectations?

3. If geographic distance or infrequent contact separate you and your father, what can you do to make the most of your relationship?
●◇

4. Do you know what expectations your father has (if any) for your relationship? What are they? Are his expectations realistic?
●◇

5. Take a few moments to try to identify times your father may have been reaching out to you, but failed. Thank God that your heavenly Father never fails and that God can help you receive your father's offer of restoration.
●◇

NOTES:

CHAPTER 11

❧❦

Hope and a Healing Community

The Christian Model of
Womanhood and Support

I was suddenly reminded of a scene from childhood: we three stair-step sisters, two years apart in age, legs dangling in a pew, our shoulders hunched over in fear, as if awaiting a blow. The preacher shouts: "It was Eve who ate that apple from the Tree of the Knowledge of Good and Evil. And in going against God's will, in eating the fruit poisoned with mortality, that woman condemned us all to exile from God's Garden. She listened to the snake and her own sinful self, instead of her sweet Lord!" We shuddered, we three terrified sisters, little descendants of Eve.

It was 1958, and we three little sinners were living in Montana. At Sunday School, our teacher, as if sensing the unbroken, fine horse flesh of such high-strung fillies, would glare at us girls as if her lectures were lassos. "Little women have to work especially hard for our Lord's redemption. We were the first in all creation to go against His divine will."

Sometimes it seemed hopeless to a nine-year-old. As the eldest sister, I was often utterly bewildered when the younger ones asked me to explain these sermonettes, as our teacher modestly called them.

"Do you think God will ever forgive us for eating that stupid apple?" my middle sister once asked me as we loped along the open range.

"Nope," I said, and suddenly felt a strange happiness within. At that moment I knew that, no matter what I did, as long as I was female I would always be Eve's daughter. I somehow intuited that being forgiven by this angry Father God might be the same as being broken—the sharp, bit of blame always turning me this way and that. Better to be a wild filly with no righteous rider.

174

> That day, when I felt the happy hopelessness of an unforgiven
> female, I wondered if this feeling was an echo of the still, small voice
> the preacher was always talking about. But when I asked my Sunday
> School teacher whether my still, small voice belonged to me or to
> God, she corrected me soundly. "Nothing about you belongs to you,"
> she pronounced. "Except for your sin."
> After that I kept my voice quiet . . . .
> I wondered what might have happened if my sisters and I had
> been blessed with a Sunday School teacher who rocked us in her
> strong arms, mothering our minds and our souls, telling us stories of
> women in the Bible who were not harlots or temptresses or slaves.[1]

This excerpt from a tragic, true-life story wrenches my heart. It is a story about sisters—broken and wounded women. Mistreated in their relationship with their earthy father. Marred by life in a not-so-perfect family. Maimed by their experience of a shame-filled Christianity, and muddled by the abortion debate. These wounds have led each woman to make painful choices in life. Each still carries the burden of that hurt. Their story stirs the ache in many women's hearts.

The author begins with a conversation she had with her mother. The forty-one-year-old mother thought she was pregnant. She asks her college-student daughter where she might get an abortion. During their talk, the daughter learns about an aborted baby boy early in her mother's marriage. His twin sister survived—she survived.

Later in the article, the author reveals that both she and her younger sister experienced unwanted pregnancies. The author miscarried. Her sister had an abortion. The author is now a pro-choice advocate. Her sister never forgave herself—she lobbies hard for the pro-life cause. Through the article, the author shares about their opposing positions and their search for healing. She looks to the feminine spirituality of ancient pagan religions. She uses a Native American ritual to "heal the wounds of my fundamentalist childhood." Her sister strives to work out her redemption and healing as an anti-abortion activist. She adheres to strict Christian fundamentalism. Both women still live in pain.

A Need for Healing

The tragedy of this story is that it is not uncommon. Many women, like the author and her sisters, have suffered from a Christian culture that has shamed women. Women should be nurtured like Esther was. Women should be empowered and emboldened to take a firm stand in a dangerous world. Instead, in the Christian culture, women have been weakened through shame. Women have been withered by poor self-esteem. Women have been wrecked by damaged boundaries. And women's lives have been wasted for lack of personal identity and worth.

All of these assaults weaken women so that they are easy prey for abusive relationships. The pain they suffer makes them vulnerable to addictions that can lead to death. In addition, these weeping and untended wounds have contributed to the tragedy of abortion. This is a far cry from a biblical view of feminine strength.

Imagine, as the author suggested, how life might have been different for these two sisters. What if they had a Sunday school teacher who rocked them in her strong arms, mothering their minds and souls? What if they had been mothered by a whole community of women who listened and understood their fears, hurts, and shame? What if their wounded hearts had been nurtured? What if those little girls had a pastor who instructed and inspired the worth of women? What if that pastor imparted and illuminated to them their true identity in Christ? What if these sisters had each seen herself as a chosen and cherished child of God? She would still be a sinner and a woman with ordinary faults, but one who has been made a saint by the sacrifice of a Savior, who values her life. Her sin debt is already paid in full. No curse or calamity from Eden's fall need ever shame her again. No more sacrifice is required. The Savior paid it all.

Jesus was very protective of the souls of children. I do not believe he is pleased with the spiritual, emotional, physical, or sexual abuse of children that has taken place within the Christian culture. Were he walking the earth today, he would enter our churches and say, "Why are you wounding my children with shame? My Church must be a safe place for all my children to heal and grow." If we claim to be Christ's community on earth, we must reject a theology of shame. Christ's community is a place of overflowing grace. It is where the sinners should be. His community is a healing and nurturing family where all of God's children grow to full maturity.

What's a Father to Do?

We began this book with the story of a father and his daughter who lived in a dangerous culture. It was a society that did not value life, particularly the life of Jews. Life in our world today isn't that much different. We still shudder at Hitler's attempt to annihilate Jews because he viewed them as less than human. Around the globe we witness the insanity of ethnic cleansing as one group attempts to wipe out another. In our own nation, we find it acceptable to end the life of the unborn simply because they are inconvenient.

What does this have to do with fathers and daughters? It has much to do with the father-daughter relationship. We no longer have the luxury of passive Christianity. Christian television, books, radio, and tapes are no substitute for active involvement in the Christian community and the culture at large. We need fathers who are spiritually and emotionally alive. We need fathers who live and demonstrate an intimate connection with the heart of God. We need fathers who feel the grief of abortion, child abuse, homelessness, divorce, and poverty. As Mordecai felt the grief of King Xerxes' edict, we need fathers who realize the life and death dangers in our world. We need fathers who call to God with their hearts and plead for mercy and deliverance.

We need fathers who reach out to the hearts of their daughters and sons. We need fathers who show concern for the hearts of children in the church and surrounding community. We need fathers who work diligently to build an emotional and spiritual bridge to their children. We need fathers who are painfully honest and unfailingly supportive of their daughters and sons. We need fathers and mothers united with their daughters and sons to become a community of people who care and make a difference. We need fathers who are bold and wise warriors able to teach their children how to survive and how to stand and fight when necessary.

Fathers like this will not arise from the Christian community until we address the weakness and woundedness that permeate our families, our churches, and our culture. The Christian community must become a safe place for the broken and abused. It must help them rise up from the ashes of their past. It must offer them hope for healing without condemnation or shame. It must be a place where the broken and immature can be nurtured to strength and prepared for service. The Christian community must be an affirming place—a people full of possibilities. In such a place, the wounded can become warriors for the cause of Christ.

This is why the story of Esther and Mordecai is so exciting to me. It illustrates what can happen in a daughter's life when her father is emotionally and spiritually available to her. It shows the unyielding power and strength of a godly woman. It also shows the power of a spiritual community that will sacrifice to nurture and support those called to take a risky stand. Through their story we see in a practical way how a daughter is nurtured and developed into a fully mature, adult woman.

As a father, I want my daughters to grow up to be strong and capable women of God. I want them to grow up with a strong sense of their identity in Christ and an intimate knowledge of him. I want them to be able to identify and express what is in their hearts. I want them to believe that their feelings, opinions, and dreams are important. I want them to have a strong sense of self-esteem—an unshakable confidence in who they are physically, emotionally, and spiritually. I want them to set secure boundaries that protect themselves from harm. I want them to be able to deal with life as it comes to them, without the temptation to survive through fantasy or addiction. And I want them to stand free from the shackles of shame and walk as women who are proud and confident.

What I desire for my daughters is something my wife and I cannot accomplish alone. It is something no parent can do alone. Such a solid foundation and potential for growth requires a strong reliance on God and the involvement of a healing community. This community starts with grandfathers, grandmothers, aunts, and uncles, but even the extended family is not enough. This healing community includes family and friends, but friends and family are not enough. The whole church community—mentors, disciples, pastors, Sunday school teachers—needs to be involved as well. God uses all of these people to nurture the spiritual and emotional development of strong and godly women.

A Community of Lifelong Support

The evangelical Christian church needs positive change in its attitude and approach to women. Women like Esther are in our congregations. They have the potential to change the world. But they need the nurture and encouragement of the Christian community.

God did not create women to carry the burden of Eve's sin. He created women to be daughters of the living God—made in his image. He gave women minds to think, strong bodies to endure life, hearts to feel, and unique gifts to accomplish his purposes. God created a woman's body as a precious temple capable of nurturing new life. The Christian community honors God as these aspects of womanhood are affirmed, respected, and nurtured.

For us to esteem women as we should, we need to examine our attitudes and beliefs about women. We need to dispense with the shame-filled, unbiblical teaching that holds so many in bondage. We need to honor and affirm that which God has created as feminine. We fathers need to face the wounds of our own hearts and open ourselves to God's healing so we may touch the hearts of our daughters.

A women's community needs to be envisioned and developed within the local church. It's purpose? To nurture the hearts of all little girls as they grow into womanhood. Women are best able to support one another as sisters united in experience, faith, and hope. A strong, loving, and healing sisterhood of women will strengthen the whole Christian community.

Join me in envisioning the growth of our Christian community. Envision the Christian community as a place where a woman's feminine nature is honored, affirmed, and nurtured throughout her life. Envision the inner strength of a woman who is a part of this emotionally and spiritually healing community. Think of the power and potential that would season her approach to life. Picture the impact she would have on her world.

The young girls who are brought into this community of women will be filled with spiritual strength. They will see integrity and valor modeled in the lives of mature women. They will be taught to connect with their feelings. They will know what it means to be a woman of God. They will hear about Hannah and the power of earnest prayer. They will be told about Abigail, and how she boldly confronted David. They will learn about Ruth and her faithful support of Naomi. They will be warned through the story of Delilah— her treachery and misuse of feminine strength. They will understand the pain and consequence that adultery caused David and

Bathsheba and all of Israel. Can you feel the tremendous spiritual potential and expression that is possible within a community of vibrant and honest women?

Imagine the community of Christian women celebrating with a young girl as she reaches puberty and transforms into a young woman. Imagine how the community of Christian women could celebrate and mark the milestone of her graduation from high school with joyful recognition of her next steps in life. They could bless her with a solemn commitment of prayer and continued support. Imagine the encouragement of phone calls, visits, and letters when she is away at college. She would feel strength and support knowing that a whole community of women are caring for her. She would feel safe to share her heart and life with other women close to her—her challenges, struggles, and disappointments. She would step into womanhood with dignity and honor rather than fear and shame. Women of all ages would stand with her mother and father to help her approach her future with hope and safety.

The community of women can help a woman develop appropriate boundaries with men. They can teach her how to distinguish between men who are safe and those who are dangerous. They can affirm her worth and help her recognize and obey the voice of caution and conscience. They can strengthen her identity and enable her to face the fears of abandonment and rejection. They can keep her from the fragile and fallible security of a destructive relationship with a young man. They can teach her the disciplines of prayer and the importance of study in God's Word. They can model a spiritual connection with the heavenly Father, her strength and hope for her life.

Imagine the increased joy when she is able to share her successes, victories, and steady progress. Imagine having support during the emptiness and loneliness that follows the breakup of a relationship, and the comfort of an understanding shoulder to cry on in times of grief, fear, and confusion.

When a woman—whatever her age—faces the start of her first job, she needs the empowerment, encouragement, and experience of other women. In a community of Christian women, she will have that and more. She will feel the delight and pride from other women for her accomplishments. She will have the benefit of their wisdom. She will be surrounded by a community of women who know her and love her and will still respect her should she stumble and fall along the way. She will be admonished to maintain strong boundaries, to reject demeaning treatment and oppressive workloads, to ask for and receive pay that is appropriate to her worth, to pursue her own business opportunities. And she will be confronted with concern if she is headed toward burn-out.

Imagine if the whole community of women were available to celebrate and nurture a young woman when she announces her engagement. The women would join with her in the months, weeks, and days before her wedding to prepare and joyfully anticipate what lies ahead. They could set aside time to bless her with their experience, counsel, and prayer. Perhaps they would have a celebration to welcome her into the sisterhood of married women.

This sense of community support opens the door for a woman to share her frustrations in her marriage, her joys, her hopes for the future. She is not alone or abandoned as she enters this new phase of her life because she can feel the commitment, love, and support of other women. She can benefit from the wisdom of a community of women as she discovers that marriage is a lifelong process. They can help her understand the ebb and flow of intimacy and growth in her relationship with her husband.

And if she announces that she is pregnant, she has a whole community of women with whom to celebrate and on whom she can depend. These women can help her give thanks for the gift growing inside her and help her ready herself for the honors and responsibilities of motherhood. As her body changes, they can share the excitement of what is happening within her body. If her baby does not live because of miscarriage, she has a community of women who affirm the reality of her loss. If her baby dies shortly before or after birth, she is surrounded by caring arms in which she can weep. When her baby is born, the community of women can pray for her, call her, make meals for her family, and support her in whatever is needed.

During those early months of motherhood, another initiation can take place in which she is blessed with respect and honor. The importance of this step in her life is recognized, and the women of the community renew their commitment to support her. They may step in to care for her baby when she is exhausted and depressed. They may listen as she seeks to understand the changes in her relationship with her husband.

If the woman faces infertility, the community of women can surround her with love and affirmation. They can comfort her in her grief. They can support her as she struggles with questions of her identity. They can listen as she tries to make decisions regarding treatment options or other alternatives. And if she faces disappointment month after month, they will be there to fortify her heart and encourage her spirit.

If a woman comes to terms with the horror of an abortion experience, the women of the Christian community can receive her with love. They can support her as she goes through the process of forgiveness and healing. This process is so much easier when a woman has the support of others who, without self-righteous judgment, will listen to her story, weep with her, mourn with her, and pray with her.

Women, who have had abortions, suffer tremendous shame in the Church. Feelings of worthlessness and fear of rejection keep these women in the shadows—in secrecy. This wound goes beyond a woman's relationship with the Christian community. Her relationship with God the Father is affected. When a woman receives forgiveness and healing, she is lifted up like a new person. She understands God's grace and love at a depth that most people never understand. Rather than being exiled from God and his people, she can become a valuable resource with much to give.

When a woman grows older, the community of women are still very important to her. As her body and hair color change, she may grieve the loss of her youth. But to the community of women, her age translates into glory. She is given a new and very important role. She grows into the position of elder within the women's community. This is not a job to be taken lightly. It is a position of honor, wisdom, and strength. It means that she has been empowered through the experience of life. Now her walk with God can benefit younger women for their lives ahead. The older she becomes, the more she has to offer.

When a woman's time on earth is over, there will be grieving among her family, friends, and the women she has loved and nurtured. Her loss will, for a time, leave an emptiness within the women's community of her church. Another woman will be called to step into her place. Yet the sadness of her loss leads to celebration because this woman of God has taken her final step of initiation. She has completed her journey in right relationship with her heavenly Father.

I do not see this as a dream or a fantasy that can never happen. I see it as a foundation for ministry that will change the hearts of women and will change the Church. I see a community of women who commit themselves to lifelong spiritual growth, rigorous honesty, spiritual and emotional intimacy, and unfailing support of one another. I see a healing community within the larger Church community. I see women being healed from the wounds of their fathers. I see those wounds of the heart being filled with a deep and vital connection with the heavenly Father.

Mended Hearts

Mended hearts won't lie
   —pain has laid them bare.
The broken souls can't boast
   —sorrow has stripped all airs.

The suffering man or woman,
   cannot judge or scold.
The honesty of scars revealed
   tell the story—bare the soul.

The torn, the tempted, the crushed
   have found new ears to hear.
They listen now and understand
   —in comfort, in care, in tears.

They will not fix, intrude, or meddle.
   No imperative, no preaching, no wind.
They are blinded by love and can only point
   to the One who mended them.[2]

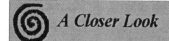 *A Closer Look*

Affirmation—The idea of affirmation is a combination of acknowledgment, acceptance, approval, support, and validation. When we affirm another person, we offer them the material from which they can build self-esteem. The components of self-esteem are acceptance (I belong), significance (I am somebody), competence (I can do something), power (I can make it happen), and virtue (I can do right).[3] Affirmation in any area of a person's life builds her self-esteem. For example, earlier I spoke of the lengthy bike trek that my daughter Rachel and I accomplished together. My presence with her affirmed her physically, and the result was a boost in every vital component of self-esteem. Acceptance—we did it together, and we belonged together. Significance—she was individually recognized because of her accomplishment, and the T-shirt proved it. Competence— she completed a difficult, twenty-five-mile bike ride. Power—her personal strength made her accomplishment possible. Virtue—the task itself was honorable because she accomplished this feat without cheating or fudging one bit.

I used a physical example with my daughter, but we can affirm others and offer the "stuff" of self-esteem in many ways. We all need to experience acceptance, significance, competence, power, and virtue in our emotional, social, intellectual, and spiritual lives. A truly healing community will seek for opportunities to affirm one another in all of these ways.

Christian Community—When I refer to the Christian community, I mean the fellowship of people united together in worship, service, and mutual encouragement because of their common faith in Jesus Christ. This can be the local church, the support group that meets in a home, two or three Christian friends gathered for coffee or a meal, or the Church around the world. Wherever Christians fellowship and come together, the Christian community exists.

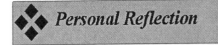 *Personal Reflection*

1. What has been your experience with the Christian community and in particular the community of Christian women? In what ways have you experienced affirmation or support? In what ways have you experienced shame or rejection? How have these experiences affected your feminine and spiritual identity?

2. What do you need from your Christian community to help you reshape your life toward godly womanhood?

3. What practical things can the Christian community provide to nurture fathers and help them grow into the men God desires them to be?

⊸◇

4. Do you have a committed group of Christian women with whom to share your life? Who are the Christian women in your life that you look up to? What is it that you see and admire about them?

⊸◇

5. Take a few moments to reflect on the lessons you have learned through this book. Ask God to continue to give you understanding about the issues important to your heart. Thank God for his perfect fatherhood and for his perfect love for you.

⊸◇

NOTES:

Appendix A

A Word about Brain Chemistry

Counseling and psychotherapy—even re-parenting and spirituality with 12-step recovery—cannot address every need. The immaturity and childishness we see in adults may actually be a problem in brain chemistry—not bad character. Impulsive behavior, hyper-activity, and fits of rage may be medical and not moral issues. And all the counseling in the world will not correct some forms of depression and moodiness.

Thanks to advancements in medicine, a certain kind of brain-imaging known as a SPECT scan can pin-point over or underactive, or damaged, areas of the brain. Doctors can use this information to prescribe medication and balance a patient's brain chemistry. This often allows the patient to experience immediate relief from life-controlling problems. Even young men with life-long conduct disorders can experience behavior change.

An imbalance in brain chemistry or a problem in the physiology of the brain can cause a person to pursue behaviors, chemicals, and relationships to sooth moods, stimulate concentration, and feel normal. Risk-taking or dare-devil behaviors can provide a large dose of adrenaline and calm the hyper-active or focus the scattered. Waking up to the "worry of the day" can provide that same fix of natural speed that allows the disorganized brain to bring order to life. But there is a cost. Risk-taking and dare-devil activity can lead to injury or death. And chronic worry can lead to an ever-present sense of doom and a constant state of alert. Tense shoulders, headaches, irritated bowels, auto-immune diseases like fibromyalgia, and chronic-fatigue can all result.

Sugar, high carbohydrate foods, and alcohol all bring a chemical change and soothing effect to the limbic system in the brain. This will also affect the reward pathways in our brain and allow us to feel good about ourselves. The person who has a problem in this area of the brain might receive compliments all day, but the good words just bounce off. They hear the compliments, but just can't accept them. But after a few drinks, a few bags of M&Ms, or a few peanut-butter and jelly sandwiches, the person can feel good about him or herself. The risk, however, is obesity, alcoholism, depression, and a host of other health and social ills.

People pleasing, care-taking, and other codependent relationships can be mood-altering experiences that trigger changes in a person's brain. The fact that we feel better when we control or enmesh ourselves in the lives of others can be a result of brain chemistry. In the end, the codependent relationship will not lead to lasting or positive changes.

If a person's problems are related to imbalance in brain chemistry or inactivity in brain function, there are specific medical interventions that can be help. For example, if you constantly get "stuck" on certain thoughts, you may have a problem with your cingulate system. If you have trouble focusing your attention you may need a prefrontal cortex prescription. If you're plagued with anxiety, the problem may lie in your basal ganglia system. If you find it hard to connect meaningfully with others, you may need to correct a faulty deep limbic system. If you can't tame your temper, your temporal lobes may be to blame. It is important to take responsibility if problems—that you have worked on in therapy or with medications—continue to persist. You may need a more accurate diagnosis with SPECT Brain Imaging. For a more detailed discussion of these problems and their treatment see the book *Change Your Brain, Change Your Life* by neuropsychiatrist Daniel Amen, M.D.

Also see Dr. Amen's website:
http://www.amenclinic.com.

Appendix B

Suggestions for Small Group Study and Support

I believe that everyone, who seeks healing from the brokenness and pain of a less-than-perfect father-daughter connection, needs the support of others. For that reason, I offer some suggestions for small group study and support. The following are common questions and concerns about the organization and make-up of a small group that is formed for the purpose of study and support.

Who should participate in group?
Anyone who relates to the topics and needs discussed in this book should participate. No one should attend as an observer. No one should attend for another person. No one should attend to provide input to the group.

Is a mixed group of daughters and fathers appropriate?
No support or study group for the father-daughter issues should be mixed. Separate groups should be formed for fathers if they desire to meet.

Where should we meet?
Many churches and community groups will provide space for support groups. A private home is a good place as well.

Who should lead the group?
Like twelve-step groups, the best form of leadership is the "group conscience." Decisions should be made by the group as a whole. Even questions of leadership and logistics should be considered together—no one left out. If a church or community organization is sponsoring the group, then existing leadership from within the church or organization would be appropriate. Still, the wise leader will take input and suggestions from the members of the study or support group.

After an introductory meeting(s) should the group be closed to newcomers and consist of only those willing to make a commitment to the group?
This is a decision left best to the group as a whole. There are good reasons to close a group and good reasons to keep a group open. A closed group provides extra safety for some. An open group provides greater access and openness to those in need outside the group.

What should be the meeting format?
Any format that is agreed upon by group is fine. I have offered a suggested group format (see page 187). A fixed routine, whatever the format, provides safety, structure, and stability week after week. There should be enough flexibility to allow the personality and special needs of the group to be expressed.

How long should the group meet?
This is a decision for the whole group. But the possibilities are broad. A group might form to go through the book rather quickly. After an initial meeting, a group could discuss one chapter a week. In this case, the members would have to read the material in advance of the meeting. Or a group might choose to proceed at a more leisurely pace. The group might read and discuss the material in the meeting, taking one section at a time. If the meeting is intended primarily for support, rather than study, the book would be used differently. A portion of the book might be read as a topic for discussion—without concern for a thorough reading or study of the text. This kind of a support group could meet indefinitely or for an agreed upon length of time.

What about a phone list? Should we share personal phone numbers with other group members and call one another for support outside the meeting?
Many twelve-step groups provide a phone list for mutual support during the week. Support from one another is always a good idea, but the decision to release personal phone numbers should always left up to each individual.

Guidelines for Sharing

A small group that has come together to support one another must be a safe place. The following guidelines for sharing can ensure that safety—if they are followed. It is important to refer to these guidelines before every meeting and to discuss them in depth at the first meeting. I've provided questions to spur group discussion and personal reflection on the guidelines.

❏ Keep your comments brief, take turns talking, and don't interrupt others.

❏ Speak personally: I, me, my—not you, we, they.

❏ Be honest, sharing both successes and struggles.

❏ Don't fix, advise, or rescue others—respect each person's right to self-expression without comment.

❏ Take responsibility—don't blame or judge others.

❏ Avoid cross talk—speak to the entire group.

❏ Keep confidence to ensure an atmosphere of safety and openness.

❏ Respect the needs of others by asking permission to express concern with a hug or a touch—many are uncomfortable with physical contact.

❏ Avoid gossip—share your own needs and refrain from talking about a person who is absent.

❏ Hold others accountable for their behavior only if they ask you to do so.

Personal Reflection

1. Which of the *Guidelines for Sharing* is most important to you? Why?

2. What do you need most from others to feel safe in a support group meeting?

3. What is your past experience with support groups? Share both your good and not-so-good experiences.

4. What do you hope to receive from this support group?

5. What do you believe you have to offer other members in the group?

Suggested Meeting Format

The following is a suggest meeting format for a small group that is formed to study this book and support one another through the process.

Opening Prayer

Any prayer that acknowledges God is appropriate. A prayer that is commonly used in twelve-steps meeting is the short version of Serenity Prayer by Reinhold Niebuhr:

> *God, grant me the serenity to accept the things I cannot change, the courage to change the things I can, and the wisdom to know the difference.*

Higher Focus

Someone from the group should come prepared to share a five minute (no more) inspirational or spiritual reading. It can be a poem, a meditation from a published source, a passage of scripture, or a short story. The important thing is to lift everyone's focus to a higher, more positive place. As the Apostle Paul said, "*Whatever is true, whatever is noble, whatever is right, whatever is pure, whatever is lovely, whatever is admirable—if anything is excellent or praiseworthy—think about such things.*"

Introduction and Personal Sharing—Highs and Lows

Go around the group and allow each person present to introduce herself (first names only) and share the high point and the low point of her previous week. Everyone should know she is free to "pass" and refrain from sharing without explanation. We share high and low points to stay in touch at a feeling level. Rather than report events or offer opinions, it is better to share feelings. When we share a high and a low, we broaden and balance our emotional connection with others.

Topic for Sharing

An agreed upon portion of the book should be read. The group may take turns reading one paragraph at time or a volunteer may read the entire portion. Everyone should know that she is free to "pass" and refrain from reading out loud.

After the reading, allow each participant to share her personal experience or feelings related to the material covered. The *A Closer Look* and *Personal Reflection* at the end of each chapter can help focus sharing. When everyone who desires to share has done so, another portion may be read as time allows.

Concluding Comments and Requests for Support

Before the meeting dismisses, everyone should have the opportunity to share one final and brief comment or make a request for support or prayer. The final comment may be an insight that was gained from the meeting. It might be a word of thanks or an affirmation. It might be a final thought related to the topic. Requests for support or prayer should be directed to the entire group. No immediate, individual response or feedback should be offered. And no group prayer should be offered for the request unless the person has asked for immediate group prayer.

Concluding Prayer

Any agreed upon prayer is appropriate. Many support groups form a circle, hold hands, and conclude with the *Lord's Prayer*:

> *Our Father, Who art in heaven, hallowed be thy name. Thy kingdom come. Thy will be done, on earth as it is in heaven. Give us this day our daily bread. And forgive us our trespasses, as we forgive those who trespass against us. And lead us not into temptation, but deliver us from evil. For thine is the kingdom and the power and the glory, forever and ever. Amen.*

Appendix C
Recovery Resources

ADD Anonymous, Website: http://www.members.aol.com/addanon/

Alcoholics Anonymous (AA) 475 Riverside Dr., New York, NY 10015 Phone: 212-870-3400; Fax: 212-870-3003 Website: http://www.alcoholics-anonymous.org

Adult Children of Alcoholics (ACA or AcoA), PO Box 3216, Torrance, CA 90510 Phone: 310-534-1815; E-mail: info@adultchildren.org Website: http://adultchildren.org

Al-Anon/Alateen Family Groups Headquarters, Inc. 1600 Corporate Landing Parkway, Virginia Beach, VA 23454-5617 Phone: 757-563-1600, 888-4Al-anon (888-425-2666); Fax: 757-563-1655 E-mail: wso@al-anon.org Website: http://al-anon.alateen.org

Clutterers Anonymous (CLA), PO Box 25884, Santa Ana, CA 92799-5884 Website: http://visi.com/~dsgood or http://clutterers-anonymous.org/resources.html

Co-Dependents Anonymous (CoDA), 105 E. Grant Road, Tucson, AZ 85705 Phone: 520-882-5705; Website: http://mpoweru.com/alano/co-depen.htm Website: http://coda-tvcc.org/index.html

Co-Anon Family Groups World Services, Inc., PO Box 12124, Tucson, AZ 85732-2124 Phone: 770-928-5122 Atlanta, GA; 714-647-6698 Orange County, CA; 818-377-4317 Los Angeles, CA; 520-513-5028 Tucson, AZ; Website: http://co-anon.org

Cocaine Anonymous (C.A.), Inc., 3740 Overland Ave., # C, Los Angeles, CA 90034 Phone: 310-559-5833; Fax: 310-559-2554; National Referral Line: 800-347-8998; Email: cawso@ca.org; Website: http://ca.org

Debtors Anonymous, PO Box 920888, Needham, MA 02492-0009 Phone: 781-453-2743; Fax: 781-453-2745 E-mail: new@debtorsanonymous.org Website: http://debtorsanonymous.org

Emotions Anonymous International (EA), PO Box 4245, St. Paul MN 55104-0245 Phone: 651-647-9712; Fax: 651-647-1593 E-mail: info@emotionsanonymous.org Website: http://emotionsanonymous.org

Families Anonymous WSO & Info.
Services, 800-736-9805

Gamblers Anonymous (GA), PO Box
17173, Los Angeles, CA 90017
Phone: 213-386-8789, 310-478-2121
Fax: 213-386-0030
E-mail: isomain@gamblersanonymous.org
Website: http://gamblersanonymous.org

Marijuana Anonymous (MA)
PO Box 2912, Van Nuys, CA 91404
Phone: 800-766-6779
E-mail: maws98@aol.com
Website: http://marijuana—anonymous.org

Narcotics Anonymous (NA)
PO Box 9999, Van Nuys, CA 91409
19737 Nordhoff Place, Chatsworth, CA 91311
Phone: 818-773-9999; Fax: 818-700-0700
E-mail: info@na.org
Website: http://wsoinc.com

Nicotine Anonymous (NicA), PO Box
591777, San Francisco, CA 94159-1777
Phone: 415-750-0328; E-mail:
info@nicotine-anonymous.org
Website: http://nicotine-anonymous.org/

Overeaters Anonymous (OA)
PO Box 44020, Rio Rancho, NM 87174-4020
6075 Zenith Ct. NE, Rio Rancho, NM 87124
Phone: 505-891-2664; Fax: 505-891-4320
E-mail: overeatr@technet.nm.org
Website: http://overeatersanonymous.org
& http://overeaters.org

Phobics Anonymous, Website:
http://pilot.infi.net/~susanf/12ofphob.htm

Pills Anonymous, Phone: 714-978-9685

Recoveries Anonymous Universal Services
PO Box 1212, East Northport, NY 11731
Phone: 516-261-1212
Website: http://r-a.org

Recovery Online (self-help groups online lists),
Website: http://recovery.alano.org/index.html

S-Anon International Family Groups (SA)
PO Box 111242, Nashville, TN 37222-1242
Phone: 615-833-3152, 800-339-0222
E-mail: sanon@sanon.org
Website: http://sanon.org

Sex Addicts Anonymous (SAA)
Website: http://sexaa.org

Sex and Love Addicts Anonymous (SLAA)
PO Box 338, Norwood, MA 02062-0338
Phone: 781-255-8825
E-mail: slaafws@aol.com
Website: http://slaafws.org

Sexaholics Anonymous (S.A.)
PO Box 111910, Nashville, TN 37222
Phone: 615-331-6230; Fax: 615-331-6901
E-mail: ca@sa.org or saico@sa.org;
Website: http://slaaws.org

Sexual Compulsives Anonymous (SCA)
PO Box 1585, Old Chelsea Station
New York, NY 10011
Int'l Info: 212-606-3778
Phone: 800-977-4325, 212-439-1123
E-mail: info@sca—recovery.org
Website: http://sca-recovery.org

Twelve Step Home Page
(resources for the online community)
Website: http://twelvestep.com

CHRISTIAN 12 STEP ORGANIZATIONS

Alcoholics for Christ
Website: http://alcoholicsforchrist.com

National Association for Christian Recovery
PO Box 215, Brea, CA 92822-0215
Voicemail: 714-529-6227; Fax: 714-529-1120
E-mail: hopehappens@earthlink.net;
Website: http://christianrecovery.com

Overcomers Outreach Inc.
520 N Brookhurst Street, Suite 121
Anaheim, CA 92801-5206
Phone: 714-491-3000; Fax: 714-491-3004
E-mail: info@overcomersoutreach.org
Website: http://overcomersoutreach.org
NOTE: Overcomers Outreach, Inc. is a
nonprofit, Christ-centered ministry dedi-
cated to helping anyone who would benefit from a twelve-step program. The organization also helps churches establish
Christ-centered twelve-step support
groups. As of this writing, there are 1,000
Overcomers Outreach groups in 50 states
and 13 countries. Internationally, Overcomers Outreach is supported by the tax-
deductible contributions of individuals
who believe in its goals or have benefited
from the program.
Overcomers Outreach is not intended
to replace such twelve-step groups as
A.A., Al-Anon, A.C.A., and so on. Rather,
the organization seeks to supplement those
programs and assist Christians who are
in recovery. Overcomers Outreach views
itself as a bridge between the twelve-step
community and churches of all denomi-
nations. Its founders are Bob and Pauline
Bartosch, who based the ministry on their
own recovery experience.
Contact Overcomers if you are interested in starting a Christian twelve-step
support group in your church.

Spirit of Hope (ADD/ADHD Support)
PO Box 53642, Irvine, CA 92619-3642
Phone: 949-733-1486; Fax: 949-733-9812
E-mail: seiden@pacbell.net

190

Appendix D
Suggested Reading

Adams, Kenneth M. Ph.D. *Silently Seduced: When Parents Make Their Children Partners*. Deerfield Beach, FL: Health Communications, Inc., 1991.

Adult Children. *The Secrets of Dysfunctional Families*. Deerfield Beach, FL: Health Communications, Inc., 1988.

Alcoholics Anonymous. *Alcoholics Anonymous, "The Big Book."* New York: Alcoholics Anonymous World Services, Inc.

—. *Twelve Steps—Twelve Traditions*. New York: Alcoholics Anonymous World Services, Inc.

Amen, Daniel, M.D. *Change Your Brain, Change Your Life*. New York: Random House, 1999.

Beattie, Melody. *Codependent No More*. New York: Harper Collins Publishers, 1987.

—. *Beyond Codependency: And Getting Better All the Time*. New York: Walker, 1990.

Boteach, Shmuel. *Kosher Sex: a Recipe for Passion and Intimacy*. New York: Main Street, 2000.

Bradshaw, John. *Bradshaw on: The Family—A New Way of Creating Solid Self-esteem*. Deerfield Beach, FL: Health Communications, Inc., 1996.

—. *Family Secrets: What You Don't Know Can Hurt You*. New York : Bantam Books, 1995.

—. *Healing the Shame That Binds You*. Deerfield Beach, FL: Health Communications, 1988.

Carnes, Patrick. *Contrary to Love: Helping the Sexual Addict*. Minneapolis, MN: CompCare Publishers, 1989.

—. *Don't Call It Love: Recovery from Sexual Addiction*. New York: Bantam Books, 1991.

—. *A Gentle Path through the Twelve Steps*. Minneapolis, MN: CompCare Publishers, 1993.

—. *Sexual Anorexia: Overcoming Sexual Self-Hatred*. Center City, MN: Hazelden, 1997.

De Becker, Gavin. *The Gift of Fear: Survival Signals that Protect Us from Violence*. Boston: Little, Brown, 1997.

Coopersmith, Stanley. *The Antecedents of Self-esteem*. San Francisco: W.H. Freeman, 1967.

Friends in Recovery. *The 12 Steps—A Spiritual Journey*. San Diego: RPI Publishing, Inc., 1994.

— with Jerry S. *Meditations for the Twelve Steps—A Spiritual Journey*. San Diego: RPI Publishing, Inc., 1993.

Goulter, Barbara and Minninger, Joan Ph.D. *The Father-daughter Dance*. New York: G.P. Putnam's Sons, 1993.

Hallowell, Edward, M.D. and Ratey, John J., M.D. *Driven to Distraction*. New York: Pantheon Books, 1994.

Halverstadt, Jonathan Scott, M.S. *ADD & Romance: Finding Fulfillment in Love, Sex, & Relationships*. Taylor Publishing Company, 1999.

Henslin, Earl R. Psy.D.(co-author). *Secrets of Your Family Tree*. Moody Press, 1991.

—. *Forgiven and Free: Learn How Bible Heros with Feet of Clay Are Models for Your Recovery*. Nashville: Thomas Nelson, [1994] 1991.

—. *Man to Man: Helping Fathers Relate to Sons and Sons Relate to Fathers*. Nashville: Thomas Nelson, 1993.

—. *The Cliff's Edge: Heaven Sent Help on a Harley—Hell Came in Other Ways*. Irvine, CA: Spirit of Hope Publishing, 2000.

Kritsberg, Wayne. *The Adult Children of Alcoholics Syndrome: from Discovery to Recovery*. Deerfield Beach, FL: Health Communications, Inc., 1986.

Millett, Craig Ballard. *In God's Image*. San Diego: LuraMedia, Inc., 1991.

Penner, Clifford. *Men and Sex: Discovering Greater Love, Passion & Intimacy with Your Wife*. Nashville: Thomas Nelson Publishers, 1997.

Scull, Charles, Ph.D., editor. *Fathers & Sons and Daughters: Exploring Fatherhood, Renewing the Bond*. Los Angeles: J.P. Tarcher, 1992.

Secunda, Victoria, *Women and Their Fathers*. New York: Delacorte Press, 1992.

Seiden, Jerry, M.A. *Divine or Distorted: God As We Understand God*. San Diego: RPI Publishing, Inc., 1993.

—. *Michael's Stable: The Best Gift Is to Belong*. Irvine, CA: Spirit of Hope Publishing, 1999.

Solden, Sari, M.S., MFCC. *Women with ADD: Embracing Disorganization At Home And In The Workplace*. Underwood Books, 1995.

Wegscheider-Cruse, Sharon. *Learning To Love Yourself*. Deerfield Beach, FL: Health Communications, Inc., 1987.

Whitfield, Charles. *Healing the Child Within*. Deerfield Beach, FL: Health Communications, Inc., 1987.

Willard, Dallas. *The Divine Conspiracy: Rediscovering Our Hidden Life in God*. San Francisco: HarperSanFrancisco, 1998.

Woititz, Janet. *Struggle For Intimacy*. Deerfield Beach, FL: Health Communications, Inc., 1985.

—. *Adult Children of Alcoholics*. Deerfield Beach, FL: Health Communications, Inc., [1983] 1991.

End Notes

Chapter 1
1. Adapted from the book of Esther. Quotations: Esther 1:18-20 (NIV).
2. Esther 2:7 (NIV).
3. Told in Genesis 27.
4. Told in Genesis 43, 44, and 45.
5. Told in Genesis 4.
6. Secunda, Victoria, *Women and Their Fathers* (New York: Delacorte Press, 1992) p.7.
7. Adapted from Esther 2:1-11, quotations from NIV.
8. Scull, Charles, Ph.D., editor *Fathers & Sons and Daughters: Exploring Fatherhood, Renewing the Bond* (Los Angeles: J.P. Tarcher, 1992) p. 99.
9. Secunda, p.9.
10. Ibid.

Chapter 2
1. The descriptions of father-daughter relationships I have used are an adaptation of the work of Barbara Goulter and Joan Minninger, Ph.D. Their concept of father-daughter relationships is presented in *The Father-daughter Dance* (New York: G.P. Putnam's Sons, 1993).
2. Ibid.
3. James 1:17 (NIV).
4. Proverbs 4:23 (NIV).
5. Ephesians 1:18 (NIV).
6. Romans 7:18-19 (NIV).

Chapter 3
1. Seiden, Jerry. *Divine or Distorted? God As We Understand God* (Irvine, CA: Spirit of Hope Publishing, 1993, 2000) pp. *Introduction xiii.*

Chapter 4
1. Adapted from Esther 2:8-20, quotations from NIV.
2. Adams, Kenneth M. Ph.D. *Silently Seduced: When Parents Make Their Children Partners* (Deerfield Beach, FL: Health Communications, Inc., 1991) pp.9-10.
3. Esther 2:11 (NIV).

Chapter 5
1. Adapted from Esther 2:19-4:3, quotations from NIV.
2. Joel 1:13 (NIV).
3. Adapted from Esther 4:48, quotations from vv. 6-8 (NIV).
4. Esther 4:11 (NIV).
5. Esther 4:13-14 (NIV).

Chapter 6
1. Adapted from Judges 4:1-22, quotations from NIV.
2. Adapted from Proverbs 31:10-31.
3. Proverbs 31:10, (NIV).
4. Millett, Craig Ballard, *In God's Image* (San Diego: LuraMedia, Inc., 1991) pp.25-27.
5. Proverbs 31:11-12 (NIV).
6. Proverbs 31:13-15 (NIV).
7. Proverbs 31:16 (NIV).
8. Proverbs 31:17 (NIV).
9. Proverbs 31:18, 20-23 (NIV).
10. Proverbs 31:25-26 (NIV).

Chapter 7
1. Adapted from Esther 4:1-5:1, quotation from NIV.
2. Esther 4:13-14 (NIV).
3. Esther 4:16-17 (NIV).
4. Adapted from Esther 5:1-3, quotation from v.2 (NIV).
5. Esther 5:8 (NIV).
6. Esther 7:3-6 (NIV).

Chapter 8
1. Author is known but chooses to remain anonymous. Used by permission.
2. Genesis 2:24.
3. John 5:1-9.
4. For further information on healing the father-son wound, see Dr. Henslin's book, *Man to Man.*

Chapter 9
1. From 1 John 1:9.
2. Luke 17:3-4 (NIV).
3. Matthew 18:22.
4. "Forgiving the Unforgivable" by Jean Callahan, *New Age Journal*, September/October 1993, p.78, which refers to *Getting Well Again*, by Carl O. Simonton, M.D., Stephanie Matthews-Simonton, and James Creighton.
5. Robin Casarjian is the author of *Forgiveness: A Bold Choice for a Peaceful Heart.* Quotation is taken from "Forgiving the Unforgivable" by Jean Callahan, *New Age Journal*, September/ October 1993, pp.78-79.

Chapter 10
1. Luke 23:34 (NIV).

Chapter 11
1. Brenda Peterson, "Sister Against Sister," *New Age Journal*, September/October 1993, pp.68,144.
2. *Mended Hearts* was written by Jerry Seiden. Used by permission.
3. The components of self-esteem are taken from Stanley Coopersmith. See his book *The Antecedents of Self-esteem* (San Francisco: W.H. Freeman, 1967).

About the Author

Dr. Earl R. Henslin is a licensed marriage, family, and child therapist. His Brea, California practice through Henslin and Associates focuses on marriage, family, and child counseling, and he conducts training sessions and seminars for professionals such as pastors, physicians, and therapists who work in these areas. He holds the doctor of clinical psychology degree from Rosemead Graduate School of Biola University, where he is a part-time instructor. He is a member of the California Association of Marriage and Family Therapists and the Christian Association of Psychological Studies. Dr. Henslin is one the founders of Overcomers Outreach, a nonprofit ministry that assists local churches in establishing twelve-step support groups. Dr. Henslin networks closely with the Amen Clinic of Behavioral Medicine. He and his staff do assessments and evaluations for SPECT Brain Imaging Scans and follow-up care.

Henslin and Associates provides outpatient treatment and networks with different inpatient treatment facilities for the treatment of adults concerned with codependency, incest, alcoholism, drug addiction, eating disorders, sexual addiction, men's issues, and other issues of dysfunctional families. A nationally acclaimed speaker, Dr. Henslin conducts seminars on these issues for churches, Christian Organizations, counseling centers, and businesses.

For information concerning treatment programs or seminars, please contact:
Earl R. Henslin, Psy.D., M.F.C.C.
745 S. Brea Blvd., Suite 23
Brea, California 92821

Other Books by Dr. Earl R. Henslin:
Secrets of Your Family Tree (co-author)
Forgiven and Free: Learn How Bible Heros with Feet of Clay Are Models for Your Recovery
Man to Man: Helping Fathers Relate to Sons and Sons Relate to Fathers
The Cliff's Edge: Heaven Sent Help on a Harley—Hell Came in Other Ways

3 8538 00001 8692

W9-ADT-105

WRITINGS FROM
The New Yorker
1927–1976

Books by E. B. White

Poems and Sketches of E. B. White
Essays of E. B. White
Letters of E. B. White
The Trumpet of the Swan
The Points of My Compass
The Second Tree From the Corner
Charlotte's Web
Here Is New York
The Wild Flag
Stuart Little
One Man's Meat
The Fox of Peapack
Quo Vadimus?
Farewell to Model T
Every Day Is Saturday
The Lady Is Cold

E. B. WHITE

WRITINGS FROM
The New Yorker
1927–1976

Edited by Rebecca M. Dale

HarperPerennial

A Division of HarperCollins*Publishers*

All the stories, reports, observations, commentaries, essays, and reviews collected here were originally published in *The New Yorker* and are copyrighted. They are reprinted here by special permission of *The New Yorker*, which reserves all rights.

A hardcover edition of this book was published in 1990 by HarperCollins Publishers.

WRITINGS FROM *THE NEW YORKER*. Copyright © 1990 by Joel White and Rebecca Dale. Introduction and Bibliography copyright © 1990 by Rebecca Dale. All rights reserved. Printed in the United States of America. No part of this book may be used or reproduced in any manner whatsoever without written permission except in the case of brief quotations embodied in critical articles and reviews. For information address HarperCollins Publishers, 10 East 53rd Street, New York, NY 10022.

First HarperPerennial edition published 1991.

Designed by Karen Savary

Library of Congress Cataloging-in-Publication Data

White, E. B. (Elwyn Brooks), 1899–1985
  Writings from the New Yorker / E.B. White.—1st ed.
    p. cm.
  ISBN 0-06-016517-0
  I. New Yorker. II. Title.
PS3545.H5187A6 1990
814'.52—dc20   89-46564

ISBN 0-06-092123-4 (pbk.)
91 92 93 94 95 RRD 10 9 8 7 6 5 4 3 2 1

CONTENTS

INTRODUCTION

While working on an independent study project at Virginia Commonwealth University in 1988, reading all of E. B. White's *New Yorker* work, I kept discovering many delightful pieces of prose that had never been collected in any of his books. This collection presents some of that work.

E. B. White is perhaps best known for his children's books *(Stuart Little, Charlotte's Web, The Trumpet of the Swan),* but he was primarily a writer for *The New Yorker,* where he wrote anonymously "Notes and Comment," "Talk of the Town," and newsbreaks, those fillers at the end of articles with wry comments on clippings from newspapers and magazines. He began sending contributions to *The New Yorker* in 1925 and writing "Notes and Comment" for it in 1926. When White moved to Maine in 1938, he started writing a monthly column, "One Man's Meat," for *Harper's Magazine* and he wrote only occasionally for *The New Yorker.* After resigning from *Harper's* in 1943, he resumed writing frequently for *The New Yorker.* The Whites divided their time between New York and Maine from 1943 until 1957, when they moved permanently to their home in Maine. He died in 1985 at the age of 86.

In his *New Yorker* work, White commented on the news and people of the time, connecting them to broader concerns. He embraced the themes he noted as Thoreau's, "man's relation to Nature and man's dilemma in society and man's capacity for elevating his spirit," and, like Thoreau, "beat all these matters together," producing "an original omelette from which people can draw nourishment in a hungry day" ("A Slight Sound at Evening," *Essays of E. B. White*). Like Thoreau, White delighted in exploring the fullness of life as an individual. Like Thoreau, he was divided between "the desire to enjoy the world (and not be derailed by a mosquito wing) and the urge to set the world straight." Moreover, White, unlike Thoreau, felt an empathic bond with humanity, a certain bond with others that Thoreau did not feel. While he was often playful in his writing, sometimes delighting in the spirit of fun for its own sake, he also dealt with important subjects, and his writing is often quite lyrical—poetry in prose form. His humor, which permeated nearly all of his writing, is the type that "plays close to the big hot fire which is Truth" ("Some Remarks on Humor," *Essays*). As we read White's work in its variety of moods, we experience his vitality, his subtle irony, his gentle but pointed satire, his unpretentious manner and admiration of simplicity, his spirit of fun, and his compassion and concern.

The pieces presented here were selected and arranged by the White family from selections and arrangements I proposed for this collection. The pieces are in roughly chronological order within each part to show a historical perspective on the United States from the Depression years through World War II and the postwar years, the evolution of *The New Yorker*'s editorial concerns, the development of E. B. White as a writer from his young voice and early promise to his more assured work and weightier subjects, and, over the years, his increasing refinement of writing style and humor.

The early pieces (twenties and thirties) examine life's little adversities and are short, frothy, witty, even sometimes flippant. The later pieces (from the forties on) are less whimsical and focus on more serious matters such as liberty, international affairs, and the environment, but even these have his graceful touch of humor. White's pieces became longer and more intricate structurally in the fifties; most of his long essays have been collected in *Essays of E. B. White*, which makes a good companion to this collection.

Most of the pieces are excerpts from "Notes and Comment," each piece bearing the date of its publication in *The New Yorker* and transcribed as it was printed in the magazine. Because "Notes and Comment" was an editorial column, White had to follow magazine policy of using "we" instead of "I." He disliked the awkwardness of the practice, saying it gave "the impression that the stuff was written by a set of identical twins or the members of a tumbling act" (Foreword, *The Second Tree from the Corner*). Despite White's preference for "I" over "we," I have not altered any of his words from the text as it appeared in *The New Yorker*. The footnotes are editorial additions; I have tried to keep them to a minimum.

Many of White's *New Yorker* and *Harper's* pieces are collected in his previously published books. His collected work, even counting this collection, contains only a small portion of the hundreds of paragraphs and essays he wrote over the years. Katherine Hall's *E. B. White: A Bibliographical Catalogue* lists 450 signed pieces and 1350 identifiable unsigned columns in *The New Yorker* from 1925 to 1976, the last year he contributed a piece (the one titled "A Busy Place" in this collection). Her bibliography is based on manuscripts White donated to Cornell University's Olin Library and on a scrapbook of his articles in various magazines put together and donated to the library by Scott Elledge, professor of English at Cornell and White's biographer. Elledge, in turn, relied on the White scrapbooks in the files at *The New Yorker*, which are the basic source for identifying which parts of the unsigned columns are White's work.

Ebba Johnson, head librarian at *The New Yorker* from 1934 to 1970, now deceased, and Helen Stark, the current librarian, deserve appreciation as the curators of those White scrapbooks. I also thank Katherine Hall, who, in her bibliography, has made information on White's work readily available. I thank Bryant Mangum, Bill Griffin, and Terry Oggel of Virginia Commonwealth University for their advice to me on this project, and I thank my family for their support. In putting together this collection, I tried to imagine how E. B. White would have wanted it done. I relied on his family and Cass Canfield, Jr., of HarperCollins (the son of his editor at Harper & Row) for advice, and I appreciate their suggestions and enthusiasm for the project. Although White is not here to speak for himself, he deserves to have the last word. In a note in Hall's bibliography concerning "Notes and Comment," he wrote how he came up with ideas for the column: "People on the staff and other people who were readers of the magazine used to submit comment ideas, and I always had a folder of these ideas and suggestions on my desk, together with clippings and stuff that I would toss into the folder from my own reading." He wished to acknowledge these "thousand mysterious and unremembered sources."

Rebecca M. Dale
1990

1

Nature

LIFE

9/1/45

AT EIGHT OF A HOT MORNING, the cicada speaks his first piece. He says of the world: heat. At eleven of the same day, still singing, he has not changed his note but has enlarged his theme. He says of the morning: love. In the sultry middle of the afternoon, when the sadness of love and of heat has shaken him, his symphonic soul goes into the great movement and he says: death. But the thing isn't over. After supper he weaves heat, love, death into a final stanza, subtler and less brassy than the others. He has one last heroic monosyllable at his command. Life, he says, reminiscing. Life.

PROHIBITED

1/25/36

THE PLANT-PATENT BUSINESS is taking right hold, apparently. We know a man who received a birthday present of a nice little azalea. Tied around the azalea's stem, like a chastity belt, was a metal tag from Bobbink & Atkins, reading, "Asexual reproduction of this plant is illegal under the Plant Patent Act." It was Number 147. Our friend, a man of loose personal habits, ripped the tag off angrily, fed it to his dachshund puppy, and sent the plant to a friend in Connecticut with instructions to bed it down warmly next to an old buck hydrangea.

SUMMERTIME

8/12/44

SUMMERTIME THIS YEAR is a ripe girl who finds herself forsaken by the boys, the ordinarily attentive and desirous boys. They are nowhere to be found; they have disappeared, the way males do, seized by some sudden mechanical flirtation, some new interest of a passing sort. Summertime is a girl who knows they will be back and who is conscious that she herself is irresistible over the long term, that her beauty and her accommodating ways have lost no fraction of their power. We had summertime practically to ourself the other afternoon, and in our guilt we lay with her in the name of all who were temporarily denied that privilege, admiring her incredible poise. The scent of her clothes was unmistakable; her sea, her sand, her sky wore the same look as ever; the insects which are her private minstrels sang the same seductive measure. We have never seen a discarded female more sure of where she stood than summertime.

SEEDS

1/12/52

OUR FIRST COMMUNICATION of the year 1952 was a card from a seed company, and this seemed a good omen. A new bush bean, rich in flavor. A new pickle, early, dark green, delicious. A new muskmelon, thick orange flesh of top quality. A new petunia, giant fringed, dwarfish. So starts the year on a note of planning and dreaming. The card went on to chide us—said no order had been received from us since 1949. That is a fantastic accusation; we virtually supported that seed house last year and the year before and the year before, back into the dim, infertile past. However, we don't expect seed companies

4

to keep accurate records; the whole business is so wild, so riotous, so complex, it's no wonder they forget who their own best friends are. If there is any doubt on that score, though, we will gladly send the management a jar of our wife's green-tomato pickle from last summer's crop—dark green, spicy, delicious, costlier than pearls when you figure the overhead.

DRESSING UP

4/20/46

ONE OF THE MALE SPARROWS in Turtle Bay garden made a wonderful discovery at quarter past nine the other morning. He found a small length of blue confetti tied in a bow. The morning was springlike, although a trifle cool, and the combination of blue confetti and blue sky stirred him up. He carried his find to the branch of a large sycamore, where he sat waiting to be photographed. (It really looked as though he had on an outsize Windsor tie.) After a minute or two, he moved on to a willow, then to Dorothy Thompson's gate, then to an ailanthus. Pretty soon the word got around and other sparrows of both sexes showed up, the ladies to admire, the men to jeer. It was fairly obvious that the owner of the blue bow tie was uncertain about his next move. He was undecided whether to start nest building, using a blue confetti bow tie as a sill piece (and face all the involvements and commitments that follow nest building), or whether just to wear the damned thing. He unquestionably was enjoying the fuss, and when the attention of the other birds flagged, he purposely dropped the bow, allowed it to spiral down almost to the fountain, then swooped and recovered it in midair. This drew a round of applause. We watched the act for twenty minutes, at the end of which time the sparrow dropped the bow again and flew away to a neighborhood saloon. It is a wearisome thing to be overdressed in the early morning.

TOMORROW SNOW

ALONE OVER A WEAKFISH in the deep noonday shadows of the Roosevelt Grill, we spelled out the strong editorials in the *News*, occasionally lighting a match to read some of the more challenging passages. Our waiter drifted over after a while and stood quietly at our side. "It's so beautiful," he murmured. "What is, Father?" we asked. "This day, this perfect soft spring day." He pointed east, where the faint luminosity of Vanderbilt Avenue showed through the blinds and gave the restaurant a ribbon of golden light. His voice had tears in it. "I've been listening to the radio," he said. "Tomorrow snow, turning to rain." He was a man carrying foreknowledge in his breast, and the pain was almost unbearable. We don't remember a winter when people followed the elements so closely and when foreknowledge so completely destroyed any chance of momentary bliss.

DISMAL?

THE MOST STARTLING NEWS in the paper on February 13th was the weather forecast. It was "Rainy and dismal." When we read the word "dismal" in the *Times,* we knew that the era of pure science was drawing to a close and the day of philosophical science was at hand. (Probably in the nick of time.) Consider what had happened! A meteorologist, whose job was simply to examine the instruments in his observatory, had done a quick switch and had examined the entrails of birds. In his fumbling way he had attempted to predict the impact of the elements on the human spirit. His was a poor attempt, as it turned out, but it was an attempt. There are, of course, no evil days in nature, no *dies mali,* and the forecast plainly showed that the weatherman had been spending his time indoors. To the intimates of rain, no day is dismal, and a dull sky is as plausible as any other. Nevertheless, the forecast indicated that the connection had been reëstablished between nature and scientific man. Now all we need is a meteorologist who has once been soaked to the skin without ill effect. No one can write knowingly of weather who walks bent over on wet days.

THE ARRIVAL OF SPRING

3/28/53

SPRING ALWAYS USED TO ARRIVE in midtown in the window boxes of the Helen Gould Shepard house. Something about the brightness and suddenness of that hyacinthine moment said Spring, something about its central location, too. The other day, we passed the ruins of the Gould house and shed a private tear for olden springtimes. Spring struggles into Manhattan by other routes these days; Rockefeller Center has pretty much taken the occasion over. Rockefeller's is different from Helen Gould's. Less homey. More like Christmas at Lord & Taylor's—beautiful but contrived. One never really knows where one will encounter the first shiver and shine of spring in the city. Often it is not in a flowering plant at all, merely in a certain quality of the light as it strikes the walls. We met ours quite a while back, late one afternoon in February, driving south through the Park; in an instant the light had lengthened and strengthened and bounced from the towers into our system, hitting us as a dram of tonic reaching the stomach, and, lo, it was spring.

WINTER BACK YARD

3/24/51

A CITY BACK YARD on many a winter's day is as shabby and unpromising a spot as the eye can rest on: the sour soil, the flaking surfaces of wall and fence, the bare branch, the doom-sprinkled sky. The tone of our back yard this past month, however, has been greatly heightened by the presence of a number of juncos, the dressiest of winter birds. Even the drabbest yard-scape achieves something like elegance when a junco alights in the foreground—a beautifully turned-out little character who looks as though he were on his way to an afternoon wedding.

PLANT THE GARDEN ANYWAY

4/24/54

WE FIND A USEFUL PARABLE in one of the farm journals, whither we turned, hoping to escape for a few moments the ominous headlines of suspicion in the papers. It was a vain hope. The first headline we encountered was "Danger in the Flower Garden." There is enough poison in a single castor bean to kill a person. The seeds of pinks cause vomiting. Sweet-pea seeds contain a poison that can keep a person bedridden for months. The night-blooming jimson has enough power in its leaves to produce delirium. Daffodil bulbs when eaten cause stomach cramps. And in the lily of the valley is a subtle substance that makes the heart slow down. But the conclusion drawn by the writer of the article, chewing absently on a daffodil bulb, was a good one. *We must plant this garden anyway*. Even in the face of such terrors, we must plant this garden. Quite a few prophets and thinkers, these days, are recommending just the opposite. They advise doing away with a garden that produces such dangers. Let's change the seed, they say.

DANBURY FAIR

SOMETHING MUST HAVE GOTTEN INTO US, because we arrived at the Danbury Fair shortly after sun-up on the first day. Nothing much had started. Freaks and crystal-gazers were still asleep in the back seats of old sedans. They slept with their clothes on. Grass in the tents was still green, untrampled.

In the Guernsey barn a calf had been born during the night. A farmhand was teaching it to suck, squirting milk into its stubborn face as it sprawled in the sweet hay. Near the door a bull was having his hair clipped, murder in his eye, murder in the awful muscles of his neck. The electric clippers made a pleasant noise that seemed to go with the good smell of cattle. When the barber was through, a farmboy asked for a hair trim. He would be going into Danbury that night, wanted to look spruce when he winked at the girls. The man cut his hair with the bull clippers. Outside, on the south end of the race course, the overhanging elms still threw long morning shadows on the track as the trotting horses were sent around for a brisk, the drivers hunched over their rumps.

The first day is really the best; you take your ease and see what goes on. The smells, when we arrived, were just starting to taint the air; the food booths were just starting to smear the first layer of terrible grease on their grills; the faces of the prize dolls were just starting to compete with "your chirce of any pretty lamp." A man in a wing collar was raking, with a tiny rake, the eleventh fairway of a tiny golf course. "Make 8o and win a free airplane ride." Madam Drielle, blonde as a birch leaf, stood in the doorway of her tent, yawning—wise with Love, Business, Marriage, Speculation, and Travel, but still a little sleepy. She hated already the faces of the people who hadn't come yet. Everywhere, sprawled on the ground, were the strange and implausible equipment of the concessionaires— things that fitted vaguely and temporarily into other things. In the big produce tent, marvellously juxtaposed, pumpkins of golden yellow, Crane bathtubs of jade green. We lolled comfortably on the running-board of a truck, watching a Holstein bull get his baptism of bluing. It is not every day one sees a bull bathed. A small lad in spectacles holds the ring of his dripping nose, while a red-cheeked washer dips his tail in bluing-water to make it white. Down the midway Betty, the inexplicable freak of nature, 5 tongues, 3 jaws, Truthful, Tangible, Thriving, Come In. In the poultry house, the sawdust soft underfoot, the birds full of dawn song, cocks in fighting trim, and the inquiring geese penetratingly audible.

It was a long, untroubled day. There is nothing like it. Sitting in the grandstand, watching, between trotting races, a trained bear riding a bicycle. All beginnings are wonderful. We rode home in the cool of the evening, wondering what a bear thinks about when he first sees a bicycle.

SAVE THE GRIZZLIES

1/23/32

A COMMITTEE HAS APPROACHED US to ask if we would help in the work of protecting and preserving the brown and grizzly bears of Alaska. Need we say we will? Once we spent six weeks in Alaska, and although we never happened to have an opportunity to protect a grizzly from the predatory old paper-pulp interests, which threaten their extinction, we always stood ready to. We are still ready. The islands of the Inside Passage, where the bears live, seemed to us lovely, perfect. We should not want one of them changed by the extinction of so much as one bear, or the establishment of even one pulp mill. Grizzlies are certainly less dangerous than the tabloids that are printed from paper pulp.

Of course it is our ill fortune always to see both sides of every question. The letter from the Committee on Protection and Preservation of Alaska Brown and Grizzly Bears was written, we notice, on paper. In other words, the Committee are using paper in their campaign against paper pulp. We think they really ought to send out their communications on parchment, preferably made from the hides of sheep especially killed for the purpose by grizzly bears. You see? We're no good in any cause. Too open-minded.

DANISH MOOSE

A DANE TOLD US the other day (and he seemed neither melancholy nor wholly cheerful) that Denmark has two moose. Denmark used to have only one moose (a bull), but a second arrived—swam over from Sweden, or took the ferry. The Danes were worried lest the new arrival prove to be a female. "Denmark is such a small country; we cannot have it too full of mooses." The second moose, however, was another bull. People felt relieved, but they know that it is only a question of time before some Swedish cow moose learns that there are extra men south of the border.

ALARM-GEESE

THE MOST STIMULATING PIECE of news we've heard since Malenkov* came to power is that the British are using geese in Malaya to fight Communist guerrillas. The geese are employed as watchdogs, to sound a warning at the approach of the foe. It happens that we have had quite a good deal to do with geese in our time, and we feel it advisable to pass along a word of caution to the British. Geese, we have found, are alert and articulate and they practically never sleep, but they are also undiscriminating, gossipy, and as easily diverted as children. For every alarum they sound to announce a guerrilla, they will most certainly utter a hundred to announce a British subaltern who is passing by. Everything and everybody interests a goose,

---

*Georgi M. Malenkov, Premier of the Soviet Union 1953–55. The British troops White refers to were stationed in Malaya during the late forties and in the fifties to fight Chinese Communist guerrillas.

and they play no favorites. Geese have their moods, too, and when geese are in one of their moods, an entire band of guerrillas could walk boldly into camp without stirring up so much as a small greeting. Furthermore, geese sometimes get together and retell old tales, and while at it they make as much noise as though they were announcing the invasion of the planet by little green men. We have an idea that the British will get some real help from geese, but if they feel obliged to act on every report a goose turns in while on duty, they're going to suffer a nervous breakdown into the bargain.

TURTLE BLOOD BANK

1/31/53

WE STROLLED UP TO Hunter College the other evening for a meeting of the New York Zoological Society. Saw movies of grizzly cubs, learned the four methods of locomotion of snakes, and were told that the Society has established a turtle blood bank. Medical men, it seems, are interested in turtle blood, because turtles don't suffer from arteriosclerosis in old age. The doctors are wondering whether there is some special property of turtle blood that prevents the arteries from hardening. It could be, of course. But there is also the possibility that a turtle's blood vessels stay in nice shape because of the way turtles conduct their lives. Turtles rarely pass up a chance to relax in the sun on a partly submerged log. No two turtles ever lunched together with the idea of promoting anything. No turtle ever went around complaining that there is no profit in book publishing except from the subsidiary rights. Turtles do not work day and night to perfect explosive devices that wipe out Pacific islands and eventually render turtles sterile. Turtles never use the word "implementation" or the phrases "hard core" and "in the last analysis." No turtle ever rang another turtle back on the phone. In the last analysis, a turtle, although lacking know-how, knows how to live. A turtle, by its admirable habits, gets to the hard core of life. That may be why its arteries are so soft.

Afterthought: It is worth noting that Chinese do not appear to suffer from arteriosclerosis nearly as much as do Occidentals, and Chinese are heavy eaters of terrapin. Maybe the answer is a double-barrelled one: we should all spend more time on a log in the sun and should eat more turtle soup. With a dash of sherry, of course.

2

The Word

VERMIN

10/7/44

The mouse of Thought infests my head.
He knows my cupboard and the crumb.
    Vermin! I despise vermin.
I have no trap, no skill with traps,
No bait, no hope, no cheese, no bread—
I fumble with the task to no avail.
I've seen him several times lately.
He is too quick for me,
I see only his tail.

THE COST OF HYPHENS

12/15/28

THE PAIN WHICH ATTENDS all literary composition is increased, in some cases, by the writer's knowing how much per word he will receive for his effort. We came upon a writer at his work recently, and were allowed to sit quietly by while he finished his stint. Quite casually he mentioned that he was getting fifty cents a word. A moment or two later his face became contorted with signs of an internal distress. With his hand poised above the machine, he seemed to be fighting something out with himself. Finally he turned to us. "Listen," he said, grimly, "do you hyphenate 'willy-nilly'?" We nodded, and saw him wince as he inserted the little mark, at a cost of half a dollar.

TRAVEL BROCHURE

THE ADVENTURE-MAD TRAVEL-BUREAU PEOPLE run a high fever all the year round, deliriously mumbling of far places regardless of season. More than any other group, they arrange life for us in neat grooves. We have just this moment been skirting through a prospectus of winter and spring trips presented to us by a dutiful and precise agent. The trips are divided into "short" and "long." "There's Mexico," says the booklet. "Ten days, $180." And "there's the Mediterranean, 29 days, $485." Our fancy flits along, jog-step, taking in the sights. And then, as a sudden afterthought, the joyous booklet writer really hits his stride. "There's the WORLD," he cries. "97 days, $833.50."

We had never had the planet laid so neatly at our feet, as though dropped there by a spaniel.

NO VERBS

ON A FETID AFTERNOON LIKE THIS, when all the nobility goes out of a writer and parts of speech lie scattered around the room among cigarette butts and crushed paper cups, we envy the gossip columnists their lot. We particularly envy them their ability to earn a living by talking in participles. You have, of course, observed this phenomenon of the American press—the sentence with no verb. From a literary standpoint it is the prose invention of the century, for it enables the writer to sound as though he were saying something without actually saying it. Thus: "Mrs. Oral Ferrous on the Starlight Roof, chatting with Count de Guiche." Or, "Captain Montmorency Squall, sitting with Mrs. Vincent Trip in a black lace gown and two ropes of pearls." The absence, in these participial items, of any predicate is extremely exciting to the reader, who figures anything might happen. Outside of the columnists, the only person we know who talks entirely in participles is a French–Italian lady who has done our laundry beautifully for years without the use of a single verb. Her sentences don't even have subjects—just participles and adverbs.

It is perhaps only fair to columnists and to the subjects of their stillborn sentences to confess that, a year or more ago, when we discovered that unfinished sentences were having a bad effect on our nerves, we took to completing all sentences under our breath—using a standard predicate. We found that the predicate "ought to be in bed" served well enough, and that is the one we still use. Almost any old predicate will do, however. The important thing is to add it.

WRITER AT WORK

3/26/27

THE WEEK HAS PRODUCED two cases of mortal man's intense itch to see, with his own eyes, a poet or a writer at work. The first case is that of the novelist who will write a book in a glass cage on a Paris boulevard—a chapter every working hour. But the second instance is even more plaintive, richer in human frailty. It concerns our own Edna Millay, who contemplates a trip to Washington. "It would be good," says a Washington news story, "to have this tender poet here in cherry blossom time and to hear her version of this glorious spectacle." (Even the theme is laid out for her, like clean linen.)

MOTIVATION

5/3/30

WHEN HE HEARD ABOUT THE National Arts Club prize for a book which would "reveal the soul of America," one of our dearest friends sat right down and got to work. He had a good plot, and seemed, when we left him, to be much interested in getting it down on paper. When, a day or two later, we saw him again, we were surprised to learn that he had given up the project. It seems that when he read about the prize in the newspaper, he thought it said thirty thousand dollars; later he looked up the clipping and discovered it said three thousand dollars. True to the soul of America, he gave the thing up immediately.

WRITING AS A PROFESSION

5/11/29

"WRITING IS NOT AN OCCUPATION," writes Sherwood Anderson. "When it becomes an occupation a certain amateur spirit is gone out of it. Who wants to lose that?" Nobody does, replies this semi-pro, sitting here straining at his typewriter. Nobody does, yet few writers have the courage to buy a country newspaper, or even to quit a city writing job for anything at all. What Mr. Anderson says is pretty true. Some of the best writings of writers, it seems to us, were done before they actually thought of themselves as engaged in producing literature. Some of the best humor of humorists was produced before ever they heard the distant laughter of their multitudes. Probably what Mr. Anderson means, more specifically, is that life is apt to be translated most accurately by a person who sees it break through the mist at unexpected moments—a person who experiences sudden clear images. A writer, being conscientious, is always straining his eyes for this moment, peering ahead and around; consequently when the moment of revelation comes, his eyes are poppy and tired and his sensitized mind has become fogged by the too-frequent half-stimuli of imagined sight. No figure is more pitiful to contemplate than a novelist with a thousand-dollar advance from a publishing house and a date when the manuscript is due. He knows he must invite his soul, but he is compelled to add: "And don't be late, soul!"

HONOR ROLL

1/11/30

THE *Nation* HAS PUT *The New Yorker* on its Honor Roll for 1929, along with Rear Admiral Byrd, the New York *Telegram*, Professor Michelson, Eva Le Gallienne, and the United States Senate. Here are the very words of the announcement: "The *New Yorker*, for being consistently amusing, good-tempered, intelligent, resourceful, and good-to-look-at." We are naturally grateful; it is the first time anybody has put us on an honor list. But after thus elevating us, the *Nation*, in an explanatory paragraph, plunges us into despair. "We had great trouble," said they, "in deciding whether to give first place, on the score of humor, to the *New Yorker* or to the Department of State. We finally gave it to the *New Yorker* on the ground that our cheerful contemporary is always good-natured, which the State Department sometimes is not. But we confess that we find the State Department a great deal funnier than the *New Yorker*." To us this comparison seems unfair. No magazine, whether weekly or annual, could ever hope to be as funny as the State Department. We defy most magazines to be as funny, even, as the Passport Bureau. In a comedic moment of history such as today, with its funny taxes, its funny prohibition, its funny prosperity, and its funny talk of peace, a mere publication whose aim is to interpret the times is somewhat at a loss to compete, in entertaining qualities, with the institutions themselves. We often feel like giving up and going home.

UNWRITTEN

4/26/30

SOMETIMES WE REGRET OUR FAILURE to write about things that really interest us. The reason we fail is probably that to write about them would prove embarrassing. The things that interested us during the past week, for example, and that we were unable or unwilling to write about (things that stand out clear as pictures in our head) were: the look in the eye of a man whose overcoat, with velvet collar, was held together by a bit of string; the appearance of an office after the building had shut down for the night, and the obvious futility of the litter; the head and shoulders of a woman in a lighted window, combing her hair with infinite care, making it smooth and neat so that it would attract someone who would want to muss it up; Osgood Perkins in love with Lillian Gish; a man on a bicycle on Fifth Avenue; a short eulogy of John James Audubon, who spent his life loafing around, painting birds; an entry in Art Young's diary, about a sick farmer who didn't know what was the matter with himself but thought it was probably biliousness; and the sudden impulse that we had (and very nearly gratified) to upend a large desk for the satisfaction of seeing everything on it slide off slowly onto the floor.

ACCELERATING CULTURE

5/21/38

A CALL HAS GONE OUT TO WRITERS to meet on Sunday in the cause of a Federal Bureau of Fine Arts. "In issuing this call," said the letter we received, "we are moved by a belief that it is the desire of all writers . . . to have the advance of culture accelerated, the base of art broadened, and the economic place of artists reasonably secure."

Here, in a sentence, is the issue. One must decide how he feels about the acceleration of culture before he can know whether he wants a Bureau of Fine Arts. It is as common to believe that culture should be accelerated as to believe that whooping cough should be retarded, yet we have never heard any devotee of the bureaucratic ideal make out a solid case for this proposed quickening. A Bureau of Fine Arts would indeed accelerate culture, in that it would provide public money for creative enterprise, and by so doing would make it easier for artists and writers to go on being artists and writers, as well as for persons who are not artists and writers to continue the happy pretence. Such a Bureau would presumably have other effects symptomatic of acceleration. The radio, for example, has immensely accelerated culture in that it has brought to millions of people, in torrential measure, the distant and often adulterated sounds of art and life. But it is still an open question whether this mysterious electrical diffusion has been a blessing to man, who appears at the moment to be most unhappy about nearly everything.

Santayana, although he won't be at the meeting Sunday, is a writer whose views on the diffusion of culture we find instructive. "Great thoughts," he says, "require a great mind and pure beauties a profound sensibility. To attempt to give such things a wide currency is to be willing to denaturalize them in order to boast that they have been propagated. Culture is on the horns of this dilemma: if profound and noble it must remain rare, if common it must become mean. These alternatives can never be eluded until some purified and high-bred race succeeds the promiscuous bipeds that now blacken the planet."

Advocates of a bureaucratic culture, in wishing to establish artists more firmly in the national economy, argue that it is to a nation's advantage to make its creative souls more comfortable financially; but here we feel they are confusing an aesthetic ideal with a social one. When two persons are in need of food, there is always the embarrassing question whether to feed the talented one first, on the somewhat questionable grounds that he may live to provide beauty for the other one (who in the meanwhile may die of starvation, or laughter). This is essentially what the Bureau proposes, and it is a proposal which naturally meets with very little opposition among writers and artists, who feel both hunger and beauty, and who can always use a little dough.

Sponsorship of the creative ideal by the government has many delightful delinquencies. It assumes, among other things, that art is recognizable in embryo—or at least recognizable enough to make it worth the public's while to pay for raising the baby. And it assumes that artists, like chickens, are responsive to proper diet. We sometimes wonder if they are. Housman, when they asked him what caused him to produce poems, said that as far as he could determine it was usually some rather inappropriate physical disability, such as a relaxed sore throat. This catarrhal theory of the creative life has always fascinated us, and it should give the government pause before setting aside too great a share of the public funds for improving the vigor of poets.

OUR CONTENTIOUS READERS

4/6/40

TO THE EDITOR OF *The New Yorker,*
Dear Sir:
Students of City College are almost certain to be misled by Bishop Manning's attack on Bertrand Russell.* They will conclude that the issue is a moral one, and that Earl Russell's sex ideas must be accepted or rejected on the score of morality. This is most unfortunate. The trouble with Russell on sex is not that he is immoral but that he is unrealistic. He is just a dreamer, putting into logical expression the immoderate hopes of men for a more elastic, carefree, and generally agreeable solution of their urgencies and their problems. College students are quick to explore any ethical concept which has the double bloom of intellectuality and sin; I think the Bishop was most unwise to invest the Russell ethics with the glamour of wickedness and to advertise the Russell code as "immoral," thereby giving it a distinction it hardly deserves. Students will certainly infer that if Russell's sex ideas are as bad as all that, there must be something to them; whereas the depressing thing about Earl Russell's code is that it doesn't work. However distinguished he may be in the world of logical thought, on the subject of sex he has always been something of an old fraud.
Let us consider two or three of the sex concepts which the Bishop dug up in his investigation. First, he quotes from Russell's "Education and the Modern World":

> I am sure that university life would be better, both intellectually and morally, if most university students had temporary childless marriages. This would afford a solution of the sexual urge neither restless nor surreptitious, neither mercenary nor casual, and of such a nature that it need not take up time which ought to be given to work.

*British philosopher and mathematician (3rd Earl Russell). His appointment as professor of philosophy at City College of New York was rescinded when Jean Kay, a taxpayer protesting his appointment, brought suit in New York's State Supreme Court against the Board of Higher Education and Justice John E. McGeehan ruled in her favor. Spearheading the opposition to Russell, William T. Manning, the Episcopal Bishop of New York, had sent a circular letter to the New York newspapers denouncing Russell's appointment. The case created public debate not only over Russell, but also over issues of academic freedom.

Now, the suggestion that to live with a girl isn't going to take up much of a student's time seems to me as fantastic a bit of philosophical hokum as I have ever encountered. Russell is a Britisher, and of course I don't know how things are in England, but I think I am safe in saying that in America nothing takes up more of a man's time than living with a girl. It is the most time-consuming thing there is. Also, I resent the implication in this passage of Russell's that sex is just something to get out of your system, that work is the important thing, and that sex is good just in proportion to the amount of a man's time it *doesn't* occupy. That's a mighty unattractive report to spread among the young, who are (rightly, I think) romantically minded, and who tend to incorporate sex into the body of the romance.

Then we come to the Earl's remark that "if a man and woman choose to live together, that should be nobody's business but their own." If the Bishop were smart, he would simply point out to students that the word to watch out for in that sentence is the word "should." Of course it *should* be nobody's business but their own. But it usually turns out to be the business of the darnedest, most unexpected people, including a young man in the same building who has been secretly in love with the girl for three years, has sublimated his passion by tearing telephone books in two, and now seizes the opportunity to hang himself with a rope made out of dozens of college pennants. Students should certainly be informed that no man, since the beginning of time, has lived with a woman without it turning out sooner or later to be somebody else's business.

Finally, there is the Earl's little essay on the psychology of adultery. "Suppose," writes Earl Russell eagerly, "a man has to be away from home on business for a number of months. If he is physically vigorous, he will find it difficult to remain continent throughout this time, however fond he may be of his wife." I think Bishop Manning should just tell the students that the matter of continence during a business trip has very little to do with physical vigor. An exceptionally vigorous man almost invariably spends himself in rather forthright, athletic ways—leaping up stairs three steps at a time, pounding on other men's desks, and putting in long-distance calls from clients' offices. It is the tired little fellow on his way home from a basal-metabolism test who is most likely to become hopelessly involved in some adulterous and unhappy circumstance quite beyond his puny control. In my professional life (I am a doctor), I have enjoyed the confidence of hundreds of adulterous persons; rarely have they shown evidences of any special vigor. As a group, they are on the anemic side.

These are only a few of the points which the Bishop has been worried about. I merely wished to suggest to him that if he wants to spike Russell's guns, he is going about it the hard way.

Yours faithfully,
WALTER TITHRIDGE, M.D.*

EDITORIAL WRITERS

3/4/44

GEORGE SELDES, in the *Saturday Review,* says he has never known of an editorial writer who wrote as he pleased. This makes us a kept man. We often wonder about our life in our bordello, whether such an existence erodes one's character or builds it. An editorial page is a fuzzy performance, any way you look at it, since it affects a composite personality with an editorial "we" for a front. Once in a while we think of ourself as "we," but not often. The word "ourself" is the giveaway—the plural "our," the singular "self," united in a common cause. "Ourself" is real. It means "over-self," which reminds us that we should try to dig up a writer named Emerson for this page.

At any rate, we have evolved (and this may interest Mr. Seldes) a system for the smooth operation of a literary bordello. The system is this: We write as we please, and the magazine publishes as *it* pleases. When the two pleasures coincide, something gets into print. When they don't, the reader draws a blank. It is a system we recommend—the only one, in fact,

---

*A pseudonym used by White.

under which we are willing to be kept. Mr. Seldes can undoubtedly prove that it comes to the same, in the end, as if we deliberately shaped our ideas to a prescribed pattern, but in order to do that he will have to write another article, so at least we've made work for somebody and are not entirely frivolous and useless. Of course, a good deal depends on the aims of a publication. The more devious the motives of his employer, the more difficult for a writer to write as he pleases. As far as we have been able to discover, the keepers of this house have two aims: the first is to make money, the second is to make sense. We have watched for other motives, but we have never turned up any. That makes for good working conditions, and we write this as a sort of small, delayed tribute to our house. Anytime Mr. Seldes wants to see writers writing as they please, he can just step off the elevator and take a gander at us. By us, of course, we mean ourself. Emerson's the name. Call us Ralph.

RAINBOW WORKERS

11/1/47

THIS MAGAZINE TRAFFICS with all sorts of questionable characters, some of them, no doubt, infiltrating. Our procedure so far has been to examine the manuscript, not the writer; the picture, not the artist. We have not required a statement of political belief or a blood count. This still seems like a sensible approach to the publishing problem, although falling short of Representative J. Parnell Thomas's* standard. One thing we

---

*Chairman of the House Un-American Activities Committee. This committee, set up as a standing committee of the House of Representatives in 1945, investigated charges of Communist influences in government and other areas of American life (such as the motion picture industry). White, as a teenager, once took Thomas's sister Eileen to a tea dance; for an account of that date see "Afternoon of an American Boy" in *Essays of E. B. White*.

have always enjoyed about our organization is the splashy, rainbow effect of the workers: Red blending into Orange, Orange blending into Yellow, and so on, right across the spectrum to Violet. (Hi, Violet!) We sit among as quietly seething a mass of reactionaries, revolutionaries, worn-out robber barons, tawny pipits, liberals, Marxists in funny hats, and Taftists in pin stripes as ever gathered under one roof in a common enterprise. The group seems healthy enough, in a messy sort of way, and everybody finally meets everybody else at the water cooler, like beasts at the water hole in the jungle. There is one man here who believes that the solution to everything is proper mulching—the deep mulch. Russia to him is just another mulch problem. We have them all. Our creative activity, whether un- or non-un-American, is properly not on a loyalty basis but merely on a literacy basis—a dreamy concept. If this should change, and we should go over to loyalty, the meaning of "un-American activity" would change, too, since the America designated in the phrase would not be the same country we have long lived in and admired.

We ran smack into the loyalty question the other day when we got a phone call from another magazine, asking us what we knew about a man they had just hired. He was a man whose pieces we had published, from time to time, and they wanted to know about him. "What's his political slant?" our inquisitor asked. We replied that we didn't have any idea, and that the matter had never come up. This surprised our questioner greatly, but not as much as his phone call surprised us. When he hung up, we dialled Weather and listened to the rising wind.

EXPEDIENCY

WE HAVE OFTEN WONDERED how journalism schools go about preparing young men and women for newspaperdom and magazineland. An answer came just the other day, in a surprising form. It came from California, via *Editor & Publisher.* We quote:

> San Francisco—Public opinion polls are scientific tools which should be used by newspapers to prevent editorial errors of judgment, Dr. Chilton Bush, head of the Division of Journalism at Stanford University, believes.
>
> "A publisher is smart to take a poll before he gets his neck out too far," he said. "Polls provide a better idea of acceptance of newspaper policies."

We have read this statement half a dozen times, probably in the faint hope that *Editor & Publisher* might be misquoting Dr. Bush or that we had failed to understand him. But there it stands—a clear guide to the life of expediency, a simple formula for journalism by acceptance, a short essay on how to run a newspaper by saying only the words the public wants to hear said. It seems to us that Dr. Bush hands his students not a sword but a weather vane. Under such conditions, the fourth estate becomes a mere parody of the human intelligence, and had best be turned over to bright birds with split tongues or to monkeys who can make change.

ACCREDITED WRITERS?

12/11/48

BEFORE A BOOK CAN BE PUBLISHED in Czechoslovakia, the publisher must submit an outline of it to the government for approval. Accompanying the outline must be written opinions of "responsible literary critics, scientists, or writers." (We are quoting from a dispatch to the *Times.*) The question of who is a responsible critic or writer comes up in every country, of course. It must have come up here when the Algonquin Hotel advertised special weekend rates for "accredited writers." We often used to wonder just how the Algonquin arrived at the answer to the fascinating question of who is an accredited writer, and whether the desk clerk required of an applicant a rough draft of an impending novel. It seems to us that the Czech government is going to be in a spot, too. No true critic or writer is "responsible" in the political sense which this smelly edict implies, and in order to get the kind of censorship the government obviously wants, the government will need to go a step further and require that the critic himself be certified by a responsible party, and then a step beyond that and require that the responsible party be vouched for. This leads to infinity, and to no books. Which is probably the goal of the Czech government.

The matter of who is, and who isn't, a responsible writer or scientist reminds us of the famous phrase in Marxist doctrine— the phrase that is often quoted and that has won many people to Communism as a theory of life: "From each according to his ability; to each according to his needs." Even after you have contemplated the sheer beauty of this concept, you are left holding the sheer problem of accreditation: who is needy, who is able? Again the desk clerk looms—a shadowy man. And behind the clerk another clerk, for an accreditation checkup. And so it goes. Who shall be the man who has the authority to establish our innermost need, who shall be the one to approve the standard of achievement of which we are capable? Perhaps, as democracy assumes, every man is a writer, every man wholly needy, every man capable of unimaginable deeds. It isn't as beautiful to the ear as the Marxian phrase, maybe, but there's an idea there somewhere.

SATIRE ON DEMAND

1/8/49

ONE OF OUR CONTEMPORARIES, the Russian humor magazine called *Crocodile,* has been under fire lately. *Crocodile* got word from Higher Up that it would have to improve, would have to bear down harder on "the vestiges of capitalism in the consciousness of the people." This directive, according to the Associated Press, came straight from the Central Committee and was unusual only for its admission that there were any such vestiges. *Crocodile* was instructed to gird on its satiric pen and by "the weapons of satire to expose the thieves of public property, grafters, bureaucrats . . ." It has never been our good fortune to observe a controlled-press satirist who is under instructions from his government to get funnier, but it is a sight we'd gladly crawl under a curtain to see. A person really flowers as a satirist when he first slips *out* of control, and a working satirist (of whom there are woefully few in any country) careens as wildly as a car with no brakes. To turn out an acceptable pasquinade is probably unthinkable under controlled conditions, for the spirit of satire is the spirit of independence. Apparently the Russian committee anticipates difficulties in stepping up humor and satire by decree. *Crocodile* used to be a weekly. From now on it will appear only every ten days. Three extra days each issue, for straining.

THE THUD OF IDEAS

9/23/50

AMERICANS ARE WILLING to go to enormous trouble and expense defending their principles with arms, very little trouble and expense advocating them with words. Temperamentally we are ready to die for certain principles (or, in the case of overripe adults, send youngsters to die), but we show little inclination to advertise the reasons for the dying. Some critics say that a self-governing, democratic people don't know what they believe; but that is nonsense. It is simply that a democratic people, who are also an impatient and restless people, feel no strong urge to define what they instinctively comprehend. Also, they do not delegate to government the power to speak for the individual. The disinclination to propagandize is characteristic. Thirty-six billions for a military program, a thin buck for a voice clarifying our aims and beliefs. Many people now think, and we agree with them, that if we are to compete successfully with the throaty call of the Communist heartland—a call as brassy as that of a tenting evangelist—we shall have to develop a bit of a whistle of our own. We already have the Soviet voice at a disadvantage, and we should exploit it. The Russians limit themselves to spreading what they call the Truth and to jamming the sounds that come from the other direction. They cannot disseminate information, because information would too often embarrass their Truth. We can do much better. We can, and should, spread the material an American reads each morning in his paper—news, definitions, letters to the editor, texts, credos, reports, recipes, aims and intentions. We must reach and astonish with our kind of reporting the millions who hear almost nothing of that sort and who hardly know it exists. We can safely leave Truth to the Kremlin, and can broadcast instead the splendid fact of difference of opinion, the thud of ideas in collision.

The Russian charge about us, which deliberately misleads so many millions of people, should be met by a greatly expanded United States Department of Correction, Amplification, and Abuse. Misinformation, even when it is not deliberate, is at the bottom of much human misery. We recall the recent ordeal of

George Kuscinkas, the fifty-six-year-old delivery man who pushed his handcart thirteen miles, far into the Bronx, because his employer had written "23rd Street" so that it looked like "234th Street." This was mere carelessness. But think of the journeys that are being made in the world by those who are pushing a heavy handcart in an impossible direction under misapprehensions of one sort and another!

We saw a piece in the paper the other day by a historian who had decided that freedom was shot because frontiers were disappearing. Freedom, he reasoned, can't survive in the congested conditions of a non-pioneering civilization. If there were anything to this theory, it would be the worst news of the week. We think the historian underestimates the vitality of the free spirit in the individual and exaggerates the role of geography. An iron curtain almost but not quite impenetrable is as challenging a frontier as a forest of virgin timber. Besides, it is perfectly apparent that freedom resides comfortably in areas of great congestion. We walked through such a street this morning.

Somehow the letters-to-the-editor page, strange and wonderful as it always is, is one of the chief adornments of the society we love and seek to clarify for the world. The privilege of writing to the editor is basic; the product is the hot dish of scrambled eggs that is America. Take the *Times* the other morning: a resounding letter headed "Awareness of Issues Asked," a studious appeal to protect forest preserves ("Let this long and difficult fight be a lesson . . ."), an indignant attack by a Gaines Dog Research man on the superstition that dog days are associated with hydrophobia, a thoughtful essay on world government, and finally a blast from a reader in Monroe, New York: "It just so happens that I attempted to transplant three plants [of orange milkweed] recently and they all had long, horizontal roots."

Such a page, together with the *Times'* sense of duty in publishing it, suggests an abiding normalcy in democratic behavior and thought, and gives the reassurance that neither Korea nor the volume of the Russian voice can unsettle this land whose citizens' torments and hopes, big and little, are aired daily in the press, this land whose roots are both long and horizontal.

THE HUMOR PARADOX

9/27/52

ADLAI STEVENSON* has been reprimanded by General Eisenhower for indulging in humor and wit, and Mr. Stevenson
has very properly been warned of the consequences by his own
party leaders, who are worried. Their fears are well grounded.
We have had long experience with humor in the literary world,
and we add our warning to the other warnings. Nothing is so
suspect as humor, nothing so surely brands a work of art or
politics as second-rate. It has been our sad duty on several
occasions in the past to issue admonitory statements concerning the familiar American paradox that governs humor: every
American, to the last man, lays claim to a "sense" of humor and
guards it as his most significant spiritual trait, yet rejects humor
as a contaminating element wherever found. America is a nation of comics and comedians; nevertheless, humor has no stature and is accepted only after the death of the perpetrator.
Almost the only first-string American statesman who managed
to combine high office with humor was Lincoln, and he was
murdered finally. Churchill is, in our opinion, a man of humor,
but he lives in England, where it doesn't count.

The New Yorker subscribes to a press-clipping bureau, and
over the years we have examined thousands of clippings from
many sources, in praise of one thing or another that has appeared in the magazine. Almost invariably, the praise begins
with a qualifying remark, pointing out that the magazine is
non-serious in nature and indicating that it takes a superior
intelligence (the writer's) to detect truth or merit in such unlikely surroundings. If it's any comfort to Stevenson, we can
assure him that in this matter of humor we have been in the
same boat with him for a long time, and that the sea has been
rough.

---

*Stevenson was the Democratic nominee for President in 1952, Dwight Eisen-
hower the Republican nominee.

AFFAIR WITH HUMOR

10/5/46

SOMEBODY, perhaps suspecting that we were having an affair with Humor, sent us the following passage from Proudhon. We reprint it in free translation, with pride and embarrassment— the sort of mixed feeling you have when walking with a pretty girl and the girl is whistled at:

> Liberty, like Reason, does not exist or manifest itself except by the constant disdain of its own works; it perishes as soon as it is filled with self-approval. That is why humor has always been a characteristic of philosophical and liberal genius, the seal of the human spirit, the irresistible instrument of progress. Stagnant peoples are always solemn peoples: the man of a people that laughs is a thousand times closer to reason and liberty than the anchorite who prays or the philosopher who argues.
>
> Humor—true liberty!—it is you who deliver me from ambition for power, from servitude to party, from respect for routine, from the pedantry of science, from admiration for celebrities, from the mystifications of politics, from the fanaticism of the reformers, from fear of this great universe, and from self-admiration.
>
> Come, sovereign, turn a ray of your light on my fellow-citizens; kindle in their soul a spark of your spirit, so that my confession may reconcile them to each other and so that this inevitable revolution may come about with serenity and joy.

Proudhon's word is *"l'ironie,"* which we have translated "humor," possibly too loosely, but at any rate with serenity and joy. After so many summers and winters living with Humor as our mistress and credit manager, seeing her blow hot and cold, running her unreasonable errands, taking her lip, we find our affection undiminished. The attachment strengthens, even as it grows more troublesome. Come, sovereign, give us a kiss. And deliver us, right this minute, from self-admiration.

3

Thoreau

THE INDIVIDUALIST

5/7/49

MAY 6TH IS THE SADDEST DAY in the year for us, as it is the day of Thoreau's death*—a grief from which we have not recovered. Henry Thoreau has probably been more wildly misconstrued than any other person of comparable literary stature. He got a reputation for being a naturalist, and he was not much of a naturalist. He got a reputation for being a hermit, and he was no hermit. He was a writer, is what he was. Many regarded him as a poseur. He was a poseur, all right, but the pose was struck not for other people to study but for *him* to study—a brave and ingenious device for a creative person to adopt. He posed for himself and was both artist and model, examining his own position in relation to nature and society with the most patient and appreciative care. "Walden" is so indigestible that many hungry people abandon it because it makes them mildly sick, each sentence being an anchovy spread, and the whole thing too salty and nourishing for one sitting. Henry was torn all his days between two awful pulls— the gnawing desire to change life, and the equally troublesome desire to live it. This is the explanation of his excursion. He hated Negro slavery and helped slaves escape, but he hated even more the self-imposed bondage of men who hung chains about their necks simply because it was the traditional way to live. Because of a few crotchety remarks he made about the factory system and because of his essay on civil disobedience, he is one of the early Americans now being taken up by Marx-

*White admired Henry David Thoreau, author of *Walden*, perhaps more than he did any other writer. In the following pieces and in "A Slight Sound at Evening" *(Essays)*, "Walden" *(One Man's Meat)*, and "The Retort Transcendental" *(Second Tree)*, White records his appreciation for *Walden:* "the book is like an invitation to life's dance."

ists. But not even these hard-working Johnnies-come-lately can pin him down; he subscribed to no economic system and his convictions were strong but disorderly. What seemed so wrong to him was less man's economy than man's puny spirit and man's strained relationship with nature—which he regarded as a public scandal. Most of the time he didn't want to do anything about anything—he wanted to observe and to feel. "What demon possessed me that I behaved so well?" he wrote—a sentence that is 100-proof anchovy. And when he died he uttered the purest religious thought we ever heard. They asked him whether he had made his peace with God and he replied, "I was not aware we had quarrelled." He was the subtlest humorist of the nineteenth century, a most religious man, and was awake every moment. He never slept, except in bed at night.

WALDEN

12/28/46

THE MOST RECENT EDITION of "Walden" is a Dodd, Mead book containing a hundred and forty-two photographs by Edwin Way Teale. It is an amusing specimen for hard-shelled Thoreauvians. In it they can hear one naturalist speaking to another across a hundred years. Mr. Teale supplies, in addition to the pictures, an excellent introduction and some background notes for each chapter. Carrying a camera, and probably bent on elevating his life by a conscious endeavor, he went out to the pond to make a photographic record of where Thoreau lived and of what he lived for. Mr. Teale rose early to catch the mists above the water. He lay in wait for the ice to break up in spring. He went out and took pictures of Brister's Spring and of Fair Haven Hill. He walked the tracks of the Fitchburg. He closed in on ground nut and swamp grass, on johnswort and wild grape. He even fired point-blank at a bean row and scored a direct hit.

"Walden" is, of course, not a book that can be illustrated. The Concord woods are both tamer and wilder than they were in 1845, and besides, Thoreau was writing not about beans but about the meaning of beans—which is hard to photograph. A person who is about to encounter the text of "Walden" for the first time should buy a small, unadorned edition, such as the pocket Oxford, which will allow him to travel light and on a high plane. I rather imagine that Henry Thoreau would feel that Mr. Teale, roaming the Concord woods on his second-hand errand, was not fronting the essential facts, not living deliberately. Nevertheless, it is easy to understand why Mr. Teale was there, easy to share his vicarious excitement and to enjoy his tardy and beautiful photographs. (I was glad to learn from one of the notes that Thoreau was thirty-six years old before he discovered that he was tying his shoes with a granny knot. A man must take courage from something these days, while tying his shoes, and that is as buoyant a thought as any.)

A book of this sort is a personal tribute rather than an illustrative work. Thoreau is the naturalist's philosopher. The extraordinary thing about him was that he so strangely combined the curiosity, the patience, and the literalness of the scientist with the poetical and critical faculty of the artist. His contribution to limnology (the study of fresh-water ponds) is recognized by scientists. And even when he was voicing man's highest aspirations in sentences of great power and intensity, a muskrat would somehow work its way into the thing. As long as there are men and muskrats, there will be readers who will ache to identify themselves with the spirit and the sense of this revolutionary book, this solid and everlasting book; and they will be drawn to Deep Cove in all weather and in all seasons, armed with whatever they can substitute for a borrowed axe. Teale took a camera.

THOREAU AND SHELTER

8/7/48

THE THOREAU SOCIETY wants contributions so it can buy the house at 73 Main Street, Concord, where Henry David Thoreau sat taking pot shots at the whole theory of shelter. We haven't decided yet whether to listen to the Society or to Henry. If we heed the Society's call, it will cost us a hundred dollars to become a one-three-hundredths owner of 73 Main, but if we take Thoreau's advice, we'll simply enclose a dollar to the Society and suggest that it exercise a little Yankee shrewdness and buy one of those large toolboxes that you see by the railroad, six feet long and three feet wide, bore a few auger holes in it, and set it up in Concord, thus memorializing not only the man but the Idea. Unless the Thoreau Society is careful, it is going to find itself with a museum on its hands—a labyrinth without a clue. Nobody would chuckle more appreciatively over this, if he were in chuckling trim, than Henry. You can hear his frogs chuckling over it any night you want to walk out to the pond.

VISITORS TO THE POND

5/23/53

WHEN SENATOR MCCARTHY* turned his attention to H. D. Thoreau, the egghead of Concord, and decided to visit the Walden country to look into the very suspicious fact of Thoreau's pondside interlude, he asked me to go along as guide. I always jump at the chance of an outing and I agreed readily. Copies of "Walden, or Life in the Woods" had been found on the shelves of libraries of the United States Information Service overseas, and the Senator was in a high state of excitement about it. He was particularly anxious that I accompany him to the pond, as he wanted me to read aloud from the pocket edition, which has fine print. Long hours of studying defamatory evidence have affected McCarthy's vision, and there are days when he can hardly see anything smaller than a subpoena.

The minute we stepped from the train at the Concord station, the indescribable innocence and beneficence of Nature began having a bad effect on my companion. It was a lovely afternoon, and I suggested that we walk out to the pond along the tracks of the Fitchburg Railroad, but McCarthy refused irritably and demanded a cab.

"I'd like to walk," I protested.

"And I want to ride," snapped the Senator. It was a contretemps.

"A contretemps!" cried a bystander, and several other Concordians, idling on the platform, gathered around to see the fun.

Seizing the opportunity, I pulled "Walden" from my pocket and turned quickly to page 119, knowing that I could use the text to mollify the Senator. "Here," I said. "We'll let Thoreau himself settle the point whether we walk or ride. Here's the passage: 'I have found that no exertion of the legs can bring two minds much nearer to one another.' "

"There you are!" said the Senator. "We ride."

---

*Joseph McCarthy, chairman of the Senate's Government Operations Committee. McCarthy held publicized hearings accusing people of sympathizing with the Communist Party. He was censured in 1954 by Senate colleagues. White frequently spoke out against McCarthy and his tactics.

As I climbed into the cab behind my strong-willed companion, I could see that his spirits were mounting because of the little incident that I had so deftly turned in his favor. At the pond, we paid off the driver and I led the Senator rapidly along the path, showing him Deep Cove and the site of the cabin. McCarthy cased the woodland quickly. He explained that he liked to "get the feel" of a person's background before going after him. As we were standing there, imbibing the past through every pore, a skunk appeared on the path, eyed us curiously, turned, and walked away. The Senator chuckled.

"What's funny, Senator?" I inquired.

"Young man," he replied (he kept calling me "young man," although I am ten years his senior), "young man, one thing you'll find out—everywhere you go in this country you'll come across a skunk." The episode seemed to please him immensely and his mood was now mellow. He was soon grilling me closely about Thoreau's character, habits, and associates.

"How big was the house?" he asked.

"Ten by fifteen," I replied.

"How big was the mortgage?"

"There wasn't any," I said, weakly. The Senator's eyes narrowed. He drew a notebook and pencil from his pocket and scribbled, "Says there was no mortgage."

"I consider it un-American not to have a mortgage," murmured the Senator, as though speaking to himself. "Besides, it's probably a lie."

"Well, this case was a little different," I explained. "The whole house cost only a little over twenty-eight dollars. That was for materials. Thoreau did the work himself."

"I'd certainly like to see a breakdown of *those* figures," muttered the Senator. So I showed him page 42 and read him the modest accounting.

Suddenly McCarthy turned on me. "Answer a simple question!" he said. "Did this man believe in the American way of life?"

"I will answer that," I replied, "if you will tell me what you mean by the American way of life."

A foxy smile spread across the Senator's face as he detected the trap I had laid for him. "Young man," he said, "I praise Americanism, I don't define it. If you define it, you lose customers. But let's get down to business. Let's get to the book!"

I was more than willing. "Walden" is the only book I own,

although there are some others unclaimed on my shelves. Every man, I think, reads one book in his life, and this one is mine. It is not the best book I ever encountered, perhaps, but it is for me the handiest, and I keep it about me in much the same way one carries a handkerchief—for relief in moments of defluxion or despair. So I was glad to get to the book at this juncture. The Senator sat down on the ground and propped himself against a log, and I joined him after kicking an empty beer can out of the way.

"Read from the chapter on Economy and from the chapter on Solitude!" commanded the Senator. "Every screwball who tries to discuss economics gives himself away, and as for solitude, that's damaging in itself. It's un-American to live alone."

Slipping the book from my pocket, I opened it to the first page and started to read, at first hesitantly, then gaining confidence.

"'When I wrote the following pages, or rather the bulk of them, I lived alone, in the woods, a mile from any neighbor, in a house which I had built myself, on the shore of Walden Pond, in Concord, Massachusetts, and earned my living by the labor of my hands only. I lived there two years and two months. At present I am a sojourner in civilized life again.'"

The familiar words had a new, strange sound—a sort of looseness, as though they were sifting down through the branches of the pines and skittering up from the surface of the lake. The Senator attended closely. He was obviously a good listener.

"'I should not obtrude my affairs so much on the notice of my readers if very particular inquiries had not been made by my townsmen concerning my mode of life, which some would call impertinent . . .'"

McCarthy leapt to his feet. "Inquiries?" he snorted. "There you are. This guy was being investigated even then, and the inquiries were being called impertinent. Brother, where have I heard *that* before! Anyway, the townspeople must have been wise to him or they wouldn't have questioned his affairs."

The Senator took out his pad and noted, "Was under fire at the time." Then he ordered me to continue reading. I complied, skipping around in the text as it suited my fancy, which is one of the privileges of anyone who reads to the blind or the near-blind.

" 'The greater part of what my neighbors call good I believe in my soul to be bad . . .' "

"Read that again, slower!" commanded the Senator.

I repeated the sentence.

"Well," drawled McCarthy, "that's a subversive statement right there. He's going against the majority opinion of the community. Anybody who does that has no kick coming if he gets investigated." The Senator grew thoughtful. He repeated the sentence slowly, savoring the words. "You know," he said, "that sentence came very near being a very sensible remark. I could edit it a little and make it into something completely American, if I wanted to. All you do is just take out three words. Listen to this: 'The greater part of my neighbors I believe in my soul to be bad.' Now you've got something! Well, I'm not going to clean up Thoreau's text for him—he's cutting his own throat fast and I'm going to let him. But it just shows what can be done if you're on the ball. Read some more!"

" 'I think we may safely trust a good deal more than we do,' " I read.

"Poppycock!" cried McCarthy. "Balderdash!" He was visibly shaken by the sound of the word "trust," and his body was racked with shudders. He flapped his head back and forth, the way a dog fights an itch, as though trying to expunge the idea of confidence from his thoughts. I waited till he subsided, then skipped a few paragraphs and read some of Thoreau's remarks about shelter and vital heat.

" 'When a man is warmed by the several modes which I have described, what does he want next? Surely not more warmth of the same kind, as more and richer food, larger and more splendid houses, finer and more abundant clothing . . .' "

"Wait a minute!" said the Senator. "Now d'ya see what I mean? This man was Communist-inspired. That accounts for his sour attitude about housing—those cracks about not wanting larger and more splendid houses, more food, finer clothing. Every good American wants a bigger house, that's for sure."

"What about the small ranch-type dwelling so popular today?" I asked, timidly. "The ranch-type house is an American manifestation, a concession to the compact-living school of which Thoreau was a founder. Thoreau was simply ahead of his time."

McCarthy uttered something unintelligible. He seemed unimpressed. I was unimpressed myself, but I felt that I had met the challenge adroitly and in a manly fashion. I turned back to the book, but my companion interrupted.

"Was this fellow ever in jail?"

"Yes," I replied.

"I thought so," said the Senator. "Why was he in?"

"Nonpayment of taxes," I said. This cheered the Senator and we were able to return to the text.

" 'For many years I was self-appointed inspector of snow-storms and rain-storms, and did my duty faithfully; surveyor, if not of highways, then of forest paths and all across-lots routes, keeping them open, and ravines bridged and passable at all seasons, where the public heel had testified to their utility.' "

" 'The public heel?' " repeated the Senator. "The Acheson* of his day, I reckon." I responded to the weak joke and we laughed together. A loon on the far side of the pond heard us and laughed back, mocking us across the water. McCarthy's face clouded at the unearthly sound. A look of anger furrowed his brow. "Nobody mocks McCarthy!" he growled. He shook his fist angrily at the bird, and tension mounted darkly in the woods. I hastily retreated to the text, wondering vaguely how this strange excursion of ours was helping the United States Information Service, which now seemed incredibly remote.

" 'I have thought that Walden Pond would be a good place for business,' " I read, " 'not solely on account of the railroad and the ice trade; it offers advantages which it may not be good policy to divulge; it is a good port and a good foundation. No Neva marshes to be filled; though you must everywhere build on piles of your own driving. It is said that a flood-tide, with a westerly wind, and ice in the Neva, would sweep St. Petersburg from the face of the earth.' "

"That does it," said McCarthy, quietly. "He's hung himself right there in a single paragraph. First he admits that his lonely hangout has advantages he's unwilling to divulge, then he bewails the loss of a Russian city. What more do I want? I can get the book yanked from overseas libraries on that one paragraph alone. The taxpayers won't have to foot the bill any longer for this kind of fruitcake. The lousy jailbird!"

---

*Dean Acheson, Secretary of State 1949–53. Although he helped create the Cold War policies of containment of communism ("negotiation through strength"), he was attacked during the McCarthy hearings for refusing to fire any of his State Department subordinates. "I will not turn my back on Alger Hiss," he said.

"Not so fast, Senator!" I put in, and rose to my full height. "When you cast aspersions on Henry David Thoreau you are impeaching a great American institution."

"What institution?"

"The motel," I replied with quiet desperation. "It is well known that the man who conceived the motel got his inspiration from Thoreau's pondside hut. In fact, you might say that the tiny Walden house was America's first motel."

I was grasping at a straw. Actually, I found myself grasping at the stalk of a smooth sumac *(Rhus glabra);* it gave way and I swayed into the bushes, fell, and buried my teeth in leafmold. McCarthy smelled a ruse and didn't even dignify my motel story with a reply. "Skip the rest of Economy," he ordered, "and get on to Solitude! On second thought, skip Solitude, too. I've had enough of this bilge. We'll go back to town."

"Along the railroad tracks?" I pleaded, sitting up and spitting leafmold.

"Along Route 126," replied the Senator. He had his way, as usual, and we trudged wearily into Concord along the highway and put up at the Inn, where we spent a restless night in a double room.

On the plane carrying us back next morning—I to New York, McCarthy to Washington—the Senator was in a thoughtful mood. He kept steering the conversation back to Thoreau.

"Frankly, what would you say was eating the guy up?" he asked. "Just what *was* on his mind?"

"A fair question," I said, stalling. "Let's see, now—what was on Henry's mind? Goodness! What *wasn't*? Well, for one thing, he was on the defensive; he felt at home in nature as well as in society, and to that extent was freakish. He had a good opinion of wildness. He liked to test ideas on his tongue before swallowing them, and was more than half convinced that a great many enterprises men commonly take for granted are merely desperate. He distrusted complexity and impedimenta as being the great thieves of time, and he believed that behind every man there rises and falls a tide that can float the British Empire like a chip."

"What the hell has the British Empire got to do with this?" asked my companion. "Was Thoreau an Anglophobe?"

"Not at all," I said. "He paid very little heed to governments—was preoccupied with the individual. He was particularly preoccupied with himself."

"I can see that. What else was eating him?"

"Well, he was suffering from the loss of a hound, a bay horse, and a turtledove."

"That sounds like sheer carelessness," replied the Senator. "Go ahead, what else was eating him?"

"He was a writer trying not to act like a writer," I continued. "He was a man possessed. He believed that the natural day was very calm; that if you followed your genius closely enough, it would not fail to show you a new prospect every hour. One of his friends described him as the captain of a huckleberry party—which I have always felt was a patronizing remark and not a very accurate one. It would be truer to say that Henry was the captain of a boarding party: he wanted to board men's minds, not to sell them a bill of goods, merely to assure them that the spirit is capable of elevation. The note he sounded was like the white-throat's—pure, wavering, full of the ecstasy of loneliness. He also advocated wearing old clothes when you had anything important to do."

"That's bad for business," mused the Senator. "The thing to do is keep producing more and better goods, and that includes clothing and accessories. What would happen if everybody just decided to wear their old clothes? There would be a slump."

"I know," I replied. "It's awfully confusing, and I sometimes wonder. Thoreau never bothered to systematize his philosophy—probably because he knew it had bugs in it; but you were asking about him, Senator, and I'm just filling you in. Henry was careful never to confuse the standard of living with the standard of furnishing. I mean, he foresaw Macy's basement, both its strength and its weakness, its bounty and its deception."

"Are you trying to tell me," roared McCarthy, "that the R. H. Macy Company is a fraud?"

"Quiet, Senator!" I said. "Nothing could be further from my intention or my belief. And let's not stray from the subject of this so interesting discussion. Thoreau felt that the ruts of tradition and conformity are deep; he spent a good deal of his life skirting them, for the pleasure of the sensation and the glory of man. He perceived that the life in us is like the water in a river—at any time it may rise to extravagant heights and drown out all our muskrats."

"I haven't *got* any muskrats!" yelled the Senator, who by this

Stockton Twp. Pub. Lib.
140 W. BENTON
STOCKTON, IL 61085

time was thoroughly exasperated by the quality of my interpretation, as well as by the eccentricity of the author. With no attempt at concealing his irritation, he made a few notes, then put the notebook away and allowed his eyelids to droop. When I thought he wasn't looking, I pulled a bottle from my pocket, drew the stopper, and took a drink.

"Whuzzat?" asked the Senator.

"That," I said, "is a draught of undiluted morning air. You can find it on page 123." I offered him the bottle. He examined the label carefully.

"I never take a drink till after twelve o'clock."

"Then you're out of luck," I replied. "This stuff will not keep quite till noonday."

I could see that the Senator's curiosity was aroused. "Well," he said, grumblingly, "I might relax and try a little if it's non-alcoholic. Understand, I never take anything that makes me tipsy." He held the bottle to his lips and drained off a deep slug. The effect was immediate and terrible. McCarthy's eyes dilated. He stiffened. Perspiration broke from neck and forehead. The hostess of the plane, noticing his distress, came alongside to offer help. She took the bottle gently from his hand. When he spoke, the words came huskily.

"Throw away!" he croaked. "Poison!"

The hostess disappeared, carrying the fateful bottle.

When the plane reached New York, my companion was still in pain. He was barely able to thank me for my services as guide. The morning air, taken neat, had been overpowering: when one's system is long deprived of that elixir, which alone has the power to cure the general sickness, the shock of the first drink is great. The truth is, the journey had been almost too much for both of us. I think it may well be my last trip to the pond. Perhaps it was just because of the presence of the Senator, but the frogs sounded all the same as I listened—no variation in their voices. It didn't used to be that way, and I don't like such ponds.

4

Liberty

ANYTHING LIKE THAT

11/26/32

A YOUNG LADY, born in Russia, confided to us that she was about to become an American citizen, and would we be her witness, for she needed someone to testify to her good character and good intentions. Greatly touched, we dressed in a semiformal manner and accompanied her to a sort of barn over on the North River. Here we were tossed about from one United States naturalization clerk to another United States naturalization clerk, and eventually wound up before a bench, an American flag, and a grim, chilly examiner. After a few routine questions, the man suddenly speeded up his voice and inquired: "Do you believe in Communism, anarchism, polygamy—or anything like that?" And before we could pry into the phrase "anything like that"—which we felt it our duty to do—our young friend had blithely answered no, and it was all over. She is now an American citizen, a very pretty one, sworn never to believe in Anything Like That.

THE CONSTITUTION

2/8/36

THAT WAS A GOOD LETTER of Thomas Jefferson's which F. P. A.* published in his column, in which Jefferson pointed out that there was nothing sacred about constitutions, and that they were useful only if changed frequently to fit the changing needs of the people. Reverence for our Constitution is going to reach droll new heights this year; yet the Constitution, far from being a sacred document, isn't even a grammatical one. "We, the people of the United States, in order to form a more perfect union . . ." has turned many a grammarian's stomach, perfection being a state which does not admit of degree. A meticulous draughtsman would have written simply "in order to form a perfect union"—a thing our forefathers didn't dare predict, even for the sake of grammar.

POLITICAL SPEECHMAKING

7/8/44

THE THING WE REMEMBER of the Republican keynote speech, as it came in over the air, is the summer heat in the long grasses of the June night outside the window, and our own feeling of sin and of futility. It was the same feeling a boy has at the county fair, on the hot midway in the suggestive summertime, as he pauses before a barker outside a girl-show tent, with the smell of fried food in his nostrils and the enticements of girls in his mind, lost in the immemorial sheepishness of humanity and its deliberate exploitation by the ancient devices

*Franklin P. Adams's column "The Conning Tower" ran in *The New York World* and later in *The New York Herald Tribune*.

54

of oratory. The keynoter in Chicago indicated that the Republicans were against aggression, New Dealism, and the man-eating shark. There was to be no more aggression because Republicans do not tolerate any evil thing like aggression. The speaker gave no indication that the reorganization of a shattered world would require anything more than a mere extension of American culture and habits, as exemplified by past and present Republicans. In the summer night, we felt that we were a million boys, armed, bloody, and tired, standing and listening to this slick spiel, outside this gaudy and unlikely tent—listening and knowing all the while that we were about to be taken.

LIBERALISM

1/17/48

"THERE IS NO LIBERAL VIEW," sighed the *Herald Tribune* as the old year died, "no really self-consistent and logical body of principle and policy." It was a doleful thought, and the old year drew a few more tortured breaths and expired.

Ever since Thanksgiving, the *Herald Tribune* has been rassling with the theme of liberalism, and there have been mornings when the struggle resembled an old-fashioned rassling match with the Devil. The *Tribune*'s feeling about the independent liberal seems to be that he comes from a good family but has taken to hanging around pool halls. His instability, his shallow charm, his unpredictable movements, his dissolute companions, all have been the subject of speculation recently in the *Tribune*'s pages, and the word that was finally trotted out to describe his fate was the word "bankrupt." Even this word, however, seemed vaguely to trouble the *Tribune*, which does not in theory approve of any sort of American insolvency, even liberal insolvency. Clearly, a dilemma. The *Tribune* met it boldly by explaining that the liberal's work was done, his victory complete, and that henceforth the "conventional party structure" would be happy to carry the whole load and take care of the situation without any help. Its editorial paid tribute to the deep moral roots of nineteenth-century liberalism and the classic insurgencies, and traced the course of liberal history from the Jefferson revolt right down to the year 1933, at which point the editorialist gulped, hawked, and spat out.

The *Tribune*'s estimate of the independent liberal sounds to us a bit on the romantic side, a bit too full of the great tradition, not quite catching the essence of liberalism. The value of the liberal in the republic is not that he is logical but that he is inquisitive. At the moment, the liberal's desperate position and his dead life seem to us neither as desperate nor as dead as the *H. T.* has been making out. There are still a good many free men around who don't think that the liberal's work is done. (They would like to, but it isn't that easy.) The independent liberal, whether walking by his wild lone or running with a pack, is an essential ingredient in the two-party system in America—as strange and as vital as the trace elements in our soil. He gives the system its fluidity, its benign inconsistency, and (in cahoots with the major political organizations) its indisputable grace. We have never believed that the independent liberal had a priority on liberal thought, or a corner on the market; he merely lives in a semi-detached house and goes out without his rubbers. The *Tribune* itself has turned in such a good liberal performance lately in its news columns that its editorial shudders have seemed all the more strange. After all, it was the *Trib* that handed over ten columns last Sunday to William Z. Foster, who has seldom needed more than twenty-five words to hang himself in and this time did it in two flat, when he described legislative debates as "ridiculous talkfests."

The liberal holds that he is true to the republic when he is true to himself. (It may not be as cozy an attitude as it sounds.) He greets with enthusiasm the fact of the journey, as a dog greets a man's invitation to take a walk. And he acts in the dog's way, too, swinging wide, racing ahead, doubling back, covering many miles of territory that the man never traverses, all in the spirit of inquiry and the zest for truth. He leaves a crazy trail, but he ranges far beyond the genteel old party he walks with and he is usually in a better position to discover a skunk. The dog often influences the course the man takes, on his long walk; for sometimes a dog runs into something in nature so arresting that not even a man can quite ignore it, and the man deviates—a clear victim of the liberal intent in his dumb companion. When the two of them get home and flop down, it is the liberal—the wide-ranging dog—who is covered with burdocks and with information of a special sort on out-of-the-way places. Often ineffective in direct political action, he is the opposite of the professional revolutionary, for, unlike the latter, he never feels he knows where the truth lies, but is full of rich memories of places he has glimpsed it in. He is, on the whole, more optimistic than the revolutionary, or even than the Republican in a good year.

The *Tribune* may be right that there is no liberal "view." But the question is whether there is still a liberal spirit. In these melancholy days of Hooper and Gallup, when it is the vogue to belittle the thought in the individual and to glorify the thought in the crowd, one can only wonder. We think the spirit is there all right but it is taking a beating from all sides. Where *does* a liberal look these days? Mr. Truman has just suggested a forty-dollar bonus for all good taxpayers, Mr. Wallace has started calling people "ordinary" and man "common," and the *Herald Tribune* has liberalism on the mat, squeezing it in the kidneys. Your true liberal is on a spot, but it isn't the first time. Two dollars says it isn't going to be the last time. We'd make it five dollars except for all this talk of bankruptcy.

VOTER SANITY

ONE OF OUR OVERSEAS READERS has dropped us a line to inform us about the qualifications for voting in England. He got into a discussion with somebody in London about the matter, and they called the reference library of the House of Commons and received the following pronouncement: "In Great Britain any adult twenty-one years of age or over may register and vote except peers and lunatics. The latter, if they have a moment of lucidity, may register and vote." Our reader passed this on to us in the hope that it might sustain us through the difficult weeks ahead. The American political scene has seldom put such a strain on the sanity of the electorate, and we have an idea that when we step up to the polls next November we will feel like one of those British voters—daft as a coot, but praying, as we draw the curtain behind us, for a moment of lucidity.

A VOICE HEARD IN THE LAND

WE HAVE A CORDIAL INVITATION from the Businessmen for Wallace* to attend a dinner on the twenty-first, *couvert* $100, and although we ordinarily try to get to political rallies, we are hesitating on this one. The invitation shows a picture of Mr. Wallace in the act of delivering a speech, and there seems to be shining around him (and coming from above) a wonderful

---

*Henry A. Wallace, Progressive Party candidate for President in 1948. Originally a Republican, Wallace had been a Democrat as Secretary of Agriculture (1933–40), Vice President of the U.S. (1940–44), and Secretary of Commerce (1945–46).

radiance. It is probably a Consolidated Edison radiance, but there is nothing in the photograph to indicate that. This radiance looks like the real thing. Halfway down the shaft of light is a caption that says, "And a voice was heard in the land." The question that naturally arises, of course, is whether this land wants a voice. A distinguishing political feature of America is that it has never had a voice; it has had a lot of hoopdedoo but no voice, and that's the way we like it. Frankie Sinatra can handle the country's voice requirements, and the political candidates can handle the hoopdedoo, and we'll take ours without radiance, please.

Mr. Wallace has had a great deal to say about the infirmities and the unfairness of the American press, and we have taken most of his remarks lying down. He keeps saying that you can't learn the truth from the papers. We agree. You can't learn the truth from the papers. You can, however, buy at any newsstand a ten-cent assortment of biassed and unbiassed facts and fancies and reports and opinions, and from them you are allowed to try to assemble something that is a reasonable facsimile of the truth. And *that's* the way we like it, too. If a "voice" should ever be heard in the land, and stay heard, an awful lot of editorial pages and news pages would take the count. We think it entirely fair to remind the Businessmen of the most recent case where a voice was heard in a land. The voice was heard, the light came straight down from above, you could learn the Truth from the papers—and the land* is now under a four-power military government.

*Nazi Germany.

POLLING

11/13/48

THE TOTAL COLLAPSE of the public opinion polls* shows that this country is in good health. A country that developed an airtight system of finding out in advance what was in people's minds would be uninhabitable. Luckily, we do not face any such emergency. The so-called science of poll-taking is not a science at all but mere necromancy. People are unpredictable by nature, and although you can take a nation's pulse, you can't be sure that the nation hasn't just run up a flight of stairs, and although you can take a nation's blood pressure, you can't be sure that if you came back in twenty minutes you'd get the same reading. This is a damn fine thing.

Hollywood, which long ago elevated the pollster above the writer, and which invariably takes a blood count before beginning a picture, must be examining the results of the 1948 Presidential election with particular interest. Book clubs, which listen to the pitter-patter of millions of hearts before deciding whether a book is any good, must be studying the results, too. We are proud of America for clouding up the crystal ball, for telling one thing to a poll-taker, another thing to a voting machine. This is an excellent land. And we see even more clearly why the movies have advanced so slowly in the direction of art: Not only have the producers been deliberately writing down to the public but they've been getting bad information into the bargain. Who knows? Maybe the people aren't so far below them as they think.

*Polls had predicted Republican candidate Thomas Dewey's election, but Democratic candidate Harry Truman won despite competition from the Progressives (Henry Wallace) and Dixiecrats, which had threatened to drain Democratic votes.

SOCIAL SECURITY

11/20/48

PRESIDENT TRUMAN SAYS he is going to increase social security. By this he means that a somewhat larger amount will be withheld from a worker's pay check each week and that the employer will be asked to match the amount. Mark Sullivan, in the *Tribune*, points out that with the value of money dropping the way it is, an increase in social security is only an apparent increase, not a real increase. Mr. Sullivan argues that the fifty cents that was withheld from your pay check in, say, 1937 would have bought you a square meal at that time, but that when you are sixty-five years old and get the fifty cents back, it may buy you only a small box of dried raisins. He says the way to increase social security is to see that the dollar doesn't shrink. The argument is sound enough. Perhaps the way to manage social security is to forget about dollars and withhold meat instead. Every employer could be required to maintain a deep-freeze unit and withhold one square meal each week for each employee. Then when an employee reaches sixty-five and starts digging around like a squirrel on a winter morning, he will dig up some frozen meat instead of a shrivelled dollar. Of course, withholding meat for security reasons would cause food prices to skyrocket and this, too, might be a social advantage, since many of us could normally be counted on to die of malnutrition before we ever reached sixty-five.

The problem of security is full of bewildering implications, pitfalls, and myths. It is paradoxical that the more secure a person gets in a material way, the less secure he may become in other ways. The least secure fellows you see around, in any age or period, are the big fellows, with their personal empires and kingdoms and all the responsibilities and ulcers that go with kinging. In a sense, the only genuinely secure person is a healthy man possessed of absolutely nothing; such a man stands aloof and safe—there is no way either to reduce his fortune or to debase his currency. But even he is not perfectly secure: his loneliness may suddenly depress his spirit, and this might endanger his health.

There is a sort of security in savagery, in that the savage

enjoys an extremely intimate and direct relationship with his supply—the berry, the root, the deermeat, the fish, the pelt. He is more truly a man of the world than is the civilized man. But he is not really secure, either; he soon notices the twinkle in a glass bead (and the possibilities of appreciation and exchange), and he fights wars with other savages (as do we all), and his security fades when the arrow is directed not at a deer but at another man.

OUR POLITICAL EXILES

8/6/49

A DOCUMENT DESCRIBING the Russian system of exile and forced labor has been produced by the British Government and is to be placed before the United Nations. It is estimated that some ten million persons in the Soviet Union are subject to compulsory work. These persons include the "unstable" elements, the "déclassé" elements. The concept of forced labor is so abhorrent to the American temperament, one wonders why there is so little concern in this country over our own system of forced idleness. The disease is the same—the difference is in the method of treating the victims. In the last couple of years, a handful of American citizens have been banished from industry for political reasons and forced into the camp of idleness. From this nucleus there can easily grow (and in fact there is growing) a group of American political prisoners. They are the "déclassé," the "unstable." Their crime is to have belonged to a wrong organization in a bygone year, to have once entertained a bubbly thought (or a second cousin at dinner), to have worn a hat backward, to have been seen by an agent at a rally. Industry is being encouraged to get shed of these unstable elements, these nebulous people. Laws are being framed to help detect and debar them. They may never have broken a law, or a piece of pottery, but they are being marched steadily, imperceptibly, toward the queer Siberia of our temperate zone. This is a dangerous exodus, an unhealthy state of mind. Perhaps a report should be placed before the U. N., but we would rather see it placed where it belongs—just a memo in the hatband of every democrat, reminding him that no country has a monopoly on political terror.

ORTHODOXY

12/30/50

FOR OURSELF, we shall resolve not to overwrite in the New Year, and to defend and exalt those principles and quirks that have carried the nation slowly up the long hill since it started: its gaiety, its resilience, its diversity, its tolerance of the divergent or the harassing idea, its respect for all men. Who is to say we are not greatly ascendant still? Because of fear, Americans have lately compromised their essential position—have published blacklists, have permitted legislative committees to presuppose what is "American," have watched them hang innocent men and women on the gallows of the newspaper headline, have winked at the meddling of congressmen in the conduct of the movies, have made the natural loyalty of the citizen ever so much more difficult by removing loyalty itself from the realm of free choice, have hinted that jobs belong chiefly to the confessed orthodox. For us, 1950 will be memorable above all other years because it was the year we once found ourself hesitating to throw something in the wastebasket, from a fleeting dread that it might be seen and misconstrued. In that one blinding moment of hesitation, the fresh air of America suddenly seemed contaminated with evil. The incident was absurd and the feeling passed, but nothing is quite absurd that happens.

Insofar as orthodoxy has gained strength, our republic has lost strength. But the loss is neither irreparable nor unusual. It is the product of war clouds—a sort of terrible mist that gathers. Luckily, many of our strongest skippers see through it. For 1951, we wish our readers health, faith, the sure eye that sees through mists, and the patience and muscle for the ascent of the most beautiful hill there is.

NEWSPAPER STRIKE

12/12/53

AT ONE POINT in the newspaper lull,* Edward R. Murrow remarked that "breakfast without a newspaper is a horse without a saddle"—an unhappy metaphor, it seemed to us. We began watching our own breakfasts, to see whether they were horses without saddles, and all we could discover was that the breakfast hour had achieved a sort of eerie serenity. Our digestion improved noticeably when the morning paper stopped arriving. Our private feeling about newspapers is a mixed one. Surely ninety per cent of all so-called news is old stuff—some of it two and three thousand years old. And surely ninety per cent of everything we read today is discouraging stuff, whether newsy or not. So the breakfast hour is the hour when we sit munching stale discouragement along with fresh toast. Except for one thing, we could take a newspaper or leave it alone. If we felt confident that liberty was secure and that democracy would remain in good health without assistance from its many admirers, we could do without a newspaper quite handily. At certain periods in our life, we've tried the experiment of not reading newspapers, and we found it put no strain on our system, since we enjoy a very low-grade curiosity and are seldom moved to keep informed of late developments. Mr. Murrow's famous opener, "This is the news," which carries the

*The International Photo-Engravers union was on strike against six New York newspapers from November 30 to December 9, 1953.

vox-humana sound of civilization-at-the-crossroads, often turns out to be a slight exaggeration. Nothing much happens from day to day. Public servants serve, felons act feloniously, demagogues croak their froggy tunes, echo answers echo (if it can get network time), and life goes on in its familiar pattern. But city dwellers without newspapers breathe an ominous air, as though the smog were descending. Liberty is not secure. Democracy does not thrive unassisted. And so, for love of these, we all swallow our bulletins at breakfast along with our marmalade.

WE'RE ALL AMERICANS

3/6/54

DR. SOCKMAN, the Methodist pastor, says the American city is more like a sand pile than a melting pot. "People are heaped together, but they do not hold together." Well, we have a letter telling us of an incident when Americans held together beautifully. The writer of the letter went, during his lunch hour, to buy stamps at the small post office in Bloomingdale's basement. Ahead of him in line was a lady who brought things to a standstill by changing her mind about what kind of stamps and envelopes she wanted, by running up a bill of more than thirty dollars, and by discovering that she didn't have thirty dollars and could she pay the balance by check? The line grew and grew. After a while, someone ventured to hope, out loud, that she wouldn't change her mind again, because he was on his lunch hour. At this, the woman turned on him and said, "You aren't even an American, are you?" The man was quite shaken by this, but the others in the line weren't, and they came to his aid instantly. "We're all Americans," shouted one of them, "and we are all on the lunch hour!"

That was no sand pile. People hold together and will continue to hold together, even in the face of abrupt and unfounded charges calculated to destroy.

A BUSY PLACE

> Our Misfortunes in Canada, are enough to melt an Heart
> of Stone. The Small Pox is ten times more terrible than
> Britons, Canadians and Indians together. . . . There has been
> Want, approaching to Famine, as well as Pestilence. . . . But
> these Reverses of Fortune dont discourage me. It was natural
> to expect them, and We ought to be prepared in our Minds
> for greater Changes, and more melancholly Scenes still.

So wrote John Adams to Abigail, in one of his mercurial
moments, June 26, 1776. We don't know how far into the future he was gazing, but if he were around today, celebrating
our two-hundredth, he would not lack for melancholy scenes.
As far as the eye can see in any direction, corruption and
wrongdoing, our rivers and lakes poisoned, our flying machines
arriving before the hour of their departure, our ozone layer
threatened, our sea gasping for breath, our fish inedible, our
national bird laying defective eggs, our economy inflated, our
food adulterated, our children weaned on ugly plastic toys, our
diversions stained with pornography and obscenity, violence
everywhere, venery in Congress, cheating at West Point, the
elms sick and dying, our youth barely able to read and write,
the Postal Service buckling under the crushing burden of the
mails and terrified by gloom of night, our sources of energy
depleted, our railroads in decline, our small farms disappearing, our small businesses driven against the wall by bureaucratic edicts, and our nuclear power plants hard at work on
plans to evacuate the countryside the minute something goes
wrong. It is indeed a melancholy scene.

There is one thing, though, that can be said for this belea-
guered and beloved country—it is alive and busy. It was busy
in Philadelphia in 1776, trying to get squared away on a sensible course; it is busy in New York and Chillicothe today, trying
to straighten out its incredible mess.

The word "patriot" is commonly used for Adams and for
those other early geniuses. Today, the word is out of favor.
Patriotism is unfashionable, having picked up the taint of chau-
vinism, jingoism, and demagoguery. A man is not expected to
love his country, lest he make an ass of himself. Yet our country,
seen through the mists of smog, is curiously lovable, in some-

what the way an individual who has got himself into an unconscionable scrape often seems lovable—or at least deserving of support. What other country is so appalled by its own shortcomings, so eager to atone for its own bad conduct? What other country ever issued an invitation like the one on the statue in New York's harbor? Wrongdoing, debauchery, decadence, decline—these are no more apparent in America today than are the myriad attempts to correct them and the myriad devices for doing it. The elms may be dying, but someone has developed a chemical compound that can be injected into the base of an elm tree to inhibit the progress of the disease. The Hudson River may be loaded with polychlorinated biophenyls, but there is an organization whose whole purpose is to defend and restore the Hudson River. It isn't as powerful as General Electric, but it is there, and it even gets out a little newspaper. Our food is loaded with carcinogens, while lights burn all night in laboratories where people are probing the mysteries of cancer. Everywhere you look, at the desolation and the melancholy scene, you find somebody busy with an antidote to melancholy, a cure for disease, a correction for misconduct. Sometimes there seems almost too much duplication of good works and therapeutic enterprise; but at least it suggests great busyness—a tremendous desire to carry on, against odds that, in July of 1976, as in June of 1776, often seem insuperable.

> But these Reverses of Fortune dont discourage me. . . . It is an animating Cause, and brave Spirits are not subdued with Difficulties.

Let us, on this important day when the tall ships move up the poisoned river, take heart from good John Adams. We might even for a day assume the role of patriot, with neither apology nor shame. It would be pleasant if we could confront the future with confidence, it would be relaxing if we could pursue happiness without worrying about a bad fish. But we are stuck with our chemistry, our spraymongers, our raunchy and corrupt public servants, just as Adams was stuck with the Britons, the Canadians, the Indians, and the shadow of Small Pox. Let not the reverses discourage us—liberty is an animating Cause (and there's not much smallpox around, either). If the land does not unfold fair and serene before our eyes, neither is this a bad place to be. It is unquestionably a busy one. Bang the bell! Touch off the fuse! Send up the rocket! On to the next hundred years of melancholy scenes, splendid deeds, and urgent business!

5

Maine

COME ONE, COME ALL

8/26/44

THERE ARE MANY FACETS of the promotional spirit which beguile us, but our favorite is the promotion of states of the Union by their development commissions. It is common practice for a state to recommend itself as a sanctuary to people of other states, extending a blanket invitation to all to come and romp in the peculiar sunlight within its borders. Maine, conscious of its paradisiacal quality, doggedly advertises its "unspoiled wilderness," presumably in the hope that millions will shortly arrive to cry in it. This is an odd quirk. Obviously, if a state valued its wildness, it would keep silent and not let the secret out among the tame. The very idea of "development" is inconsistent with natural beauty, and there is, of course, little likelihood that the Maine woods will be thoroughly appreciated by Maine until after they no longer exist, except in the joists and rafters of the wayside soft-drink parlors.

Bill Geagan, a sportswriter for the Bangor *News*, wrote a column the other day in strong contrast to the rich prose of the vacation ads. He was describing a Maine trout stream before the black flies entered the scene to distract his attention: "I found unsightly dumps that contained rusted bedsprings, tin cans, automobile seats and tires, iron wagon-wheel tires, burlap sacks, washtubs, barrel hoops, medicine and beer bottles, rotten potatoes, and wornout corsets. . . . It should be remembered that the future of this great State of ours . . ."

And so on. Nowadays the journey a man makes to escape from his own rusty bedsprings is a long one, and in every coppice lurks a development commission.

71

BLENDING IN

THE GERMANS, who do things well up to a certain point, made two serious mistakes in their latest attempt to land saboteurs in this country. They picked Maine, which was one mistake. And they dressed the lads in topcoats, which was another. Maine people, as young Master Hodgkins pointed out, don't wear topcoats in winter. In that cold climate the topcoat has long been recognized as a fraudulent garment—open at the sleeves, open at the neck, open at the bottom, drafty as a north chamber. The spies were immediately spotted as "from away."

The coast of Maine, viewed from a chart, must have seemed to the Germans the perfect place to put someone ashore—a long coastline, rocky, wooded, and difficult. But the people who live in the villages on Maine's coast are members of the oldest bureau of investigation in existence—they have the eyes, the ears, and the curiosity of hunters and fishers, and whatever or whoever comes ashore or goes afloat, man, bird, or beast, in whatever kind of weather, is duly noted and entered in the book of days.

Probably Germans like to do things the hard way. They get a kick out of running a submarine into an American bay in a snowstorm and unloading a couple of spy-school graduates carrying invisible ink, who later turn up at a table in Leon & Eddie's. A more sensible, and much simpler, way to get saboteurs into this country would be to parachute them down into Bryant Park at high noon, in fancy clothes, from a plane trailing a streamer advertising a Broadway show. The cops would chalk it up to press-agentry, and after the spies had satisfied a couple of autograph hounds, they could walk away and proceed to the serious business of blowing up the Kensico Dam and releasing the lions from the Zoo.

PULPWOOD

9/4/48

WE WERE BAITING a flounder hook with a clam belly the other afternoon when we looked up and saw an LCT* entering the cove. For an instant we thought perhaps things had started up all over again, but when the captain dropped anchor and cut his engine, we could hear a baby cry and, as the craft swung to the wind, could see that there were no tanks aboard. An hour or two later, when the tide served, the anchor came up and the boat headed for the beach—straight at a pile of pulpwood. The ramp rattled down, a truck appeared from the woods, and in short order the landing craft was being loaded with pulpwood, presumably for the nearest paper mill, which is owned by Time, Inc. The operation continued for about an hour. When the tide turned, the ramp came up. The captain backed away and anchored again in deep water. Darkness and mosquitoes enfolded the gaunt black hull. We noticed that, like some of the sentences in *Time*, she lay stern to the wind.

Early next morning the craft hit the beach again and resumed loading pulpwood. It was an awesome sight, this tentacle of empire reaching out into so remote and quiet a spot; and it was a fearsome sound, the throbbing engines of an old, dead war furnishing the paper for new conquests in the magazine field. Awesome or not, the LCT proved a handy rig for loading pulpwood, and a pleasant visitor in the cove. We got one flounder. Luce got, we should judge, about sixty cord.

*Landing Craft Tank. See pp. 298–99 in *Letters of E. B. White* for letters discussing this piece. After he wrote it, White found out that the landing craft was headed not for the mill at Bucksport, Maine owned by Time-Life, but rather for a mill in Brewer, Maine.

LATE AUGUST

9/3/49

FOR US THE PRETTIEST DAY in all the long year is the day that comes unexpectedly at the end of August in the country. It is a cool day, freshly laundered (as though straight from the Bendix* of the gods), when the airs, the light, and a new sound from the grasses give the world a wholly changed character. On this day, summer, languishing but not really sick, receives her visitors with a certain deliberateness—a pretty girl who knows she doesn't need to stay in bed. The yellow squash illuminates the aging vine, the black-billed cuckoo taps out his hollow message in code (a series of three dots), and zinnias stand as firm and quiet as old valorous deeds. This is the day the farmer picks up the first pullet egg, a brown and perfect jewel in the grass; the day a car stops and a man gets out and tacks up a poster advertising the county fair. You couldn't get us to swap this one day for any six other days.

CHANGE OF SEASON

10/13/51

THE CHANGE-OF-SEASON EDITOR of *Time* sat down the other day, closed his eyes, opened them again, and wrote his mood piece on the coming of autumn to the U. S. The piece was headed "Stain in the Air." "Autumn," said *Time*, "came to the U. S. last week with a souse of wet snow on Denver, a spatter of cold rain on South Dakota's Black Hills, a chill wind in Chicago that moved on to New York. . . . It was a time of transition and suspension. Along New England's shores, the squeak of a

*Bendix Home Appliance Co. produced home laundry equipment.

fisherman's oars against thole pins sounded lonely and clear in the fog of early morning. . . . On the Pacific Coast, nights had turned cold. . . . In Texas river bottoms the sweet gum trees were tinged with yellow." Then followed a quick estimate of UStemper* at applefall, ending, "In the uneasy air of 1951's autumn, a sense of wrong stained the air like smog."

This piece, ranging so widely and concluding so sadly, depressed us, and we felt wave after wave of Wrongsense lapping at our shingle. But right in the middle of feeling so bad we realized that, by a lucky chance, we were in an excellent position to check one of *Time*'s items—the one about the squeak of a fisherman's oars against thole pins along New England's shores. We just happened to *be* on a New England shore; furthermore, the hour was early and the morning was foggy. Cocking our ears, we soon picked up the sounds made by a departing fisherman. What we heard, of course, was first the scraping of the conventional galvanized rowlock in its galvanized socket, then, a few moments later, the crisp explosions of a six-cylinder Chevrolet conversion, whose cheerful pistons were soon delivering more thrusts per minute than there are thole pins in all of Maine. The collapse of this single *Time* item when checked against the facts restored our sense of well-being, and we went in to breakfast wondering whether those Texas sweet-gum trees were tinged with yellow or with robin's-egg blue.

*Time magazine frequently coined words in this manner. But that was not their only sin. Retaliating for *Fortune*'s 1934 profile of *The New Yorker*, Wolcott Gibbs in a parody profile of Henry Luce, *Time*'s editor, imitated *Time*'s inversion of normal sentence structure: "Backward ran sentences until reeled the mind."

6

One World

INIMICAL FORCES

4/8/33

EINSTEIN IS LOVED because he is gentle, respected because he is wise. Relativity being not for most of us, we elevate its author to a position somewhere between Edison, who gave us a tangible gleam, and God, who gave us the difficult dark and the hope of penetrating it. Not long ago Einstein was here and made a speech, not about relativity but about nationalism. "Behind it," he said, "are the forces inimical to life." Since he made that speech we have been reading more about those forces: Bruno Walter forbidden by the Leipzig police to conduct a symphony; shops of the Jews posted with labels showing a yellow spot on a black field. Thus in a single day's developments in Germany we go back a thousand years into the dark, while a great thinker, speaking not as Jew but as philosopher, warns us: these are the forces inimical to life.

COMMON ENEMY

10/12/35

STATESMEN AND HISTORIANS have long known that a common enemy is the most solidifying thing a nation can have, welding all the people into a happy, united mass. We saw how true that was in our own home last week when we discovered that the place we had moved into had cockroaches, or, as the cook calls them, cackaroachies. We discovered them late one night when we went down into the pantry and snapped on a light; since then, the household has warred against them with a high feeling of family unity and solidarity, sniping at them with a Flit gun, rubbing poisonous paste on bits of potatoes for them to eat, the house full of great singleness of purpose and accord. No wonder a dictator, when he feels uneasy, looks around for something for his people to squash.

SCRAP IRON

4/3/37

OLD, DEAD AUTOMOBILES, moldering in roadside grave-yards, have long been a worrisome sight in this country. We peer into glade and glen, and find bodies decomposing there, stripped of tires and batteries. Foreigners, visiting us, are appalled at the spectacle, and write letters home to their papers about American wealth and waste. But today these carcasses lie uneasily in their burial grounds, preyed upon by grave robbers of a new sort. The price of scrap iron and steel has risen tremendously—it seems there is a European demand: iron is wanted for the wars, and the stealthy junkman arrives to pluck the ancient Overland from the caress of raspberry vine and nettle. At his approach, field mice flee their nest in the cushions. Iron for the wars! Somewhere a peasant saves his broken spade for the government collector; somewhere a bride melts down her wedding ring for God and country; somewhere someone's old family sedan goes to its great adventure. The iron we could not quite destroy will serve destruction yet. Scrap iron, scrap steel, scrap gold. Scrap life.

VIGIL

9/2/39

THIS WILL BE ONE OF THOSE mute paragraphs written despite the impossible interim of magazine publication, handed over to a linotyper who has already heard later news. Today is Sunday, August 27th. Perhaps you don't remember that far back, you who presumably now dwell in a world which is either at peace or at war. It is three o'clock in the morning. The temperature in New York is 70 degrees, sky overcast. The long vigil at the radio is beginning to tell on us. We have been tuned in, off and on, for forty-eight hours, trying to snare intimations of our destiny, as in a butterfly net. Destiny, between musical transcriptions. We still twitch nervously from the likelihood of war at 86 on the dial to the possibility of peace at 100 on the dial. The hours have induced a stupor; we glide from Paris to London to Berlin to Washington—from supposition to supposition, lightly. (But that wasn't a supposition, that was the Hotel Astor.) The war of nerves, they call it. It is one of those phrases that catch on. Through it all the radio is immense. It is the box we live in. The world seems very close at hand. ("Countless human lives can yet be saved.") We sit with diners at the darkened tables in the French cafés, we pedal with the cyclists weekending in the beautiful English countryside, we march alongside the German troops approaching the Polish border, we are a schoolboy slipping on his gas mask to take shelter underground from the raid that hasn't come, we sit at the elbow of Sir Neville* as he presents the message to the British Cabinet (but what does it say?). Hour after hour we experience the debilitating sensation of knowing everything in the world except what we want to know—as a child who listens endlessly to an adult conversation but cannot get the gist, the one word or phrase that would make all clear. The world, on this Sunday morning, seems pleasingly unreal. We've been reading (between bulletins) that short story of Tomlinson's called "Illusion: 1915," which begins on a summer day in France when the bees

*Neville Chamberlain, Prime Minister of Great Britain 1937–40. His policies of appeasement of the Germans ("peace in our time") such as the 1938 Munich Pact, though supported by many at the time, failed to discourage Hitler's expansionism.

were in the limes. But this is Illusion 1939, this radio sandwich on which we chew, two bars of music with an ominous voice in between. And the advertiser, still breaking through: "Have you acquired the safety habit?" Moscow is calling New York. Hello, New York. Let me whisper I love you. They are removing the pictures from the museums. There was a time when the mere nonexistence of war was enough. Not any more. The world is in the odd position of being intellectually opposed to war, spiritually committed to it. That is the leaden note. If war comes, it will be war, and no one wants that. If peace is restored, it will be another arrangement enlarging not simply the German boundary but the Hitler dream. The world knows it can't win. Let me whisper I love you while we are dancing and the lights are low.*

SUPREMACY

3/27/43

THE LEAST SATISFYING ESSAY we have seen on the subject of isolation was written by an advertising man for an airplane company. He described the shrinking of the world, the ease with which anyone could hop from one point on the earth to any other point. He concluded with the curious observation that, the world being what it is today, the United States should see to it that it (the U.S.) achieves unquestioned supremacy of the air in the postwar world.

This conclusion, mystical and spooky though it is, seems to be a fairly common one. We find it hard to arrive at, either logically or superstitiously. If it appears necessary to an American that America should assume control of the air, then presumably

*Germany invaded Poland on September 1, 1939. Great Britain and France declared war on Germany on September 3.

it seems necessary to an Englishman that England should, and to a Russian that Russia should, and to a German that Germany should. The postwar world thus becomes simply an extension of the prewar world, same rules, same outlook. We should all get out our little book on logic and study hard. The answer must be in there somewhere.

LIBERATION OF PARIS

9/2/44

PROBABLY ONE OF THE DULLEST stretches of prose in any man's library is the article on Paris in the Encyclopædia Britannica. Yet when we heard the news of the liberation, being unable to think of anything else to do, we sat down and read it straight through from beginning to end. "Paris," we began, "capital of France and of the department of Seine, situated on the Ile de la Cité, the Ile St. Louis, and the Ile Louviers, in the Seine, as well as on both banks of the Seine, 233 miles from its mouth and 285 miles S. S. E. of London (by rail and steamer via Dover and Calais)." The words seemed like the beginning of a great poem. A feeling of simple awe overtook us as we slowly turned the page and settled down to a study of the city's weather graph and the view of the Seine looking east from Notre Dame. "The rainfall is rather evenly distributed," continued the encyclopædist. Evenly distributed, we thought to ourself, like the tears of those who love Paris.

U. N. ARROW

THE SUBTLEST SIGN in town is on an "L" pillar at Forty-eighth Street and Third Avenue. The sign reads, "UNITED NATIONS," and there is an arrow. The arrow is vertical—one of those conventional highway "straight ahead" indications. A hurried motorist probably would interpret this without trouble and would keep going toward the East River Drive; but we were on foot, and far gone in meditation, and for us the arrow distinctly pointed straight up past the dingy railroad tracks and on into Heaven.

THE UNIVERSAL THEME

4/3/48

THE RESURRECTION IS VISIBLE in the back yard in the green spear breaking ground, and it is audible in the choirs in the churches. The sparrow selects a piece of dull string for the resurrection; the stroller selects a bright necktie. The zealot overhauls his set of ideas and finds rebirth in running his fingers through them, as the gardener takes strength from touching the earth. The theme of freedom emerges like a woodchuck after a long winter of cold and crisis, and is reborn under sombre skies.

Out at Lake Success,* the peepers celebrate love and the unity of earth, the talkers celebrate hate and division. Professor Cantril, of Princeton, has been named by Unesco† to inquire into tensions and to study ways to stimulate respect among

*Meeting place for the United Nations.
†Unesco: United Nations Educational, Scientific, and Cultural Organization.

nations for each other's ideals. He will examine influences that predispose toward nationalism. He will be a busy man. Almost everything one reads and hears these days predisposes toward nationalism; only the peepers and the green spears publish the universal theme. The nation steams like a cup of hot coffee, and the patriot's spectacles become fogged, so that he sees nothing except through the mind's eye, merely feels the strong, warm liquid going into his stomach, stimulating his glands.

In Town Hall the other night, at a radio forum, we heard a man in the audience address the moderator: "Isn't it true, sir, that in the last analysis this boils down to the old struggle between freedom and tyranny?" All around him heads nodded gratefully, everyone relieved to have life clarified in a moment of revelation. Anti-Communism is strong drink. Already the lines are being drawn tighter; already fear produces symptoms of the very disease we hope to fight off: the preoccupation with loyalty, the tightening of censorship, the control of thought by legislative committee, the readiness to impute guilt by association, the impatience with liberalism. The tyrant fear, pricking us to fight tyranny. This time, we suspect, there is more on the stage than the old familiar conflict between freedom and tyranny. The playwright is subtly ambitious and carries another theme along, and we are about to witness the death scene of nationalism to boot. This is the big act, and we who live in this decade are the favored few.

A week or two ago, in *Life*, Dorothy Thompson published a letter she had from Jan Masaryk,* whose suicide pointed the dilemma of millions of free-spirited men who find themselves in circumstances for which they feel partially responsible and from which they see no escape. The letter revealed Masaryk's self-doubts and his presentiment of the spiritual impasse toward which he was headed. It was dated November 15th. "I have been toying with the idea," he wrote, "to let myself go at one of the closing sessions of the General Assembly and call out a warning to all those self-centered nationalists assembled in

*Masaryk, Czechoslovakian minister for foreign affairs, represented Czechoslovakia at the San Francisco Conference of the United Nations in 1945 and managed to remain in power after the Communist coup in February 1948. He died March 10, 1948, from a fall from an apartment window in Prague; the Communist government announced it as a suicide.

the 'Flushing-Success' area. It is the question of timing that worries me."

He did not let himself go, and no one is wise enough to say whether his timing would have been good or bad. But most of us can feel something of the paralysis of that doubt, something of the pulsation of that intent.

The essential antagonism between the Russian world and the Western world is in the emphasis each places on responsibility. Both capitalism and socialism accept certain responsibilities, avoid others. Socialism holds itself responsible to the people for the use and management of resources, and in so doing is likely to wind up (as it has in Russia) by managing everything, including the citizen's private life, his thoughts, his arts, and his science. This is wholly repugnant to democratic capitalists, whose system accepts the responsibility for guarding civil liberties and is notably cavalier about private concentrations of economic power, despite the fact that the destinies of the people are tied up in them. And so the antagonism grows—each system both ambitious and fearful, largely because of the presence of the other. The argument about responsibility seems ready to boil over into a mess that, for utter *ir*responsibility, would make the gaudiest robber barons of capitalism and the most ruthless tyrants of Communism look like pikers.

The question of responsibility is a pervasive one. The United Nations, lacking both money and force, and being merely a set of nations with their fingers crossed, has not been able to assume much responsibility for humanity. The "self-centered nationalists" whom Jan Masaryk hesitated to warn are not all of them deliberately self-centered, but the Charter offers little chance for any delegate to be anything but centered on self and nation.

We recommend to Professor Cantril, in his search for things that predispose toward nationalism, that he reexamine the principles of the Charter. The Charter specifies "coöperation." Yet small nations coöperate reluctantly and big nations do not coöperate at all. The Charter advertises "sovereign equality." But equality is a myth. A voting procedure based on equality is an exasperation to strong nations and not much comfort to weak ones. Ask any western European nation about its sovereign equality when the shadow of Russian expansion stretches across it from the east and the gleam of American dollars strikes it from the west. Ask the ghost of Masaryk. The Charter seeks collective security by the prevention of aggression, but nobody has ever figured out how to prevent aggression by disciplining nations, and we are all less secure, singly and collectively, than we were three years ago.

It seems to us that the people of our country and of many other countries believe in the purposes of the United Nations but are baffled and discouraged by its principles. As long as we're an independent nation, we have to pursue a national policy. But if the people say so, our foreign policy can be broadened to express a universal principle even while acting to preserve a national ideal. Anti-Communism is our necessary foreign policy at the moment, but it is negative and it is incomplete. The long-term policy of the United States should be to end the anarchy of sovereign states and to build the government of free people. We ask the delegates to take a stroll some evening, leave the hall and go over to the lake, and listen to the lovesick little frog, *Hyla crucifer,* for the sound of the correct principle.

EAGLES AND BEARS

11/26/49

MR. McNEIL* AND MR. VISHINSKY exchanged fables last week, thereby charming the United Nations with a fresh obliquity of expression. We were glad to see this trend, and we commend to the delegates the fable of the Raccoon and the Fresh-Water Mussel. It goes like this:

---

*Hector McNeil, Minister of State for Great Britain, headed the British delegation to the U. N. Andrei Y. Vishinsky was Foreign Minister of the U.S.S.R.

After the long bloodiness of the jungle, the animals assembled their delegates in the council place to put an end to the scourge of trouble and to establish a community of beasts, devoid of tooth and fang, free from the legacy of fear. Delegates were soon making speeches, among the longest of which were the speeches of the Bear, the Eagle, and the Lion.

"It is quite clear," said the Bear, pounding the table with his paw, "that the Eagles are up to no good. Everything Eagles do is warlike and wrong. Lions are bad, too. The jungle would be an excellent place if all animals would act more like Bears and would turn matters over to the head Bear. Bears are the thing."

The animals listened attentively to this speech and the Raccoon applauded loudly. Then the Eagle rose and opened his beak.

"The trouble with Bears," said he, "is that they keep too much to themselves. I would like to see Bears mingle more. Because a Bear likes raspberries, it doesn't mean *I* like raspberries. Because Bears sleep in winter, must an Eagle who stays awake be called stupid?"

"Good speech," said the Lion. "Jolly good. Furthermore, time runs out."

There followed a few other speeches by minor animals and then the delegates withdrew to their personal jungles.

The first to get home was the Eagle.

"What happened?" asked all the Eagles.

"If you were listening to your radios, you know what happened," answered the Eagle. "There will be a rebroadcast at ten-thirty this evening for anybody who missed the proceedings."

The Lion was the second to get home.

"What happened?" asked all the Lions.

"Here—read all about it," said the Lion, handing them copies of the London *Times*.

The Bear was the last to get home.

"What happened?" asked all the Bears.

"Well," said the Bear, "I simply told the other animals how the Eagles and the Lions were preparing for war. I explained that the jungle would be all right if everybody would be more like Bears and would turn things over to the head Bear. I made it clear that Bears are the thing."

"What did the others say to that?" asked the delighted Bears.

"What did they say?" said the Bear. "Say? Why, they said the same old stuff. What they said was propaganda. You Bears don't need to know what they said, because it is without meaning." And the old Councilbear smiled. That night, when some of the more inquisitive of the Bears turned on their radios, all they heard in their radio sets was the sighing of the wind in the treetops.

The debate continued for several months. Each jungle session saw the Bears, the Lions, and the Eagles at odds. After each session, the Council-animals returned and made their familiar reports. Once in a while a very small animal would make a speech—a Chipmunk, or a Water Beetle—but nobody paid much attention. Everyone concentrated on Lions, Bears, and Eagles.

The Eagles worried so much about what the Bears were doing they got ulcers. Some Eagles had to sip milk in the middle of the morning. It was humiliating. The Bears, on the other hand, worried about what the Eagles were up to. The more they worried, the closer they kept to themselves. They would sleep for months at a time, hibernating, in the wintertime of fear.

The Eagles, sensing trouble, sharpened their talons and stockpiled steel toenails. The Bears, sensing trouble, sharpened their teeth and stockpiled brass claws. Everyone in the jungle was acutely unhappy, except, of course, the Chickadees, who never allowed anything to depress them. The small animals were restless, realizing that the jungle was overburdened with strong Bears lying low, strong Eagles flying high. It was a bad situation. However, things weren't impossible. Bears didn't really dislike Eagles, and the Eagles didn't really dislike Bears. It was all on paper—or in the mind.

It wasn't till the day a Raccoon ate a Fresh-Water Mussel that the lid blew off.

"You can't do that to a Mussel!" screamed an Eagle.

"Why not?" asked the Raccoon, who had acted on impulse.

"Because it's unkind and because I have an arrangement with Fresh-Water Mussels," said the Eagle.

"Never heard of it," said the Raccoon.

"Well, lay off Fresh-Water Mussels! Who strikes a Fresh-Water Mussel strikes me!" screamed the Eagle. "Death to Raccoons!"

"O.K.," said the Raccoon, "death to Eagles!"

"This concerns me," said the Bear. "Raccoons are my little

brothers. Who strikes a Raccoon strikes me. Death to the people who strike Raccoons!"

"O.K.," cried the Eagles, who were immediately joined by the Lions, "death to Raccoons *and* Bears!"

In almost no time, the Bears and the Eagles and the Lions tangled, and were joined by Water Beetles, Chipmunks, Moles, Luna Moths, Porcupines, Jackals, Ladybugs, Sloths, Barn Swallows, and Whirling Mice. It was a mess. The Eagles and the Bears were the only ones that had real power, and they fixed everything quick. For the next three or four million years, the jungle was silent and relaxed. Only the sound of the wind disturbed it—and the small whirring noise in some of the radio sets abandoned by the dead Bears.

SNOWSTORMS

12/22/51

THERE WAS A FLURRY OF SNOW one morning recently—a sudden gaiety and white charm at breakfast time, the snow descending prettily across roof and wall. The moment we saw this cheerful sight, this unexpected bonus, our mind rocketed back to a time in childhood, a morning unforgettable because of snow. The snow that day arrived in blizzard force; at eight o'clock the fire siren, muffled by the blast, wailed the "No School Today" signal, and we retired in ecstasy to a warm attic room and to Meccano. The thing we remember is the coziness, the child's sense of a protective screen having been quickly drawn between him and his rather frightening world. This feeling was perfectly reproduced for us the other morning. For about five minutes, the snow seemed quite capable of insulating us from all harm, from every trouble, from evil itself, and we were again in the warm, safe attic with a straightforward problem in mechanical engineering.

The Russians are trying, with their curtain, to draw the protective screen and make it snow forever in the world, for their special benefit. They long for the sense of security that circumstances and their own stubbornness have denied them. A childish surrender to unreality, the curtain not only does not shut out evil, it *is* evil. The curtain is not merely the screen that makes it impossible for the West to relax its arms, it is itself the core of Russian armament. It is poison gas in political form.

There ought to be a healthy debate going on today—a debate between capitalism and socialism, between individualism and statism. The curtain has prevented this debate from taking place, and although there is plenty of talk in the forum, we are really stuck with the fact of having no discussion. The Russians do not qualify as debaters, because they have boxed their argument, sealed their people, and turned out the house lights. In consequence, the delegates to the United Nations stand around and talk about peace and disarmament—subjects on which there is no real difference of opinion. (Everybody loves peace by the terms of the contract, and nobody can risk disarming under the conditions created by the curtain.)

An interesting experiment would be to place the curtain itself on the agenda. It is not a secondary matter, to be buried in committee; it is the big thing. The U. N. cannot much longer pretend that questions can be genuinely discussed under Russia's terms—with all ideas being halted at the border, with writers being instructed how to write, with radio being jammed. Such "discussions" are farcical, and are quite expensive, too. The United States has proposed that the curtain be opened just enough to allow inspectors to walk through and look about for concealed weapons. That begs the issue. The free nations of the U. N. should ask Russia to show cause why her curtain should not be abandoned—not as an approach to disarmament but as a precondition of further debate on anything at all. The curtain is the one topic that must acutely embarrass the Soviet lords, it is such a telltale device: evidence of their fear, symbol of their immaturity, and sure sign of their contempt for people. The curtain is their private snowstorm, behind which they hope to withdraw and play with their construction set.

PIRANHAS

11/29/52

THERE'S A TROPICAL-FISH STORE in this vicinity, and one of the tanks contains a solitary piranha—a little fish that looks something like a sunfish. The price tag says $25—quite a sum for a three-inch pet that sulks in a watery corner, slowly waving its pectorals. However, the piranha has this to be said for it: it is a man-eater. Fierce, remorseless, and with a taste for the flesh of warm-blooded animals, it will attack furiously. We pass the fish store almost every day on our way to work, the blood flowing warm in our veins, the prospect of another day at a typewriter filling our head with suicidal fancies, and we always stop for a moment in front of the piranha. We like having a murderous fish in the neighborhood; it is reassuring to know that all we have to do is dive into a nearby tank to be stripped flesh from bone in a matter of minutes.

A glance at the calendar, a glimpse of Gristede's,* set us exploring our private reserves of gratitude and adoration. To forget the world's abundance, even briefly and in a moment of spiritual penury, is to lose one's toehold on the ladder. The sun rises, the leaves fall, the park grows cold, the springs flow, the birds rip by on knowing wings, the pumpkin accedes to the throne, and men prepare. For what do they prepare? Unlike birds, trees, sun, they prepare for war—or else they prepare for they know not what, which is almost the same thing. They prepare, perhaps, for cold. Fearing the worst, they prepare for the worst. But there is still room for thanks—not for the pass we've reached but for the setting against which we've reached it, a backdrop beyond compare, a scene of wild and illimitable promise, a revolutionary cyclorama of cleverly concealed progress, with good men holding firm. Wanted: a third act. Until we know that the playwright has collapsed or gone in with the piranha, until we know that all's behind, we shall innocently assume that all is ahead, and render thanks, at the customary time and in the customary way, for the privilege of a walk-on part in the show.

*Chain of food stores.

CITIZEN OF THE WORLD

12/19/53

OUT IN SUMMIT, NEW JERSEY, the students of the Junior High recite a school pledge at their assemblies, and the pledge used to start, "I, a student of Summit Junior High School and a future citizen of the world, promise to obey and uphold the laws of my country and school." The Veterans of Foreign Wars got wind of this dangerous condition and persuaded the school authorities to strike out the offensive phrase "citizen of the world." The school children must, therefore, have been surprised the other day when the same phrase popped up in President Eisenhower's address to the United Nations. "The atomic age," he said, "has moved forward at such a pace that every citizen of the world should have some comprehension, at least in comparative terms, of the extent of this development." Clear case of the President of the United States going over the heads of the Veterans of Foreign Wars. We don't know what the next step of the school authorities should be—give up assemblies, perhaps, as being a breeding ground for difference of opinion.

FRIENDSHIP CARDS

6/19/54

A GREETING-CARD FIRM has sent us some statistics about the expression of friendship and good will in America. The figures are staggering. In 1953, some three and a half billion cards were mailed, carrying greetings of one sort or another. Friendships ranked high on the list, along with Get Well Soons, Happy Birthdays, and Merry Andsoforths. For a firm dealing in the emotions of love and affection, the statistician's mind runs

93

on very strange matters indeed. Thus we read that the money spent on "friendship" in 1953 would "pay for a battleship." And if stacked one atop another in their envelopes, those three and a half billion messages of love would "make a pile so high that even the Russians couldn't invent a guided missile that could get over the top of it. It would be 4,375 miles up in the ionosphere." There seems to be something wrong here somewhere. Perhaps we should simply stack these friendship cards instead of mailing them, thus warding off unfriendly missiles. Or perhaps we're sending cards to the wrong people. Why doesn't some enterprising greeting-card firm get up a mailing list of our "enemies" (there must be billions of them), to whom a friendship card would come as a real surprise? The money spent on the cards would still pay for a battleship, but if the cards worked, the battleship might never have to open fire.

HUNGARIAN REVOLT

12/22/56

A FEW YEARS AGO, when Joseph Stalin was still alive, we tried to write a Christmas allegory in the form of a playlet. It didn't come off. But we are reminded of it this year because of recent events in Europe. Our story was about a Russian emissary to the United States who goes back to his homeland at Christmas to check in. As a gag, he brings Stalin a gift of a luminous candy cane from America. The cane arouses the Marshal's curiosity. He pumps his man about life in the United States, and the two of them have a few drinks. Stalin wants to know what Christmas is like over here. He asks to be filled in on the story of the Nativity, and the emissary tells it, rather blunderingly. Stalin wants to know why the candy cane shines. "They doctor it up with something, I guess," the fellow says. The two men get a bit drunk. And before the underling leaves, he tells his boss that, actually, it isn't just candy canes that act this way. A lot of things in America seem to be sort of luminous; things just get looking lighter than they should—streets, buildings, the sky, the faces of little girls in the park when they buy the popcorn and the pigeons fly up and the wings of birds are all around them. The emissary leaves after a while. Stalin is furious at the inadequacy of the man's explanation, the rambling tale of unexplained luminosity. The room grows dark. The cane, hanging on a hat tree, shines in the gloom, a bright inverted J. Finally, after making several attempts to eat the cane and being scared off by the possible consequences, he rings for an aide and orders the hated object removed. He tells the aide to bury the cane—secretly, so none shall see the light from it.

As you can gather from the synopsis, this wasn't much of an allegory. But now, in 1956, at Christmas, a candy cane does indeed hang in the Kremlin on the hat tree. The cane is a luminous one, and sheds the old, disturbing, familiar light. It is of Hungarian manufacture,* brought back by an emissary, and not as any gag, either. The presence of this object gives the 1956 Christmas a different look from any Christmas the world has had in a long, long while. Mr. Stalin is dead, and few are the mourners. His successors, the heads of state, will be afraid to eat this luminous cane, because of the mysterious nature of its ingredients, and they will be unable to get a satisfactory explanation of what makes it shine. (The light generated by men on their way toward freedom has never been really explained.) And even though the heads of state bury the disagreeable object, which they will surely try to do, there is no assurance whatever that it will stay down, or that somebody will not have caught a gleam from it on its way to the graveyard.

*Following a student revolt in Budapest in October 1956 that resulted in the formation of a new government headed by Imre Nagy, Soviet tanks entered the city on November 4, crushing Hungary's brief revolution. The emissary is probably Pal Maleter, a general of the revolutionaries, who was arrested by the Soviets while on a mission negotiating Soviet withdrawal from Hungary.

KHRUSHCHEV AND I
(A STUDY IN SIMILARITIES)

9/26/59

UNTIL I HAPPENED TO READ a description of him in the paper recently, I never realized how much Chairman Khrushchev and I are alike. This fellow and myself, it turns out, are like as two peas. The patterns of our lives are almost indistinguishable, one from the other. I suppose the best way to illustrate this striking resemblance is to take up the points of similarity, one by one, as they appear in the news story, which I have here on my desk.

Khrushchev, the story says, is a "devoted family man." Well, now! Could any phrase more perfectly describe me? Since my marriage in 1929, I have spent countless hours with my family and have performed innumerable small acts of devotion, such as shaking down the clinical thermometer and accidentally striking it against the edge of our solid porcelain washbasin. My devotion is too well known to need emphasis. In fact, the phrase that pops into people's heads when they think of me is "devoted family man." Few husbands, either in America or in the Soviet Union, have hung around the house, day in and day out, and never gone anywhere, as consistently as I have and over a longer period of time, and with more devotion. Sometimes it isn't so much devotion as it is simple curiosity—the fun of seeing what's going to happen next in a household like mine. But that's all right, too, and I wouldn't be surprised if some of the Chairman's so-called devotion was simple curiosity. Any husband who loses interest in the drama of family life, as it unfolds, isn't worth his salt.

Khrushchev, the article says, "enjoys walking in the woods with his five grandchildren." Here, I have to admit, there is a difference between us, but it is slight: I have only three grandchildren, and one of them can't walk in the woods, because he was only born on June 24th last and hasn't managed to get onto his feet yet. But he has been making some good tries, and when he does walk, the woods are what he will head for if he is anything like his brother Steven and his sister Martha and, of course, me. We all love the woods. Not even Ed Wynn loves the woods better than my grandchildren and me. We walk in them at every opportunity, stumbling along happily, tripping over windfalls, sniffing valerian, and annoying the jay. We note where the deer has lain under the wild apple, and we watch the red squirrel shucking spruce buds. The hours I have spent walking in the woods with my grandchildren have been happy ones, and I hope Nikita has had such good times in his own queer Russian way, in those strange Russian woods with all the bears. One bright cold morning last winter, I took my grandchildren into the woods through deep snow, to see the place where we were cutting firewood for our kitchen stove (I probably shouldn't tell this, because I imagine Khrushchev's wife has a modern gas or electric stove in her house, and not an old wood-burner, like us Americans). But anyway, Martha fell down seventeen times, and Steven disappeared into a clump of young skunk spruces, and I had all I could do to round up the children and get them safely out of the woods, once they had become separated that way. They're young, that's the main trouble. If anything, they love the woods too well.

The newspaper story says Khrushchev leads a "very busy" life. So do I. I can't quite figure out why I am so busy all the time; it seems silly and it is against my principles. But I know one thing: a man can't keep livestock and sit around all day on his tail. For example, I have just designed and built a cow trap, for taking a Hereford cow by surprise. This job alone has kept me on the go from morning till night for two weeks, as I am only fairly good at constructing things and the trap still has a few bugs in it. Before I became embroiled in building the cow trap, I was busy with two Bantam hens, one of them on ten eggs in an apple box, the other on thirteen eggs in a nail keg. This kept me occupied ("very busy") for three weeks. It was rewarding work, though, and the little hens did the lion's share of it, in the old sweet barn in the still watches of the night. And before that it was haying. And before haying it was baby-sitting—while my daughter-in-law was in the hospital having John. And right in the middle of everything I went to the hospital myself, where, of course, I became busier than ever. Never spent a more active nine days. I don't know how it is in Russia, but the work they cut out for you in an American hospital is almost beyond belief. One night, after an exhausting day with the barium sulphate crowd, I had to sit up till three in the morning editing a brochure that my doctor handed me—something he had written to raise money for the place. Believe me,

I sank down into the covers tired *that* night. Like Khrushchev, I'm just a bundle of activity, sick or well.

Khrushchev's wife, it says here, is a "teacher." My wife happens to be a teacher, too. She doesn't teach school, she teaches writers to remove the slight imperfections that mysteriously creep into American manuscripts, try though the writer will. She has been teaching this for thirty-four years. Laid end to end, the imperfections she has taught writers to remove from manuscripts would reach from Minsk to Coon Rapids. I am well aware that in Russia manuscripts do not have imperfections, but they do in this country, and we just have to make the best of it. At any rate, both Mrs. Khrushchev and my wife are teachers, and that is the main point, showing the uncanny similarity between Khrushchev and me.

Khrushchev, it turns out, has a daughter who is a "biologist." Well, for goodness' sake! *I* have a *step*daughter who is a biologist. She took her Ph.D. at Yale and heads the science department at the Moravian Seminary for Girls. Talk about your two peas! Incidentally, this same stepdaughter has three children, and although they are not technically my grandchildren, nevertheless they go walking in the woods with me, so that brings the woods total to five, roughly speaking, and increases the amazing similarity.

Khrushchev's son is an "engineer," it says. Guess what college my son graduated from! By now you'll think I'm pulling your leg, but it's a fact he graduated from the Massachusetts Institute of Technology. He hasn't launched a rocket yet, but he has launched many a boat, and when I last saw him he held the moon in his hand—or was it a spherical compass?

"The few hours Khrushchev can spare for rest and relaxation he usually spends with his family." There I am again. I hope when Khrushchev, seeking rest and relaxation, lies down on the couch in the bosom of his family, he doesn't find that a dog has got there first and that he is lying on the dog. That's my biggest trouble in relaxing—the damn dog. To him a couch is a finer invention than a satellite, and I tend to agree with him. Anyway, in the hours I can spare for rest, it's family life for me. Once in a great while I sneak down to the shore and mess around in boats, getting away from the family for a little while, but every man does that, I guess. Probably even Khrushchev, devoted family man that he is, goes off by himself once in a great while, to get people out of his hair.

Already you can see how remarkably alike the two of us are, but you haven't heard half of it. During vacations and on Sundays, it says, Khrushchev "goes hunting." That's where I go, too. It doesn't say what Khrushchev hunts, and I won't hazard a guess. As for me, I hunt the croquet ball in the perennial border. Sometimes I hunt the flea. I hunt the pullet egg in the raspberry patch. I hunt the rat. I hunt the hedgehog. I hunt my wife's reading glasses. (They are in the pocket of her housecoat, where any crafty hunter knows they would be.) Nimrods from away back, Khrush and I.

Khrushchev has been an "avid reader since childhood." There I am again. I have read avidly since childhood. Can't remember many of the titles, but I read the books. Not only do I read avidly, I read slowly and painfully, word by word, like a child reading. So my total of books is small compared to most people's total, probably smaller than the Chairman's total. Yet we're both avid readers.

And now listen to this: "Mr. Khrushchev is the friend of scientists, writers, and artists." That is exactly my situation, or predicament. Not all scientists, writers, and artists count me their friend, but I do feel very friendly toward Writer Frank Sullivan, Artist Mary Petty, Scientist Joseph T. Wearn, Pretty Writer Maeve Brennan, Artist Caroline Angell, Young Writer John Updike—the list is much too long to set down on paper. Being the friend of writers, artists, and scientists has its tense moments, but on the whole it has been a good life, and I have no regrets. I think probably it's more fun being a friend of writers and artists in America than in the Soviet Union, because you don't know in advance what they're up to. It's such fun wondering what they're going to say next.

Another point of similarity: Mr. Khrushchev, according to the news story, "devotes a great deal of his attention to American–Soviet relations." So do I. It's what I am doing right this minute. I am trying to use the extraordinary similarity between the Chairman and me to prove that an opportunity exists for improving relations. Once, years ago, I even wrote a book* about the relations between nations. I was a trifle upset at the

*The Wild Flag. (Boston: Houghton, 1946).

time, and the book was rather dreamy and uninformed, but it was good-spirited and it tackled such questions as whether the moon should be represented on the Security Council, and I still think that what I said was essentially sound, although I'm not sure the timing was right. Be that as it may, I'm a devoted advocate of better relations between nations—Khrush and I both. I don't think the nations are going about it the right way, but that's another story.

"No matter how busy Khrushchev is," the article says, "he always finds time to meet Americans and converse with them frankly on contemporary world problems." In this respect, he is the spit and image of me. Take yesterday. I was busy writing and an American walked boldly into the room where I was trying to finish a piece I started more than a year ago and would have finished months ago except for interruptions of one sort and another, and what did I do? I shoved everything aside and talked to this American on contemporary world problems. It turned out he knew almost nothing about them, and I've *never* known much about them, God knows, except what I see with my own eyes, but we kicked it around anyway. I have never been so busy that I wouldn't meet Americans, or they me. Hell, they drive right into my driveway, stop the car, get out, and start talking about contemporary problems even though I've never laid eyes on them before. I don't have the protection Khrushchev has. My dog welcomes any American, day or night, and who am I to let a dog outdo me in simple courtesy?

Mr. Khrushchev, the story goes on, "has a thorough knowledge of agriculture and a concern for the individual worker." Gee whizz, it's me all over again. I have learned so much about agriculture that I have devised a way to water a cow (with calf at side) in the barn cellar without ever going down the stairs. I'm too old to climb down stairs carrying a twelve-quart pail of water. I tie a halter rope to the bail of the pail (I use a clove hitch) and lower the pail through a hatch in the main floor. I do this after dark, when the cow is thirsty and other people aren't around. Only one person ever caught me at it—my granddaughter. She was enchanted. Ellsworth, my cow, knows about the routine, and she and her calf rise to their feet and walk over to the pail, and she drinks, in great long, audible sips, with the light from my flashlight making a sort of spot on cow and pail. Seen from directly above, at a distance of only four or five feet, it is a lovely sight, almost like being in church—the great head and horns, the bail relaxed, the rope slack, the inquisitive little calf attracted by the religious light, wanting to know, and sniffing the edge of the pail timidly. It is, as I say, a lovely, peaceable moment for me, as well as a tribute to my knowledge of agriculture. As for the individual worker whom Khrushchev is concerned about, he is much in my mind, too. His name is Henry.*

Well, that about winds up the list of points of similarity. It is perhaps worth noting that Khrushchev and I are not *wholly* alike—we have our points of difference, too. He weighs 195, I weigh 132. He has lost more hair than I have. I have never struck the moon, even in anger. I have never jammed the air. I have never advocated peace and friendship; my hopes are pinned on law and order, the gradual extension of representative government, the eventual federation of the free, and the end of political chaos caused by the rigidity of sovereignty. I have never said I would bury America, or received a twenty-one-gun salute for having said it. I feel, in fact, that America should not be buried. (I like the *Times* in the morning and the moon at night.) But these are minor differences, easily reconciled by revolution, war, death, or a change of climate. The big thing is that both Khrushchev and I like to walk in the woods with our grandchildren. I wonder if he has noticed how dark the woods have grown lately, the shadows deeper and deeper, the jay silent. I wish the woods were more the way they used to be. I wish they were the way they could be.

*Henry Allen, White's indispensable helper on the Maine farm.

MOON LANDING

THE MOON, it turns out, is a great place for men. One-sixth gravity must be a lot of fun, and when Armstrong and Aldrin* went into their bouncy little dance, like two happy children, it was a moment not only of triumph but of gaiety. The moon, on the other hand, is a poor place for flags. Ours looked stiff and awkward, trying to float on the breeze that does not blow. (There must be a lesson here somewhere.) It is traditional, of course, for explorers to plant the flag, but it struck us, as we watched with awe and admiration and pride, that our two fellows were universal men, not national men, and should have been equipped accordingly. Like every great river and every great sea, the moon belongs to none and belongs to all. It still holds the key to madness, still controls the tides that lap on shores everywhere, still guards the lovers who kiss in every land under no banner but the sky. What a pity that in our moment of triumph we did not forswear the familiar Iwo Jima scene and plant instead a device acceptable to all: a limp white handkerchief, perhaps, symbol of the common cold, which, like the moon, affects us all, unites us all.

*During the Apollo 11 mission, Neil Armstrong and Edwin "Buzz" Aldrin took the first steps on the moon July 20, 1969 ("One small step for man, one giant leap for mankind").

7

Body and Mind

HUNGER

4/4/31

YESTERDAY IN THE GRAYBAR BUILDING I bumped into my friend Philip Wedge, looking like the devil. The sight of him gave me a start—he was horribly thin, nothing but skin and bones.

"Hello, Wedge," I said. "Where is the rest of you?"

He smiled a weak smile. "I'm all right."

We chatted for a few moments, and he admitted he had lost almost forty pounds; yet he seemed disinclined to explain. Had it been anybody but Philip Wedge, I would have dropped the subject, but this queer skeleton fascinated me and I finally persuaded him to come along to lunch. At table, we got to the root of the thing quickly enough, for when the waiter appeared Wedge simply shook his head.

"I don't want anything."

"Good Lord," I said, "why not?"

Wedge fixed his eyes on me, the hollow gaze of a death's-head. "Look here," he said, sharply, "you think I'm broke, or sick. It happens I'm neither. I can't eat food, and I'm going to tell you why."

So while I listened he poured it out, this amazing story. I shall set it down as it came from him, but I cannot describe his utter emaciation of body, his moribundity of spirit, as he sat there opposite me, a dying man.

"It wasn't so bad," he began, "while I still had coffee. Up to a few weeks ago I used to get along pretty well on coffee. Practically lived on it. Now even coffee is gone."

"Gone?" I asked.

"Full of rancid oil," said Wedge, drearily. "In its natural state the coffee bean contains a certain amount of oil. This gets rancid, same as any oil." He drew from his pocket an advertise-

105

ment telling about rancid oil in coffee. When I had read it, he folded it and returned it to his pocket.

"I haven't always been this way," he continued. "I used to eat what was set before me. I believe it all started when I learned about marmalade's being made out of bilgewater."

"Out of what?" I gasped.

"Bilgewater. I was only fourteen. A friend of my father's, visiting at our house, told us. The oranges are brought to Scotland from Spain in the holds of ships. During the voyage the oranges float around in the bilge, and when they are unloaded the bilgewater is dumped out with them. The manufacturers find that it gives the marmalade a rich flavor."

"Holy Moses," I murmured. Wedge raised his hand.

"I could never eat marmalade after that. Wouldn't have mattered, of course, but soon other foods began to be taken from me. A year later I learned about wormy pork. Saw an item in the paper. Whole family wiped out, eating underdone pork. Awful death. I haven't had a mouthful since."

I glanced down at my plate and gently pushed it to one side.

"Used to be crazy about cheese," Wedge went on. "Did you ever see the bulletin that the Department of Agriculture issued in regard to mold? If you sniff mold it starts to grow in your lungs, like seaweed. Sometimes takes years but finally gets you. I gave up everything that might be moldy, even bread. One night I was opening a bottle of French vermouth, and the top of the cork was alive with mold. I haven't had a peaceful moment since. Jove, it seems as though every day I learned something awful about food. Ripe olives—every time I opened a newspaper, one or two dinner parties poisoned, people dying like rats. Sometimes it was éclairs. In 1922 I learned about what happens if you eat spinach from a can."

Wedge looked at me steadily.

"The vaguest rumors used to prey on my mind: casual remarks, snatches of overheard conversation. One time I came into a room where a radio was going. A speaker was ending his talk: '. . . or sulphuric acid from dried apricots, or the disintegration of the spleen from eating a poor grade of corn syrup.' That was all I heard. Haven't touched any dried fruit or any syrup since.

"Maybe you recall the track meet some years ago in Madison

Square Garden, when Paavo Nurmi* collapsed. Put his hand to his side, threw back his head, and collapsed. That was veal. Still, even with wormy pork and veal gone, my diet wasn't so bad until I found out about protein poisoning: somebody ate meat and eggs and nuts, and swelled up. I gave up all meat and all eggs, and later all nuts. At meals I began to see not the food that was actually before me—I'd see it in its earlier stages: oysters lying at the mouths of typhoid rivers, oranges impregnated by the citrus fly, gin made from hospital alcohol, watercress in drainage ditches, bottled cherries dipped in aniline dyes, marshmallows made of rotten eggs, parsley vines covered with green caterpillars, grapes sprayed with arsenate of lead. I used to spend hours in my kitchenette testing cans of foodstuffs to see if the cans sat flat. If a can doesn't sit flat, it has an air bubble in it, and its contents kill you after a few hours of agony.

"I grew weaker right along, hardly took a mouthful of any-thing from day to day. I weigh ninety-five now. All I've had since yesterday morning is a graham cracker. I used to drink quite a lot—alcohol kept me going. Had to quit. Fragmentary bits of gossip I picked up: '. . . lay off the Scotch in the West Forties,' 'The liqueurs contained traces of formaldehyde,' '. . . she died of fusel oil in homemade wine.' I even gave up cigars when I heard how they were made. You know how the ends of cigars are sealed?"

I nodded.

"Life is hell these days. I'm wasting away fast, but it's better than eating things you're scared of. Do you know what happens inside the human stomach when fruit is eaten in combination with any of the root-vegetables such as carrots, turnips . . . ?" Wedge's voice was failing. His eyelids drooped.

I shook my head.

"Enough gas is formed to inflate a balloon the size of . . ."

Wedge swayed in his chair, then slumped down. The poor chap had fainted. When he came to, I held a glass of water to his lips, but he motioned it away.

"Not potable," he murmured. "Reservoirs . . . too low." Then he fainted again. In the sky over Forty-third Street a buzzard wheeled and wheeled on motionless wings.

---

*Finnish long-distance runner, winner of nine gold medals in the 1920, 1924, and 1928 Olympics.

UP AND DOWN

3/13/37

FEELING FIT AS A FIDDLE, we dropped into the Psychiatric Institute the other afternoon, to pay a small call. Maybe you don't know it, but the Institute has two entrances—one on Riverside Drive, another about a hundred feet above on 168th Street. Anyway, we entered from 168th Street, stepped into the elevator, and asked for the sixth floor. Just as we were bracing ourself for the ascent, the car dropped out from under us, descended a flight or two, the door flew open, and the operator (who by this time we suspected was one of the patients) waited for us to get out.

"Sixth floor," he said, sternly.

We stepped out, gibbering, and it *was* the sixth floor. Luckily we come from hardy stock and can withstand colossal japes like that; but we should think it would be tough on the nervous patients of the Institute, particularly those that are troubled by little men who chase them up airy mountains, down rushy glens.

MY PHYSICAL HANDICAP, HA, HA

6/12/37

SIX MONTHS AGO I began to suffer from dizziness. It is an unhinging of the equilibrium, a condition of the body which gives rise to queer street effects, dreams, and fancies. I will be walking along the street, say, and will take three normal steps in a forward direction; then, as I am about to set my foot down for the fourth step, the pavement moves an inch or two to the right and drops off three-quarters of an inch, and I am not quick enough for it. This results in my jostling somebody on my left, or hitting the corner of the Fred F. French Building a glancing blow. It was fun for a few days, but I have recovered from the first fine ecstasy of dizziness, and am getting bored with it. Once I sidled into a police horse, and he gave me back as good as I gave him.

Although I am sick of my dizziness, I can't say my friends are. They still go into gales of laughter over my infirmity, and if I had lost both legs and travelled in a tiny cart drawn by a span of Baltimore orioles, I don't think I could give them more pleasure. I have consulted doctors, but doctors lose interest in any man who sticks to the same story. At first they were suspicious of my teeth, so I let them have a couple to calm them down. Then they fooled around with some flora they claim grow in the intestines, but they soon learned they were in a blind alley. Several of my friends have tried amateur witchcraft on me, including one lady who insists that my trouble is psychological; she says I stagger through streets because, deep in my heart, I loathe streets. She is, of course, a mad woman. If there's anything I enjoy (or used to), it's messing around the streets.

After listening to friends and doctors, I have drawn my own conclusion about my staggering. I am of the opinion that I have simply lost the knack of walking. Is that so incredible? A biped's ability to get along smoothly on only two legs has always seemed implausible to me. What if I say I've lost the trick? I don't think such an explanation is half so crazy as that I ought to have my tonsils out—which is the most far-fetched idea I ever heard of.

However, I didn't sit down to write about my physical disability; I sat down to write about how I amuse myself now that I am handicapped. At first it was no easy matter. I couldn't work; and while that in itself is amusing, it isn't everything. For a while I had a bad time, but one day, thumbing through a copy of *Hygeia*, I ran onto a list of things to do—a page of suggestions called "Suggested Activities for Persons With Impaired Health or Physical Handicaps," and for the first time I really felt as though I had hold of something.

The list was alphabetical, and apparently had been running as a serial, because in my copy (the April number) the list started with the "J"s and went through the "P"s. I lit a cigarette, snuggled into the couch, where I wouldn't feel dizzy, and began in earnest:

Jail, help families whose father or mother is in

This suggestion, though ingenious, I discarded. I had never helped anybody whose father or mother was in jail even when I was well, and it would be a queer time to start just because I happened to feel bad myself. I continued:

Jam, exhibit for state fair
Journalism, study for

This was getting closer. I ordered currants, raspberries, gooseberries, ten pounds of sugar. They are still around the house, mute reminders of my jam-making days. But I didn't stop with the "J"s, I went on to the "K"s.

Keep watch for the milkwagon horse
Knit, knit, knit, be one of the millions
Kitchen aprons, sell to tourists

I didn't see why I should sell the only kitchen apron in the house to tourists, especially since I contemplated making jam; but it *was* fun knitting and being one of the millions. I did that for two or three days, till I got complained about. In odd moments, I watched for the milk horse, and he for me. Life was indeed straightening out.

Then came the "L"s:

Languages, study by phonograph records and textbooks
Lease your barn for a summer theatre
Leather tooling
Listening ear (Manhattan cocktail at 5 A.M.)

And the "M"s:

Marmosets, breed
Milkwagon horse, keep watch for the
Mineralogy, study on your walks in wood (with hammer along)
Minks, breed
Missing antiques, hunt for
Mothers, adult education for young
Mothers of several small children, watch
Music, study, compose, teach

I let my barn, tooled a little leather, and one morning I arose at five o'clock and mixed myself a Manhattan. It made the day.

Even the marmosets, breeding steadily among themselves, seemed less quarrelsome seen through alcohol's beneficent haze. Streets, and street staggering, began to seem a long way off. I found that a man can occupy himself pleasantly without walking all over town. Quietly, through the long spring evenings, I watched a mother of several young children, and she returned the stare. My minks were sterile but good company. The only "M" that let me down was the mineralogy walks—for me they would have been only another dizzy stagger. And besides, I never carry a hammer. Not after what I've read in the papers.

I'm down to the "N"'s now:

Newspapers, sell
Newspapers, send forgotten lines of poem to inquirer in
Night popstands at summer theatre, sell hot coffee or sandwiches
Nurse, have a versatile

There seems to be something for a handicapped man in all these suggestions. The last one practically has my name written on it.

LIFE PHASES

2/20/37

WE ARE NOT SURE we agree with President Roosevelt that seventy is the age when a Supreme Court judge should retire. If we must establish an arbitrary pension age, it should be either fifty or ninety, but not seventy. At seventy, men are just beginning to grow liberal again, after a decade or two of conservatism. Their usefulness to the state is likely to improve after the span of life which the Bible allows them is complete. The men of eighty whom we know are on the whole a more radical, ripsnorting lot than the men of seventy. They hold life cheaply, and hence are able to entertain generous thoughts about the state. It is in his fifty-to-seventy phase that a man pulls in his ears, lashes down his principles, and gets ready for dirty weather. Octogenarians have a more devil-may-care tactic: they are sometimes quite willing to crowd on some sail and see if they can't get a burst of speed out of the old hooker yet.

A man's liberal and conservative phases seem to follow each other in a succession of waves from the time he is born. Children are radicals. Youths are conservatives, with a dash of criminal negligence. Men in their prime are liberals (as long as their digestion keeps pace with their intellect). The middle-aged, except in rare cases, run to shelter: they insure their life, draft a will, accumulate mementos and occasional tables, and hope for security. And then comes old age, which repeats childhood—a time full of humors and sadness, but often full of courage and even prophecy.

GUILTY GUMS

12/17/49

NOW THAT CHILDREN'S TEETH can be protected by adding fluorine to their drinking water, dentists are casting around for some new place to sink their drills. It looks as though they may have found it, too. Last week, Dr. Robert S. Gilbert told his fellow-dentists that a patient's open mouth is a stage on which is enacted the drama of his emotional life. Plenty of people who complain of toothache are just upset, and he (Gilbert) has himself cured a man whose teeth were hurting because of guilt feelings about a dead sister. This is wonderful news, this broadening of the scope of dentistry. We, in our own lifetime, have seen dentistry come a long way. We recall clearly the days when a cavity was a hole that a dentist could feel by poking about with his pry. Then came X-ray, and a cavity was something that the dentist could see on the negative but the patient couldn't, and dentists would drill according to a plotted position on a chart, crashing their way through fine, sturdy old walls of enamel to get to some infinitesimal weakness far within. Now dentists are in search of guilt, not caries, and go rummaging around among the gums for signs of emotional instability. The toothpaste people will undoubtedly follow along—guilt paste, fear paste, and old Doc Lyon's psychosomatipowder.

RADIOGRAPHY

2/24/51

MODERN MEDICINE has led us down many a dead-end street, up many a stagnant backwater, following health's gleam. None of our previous excursions, though, can match last week's trip, which ended in a brand-new radiography room where the operator, a young lady, was unfamiliar with the new, bigger, faster machine and candidly admitted it. It was there, in that fateful chamber, that the old art of healing, long in decline, seemed at last to expire.

Strangely enough, our journey had started with a simple nosebleed the day before. The bleeding persisted, so our doctor suggested that we get the offending blood vessel cauterized. Obediently, we got it cauterized—a simple, early-morning nasal tuneup in the gay East Seventies. The treatment, of course, induced sneezing, and we sneezed steadily and happily while riding downtown to the office. As we stepped from our cab, we were suddenly stricken with an enormous back pain. (In middle life, the human back is spoiling for a technical knockout and will use the flimsiest excuse, even a sneeze, to fall apart.) When our pain failed to subside, we phoned our doctor and reported it, and he ordered us to start upstream again next morning, to be interviewed and photographed. This trip, as it turned out, consumed exactly five hours and wrote a new chapter in ordeal by radiography.

Some temperaments are probably well adapted to the role of guinea pig—to standing or lying in unnatural poses while somebody tries to get the hang of a new camera—but ours is not one of them. Gowned in the classic cotton tie-back frock of the X-ray victim—the frock with the plunging hipline—we exposed our bony structure for countless takes and retakes while the operator tentatively fooled with the new knobs, fought the new adjustments, and shook her pretty head over the new formulae for exposure. The machine, with its baffling wall charts, was obviously too complex for the human mind to grasp, and our sympathy at this point was with the girl. After all, we told ourself, it's no worse than taking a trial spin in a space ship, with Ed Wynn at the controls (and his bright, childish laughter at the takeoff).

An hour passed—with intervals of sitting outside in the hall waiting for plates to be developed. Gradually the idea assailed us that we were absorbing more rays than a Bikini* goat. Our back pain was almost gone—just a memory, really. Our nose showed not a trace of blood. But our condition was bad, and if we had been running the joint we would have placed ourself immediately on the critical list and prescribed massive doses of whiskey.

When the first two series of pictures failed to reveal a human spine, the operator called for help. A new girl showed up, and a conference was held, in which we were invited to join. "What d'ya say we just forget these *new* charts," murmured the consultant, "and use the old one that we always used to use" (the one, we presumed, that went with the other machine—the old, slow, reciprocating job of yesteryear). At this idea the girls brightened perceptibly, and one of them put the matter squarely up to us. "Don't you think," she asked, "that there's nothing like the old *tried* formulas?"

We mustered a tiny smile and nodded, and she disappeared behind her lead wall. "Stop breathing!" she commanded, speaking through the slot in the wall. We stopped breathing. The vast machine, goaded by the old, tried formula, retched

*The Bikini Islands in the Pacific were the site of two peacetime atomic bomb tests in July 1946 ("Operation Crossroads").

and wheezed and bored through us. "Breathe!" she cried. But there was no zest for breath any more, no grounds for inhalation, and we walked airily away, trailing the grotesque gown, along the endless corridor, toward the last dressing room.

If any doctor wants us again, he will first have to start up the breathing.

THE COLD

11/10/51

WE ARE AT THIS WRITING IN BED, entertaining our first cold of the 1951–52 virus season. It would greatly satisfy our curiosity to know at precisely what moment the virus gained entrance and took hold—for there must have been such a moment, such a division point. Prior to that moment, we were a whole man; subsequent to it, and until the symptoms appeared, we were the unwitting host to evil and corruption. One wonders about all such tremendous turning points: the moment when a child is conceived, the moment when the tide stops flooding and starts ebbing. We have often wondered at precisely what moment in life our defenses were successfully breached by another, deadlier virus—the point that marked the exact end of youth's high innocence and purity of design, the beginning of compromise, acquiescence, conformity, and the general lassitude of maturity. There must in every person's life (except a few rare ones) have been such a moment. In the case of the cold, the lag between the penetration of the disease and the appearance of the symptoms is a matter of hours; in the case of the other virus, a matter of years.

Statisticians have computed the very great interruptive strength of the common cold in our society, have shown how it slows the wheels of industry. That is only one side to the virus, however. We are such docile creatures, normally, that it takes a virus to jolt us out of life's routine. A couple of days in a fever bed are, in a sense, health-giving; the change in body temperature, the change in pulse rate, and the change of scene have a restorative effect on the system equal to the hell they raise. We heard once of a man who went to bed with a cold one day and never got up again. The seizure was soon over and his health restored, but the adventure of being in bed impressed him deeply and he felt that he had discovered his niche at last.

Medical science understands this paradox of the virus, and virus diseases are now the white hope of cancer research. (It has already been shown that they tend to congregate in cancer cells.) Thermometer in mouth, we await the day of victory, when the common cold, which has long been the butt of our anger, will emerge as the knight that slew the dragon.

CRICKET-IN-THE-EAR

9/13/52

MID-SEPTEMBER, the cricket's festival, is the hardest time of year for a friend of ours who suffers from a ringing in the ears. He tells us that at this season it is almost impossible, walking or riding in the country, to distinguish between the poetry of earth and the racket inside his own head. The sound of insects has become, for him, completely identified with personal deterioration. He doesn't know, and hasn't been able to learn from his doctor, what cricket-in-the-ear signifies, if anything, but he recalls that the Hemingway hero in "Across the River and Into the Trees" was afflicted the same way and only lasted two days—died in the back seat of an automobile after closing the door carefully and well. Our friend can't disabuse himself of the fear that he is just a day or two from dead, and it is really pitiful to see him shut a door, the care he takes.

HOSPITAL VISIT

2/16/57

MODERN MEDICINE IS A WONDERFUL THING, but we doubt whether it ever catches up with modern man, who is way out in front and running strong. One morning at the hospital, the *Times* was delivered to our breakfast table (by a woman tall enough to reach to that dizzy height) and we turned idly to an article on tranquillizers, headed "WARNS OF HEALTH PERIL." Clinicians, the article said, have found some of the effects of the drugs to be Parkinsonism, allergic dermatitis, constipation, diarrhea, jaundice, and depression. We finished our frozen juice and turned to face an entering nurse, who presented us with a tiny paper cup containing a white pill. "Take this," she said, smiling a knowing smile. We bowed and she left. We picked up the pill, examined it closely, and there, sure enough, was the familiar monogram of Miltown. Dutifully we swallowed it, and immediately felt the first symptoms of Parkinson's disease, the first faint flush of yellow jaundice. Then we looked back at the tray and noticed that our morning milk had arrived in a wax-paper carton—the same sort of carton that was in the news some months ago, suspected by scientists of being carcinogenic. Recklessly we poured the milk and raised the glass to our image in the mirror. "Cheers!" we croaked, and fell back onto the pillows, in the last stages of allergic dermatitis.

The curative value of a hospital, for us, is that it keeps us busy. In our normal life in the outside world, we seldom have anything to do from morning till night and we simply wander about, a writer who rarely writes, lonely and at peace, getting through the day cunningly, the way an alcoholic works his way along from drink to drink, cleverly spaced. But once we're in a hospital, the nights and days are crowded with events and accomplishment. Supper is at six, breakfast at nine, which means that for about fifteen hours we subsist in a semistarved condition, like a man in a lifeboat; and when our stomach is empty our mind and heart are full, and we are up and about, doing housework, catching up on correspondence, outwitting the air-conditioning system, taking sleeping pills, reading names on nurses' badges, arranging flowers, picking up after

117

the last tenant, fighting the roller shade that has lost its spring, making plans for death, inventing dodges to circumvent therapy, attaching a string to the bed table to render it accessible to the immobilized patient, flushing undesirable medication down the toilet, prying into the private affairs of the floor nurse, gazing out at the wheeling planets and the lovely arabesques of the Jersey shore. Dawn comes, and an early nurse, to test with her little fingers whether our heart still beats. And then we shave and practice counting to fifteen, so that when they jab us with Sodium Pentothal and ask us to count, we can race them to the knockout. Busyness is really the solution to a man's life, in this cold sunless clime. And a hospital is the place.

THE ICE DANCE

3/23/35

THE WINTER ends on a clear, high note with the fabulous ice extravaganza at the Garden.* Skating, which has a sort of cold purity anyway, has suddenly come to be one of the most exciting expressions—to us the ice dance is potentially a greater thing than the dance. If we were a student of the dance, we'd sell our little shoon and buy ourself a pair of skates; there is a sublimity about skating, cold as a fountain, warm-blooded as love, extra-dimensional, an ecstatic emancipation which Maude Adams hinted at when, trussed up by a wire, she flew across the stage and translated every child's dream. A few skaters have begun to realize what can be done in musical interpretation, have given up acrobatics and grapevines, and

*The Skating Club of New York sponsored a sold-out international ice-skating show March 13, 1935 at Madison Square Garden benefiting Bellevue Hospital Social Relief Service. Vivi-Ann Hulten was the Swedish skater, Louise Bertram and Stewart Reburn the Canadian skaters. Maude Adams was an American actress who played Peter Pan on stage in 1905.

settled down to set their skates to music. We remember Grafstrom, the Swede; he was an inspired dancer, the first we ever saw. The other night Miss Hulten, also of Sweden, gave a beautiful exhibition, and so did a pair from Toronto, dancing to "Isle of Capri." The Garden, in half-darkness, seemed to cohere, faces in shadow, the spotlight trailing the silvery course of the dance—a really thrilling thing to watch. Ice is an odd substance to have at last freed the body in its persistent attempt to catch up with the spirit.

8

Science

MYSTERIES OF LIFE

9/22/28

ABOUT ONCE A YEAR the human soul gets into the papers, when the British scientists convene. Once a year the mystery of life, the riddle of death, are either cleared up or left hanging. The reports of the learned men enthrall us, and there have been moments when we've felt that we were really approaching an understanding of life's secret. We experienced one of those moments the other morning, reading a long article on the chemistry of the cell. Unfortunately, when we finished we happened to glance into our goldfish tank and saw there a new inhabitant. Frisky, our pet snail, had given birth to a tiny son while our back was turned. The baby mollusk was even then hunching along the glassy depths, wiggling his feelers, shaking his whelky head. Nothing about Frisky's appearance or conduct had given us the slightest intimation of the blessed event; and gazing at the little newcomer, we grew very humble, and threw the morning paper away. Life was as mysterious as ever.

SEEING THINGS

2/18/28

THE NEW REPTILE HALL was officially opened a few days ago in the Museum of Natural History and we visited it amidst a group of youngsters who kept crying "Good night!" and their mothers who kept murmuring "Mercy!" The place is like that. It might be called the Conan Doyle Hall, with certain exhibits marked: "Strong Influence of Lewis Carroll." Things out of the dead worlds of Sir Arthur's writings and Mr. Carroll's "Looking Glass" are here but you have to accept the word of eminent scientists that they once lived. Place of honor goes to the dragon lizards which, brought from the Dutch West Indies, lived for a while at the Bronx Zoo. They look like dinosaurs reduced nine-tenths and, in fact, were spotted for dinosaurs by excited travellers who saw them rear up on their hind legs at a distance and gave the Sunday papers an annual feature story for ten years until the Museum went down and caught a few. The largest is nine feet long.

Even taking into account the grimly handsome Sphlenodon, which looks exactly like William Boyd in the last act of "What Price Glory," we like most the group of fat Brazilian horned frogs which have soft velvety black and green heads and must have been cronies of Tweedledum and his brother. Some of the exhibits tie up neatly with literature, such as the Russell's Viper, which has the title rôle in the Sherlock Holmes story, "The Speckled Band," and the tiny mongoose which is the Rikki-tikki-tavi of Kipling's tales. The mongoose is shown snapping its fingers at a King Cobra, which mongooses devote their life to chivvying about and killing, thus becoming, in our opinion, the world's bravest animal.

In one case reposes the world's largest frog, and although right next door is a tiny reptile whose sex life and fighting skill are described minutely, the sign by the world's largest frog frankly says, "Nothing is known of its habits," thus giving us an example of the oddities of scientific research to ponder about the rest of our life. All the snakes are here, including one with no card telling what it is, and the Green Mamba, which is as lovely as a jade necklace and as poisonous as the devil. The snake that interested us most, though, is the Pine Snake, for this is the one the lady snake charmers play with, and it is described as harmless and of very gentle disposition, the worst it ever does being to make a noise like a hot iron plunged into water.

We never go to the Museum but we look up two favorite exhibits of ours. One is the incredible raccoon bear, a cross between those two animals and, we like to believe, a sheer figment of the craftsmanship of the whimsical doctor who said he found one in Tibet. The other is the thirty-six-ton siderite which Peary* brought back from Greenland after two vain tries. The sign tells of the immensity of the task and relates that the mammoth hunk of almost pure iron was finally brought here and given to the museum. But how this was done is left to our imagination, which never fails to be both interested and baffled.

TECHNOLOGICAL PROGRESS

7/13/35

ON A ROCKY ISLAND in the blue sea, shining white, its tall tower naked and beautiful in the sun, a lighthouse stood, abandoned. We passed by in a boat, remembering when the place was full of life, the keeper tending his light and drawing his pay, his wife hanging out flannel drawers to the seabreeze, his children, like Captain January's daughter, roving the island, watching the ships. Now, in the channel, three or four hundred yards off the rocks, is a gas buoy, winking its mechanical warning, supplanting a whole family. To us, an idle mariner on a painted ocean, the empty lighthouse seemed a symbol of all that is going on in the world: new devices putting men and their families out of work. As we passed the forsaken island and stared at the boarded-up windows and thought about the fam-

*Robert Edwin Peary, arctic explorer who reached the North Pole April 6, 1909.

ily applying for relief and the Congress worrying about new taxes to provide the dole, we wondered whether it wouldn't just have been simpler, somehow, for the government never to have bought a gas buoy. Is it really cheaper to support a lighthouse keeper on relief than to support him in his lighthouse? Science, blessing us with gas buoys, is a hard master and perhaps an evil one, giving us steel for flesh, dole for wages, solving every problem save the essential one: what to do about the pride of a former lighthouse-keeper, who doesn't want relief, who wants bread earned by toil, seeing his light shine afar.

Of course, the defenders of scientific progress claim that for every displaced victim of technology, there is a new job opening up—if not in the service industries, or in entertainment, then in the field of invention. Maybe this is true. Certainly there are some queer new jobs that one hears about these days. There is the engineer, for instance, who carved out a niche for himself in the world by devising an apparatus which copes with the problem of the flies which hover by the thousands over the manure beds on mushroom farms. A huge fan sucks the flies across a refrigerating coil, which chills them and drops them, dormant, into large milk cans. The lids are then clamped on the milk cans and the flies are shipped to frog-growers, who chill them again and serve them, with a dash of bitters, to frogs. Maybe some ex-lighthouse-keeper can busy himself, in our brave new world, by thinking up something nifty like that.

GRAVITY

4/3/37

IT SEEMS AS THOUGH NO LAWS, not even fairly old ones, can safely be regarded as unassailable. The force of gravity, which we have always ascribed to the "pull of the earth," was reinterpreted the other day by a scientist who says that when we fall it is not earth pulling us, it is heaven pushing us. This blasts the rock on which we sit. If science can do a rightabout-face on a thing as fundamental as gravity, maybe Newton was a sucker not to have just eaten the apple.

There's one thing about this new gravitational theory, though: it explains the fierce, frenzied noise that big airplanes make, fighting their way through the inhospitable sky. We now know that a plane, roaring through the air, is not straining against the attraction of one friendly earth, but is sneering loudly at the repulsion of innumerable stars.

SILENCE OF THE SPHERES

10/30/48

ASTRONOMY IS NO LONGER a mere matter of gazing at the stars; one must listen to them, too. The Milky Way sends on a frequency of 14.2 megacycles. The other galaxies and the sun maintain a tighter broadcasting schedule than N. B. C. There is, in fact, a sort of cosmic signal always going out to the earth, and the new equipment of our astrophysicists enables them to hear it as plainly as a soap opera. It sounds, in the words of a Harvard listener, "like a combination of gravel falling on the roof and the howling of wolves." If we remember right, the *silence* of the spheres had something to do with the conversion of Pascal: he discovered faith when he became conscious of

silence. Little did he know how noisy his world was, how deceptive silence can be (and the nearness of wolves and the steady
rain of gravel).

The time in our own life when we came closest to being
convinced by silence was one time at sea in a light fall of snow.
We heard nothing—no gravel, no wind, no wave, no wolves, no
bell buoy. It was convincing and it was beautiful. We are sorry
to learn, at this date, that there was nothing to it.

HOT PIPES

3/1/52

WE READ A NEWS STORY the other day telling about the
withdrawal of a group of young atomic scientists from the
world. When the doors closed behind them, these fellows entered a life as pure and as remote as that of a monk on a
mountaintop. Instead of disappearing into puffs of cumulus
clouds, they vanished into the swirling mists of secrecy. It gave
us quite a turn, secrecy being the slow death of science, purity
its most debilitating quality. Science can't possibly serve people
well till it belongs openly to all and associates itself with wisdom
and sense—those contaminating but healthful influences.

We saw a remarkable example, recently, of an architect's
remoteness from the world—as though he had withdrawn to
his own private mountaintop. We chanced to pay a visit to a
student's dormitory room in an engineering college, to see how
things were going. The building was a modern one, and of
course the designer must have had access to the vast storehouse
of technical knowledge that the institution had assembled
through the years, so we expected to find something pretty
good in the way of digs—something sensible, if modest. What
we found was an immaculate little torture chamber suitable for
cremating a cat in. The temperature was 92°. Two large steam-

pipes extended from floor to ceiling. These supplied constant heat, day and night. The only way to subdue the hot pipes was to open the window. The only place the bed would fit was under the window. The student admitted, under close questioning, that his living conditions were less than marginal and said he'd already been to the infirmary with a stiff neck caused by extreme exposure. He was not at all disgruntled, however, and was at work on a counter architectural wonder of his own—a system of baffles to carry the cold outside air directly onto the hot pipes, bypassing the bed, confounding the original designer, raising the institution's fuel bill, and investing the room with a Goldbergian quality proper to youth. We looked over his schedule while we were there. One of his courses was something called Heat Engineering. Probably the architect who designed the room took the same course, years ago, and got honors. But it isn't enough that a designer understand Heat Engineering to save humanity, he must have once slept next to a hot pipe.

FRED ON SPACE

11/16/57

WHEN THE NEWS BROKE about the dog in the sky, I went down into the shabby woods below my dump to see if Fred's ghost was walking. Fred* is a dead dachshund of mine. He is restless in death, as he was in life, and I often encounter his

---

*White said of Fred, "Of all the dogs whom I have served I've never known one who understood so much of what I say or held it in such deep contempt." Fred was a main character in several essays: "Bedfellows" and "Death of a Pig" (*Essays*) and "Dog Training" and "A Week in November" (*One Man's Meat*). Fred was a spirited individualist and White continued to admire him long after his death in 1948. The "dog in the sky" Fred and White are discussing in this piece was the first animal launched in a space capsule (the Soviets' Sputnik 2, November 1957).

ghost wandering about in the dingle where his grave is. There are a couple of wild apple trees down there, struggling among hackmatacks to gain light. A grapevine strangles one of these trees in its strong, purple grip. The place is brambly, rank with weeds, and full of graves and the spirits of the departed. Partridges like it, and so do skunks and porcupines and red squirrels, so it is an ideal spot for Fred's ghost. I went down because I felt confused about the Russian satellite and wanted to interview Fred on the subject. He was an objectionable dog, but I learned a lot from him, and on this occasion I felt that his views on outer space would be instructive.

Fred's ghost was there, just as I suspected it might be. The ghost pretended not to notice me as I entered the woods, but that was a characteristic of Fred's—pretending not to notice one's arrival. Fred went to Hell when he died, but his shade is not touchy about it. "I regret nothing," it told me once. The ghost appeared to be smoking a cigar as I bearded him for the interview. The interview follows, as near as I can recapture it from memory:

Q—The Soviet Union, as you probably know, Fred, has launched a second rocket into space. This one contains a female dog. Would you care to comment on this event?

A—Yes. They put the wrong dog in it.

Q—How do you mean?

A—If they wanted to get rid of a dog the hard way, they should have used that thing you have up at the house these days—that black puppy you call Augie. There's the dog for outer space.

Q—Why?

A—Because he's a lightweight. Perfect for floating through space, vomiting as he goes.

Q—Vomiting? You think, then, that nausea sets in when the pull of gravity ceases?

(Fred's lips curled back, revealing a trace of wispy foam. He seemed to be smiling his old knowing smile.)

A—Certainly it does. Can you imagine the conditions inside that capsule? What a contribution to make to the firmament!

Q—As an ex-dog, how do you feel about space in general? Do you think Man will emancipate himself by his experiments with rockets?

A—If you ask me, space has backfired already.

Q—Backfired?

A—Sure. Men think they need more space, so what happens? They put a dog in a strait jacket. No space at all, the poor bitch. I got more space in Hell than this Russian pooch, who is also sick at her stomach. Hell is quite roomy; I like that about it.

Q—The Russian dog is said to be travelling at seventeen thousand eight hundred and forty miles an hour. Do you care to comment on that?

A—Remember the day I found that woodchuck down by the boathouse? Seventeen thousand miles an hour! Don't make me laugh. I was doing a good eighteen if I was moving at all, and I wasn't orbiting, either. Who wants to orbit? You go around the earth once, you've had it.

Q—News accounts from Moscow this morning say the space dog is behaving quietly and happily. Do you believe it?

A—Of course not. There's a contradiction in terms right there. If the bitch was happy, she wouldn't be quiet, she'd be carrying on. The Russians are a bunch of soberpusses; they don't know what clowning means. They ring a bell when it's time for a dog to eat. You never had to ring a bell for me, Buster.

(This was quite true. But I felt that I would learn nothing if Fred's ghost started reminiscing, and I tried hard to keep the interview on the track.)

Q—The Russians picked a laika to occupy the space capsule. Do you think a dachshund would have been a wiser choice?

A—Certainly. But a dachshund has better things to do. When a car drives in the yard, there are four wheels, all of them crying to be smelled. The secrets I used to unlock in the old days when that fish truck drove in! Brother! If a dog is going to unlock any secrets, don't send him into space, let him smell what's going on right at home.

Q—The fame of the Russian dog is based on the fact that it has travelled farther from the earth than any other living creature. Do you feel that this is a good reason for eminence?

A—I don't know about fame. But the way things are shaping up on earth, the farther away anybody can get from it these days, the better.

Q—Dog lovers all over the world are deeply concerned about the use of a dog in space experiments. What is your reaction?

A—Dog lovers are the silliest group of people to be found anywhere. They're even crazier than physicists. You should hear the sessions we have in Hell on the subject of dog lovers! If they ever put a man in one of those capsules for a ride out yonder, I hope it's a dog lover.

(Fred's shade thinned slightly and undulated, as though he was racked with inner mirth.)

Q—This satellite with a dog aboard is a very serious thing for all of us. It may be critical. All sorts of secrets may be unlocked. Do you believe that man at last may learn the secret of the sun?

A—No chance. Men have had hundreds of thousands of years to learn the secret of the sun, which is so simple every dog knows it. A dog knows enough to go lie down in the sun when he feels lazy. Does a man lie down in the sun? No, he blasts a dog off, with instruments to find out his blood pressure. You will note, too, that a dog never makes the mistake of lying in the hot sun right after a heavy meal. A dog lies in the sun early in the day, after a light breakfast, when the muscles need massaging by the gentle heat and the spirit craves the companionship of warmth, when the flies crawl on the warm, painted surfaces and the bugs crawl, and the day settles into its solemn stride, and the little bantam hen steals away into the blackberry bushes. That is the whole secret of the sun—to receive it willingly. What more is there to unlock? I find I miss the sun: Hell's heat is rather unsettling, like air-conditioning. I should have lain around more while I was on earth.

Q—Thank you for your remarks. One more question. Do you feel that humans can adapt to space?

A—My experience with humans, unfortunately, was largely confined to my experience with you. But even that limited association taught me that humans have no capacity for adapting themselves to anything at all. Furthermore, they have no *intention* of adapting themselves. Human beings are motivated by a deeply rooted desire to change their environment and make *it* adapt to them. Men won't adapt to space, space will adapt to men—and that'll be a mess, too. If you ever get to the moon, you will unquestionably begin raising the devil with the moon. Speaking of that, I was up around the house the other evening and I see you are remodelling your back kitchen—knocking a wall out, building new counters with a harder surface, and installing a washing machine instead of those old set tubs. Still at it, eh, Buster? Well, it's been amusing seeing you again.

Q—One more question, please, Fred. The dog in the capsule

has caused great apprehension all over the civilized world. Is this apprehension justified?

A—Yes. The presence anywhere at all of an inquisitive man is cause for alarm. A dog's curiosity is wholesome; it is essentially selfish and purposeful and therefore harmless. It relates to the chase or to some priceless bit of local havoc, like my experiments in your barnyard with the legs of living sheep. A man's curiosity, on the other hand, is untinged with immediate mischief; it is pure and therefore very dangerous. The excuse you men give is that you must continually add to the store of human knowledge—a store that already resembles a supermarket and is beginning to hypnotize the customers. Can you imagine a laika sending up a Russian in order to measure the heartbeat of a man? It's inconceivable. No dog would fritter away his time on earth with such tiresome tricks. A dog's curiosity leads him into pretty country and toward predictable trouble, such as a porcupine quill in the nose. Man's curiosity has led finally to outer space where rabbits are as scarce as gravity. Well, you fellows can have outer space. You may eventually get a quill in the nose from some hedgehog of your own manufacture, but I don't envy you the chase. So long, old Master! Dream your fevered dreams!

9

The Academic Life

NO CRACKPOTS?

9/12/42

WE NOTICED, with some misgivings, that the American Federation of Teachers put out a warning the other day that there would be no "crackpots" admitted to its membership. Only those teachers would be admitted who would be a credit to the Federation and instill in boys and girls an abiding loyalty to the ideals and principles of democracy. But as we understand it, one of the noblest attributes of democracy is that it contains no one who can truthfully say, of two pots, which is the cracked, which is the whole. That is basic. The Federation better welcome all comers, and let pot clink against pot.

Education is such a serious matter, we speak of it with trepidation. We remember, with sober and contrite heart, that our educational system was responsible for (among others) the group of citizens who for two years did everything in their power to prove that the war which was going on did not involve us, that nothing was happening abroad which was of any consequence in our lives, that the earth was not round. Those people—millions of them—were all educated in American schools by non-crackpots. They were brought up on American curricula. They damn near did us in. They are ready again to do us in, as soon as an opening presents itself—which will be immediately after hostilities cease. On the basis of the record, it would seem that we need what crackpots we can muster for education in our new world. We need educators who believe that character is more precious than special knowledge, that vision is not just something arrived at through a well-ground lens, and that a child is the most hopeful (and historically the most neglected) property the Republic boasts.

ACADEMIC FREEDOM

2/26/49

WHEN THE PROFESSORS were dismissed from the University of Washington,* the president remarked that allegiance to the Communist Party unfitted a teacher for the search for truth. The argument, it seemed to us, had a certain merit. To pursue truth, one should not be too deeply entrenched in any hole. It is best to have strong curiosity, weak affiliations. But although it's easy to dismiss a professor or make him sign an affidavit, it is not so easy to dismiss the issue of academic freedom, which persists on campuses as the smell of wintergreen oil persists in the locker rooms. In this land, an ousted professor is not an island entire of itself; his death diminishes us all.

There is no question but that colleges and universities these days are under pressure from alumni and trustees to clean house and to provide dynamic instruction in the American way of life. Some institutions (notably Washington University and Olivet College) have already taken steps, others are uneasily going over their lists. Professors, meanwhile, adjust their neckties a little more conservatively in the morning, qualify their irregular remarks with a bit more care. The head of one small college announced the other day that his institution was through fooling around with fuzzy ideas and was going to buckle down and teach straight Americanism—which, from his description, sounded as simple as the manual of arms. At Cornell, an alumnus recently advocated that the university install a course in "Our Freedoms"—possibly a laudable idea but one that struck us as being full of dynamite. (The trouble here is with the word "our," which is too constricting and which would tend to associate a university with a national philosophy, as when the German universities felt the cold hand of the Ministry of Propaganda.) President Eisenhower† has come out with

---

*Herbert J. Phillips and Joseph Butterworth were dismissed because of membership in the Communist Party; Ralph H. Gundlach, who denied that he was a member, was dismissed for "neglect of duty" and an "ambiguous" relationship to the party. Three other professors who admitted that they were once members of the party but had left it were placed on probation. The University of Washington's president was Raymond B. Allen.

†Dwight D. Eisenhower was president of Columbia University from 1948 to

a more solid suggestion, and has stated firmly that Columbia, while admiring one idea, will examine all ideas. He seems to us to have the best grasp of where the strength of America lies.

We on this magazine believe in the principle of hiring and firing on the basis of fitness, and we have no opinion as to the fitness or unfitness of the fired professors. We also believe that some of the firings in this country in the last eighteen months have resembled a political purge, rather than a dismissal for individual unfitness, and we think this is bad for everybody. Hollywood fired its writers in a block of ten. The University of Washington stood its professors up in a block of six, fired three for political wrongness, retained three on probation. Regardless of the fitness or unfitness of these men for their jobs, this is not good management; it is nervous management and it suggests pressure. Indirectly, it abets Communism by making millions of highly fit Americans a little cautious, a little fearful of having naughty "thoughts," a little fearful of believing differently from the next man, a little worried about associating with a group or party or club.

A healthy university in a healthy democracy is a free society in miniature. The pesky nature of democratic life is that it has no comfortable rigidity; it always hangs by a thread, never quite submits to consolidation or solidification, is always being challenged, always being defended. The seeming insubstantiality of this thread is a matter of concern and worry to persons who naturally would prefer a more robust support for the beloved structure. The thread is particularly worrisome, we think, to men of tidy habits and large affairs, who are accustomed to reinforce themselves at every possible turn and who want to do as much for their alma mater. But they do not always perceive that the elasticity of democracy is its strength—like the web of a spider, which bends but holds. The desire to give the whole thing greater rigidity and a more conventional set of fastenings is almost overwhelming in these times when the strain is great, and it makes professed lovers of liberty propose measures that show little real faith in liberty.

We believe with President Eisenhower that a university can

1952; in 1950 he took a leave of absence from Columbia to serve as Supreme Allied Commander of the North Atlantic Treaty Organization. In 1952 he was elected President of the United States.

best demonstrate freedom by not closing its doors to antitheti-
cal ideas. We believe that teachers should be fired not in blocks
of three for political wrongness but in blocks of one for unfitness. A campus is unique. It is above and beyond government.
It is on the highest plane of life. Those who live there know the
smell of good air, and they always take pains to spell truth with
a small "t." This is its secret strength and its contribution to the
web of freedom; this is why the reading room of a college
library is the very temple of democracy.

SELECTING SCHOOL BOOKS

10/8/49

THE BOARD OF EDUCATION has twenty-three criteria for
selecting textbooks, library books, and magazines for use in the
public schools. We learned this by reading a fourteen-page
pamphlet published by the Board explaining how it makes its
choice. One criterion is: "Is it [the book or magazine] free from
subject matter that tends to irreverence for things held sacred?" Another criterion is: "Are both sides of controversial
issues presented with fairness?" Another: "Is it free from objectionable slang expressions which will interfere with the building of good language habits?"

These three criteria by themselves are enough to keep a lot
of good books from the schools. Irreverence for things held
sacred has started many a writer on his way, and will again. An
author so little moved by a controversy that he can present
both sides fairly is not likely to burn any holes in the paper. We
think the way for school children to get both sides of a controversy is to read several books on the subject, not one. In other
words, we think the Board should strive for a well-balanced
library, not a well-balanced book. The greatest books are heavily slanted, by the nature of greatness.

As for "the building of good language habits," we have gone

carefully through the pamphlet to see what habits, if any, the Board itself has formed. They appear to be the usual ones—the habit of untidiness, the habit of ambiguity, the habit of saying everything the hard way. The clumsy phrase, the impenetrable sentence, the cliché, the misspelled word. The Board has, we gather, no strong convictions about the use of the serial comma, no grip on "that" and "which," no opinion about whether a textbook is a "text book," a "text-book," or a "textbook." (The score at the end of the fourteenth was "text book" 5, "text-book" 11, "textbook" 5.) It sees nothing comical, or challenging, in the sentence "Materials should be provided for boys and girls who vary greatly in attitudes, abilities, interests, and mental age." It sees no need for transposition in "Phrases should not be split in captions under pictures." It sees no bugs in "The number of lines should be most conducive to readability." And you should excuse the expression "bugs"—a slang word, interfering with the building of good language habits.

We still have high hopes of getting *The New Yorker* accepted in the schools, but our hopes are less high than they were when we picked up the pamphlet. We're bucking some stiff criteria— criteria that are, shall we say, time-tested?

THE LIVING LANGUAGE

2/23/57

BETWEEN BERGEN EVANS on the television and a man named Ellsworth Barnard* in the papers, English usage has become hot news; the rhetorical world is almost as tense, at the moment, as the Middle East. Professor Barnard wrote a piece

---

*Evans hosted "The Last Word" on CBS; Bernard's article in the New York *Times*, "Good Grammar Ain't Good Usage" (17 Jan. 1957: VI, 20), brought a number of responses from readers, some of which the *Times* printed (10 Feb. 1957: VI, 15).

in the *Times* a while back thumbing his nose at grammar and advising teachers to quit boring their pupils with the problem of "who" and "whom." The Professor was immediately ambushed by grammarians and purists in great numbers, and their shafts came zinging from behind every tree in the forest. Meanwhile, Bergen Evans and his panelists were stirring up the masses and egging them on to err. Mr. Evans believes that the language is a living thing and we mustn't strangle it by slavish attention to the rules. Winston Cigarettes, of course, backs him to the hilt, as a cigarette should.* Our prediction is that along Madison Avenue bad grammar, as an attention-getter, will soon be as popular as mutilation—which started with an eye patch and rapidly spread to arms and legs. As Arthur Godfrey sometimes remarks, in one of his contemplative moments, "Who's sponsoring this mess?"

The New Yorker has been up to its ears in English usage for thirty-two years (thirty-two years this very week) and has tried to dwell harmoniously in the weird, turbulent region between a handful of sober grammarians, who live in, and an army of high-spirited writers, who live wherever they can get a foothold. The writer of this paragraph, who also lives in, has seen with his own eyes the nasty chop that is kicked up when the tide of established usage runs against the winds of creation. We have seen heavy, cluttery pieces, with faults clinging to them like barnacles, lifted out of their trouble by the accurate fire of the grammarian (who has the instincts of a machine gunner), and we have also seen the blush removed from a peach by the same fellow's shaving it with an electric razor in the hope of drawing blood. Somewhere in the middle of this mess lies editorial peace and goodness, but, like we say, it's a weird world. Through the turmoil and the whirling waters we have reached a couple of opinions of our own about the language. One is that a schoolchild should be taught grammar—for the same reason that a medical student should study anatomy. Having learned about the exciting mysteries of an English sentence, the child can then go forth and speak and write any damn way he pleases. We knew a countryman once who spoke with wonderful vigor and charm, but ungrammatically. In him the absence

*Winston's advertising jingle was "Winston tastes good like a cigarette should."

142

of grammar made little difference, because his speech was full of juice. But when a dullard speaks in a slovenly way, his speech suffers not merely from dullness but from ignorance, and his whole life, in a sense, suffers—though he may not feel pain.

The living language is like a cowpath: it is the creation of the cows themselves, who, having created it, follow it or depart from it according to their whims or their needs. From daily use, the path undergoes change. A cow is under no obligation to stay in the narrow path she helped make, following the contour of the land, but she often profits by staying with it and she would be handicapped if she didn't know where it was and where it led to. Children obviously do not depend for communication on a knowledge of grammar; they rely on their ear, mostly, which is sharp and quick. But we have yet to see the child who hasn't profited from coming face to face with a relative pronoun at an early age, and from reading books, which follow the paths of centuries.

10

Business

DOG EAT DOG

4/1/33

MOST IMPERATIVE OF RECENT MISSIVES was a letter from *Forbes,* reminding us that we are not a bluebird. "You are not a bluebird," the letter said, gruffly, and then added, "you are a business man." There was a kind of finality about this news, and we read on. "Business is a hard, cold-blooded game today. Survival of the fittest. Dog eat dog. Produce or get out. A hundred men are after your job." If *Forbes* only knew it, goading of this sort is the wrong treatment for us. We are not, as they say, a bluebird. Nobody who reads the *Nation* regularly, as we do, can retain his amateur bluebird standing. As for business, we agree that it is a hard, cold-blooded game. Survival of the fittest. Dog eat dog. The fact that about eighty-five per cent of the dogs have recently been eaten by the other dogs perhaps explains what long ago we noticed about business: that it had a strong smell of boloney. If dog continues to eat dog, there will be only one dog left, and he will be sick to his stomach.

STRIKES

8/6/27

AS WE RODE COMFORTABLY in the subway on the day set for the transit strike, the thought came to us that strikes are not what they used to be. We mourn the old days when workers would quit their jobs in a spontaneous burst of rebelliousness and high blood-pressure. Lately, strikes have been produced in the calm manner of musical comedies, with advance announcements of the cast, date of opening, and photographs of the strike-breakers learning their duties from the smiling, expectant strikers. The police are notified in advance that riots will begin at 2:30, the same as any matinée. No wonder labor is disgruntled; it's as bad as community singing.

PREDATORY

3/19/27

AS PERNICIOUS A PIECE OF chicanery as was ever perpetrated is the inspired work of one H. W. Miller, who gave up his seat on the Stock Exchange recently, and since then has been devoting his time to calling upon friends during office hours, seemingly for no particular reason. He shows up unannounced, relaxes in a chair, talks half an hour about curiously dull subjects, makes it clear that he is in no hurry, and finally makes a vague exit without giving any reason for having dropped in. This has left his friends weak, irritable, and bewildered.

It now turns out that the merry stock merchant, finding himself relieved of work, deliberately armed himself with a sheaf of inanities, stale jokes, and platitudes, and set forth to avenge himself heartily for all the time he had been unnecessarily interrupted during business for the past ten years.

"I am going to do this for two weeks," he said when cornered, "and then I'm going to the country."

This, in our judgment, has something of the fine deliberateness of the bored ex-aviator who bought a Ford when the war was over, installed an airplane engine and a very loud horn, took aboard some ballast, and went abroad in the land insultingly showing his dust to every Lincoln and Stutz from here to Yosemite. That is the actual case, although we don't know the man's name. We do know that he occupied himself pleasantly that way for more than a year, hiding down lanes and waiting for his prey.

WHAT EVERY ADULT SHOULD KNOW

12/31/27

INSURANCE SALESMEN HAVE ALWAYS BEEN glamorous in our eyes, because they go to places we wouldn't dare go and face odds that would make us quail. While we were lunching with one of these dare-devils last week (he had been in our psychology class at college) he unexpectedly confessed all. He told us that the reason it is possible to make what seem to be impossible sales is that the average man secretly believes he can argue the hide off any salesman, and likes to hear himself try. Once he starts arguing, he hangs himself.

After listening to our friend's disclosures, we are in a position to reveal the cardinal principle for insulating oneself against insurance. It is: always make the wrong answer to the salesman's questions, which are all scientifically designed to bring forth the answer Yes. Your salvation lies in saying No. He will, of course, expect you to take the soundness and the general worthiness of the idea of insurance for granted. This never comes into question. Then he will start off very candidly with some such disarming question as this:

"Now, Mr. Fish, as you know I have come to see you about insurance. I assume, sir, that a man of your business integrity has already made provision against unforeseen circumstances, *haven't you?*" (You say Yes.) "Just as a matter of sound business sense you have created an estate for the protection of your wife, *haven't you?*" (You say Yes.) "Furthermore, I assume that you wish your son Roger to enjoy the educational advantages in life that he deserves, *don't you?*" (Another Yes.)

Well, if you say Yes to all these questions you are a goner because he has a whole string of others calling for affirmative answers which lead inevitably to the execution of a policy. The only safe answer, as we said, is No. If you say No he will still go on trying to sell you insurance but he will be too stunned and dazed to accomplish anything.

A good variation is to say, when the salesman refers to your wife: "I left my wife last week." When he speaks of your son, who will soon be ready for college, bite your lips and say that unfortunately your marriage was childless.

Our friend also informs us that in this business they no longer use the term "to sign" a thing; they say: "to write your name." The word "sign" has come to have a sinister tone. Don't let this trick fool you—writing your name is just as binding.

TADPOLES AND TELEPHONES

6/2/28

THERE WAS A LARGE BOWL of tadpoles in the window of the Telephone Building as we came wandering along, lonely as a cloud. We stopped of course—we stop for anything in windows, particularly tadpoles. A sign said: THE TADPOLE REMINDS US. It told how the unfortunate creature, gloomily metamorphic, is forced to rise at intervals to the surface of the water in order to breathe; and it compared his fate to that of the unfortunate business man who has no telephone on his desk and has to rise and leave his work whenever there is a call. It was a fine and a beautiful little object lesson, and we stood enthralled for fifteen minutes, hoping to verify the truth of this neat biological phenomenon, brooding on its neat analogy. The tadpoles, however, seemed not to rise: they rested lazily on the bottom. After ten minutes of waiting we began to shift uneasily from one foot to the other. Still no tadpoles rose to the surface. Could the Telephone Company be wrong? The truth finally seeped into our consciousness: the tadpoles had sensibly *given up* rising to the surface, wise little frogs! We departed, vowing never to answer the phone again.

TRUTH-IN-ADVERTISING

7/11/36

THE TRUTH-IN-ADVERTISING movement has just celebrated its silver jubilee, and everybody laughed when it stepped up to the piano. Advertising is almost the only profession which has spent twenty-five years worrying about its own good character. Most types of enterprise never give truth a second thought, but advertising people are not like that: they keep truth in front of them all the time, brooding dreamily about it while writing the long, long drama of mouth hygiene. They worry so furiously about truth, one suspects they read each other's copy. All this is confusing to the consumer, who has a double responsibility toward advertising, being obliged to read it and keep up with it and buy products on the strength of it, and at the same time sympathize with the advertiser's devotion to truth.

In our opinion, nobody has done justice, artistically, to advertising. It is patently America's major contribution to present-day culture; yet the only books, analytical or critical, we have seen on the subject have been either textbooks, which are dull and special, or books debunking advertising, which are ill-tempered, humorless, and out-of-date before they get into print. The key to the advertising heart (and none of the writers on the subject seems to have grasped this) is this very search for elusive truth, the kind of search that took Byrd to the South Pole even though he knew there was nothing there, the kind of search which after twenty-five years still takes its pilgrims to Boston to a meeting of the Advertising Federation of America, there to rededicate themselves to the principles of the Baltimore convention of 1931. It is this feeling for truth which sets up a local irritation in the breasts of those who have given themselves to the fantasia of depilatories and emollients. They know that the hair must be removed from ladies' arms and men's jowls, yet in the pain of literary composition they find themselves kin to Edgar Allan Poe and Arthur Guy Empey. They are obliged to express an idea on paper, and this takes them into the world of literary creation, artistic jealousy, and truth.

The consumer, if left to his own devices, would no more expect truth in advertising than he would expect honesty in parenthood; after all, it is reasonable to suppose that a manufacturer is biassed about his own product, in the same way that a parent is over-appreciative of his own child. "Advertising," said Mrs. William Brown Meloney at the silver jubilee of truth, "must be the herald of the new and greater world into which we are entering." And one suddenly gets a picture of the devotees exhausted by their zeal, entering into the new and greater world by getting a lift from a nationally advertised cigarette.

Advertisers are the interpreters of our dreams—Joseph interpreting for Pharoah. Like the movies, they infect the routine futility of our days with purposeful adventure. Their weapons are our weaknesses: fear, ambition, illness, pride, selfishness, desire, ignorance. And these weapons must be kept bright as a sword. We rise to eat a breakfast cereal which will give us strength for the tasks of the day; we vanquish the excesses of the night with an alkaline fizz; we cleanse our gums, stifle our bad odors, adorn our diseased bodies, and go forth to conquer—

cheered on with a thousand slogans, devices, lucubrations. What folly for our leaders to meet in Boston in quest of an unwonted truth! We live by fiction. By fiction alone can Man get through the day.

RAVISHED LIPS

4/10/37

WE DO NOT PROFESS TO understand the philosophy of merchandising, but we are willing to go on studying it, just as we have for many years. On the radio we heard a voice say that Angelus lipstick kept lips "ravishing yet virginal." It seems to us highly important to examine this apparent contradiction and to find out where the manufacturer really stands on the question, what his desires and hopes are for the girls who use his product. Does he want them to be ravished, or does he want them to remain virgins? If his desire is that they look ravishing, yet remain untarnished, then what are his feelings, if any, toward the males for whose benefit the cosmetic is applied and whose lot it is to be attracted yet repelled? We think the public has a right to inquire into these things, and be instructed. It is possible that a manufacturer of lipstick has no genuine interest in the potentials of his product. It is also possible that we men, faced with women who are equipped to be both maid and wanton, are deliberately being taken for a sleigh ride.

Bourjois, the scent-maker, points out that romance doesn't just happen: it is won by wearing a perfume called Evening in Paris. And there is the daring new odeur, Gabilla's Sinful Soul, exotic and naughty. One would say that ladies are now enabled to ask, in the language of the odeur, for love licit or illicit, for enduring fidelity or for the wanton tweak. Let us hope that the ladies, with their fragrances, are not embarrassed by a too great confidence in the New York male's sense of smell, debauched as it is by blowing dust, burned motor fuels, and desiccating office heat. How can the ladies tell, anyway, what smells are associated with romance in a gentleman's subconscious? For one is the torpid, alkaline smell of the Interborough; for another, the pure prickle of new linen unfolded by hands suddenly adored; for another, the drying of wet wool before a great fire. Perhaps Elizabeth Arden is wisest—she wants the ladies to smell like a rolling Kentucky landscape, which really takes in quite a lot.

WHAT? THEY DON'T WORK?

7/3/43

THE PAPERS CARRIED only the most modest account of the Federal Trade Commission's complaint against Carter's Little Liver Pills; to wit, that they had no therapeutic effect on the liver. We don't understand the complacency with which the nation received this news, threatening, as it does, to affect millions of lives and organs. From the early days of medicine men and snake oil, the sluggish liver has been an inseparable part of the American dream—the sluggish liver, the healing pill. Our mountains and plains, our cities and villages, were conquered and built by men who had sluggish livers and the means of curing them. The famous little pills travelled the uncharted alimentary canal by the untold billions, and their fame shone forth from the sides of barns and warehouses from one end to the other of this vast and bilious empire. Suddenly we are informed, in one blinding sentence of our government's charge, that not one pill ever reached its destination, not one ever made contact with the human liver, and that the whole thing has been a magnificent delusion. It was as though we had heard one morning that Broadway had in reality never made contact with Forty-second Street, or that Niagara Falls had no actuality but was a mere fiction of lovers. We fail to see why the

Times didn't give the story what it was worth—an eight-column head on the first page: CHARGE CARTER'S PILLS MISSED VITAL ORGAN—130,000,000 PEOPLE REPORTED STILL SLUGGISH.

If the Federal Trade Commission's charges are proved, the early advertising man who first had the Carter's Little Liver Pills account should certainly receive some sort of Congressional decoration for his unique contribution to American hokum. He should be posthumously awarded the coveted ribbon of the Order of the Purple Phrase.

STOCK MARKET ZIGZAGS

3/26/55

WE DON'T FULLY SUBSCRIBE to the bald statement that confidence in this country's economy can be lost in a day. There are tangible assets that are not easily wiped out—the soil, the climate, the industrial vigor, the immense spirit of a people who won freedom through revolutionary zeal and are still willing to work at it. And there are intangibles that give the economy fertility and vitality. The stock market, which is a sort of horse track without the horses, does not deserve its wide reputation as a barometer. It sometimes sows the hurricane, instead of reporting the breeze. It is naturally flighty, because traders are noncreative people who rely for their security on the creativeness of others and who are therefore uneasy. Winchell* mentions a stock by name and a rainbow appears in the sky over Wall Street. But what the market does symbolize, in its nervous way, is the health-giving flexibility of capitalism—the trait that keeps our economy delicately balanced but that makes it a far better servant of the people than the state-driven

---

*Walter Winchell, news commentator.

economies that have hardly any elasticity at all. The other day, in San Diego, the American economy even adjusted to springtime: work was halted on a seven-million-dollar building project to give a dove time to hatch her eggs. Our confidence in a society that observes this sentimental ritual and practices this fiscal folly cannot be toppled in a day. To talk of peace is not enough; we must hatch the egg of the dove.

SPLIT PERSONALITIES

2/19/55

IN THIS AGE OF TELEVISION, this day of the spoken word and the fleeting image, we find ourself taking satisfaction in the printed word, which has a natural durability. Whenever we watch TV, we are impressed by two things: its effectiveness and its evanescence. It glides by and is lost. The printed word sticks around—you can walk into any library thirty years later, and there (for what it may be worth) it is.

The most puzzling thing about TV is the steady advance of the sponsor across the line that has always separated news from promotion, entertainment from merchandising. The advertiser has assumed the role of originator, and the performer has gradually been eased into the role of peddler. This is evident everywhere. The voices of radio and television are the voices of quick-change artists; they move rapidly from selling to telling and back to selling again. They are losing their sharpness because they have divided their allegiance. In 1925, when *The New Yorker* was born, an artist was an artist, a writer was a writer, a newsman was a newsman, an actor was an actor. Today, every one of these people has developed a split personality and is hawking something besides his talent. A newscaster appears on the screen, and for a moment you don't know whether he has tidings about some offshore islands or tidings about an automobile's rear end. Usually he has both. A girl breaks into song, and for a moment you can't quite pin down the source of her lyrical passion. It could be love, it could be something that comes in a jar. Conscious or unconscious, there is an attempt to blur the line that the press has fought to hold. The line would have disappeared long since were the human voice capable of sounding the same in both its roles, but it isn't. When a man speaks words he has been paid to utter, praises something he gets money for praising, his voice invariably gives him away; it simply lacks the accents that reinforce a voice when it is expressing something that comes straight from head or heart. It seems odd to us that commerce should aspire to violate the line, blend the two voices. Yet it does. If the line were to disappear, if the voices should become indistinguishable, the show would be over.

MARKET WATCHERS

12/18/54

ON OUR WAY TO WORK in the morning, we sometimes pass one of those temples where men sit meditating with their hats on, watching ticker reports projected on a screen. We stopped for a moment the other morning to kibitz: through the window we watched the watchers at their watching. The ticker was bringing news of cloudy conditions in the Middle West; rain was expected within forty-eight hours and might have an effect on winter wheat. The watchers, some of whom looked as though they were merely taking refuge indoors from a rain of their own making, absorbed this piece of information solemnly. One man, nursing a cigar, closed his eyes as he tried to conjure up the significance of distant rain on distant wheat. What a strange little band of tardy pioneers they seemed, sifting the wind that failed to touch their cheeks as it blew across prairies they would never see! How sad they looked, these early-morning waifs—no parents, no homes, only a lighted screen on which prices rose and fell amid tidings of great gain!

11

Curiosities and Inventions

HOTSPUR THE SWIFT

3/16/29

TO TELL YOU WHAT make of car Hotspur is, would be to make General Motors insanely jealous. That I must not do. Suffice it to say that Hotspur is a small car, whose leather seats smell. Even the rumble-seat smells, although it is right out in the open.

"Do the seats smell that way just while they are new," I asked the salesman, "or will they always smell that way?"

"You won't notice it after the first five hundred miles," he replied.

"I think my friends will, though," I said.

It's four weeks since I drove Hotspur out of the agency, his windshield plastered with printed directions, his nickel head-lights catching the last gleam of the twilight, his gas swashing around audibly in the gas tank, his right front fender grazing a lady on the sidewalk. They have been four ecstatic weeks. I have obeyed the rules which I found on the windshield, have reli-giously kept Hotspur down under thirty-five miles an hour, and now my purgatory nears an end, and I will soon be able to open him up to his full forty. The smell still lingers, and even on an open road, brisking right along, I can shut my eyes, inhale, and imagine I am seated in the lobby of a second-rate hotel.

My friends twit me about this smell, just as I expected they would. At first I was sensitive about it and was at the mercy of my joking passengers, but now I forestall their remarks. The moment a guest enters my automobile I turn immediately to him with my nose in the air and inquire: "Have you been around a stable, by any chance?" or: "Have you, do you sup-pose, something on the bottom of your shoe?" This unsettles the guest and usually he has a miserable time the entire trip.

Hotspur has other traits which my friends have found amusing, but it's surprising how quickly one builds up a defence against jests. Time was when almost anybody could have annoyed me by referring to a certain strange vibrant sound that occurs in Hotspur when he attains a middling speed. It is a noise which comes over him just at twenty-eight miles an hour—it hits him suddenly, and reminds me of the pleasant sound that wagons make when, from afar, you hear them crossing a wooden bridge in the country. When my friends mention the noise, I explain that it is a "harmonic," a sympathetic overtone that can occur only at a certain speed; with this as my theme I go on at some length, telling about musical harmonics and how, when you play a note on the piano, the octave will also vibrate, and I recite, too, instances of church windows being broken by organ notes, and other interesting phenomena of sympathetic vibration, until my friends soon become so absorbed in my discourse that they forget Hotspur's extraordinary unquiet. (Either that or they get out of the car altogether and beat their way home across country.)

So far, the rumble-seat has been used only by women and children. Opinions have differed about it. For the most part, the children have enjoyed it—welcoming, as children do, the terrible exposure in midwinter, the possibility of pneumonia and release from school, the sense of utter helplessness and bounce. The only lady who ever ventured into the rumble skinned her right knee getting in and her left knee getting out, thus preserving a kind of rough symmetry through it all. A day or two later I happened to be asking her to marry me, and mentioned that if she were my wife she could always ride in the rumble. "And open up all the old wounds?" she said, sadly.

She was a lovely person. I will always remember her. I will remember how she turned to me with a heroic little smile on her lips and said:

"The seat would be more comfortable if you wouldn't keep so many empty boxes and crates in there."

"But there aren't any empty boxes and crates in there," I replied, astounded.

"No, I suppose not," she continued, thoughtfully, "and yet that's the impression one gets, somehow."

A month has worked great changes in Hotspur's appearance. His nickel trimmings, that once blinded me with their early radiance, have toned down to the color and sheen of old candy-wrappers. His fenders, at first richly ebon, are now a pale pavement blue. In spirit, though, he is the same car. Lately it has seemed to me that he senses the approach of spring, for sometimes, setting forth with him on one of those clear mornings that bleed the heart with the prick of distant and unmistakable crocuses, I have felt a little earthly shiver run through his frame, and he has leapt ahead with an urgency more than mechanical, an internal expansion not unlike my own.

BUY A BATTLESHIP?

11/30/29

WE ONCE SERIOUSLY CONSIDERED purchasing the Leviathan* when it was on sale. Somehow we never went through with it. Now we see by the papers that the government is going to sell three obsolete cruisers at public auction. One of these would suit our needs even better than the Leviathan. We suspect it would be a lot of fun to own a battleship, be it ever so obsolete. It would bolster our ego. How pleasant to overhear young ladies whispering: "Not the Mr. Tilley who has the battleship?" Pleasant, and advantageous socially. It would be pleasant, too, to make use of our ship in connection with the sporadic activities of the regular Navy. We would like to come on a sham battle on a foggy day and sneak in with *our* cruiser to participate, first on one side then on the other, annoying admirals, confusing the issue. It may not be too late. About how much would a battleship be?

---

*German ocean liner (originally "Vaterland") that was turned into an Allied troop transport during World War I, then into a transatlantic passenger liner. It was scrapped in 1937.

ANIMAL VOICES

2/8/30

WHEN THE NOON WHISTLE BLOWS in Bronx Zoo, it starts the wolves howling. They point their noses high, their breath curls upward on the cold air, and they give tongue in the primeval forests of their cage. Movie people have been trying to record this performance in sound pictures, but without any luck—the wolves refuse to howl into a microphone. It's one of the little city problems that haven't been solved yet.

Animals are rather hard to take in sound pictures, Dr. Ditmars, the snake man, tells us. He has been making sound records of their voices for synchronization with his own moving pictures, and has recorded the sounds of most of the animals in the Park. Lions are disappointing—they sound like a cow, no majesty, only vaguely sad. Metro-Goldwyn-Mayer made a sound record, for its trademark lion, but gave it up, it sounded so feeble and un-metro-goldwyn-mayer. Camels are difficult, and better results are obtained by having a man make a noise like a camel than by taking the camel's voice itself. Strangely enough, one of the best sound artists is the rattlesnake—the sound record of a rattler is perfect. Dr. Ditmars experimented with a wooden rattle in front of the microphone, but could get nothing as good as the real thing. The hiss of the cobra is also rather nice.

A major difficulty is getting the animal to make any sound at all, animals having a penchant for absolute silence. There are different ways of stimulating them. To make a monkey scream with horror, you show it a live snake. To make it chatter with glee, you show it a banana. Tree toads won't perform until you begin sawing up a piece of bronze with a hacksaw—and that spoils the record. Dr. Ditmars wanted to make a katydid record and found that the only way he could induce the katydids to make their monotonous music was by placing other katydids on the outside of his studio, so that his subjects could hear the low distant sound of their love-making. This required a lot of katydids, and necessitated a trip to Wurtsborough Mountain in Jersey, where katydids can be captured at night in the scrub oaks on the mountainside.

According to Dr. Ditmars, the cleanest and most satisfactory way to record animal sounds is to stay away from the animals altogether, and summon a man named Phil Dwyer, who will make any noise you ask for, and who doesn't require any stimulus such as bananas or distant love-making. This Mr. Dwyer was the camel in a fine camel picture made by one of the movie companies. It would have been a great success as a topical picture except that in making up the film they put the camel voice (a mournful and very loud braying noise) on a kangaroo record. The result was surprising, zoölogically, but the braying kangaroo appeared in two Broadway houses before the film company discovered its mistake. Natural history note: kangaroos do not make any noise.

THEN AND NOW

12/9/33

WE RAN ACROSS A 1908 Schwartz catalogue in the course of the week, and it was a lot of fun to compare it with the 1933 catalogue. Fundamentally, toys don't change as much as we imagine. In the current catalogue, for example, you read about a submarine "that dives and rises just like real ones." This seems like ultra-modernity till you turn to the 1908 list and find the same submarine, for slightly less money. The same is true of a diver—a little man who goes to the bottom. Schwartz has one today for $1.50. You could have had a nice five-inch diver in 1908 for forty cents. There was a swimming doll in 1908, identical with today's swimming doll except for her bathing suit, which had a long skirt. There was a very good fireboat in 1908, which threw a stream of water, and a very good cow which gave milk. The 1933 catalogue speaks of a doll that "breathes," but that idea isn't new, either. There used to be a doll that drank milk and wet its pants, and there still is. Farm sets haven't changed; and 1908 was full of jigsaw puzzles, bagatelle, and steam launches. Anchor blocks, those memorable little stone building blocks whose yellow arches, blue turrets, and red cubes formed the framework of our own childhood, are still going strong today; and to our notion nothing has come along which can touch them, in either beauty or practical possibilities.

Toys have, of course, been de-luxed up considerably. Take the Irish Mail, a standard juvenile vehicle even in this scooter age. In 1908, evidences of effeteness were already apparent in the Irish Mail: a model came out called the Fairy Auto Car, which we remember very well because it had a clutch. Equipped with "cushion tires," it sold for $13.50. Today, Schwartz sells a de-luxe Mail, equipped with Goodyear pneumatic balloon tires, electric lights and horn, and front-wheel drive, for $38. The 1933 express wagon has streamlined wheel housings, like a pursuit plane, and one of the 1933 toy coupés is radio-equipped—that is, it gives forth music, like a taxicab. Locomotives on the modern electric railways give forth a chugging noise.

The toy that seems to have gone completely by the board is the tricycle, and by tricycle we don't mean velocipede. We mean the tricycle your sister had, with the two big rear wheels and the one little front wheel and the sway-back frame which gave it its ladylike appearance. The 1908 catalogue featured tricycles, but you never see one today. It took little girls many years to discover that the tricycle was a mechanically inefficient device requiring four times the steam to make it go that it ought to, but they finally found out.

Toys now are sanitary, de-luxe, and faithful miniatures; and a good many of life's little hazards have been eliminated for today's batch of youngsters. We are thinking particularly of the motorboat which goes a hundred and fifty feet, "then turns around and comes back." Maybe we are crazy, but for us the rich charm of a mechanical boat used to be the delicious problem of retrieving it from mid-pond.

FITTING IN

6/9/34

THE COMPLAINT ONE OF OUR FRIENDS makes about modern steel furniture, modern glass houses, modern red bars, and modern streamlined trains and cars is that all these *objets modernes,* while adequate and amusing in themselves, tend to make the people who use them look dated. It is an honest criticism. The human race has done nothing much about changing its own appearance to conform to the form and texture of its appurtenances. Our professors of eugenics have dodged the whole issue. At the Chicago Fair, the noticeable thing about the circular houses of tomorrow was not how funny the houses looked but how funny the people looked in them. Must the next generation be as structurally inefficient, as architecturally inappropriate, as the present? Babies even at this late date are born with ears that stick out and catch the wind; the back of their head fails to come to a long sharp point. It often seems to us that the only people who really fit into the modern picture are certain department-store dummies and occasionally a pattern figure in a fashion magazine. The rest of us definitely don't belong.

SOOTHING THE CHICKENS

5/15/37

THE IMPERSONAL, disjointed sound which radio in large doses makes immunizes the listener. We happen to know one set-owner who has found a practical use for this curious property. He is a Massachusetts poultry farmer who goes in for large-scale egg-raising. He discovered that if his hens were disturbed by a sudden noise in the night, egg production fell off sharply next day. So now he keeps a radio going quietly night and day among his hens, immunizing them against the virus of sound. It works perfectly. Let a door squeak on its hinges; the hens accept it as a sound effect. Somehow it gives us a secret, deep pleasure to know that a dramatized news broadcast, aimed to unnerve the rest of us, is definitely reassuring to a lot of sleepy fowl, dreaming of hawks and weasels in a henhouse far away.

THE OLD AND THE NEW

6/19/37

IN AN EXCURSION along U. S. Highway 1 last weekend, we noted two interesting building operations. One was a theatre being built in the shape of a barn. The other was a restaurant being built in the shape of a diner. It is amusing to see these American forms, which were the result of vicissitudes, being perpetuated after the need is over. Heredity is a strong factor, even in architecture. Necessity first mothered invention. Now invention has some little ones of her own, and they look just like grandma.

REVOLVING DOORS

SOMEBODY HAS PATENTED a revolving door equipped with
an electric eye to start it going at "the right moment." In our
opinion there is no "right moment" for a door to begin revolving; almost always it's an unhappy compromise between two
opposing factions, one trying to get into the building, the other
trying to get out. The "right moment" never arrives, although
we have seen neurotics hanging around the outskirts hopefully
waiting for it. A revolving door is simply an ingenious trap
which most people have learned to spring without getting
killed. What a revolving door needs is not an electric eye but
a steel grabhook to help hesitant ladies and a centrifugal governor to foil the ambitions of human dynamos. An electric eye for
a revolving door would need to be fitted with bifocals, because
one person's right moment is another person's Dunkirk.*

PERILS OF THE SEA

OWNERS OF SMALL BOATS know that yachting on Long Island Sound has its perilous moments—the sudden squall, the
untried guest, the parted halyard, the accidental jibe, the over-
shot mooring, the eagle-eyed audience on the clubhouse porch.
It has its terrible overheated days, too, when the sail mildews
because nobody is there to dry it, afternoons when the wind
dies and the tide runs foul at the harbor mouth. Having come
safely through a summer of trials and dangers afloat, a lady we

*Over 300,000 Allied troops were evacuated from France at this seaport in May
1940. France surrendered to Germany in June 1940.

know, captain of an eighteen-foot sailboat, sat down the other evening in the lee of her radio to refresh her memory by reading over the insurance policy she had blithely taken out last spring. For twenty-seven dollars the company had watched over her all season and would continue to watch until the policy expired. "Touching the adventures and perils," she read, "which we, the Assurers, are contented to bear, and do take upon us, they are of the seas, men-of-war, fire, enemies, pirates, rovers, assailing thieves, jettisons, letters of mart and counter-mart, reprisals, takings at sea, arrests, restraints and detainments of kings, princes, and people, of what nation, condition, or quality soever, barratry of the Master and Mariners, and of all other like perils, losses, and misfortunes that have or shall come to the hurt, detriment, or damage of said yacht or any part thereof." Well, it had been quite a summer. The detainment of a prince, she decided, must have been the day she took that Rye man for a sail and his right arm became unmanageable.

MAKING DO

8/11/45

A FEMALE FRIEND of ours recently moved into a small apartment so full of defects as to be really quite charming. One rather obvious feature was that the place lacked kitchen shelves. After watching the pitiful and on the whole rather frightening preparations her husband made for remedying this defect (he went out and bought some twenty-penny spikes and a bottle of New England rum), our friend decided she would manage *without* kitchen shelves. She got looking around the apartment and observed that the bookshelves in the living room had four or five inches of space behind the books. Quieting her husband, she arranged her supply of canned goods neatly. For extra convenience, she alphabetized everything. Asparagus is behind Sherwood Anderson, cherries behind Conrad, peaches behind Proust. She is as happy as a child about all this.

GET A HANDLE ON IT

3/13/48

TOO OFTEN WHEN YOU LIFT SOMETHING, your hand clutches an unsuitable shape. Seize any teapot, tennis racket, or oxyacetylene blowpipe, and what have you got? A plain handle. Your own marvellously curved digits are wrapped around an unmolded surface, stresses and strains all wrong, and the tea (or oxyacetylene gas) nothing but an awkward struggle. Happily, this state of affairs is about to end. A man named Thomas Lamb has invented a handle consistent with America's destiny, a handle to fit the hand. Soon you will be lifting something—a coal shovel, a machete—and your cunning digits will enfold the new Lamb Wedge-Lock Handle, designed to meet the human grasp as intimately as an ice skater's tights meet a cold leg.

We attended the unveiling of the Lamb handle last week in a small, white, odorless Prest-Glass room in the Museum of Modern Art. The Modern has a rather dreadful knack of giving an oversoul to a ripsaw and imbuing the future with undigested beauty. The blood pounded in our temples as we stared at a diagram of a gorilla's paw and heard the bells of St. Thomas next door, scattering "Lead, Kindly Light" into Fifty-third Street. As far into the future as we could see, there were only perfect handles. Man, the sign said, has achieved dominance through brain and hand, but his hand is still wrapped around the most outrageous old surfaces—plain old suitcase handles, plain old canoe paddles, plain old telephone receivers. No shape to anything the hand slips around unless you want to count a woman's waist. Fitted with the new Lamb Wedge-Lock Handle, your stewpot, your golf club, your castrating knife will take on new meaning. Fatigue and strain noticeably reduced.

We can report that the Lamb looks like any other handle except that it is grooved to take thumb and forefinger and is a bit thicker in some places than in others. It looks like a handle that has softened in the hot weather, been used, and then hardened again in the cold. The Modern always does things up brown, and there was a wall with projecting Wedge-Lock handles, where you could *push* with a Wedge-Lock handle, *pull* with a Wedge-Lock handle, and *twist* with a Wedge-Lock handle. People gravely pushed, pulled, twisted. The handles soon grew sweaty and gave us a queer feeling of the New Sweat. When your hand is around a Lamb, it feels almost too good—a little too pat, you might say. Also, it gives a slight trapped sensation, as when you grasp a bowling ball.

The handle is in production and you will soon be meeting up with it if you are the sort of person that ever takes hold of anything. We found, on trial, that the handle has one disadvantage: unless you seize it in the right place, you're out of the groove and might as well have hold of the wrong end of a gimlet. We strongly recommend, though, that the Brooklyn Dodgers look into it and try a Lamb Wedge-Lock bat handle. If the claims mean anything, it ought to add a hundred feet to any clean drive. Might mean the pennant.

We rode home, after the unveiling, in a crosstown bus, wedged in and hanging fast to an old, unmolded metal strap. Our palm resented every inch of the journey. Hardly anyone in the bus seemed truly happy.

HAND THROTTLE

9/25/48

THIS TOWN IS FULL of persons who sleep fitfully on expensive innerspring mattresses that have been stiffened (or decontaminated) by expensive plywood bedboards, thus giving the sleepers' spines a solid support. These same bewitched persons, who paid through the nose for one slice of modernity only to discover that they had to go back and buy another slice to take the curse off it—these same persons, having brought their beds up to date with a bedboard, may now bring their automobiles up to date with a gadget called a Hande-Feed Finger Tip Gas Control. A mail-order firm in St. Louis is advertising it. It is installed in fifteen minutes. It costs $5.95. The manufacturer claims that it will enable you to relax while you drive—no toe on the accelerator. And if you are an old, old man, it may occur to you that what you are buying as an extra for your modern car is simply the hand throttle that used to be standard equipment on all cars in the days before streamlining set in. These are gay times. A man pays three thousand dollars for a new car, and then shells out an additional $5.95 for a hand throttle. Still, it's a hopeful sign. If auto-gadget makers are beginning to dig into the past for new ideas, maybe they'll come up with a lot of things. We may yet be able to buy special mail-order fenders that permit a car to be parked without the help of radar, and a special mail-order driver's seat that affords the pilot a view of the thirty feet of road immediately ahead of his front bumper.

TAKING IT WITH YOU

IN A RECENT ISSUE OF *The New Yorker,* an advertisement of Oshkosh luggage mentioned that prices ranged "from $25 to $5,000." It seemed like a sweet range, so we wrote Oshkosh and asked which unit they were holding for five thousand dollars. We got back a nice letter saying that it is a special trunk made of alligators and goats. It has thirty-two hangers. Bottom slats are hickory. Covering is alligator. Hardware is triple gold-plated. Lining is imported goatskin, color of Dubonnet. Oshkosh didn't say where the goatskins are from, but we assume they're from Greece, from the original Raymond Duncan milking herd. The trunk enjoys the following equipment, and so would you if you owned the trunk: gold-plated rib-rod trolley, electric iron, ironing board, tilting shoe boxes, corduroy laundry bag, silk curtains, built-in radio with self-charging battery, and a small bar. Every rivet is gold-plated, and the best thing of all is that the trunk has twelve ball-bearing roller casters. "A child can push it around." Oshkosh introduced this child rather suddenly and we didn't catch the little fellow's name, but we can see him at his deadly work—pushing the trunk around and around the room in Shepheard's Hotel while the trunk's radio blares the latest news of inflation in America and the child's father tries to overtake the trunk's bar so that he can pour himself a drink and the child's mother stands in the vortex wondering whether they hadn't better try to sell the trunk to a Cairo dentist for the gold there is in it.

TELEVISION

12/4/48

LIKE RADIO, television hangs on the questionable theory that whatever happens anywhere should be sensed everywhere. If everyone is going to be able to see everything, in the long run all sights may lose whatever rarity value they once possessed, and it may well turn out that people, being able to see and hear practically everything, will be specially interested in almost nothing. Already you can detect the first faint signs of this apathy. Already manufacturers are trying to anticipate it, by providing the public with combination sets that offer a triple threat: radio, record playing, and television—all three to be turned on at once, we presume.

Television, when it gets going, will almost certainly pick up and throw into one's home scenes it didn't reckon on when it set up its camera. There have already been examples of this. In London not long ago, a television broadcaster was giving his impressions of the zoo when a big lizard bit him on the finger. The technicians in charge of the broadcast, delighted at this turn of events, kept their camera trained on the spurting blood. Thus what had begun as a man's impression of an animal ended as an animal's impression of a man, and a few drops of private blood gained general currency and became a great pool of public blood, and the world immediately contained more persons who had seen a lizard bite a man.

AIR-CONDITIONED FIRES

9/12/53

AS YOU APPROACH the taproom of the Holland House Taverne, in Radio City, pressing forward through the small, air-conditioned American foyer toward the distant Dutch retreat, you pass a fireplace in which an electric fire burns cheerfully in a coal grate. Somehow this combination of fire and ice, of heat and chill, of winterproofing in the midst of summerproofing, brings to a head the American Way in a single interior. It is an architectural banana split, a perfect case of the debauchery of design. A menu printed almost entirely in Dutch adds a fillip to a completely American occasion of lunatic splendor and comfort. There is something so wonderfully insatiable about this culture of ours. The other day, as we paused in front of the Holland House fire a moment to recover from the ninety-five-degree heat of the streets and to wait for a friend, we reached in our pocket and found there a letter from an engineering firm in Chicago telling us of a device for cutting king-size cigarettes in half. ("Stop cigarette waste. Save 25 cents a day. Combination case and cutter cuts king-size cigarettes in half—for 40 quick, always fresh smokes.") Probably the man who thought up the idea of adding a cubit to the stature of a cigarette believed he had hit on something that was for the ages. It seems doubtful whether he envisioned that in a few short years somebody would come up with the revolutionary idea of cutting the longer cigarette down to size. ("Smoke the half you throw away!") At any rate, we wished we had a cutter. We would have liked to spend a languorous afternoon there by the glowing coals in the air-conditioned room, nursing a bottle of Heineken's beer and slowly slicing cigarettes and allowing them to fall onto the ashless hearth of the heat-free fire.

BRANDY KEGS

PLENTY OF STORES sell dog supplies—rubber bones, baskets, vitamins, leashes—but Abercrombie & Fitch doesn't stop there. For the past few days Abercrombie has displayed in one of its windows a brandy keg for a St. Bernard's collar. This object, so nicely made, so brilliantly unlikely, holds a curious fascination for us, a man who has been lost in the snows of Forty-fifth Street these many years and whom no dog has succored. We stand and gaze at it every time we pass, admiring its brass bindings and its strap of well-dressed leather. Only a store with a lot of guts would try to pay a high midtown rent by selling brandy kegs for St. Bernards. Of course, New York is a town of eight million inhabitants, many of them buying fools, but even so whole hours must slip by without anybody's dropping in to pick up a keg for a St. Bernard. Another thing that impresses us is the size of the keg. Its girth is about that of a dachshund puppy, and we would say that its capacity is very close to a quart. That's a lot of brandy for a half-frozen man to take aboard—and the least a snowbound man can do if a dog shows up with a drink is drink it.

When Churchill* retired the other day, we felt like sending him something—some gift in appreciation of his having once saved our life. Perhaps a St. Bernard, complete with brandy, would be the perfect present—a dog that would shuffle along at his side as he strolls the grounds of Chartwell, a sort of four-legged hip flask, keeping him supplied with his favorite comfort in the frightening blizzard of old age. We shall have to think about it, though; it's not the sort of project a person should rush into, however much it might stimulate Abercrombie, however deep our sense of gratitude to this great man.

---

*Winston Churchill, Prime Minister of Great Britain 1940–45.

GRANDFATHER CLOCKS

2/23/57

ON TV THE OTHER MORNING we heard the old song about the grandfather's clock and how it "stopped short, never to go again, when the old man died." It's a ghostly tale, all right, and we don't intend to challenge its authenticity. We do know one thing about a grandfather's clock, though, from close association: even when you take the weights off, thus depriving it of its source of strength, the clock doesn't stop short. The last time we removed the weights from ours, the clock kept going for ten minutes, from sheer force of habit, or of character, or both, plus the disinclination of all things, animate or inanimate, to let go of life. We were greatly impressed by this extra ten minutes of timekeeping by a clock that had had its jugular cut—more ghostly, in a way, than if we ourself had died and the clock had stopped short. This clock belonged originally to an ancestor of our wife's, who had it built (of cherry) to furnish a house in Stockbridge, Massachusetts, about a hundred and sixty years ago. It still keeps perfect time. In our house, instead of setting the clock by the radio, we set the radio by the clock. (How's that for a ghostly tale?)

12

Christmas Spirit

MIDNIGHT MASS

12/26/36

EVERYONE HAS ONE CHRISTMAS he remembers above all others, one blindingly beautiful occasion. Ours is a Christmas Eve, during calf love, when we made the (for us) adventurous pilgrimage to a midnight Mass in a Catholic church. Churchgoing in our family had always been in the honest gloom of a Protestant Sunday morning, and we must hasten to explain that the purpose of this clandestine night expedition was far from religious; we simply had reason to suspect that if we visited that church at that hour, we would catch a glimpse of our beloved. Snow began to fall at sundown, and fell quietly all evening. The snow, the lateness of the hour, the elaborate mysteries of the Mass (we had never seen the inside of a cathedral before), together with the steady burning vision of the back of Her neck whom we adored, and then the coming out into the snow alone afterward, with the street lamps veiled in white: this indeed was a holy time.

WOOLWORTH MADONNA

12/26/36

SHOPPING IN WOOLWORTH'S, in the turbulent days, we saw a little boy put his hand inquiringly on a ten-cent Christ child, part of a crèche. "What is this?" he asked his mother, who had him by the hand. "C'mon, c'mon," replied the harassed woman, "you don't want that!" She dragged him grimly away—a Woolworth Madonna, her mind dark with gift-thoughts, following a star of her own devising.

RELATIVE PRONOUNS

12/25/48

WE HAD A SCROOGE in our office a few minutes ago, a tall, parched man,* beefing about Christmas and threatening to disembowel anyone who mentioned the word. He said his work had suffered and his life been made unbearable by the demands and conventions of the season. He said he hated wise men, whether from the East or from the West, hated red ribbon, angels, Scotch Tape, greeting cards depicting the Adoration, mincemeat, dripping candles, distant and near relatives, fir balsam, silent nights, boy sopranos, shopping lists with check marks against some of the items, and the whole yuletide stratagem, not to mention the low-lying cloud of unwritten thank-you letters hanging just above the horizon. He was in a savage state. Before he left the office, though, we saw him transfigured, just as Scrooge was transfigured. The difference was that whereas Scrooge was softened by visions, our visitor was soft-

---

*Harold Ross, editor of *The New Yorker* from its founding in 1925 to his death in 1951.

ened by the sight of a small book standing on our desk—a copy of Fowler's "Modern English Usage."

"Greatest collection of essays and opinions ever assembled between covers," he shouted, "including a truly masterful study of *that* and *which.*"

He seized the book and began thumbing through it for favorite passages, slowly stuffing a couple of small gift-wrapped parcels into the pocket of his greatcoat.

"Listen to this," he said in a triumphant voice. " 'Avoidance of the obvious is very well, provided that it is not itself obvious, but, if it is, all is spoilt.' Isn't that beautiful?"

We agreed that it was a sound and valuable sentiment, perfectly expressed. He then began a sermon on *that* and *which,* taking as his text certain paragraphs from Fowler, and warming rapidly to his theme.

"Listen to this: 'If writers would agree to regard *that* as the defining relative pronoun, and *which* as the non-defining, there would be much gain both in lucidity and in ease. Some there are who follow this principle now; but it would be idle to pretend that it is the practice either of most or of the best writers.' "

"It was the practice of St. Matthew," we put in hastily. "Or at any rate he practiced it in one of the most moving sentences ever constructed: 'And, lo, the star, which they saw in the east, went before them, till it came and stood over where the young child was.' You've got to admit that the *which* in that sentence is where it ought to be, as well as every other word. Did you ever read a more satisfactory sentence than that in your life?"

"It's good," said our friend, cheerfully. "It's good because there isn't a ten-dollar word in the whole thing. And Fowler has it pegged, too. Wait a minute. Here. 'What is to be deprecated is the notion that one can improve one's style by using stylish words.' See what I mean about Fowler? But let's get back to *that* and *which.* That's the business that really fascinates me. Fowler devotes eight pages to it. I got so excited once I had the pages photostatted. Listen to this: 'We find in fact that the antecedent of *that* is often personal.' Now, that's very instructive."

"Very," we said. "And if you want an example, take Matthew 2:1: '. . . there came wise men from the east to Jerusalem, saying, Where is he that is born King of the Jews?' Imagine how that simple clause could get loused up if someone wanted to change *that* to *who*!"

"Exactly," he said. "That's what I mean about Fowler. What was the sentence again about the star? Say it again."

We repeated, "And, lo, the star, which they saw in the east, went before them, till it came and stood over where the young child was."

"You see?" he said, happily. "This is the greatest damn book ever written." And he left our office transfigured, a man in excellent spirits. Seeing him go off merry as a grig, we realized that Christmas is where the heart is. For some it is in a roll of red ribbon, for some in the eyes of a young child. For our visitor, we saw clearly, Christmas was in a relative pronoun. Wherever it is, it is quite a day.

HOLIDAY GREETINGS

12/20/52

FROM THIS HIGH MIDTOWN HALL, undecked with boughs, unfortified with mistletoe, we send forth our tinselled greetings as of old, to friends, to readers, to strangers of many conditions in many places. Merry Christmas to uncertified accountants, to tellers who have made a mistake in addition, to girls who have made a mistake in judgment, to grounded airline passengers, and to all those who can't eat clams! We greet with particular warmth people who wake and smell smoke. To captains of river boats on snowy mornings we send an answering toot at this holiday time. Merry Christmas to intellectuals and other despised minorities! Merry Christmas to the musicians of Muzak and men whose shoes don't fit! Greetings of the season to unemployed actors and the blacklisted everywhere who suffer for sins uncommitted; a holly thorn in the thumb of compilers of lists! Greetings to wives who can't find their glasses and to poets who can't find their rhymes! Merry Christmas to the unloved, the misunderstood, the overweight. Joy to the authors of books whose titles begin with the word "How" (as though they knew)! Greetings to people with a ringing in their ears; greetings to growers of gourds, to shearers of sheep, and to makers of change in the lonely underground booths! Merry Christmas to old men asleep in libraries! Merry Christmas to people who can't stay in the same room with a cat! We greet, too, the boarders in boarding houses on 25 December, the duennas in Central Park in fair weather and foul, and young lovers who got nothing in the mail. Merry Christmas to people who plant trees in city streets; merry Christmas to people who save prairie chickens from extinction! Greetings of a purely mechanical sort to machines that think—plus a sprig of artificial holly. Joyous Yule to Cadillac owners whose conduct is unworthy of their car! Merry Christmas to the defeated, the forgotten, the inept; joy to all dandiprats and bunglers! We send, most particularly and most hopefully, our greetings and our prayers to soldiers and guardsmen on land and sea and in the air—the young men doing the hardest things at the hardest time of life. To all such, Merry Christmas, blessings, and good luck! We greet the Secretaries-designate, the President-elect: Merry Christmas to our new leaders, peace on earth, goodwill, and good management! Merry Christmas to couples unhappy in doorways! Merry Christmas to all who think they're in love but aren't sure! Greetings to people waiting for trains that will take them in the wrong direction, to people doing up a bundle and the string is too short, to children with sleds and no snow! We greet ministers who can't think of a moral, gagmen who can't think of a joke. Greetings, too, to the inhabitants of other planets; see you soon! And last, we greet all skaters on small natural ponds at the edge of woods toward the end of afternoon. Merry Christmas, skaters! Ring, steel! Grow red, sky! Die down, wind! Merry Christmas to all and to all a good morrow!

FEED THE BIRDS!

12/26/53

AT CHRISTMAS ONE SHOULD think about birth—an easy task for us, since we have just returned from a pilgrimage to see a newborn child.* Instead of following a star, we simply followed directions given us by the child's parents; took the ten-o'clock train, and found the infant in Boston, where it lay behind glass in a hospital. No shepherds were abiding there, but there was a nurse in a mask attending, and the glory of the Lord shone round about—a child seen through a glass clearly. Like all very new infants, this one appeared to be clothed in innocence and wisdom, probably more of each than he will ever attain again in his life. In the conventional manner, we brought gifts—a flowering plant, a bottle of wine. Then we went out to the Public Gardens to see Mary and Jesus on the island in the lake, a pale-blue Madonna and Child, with ducks circling around. A Boston lady in a shabby coat fed pigeons and sparrows near us where we sat, and she was soon joined by another lady, in a fur cape, who also had crumbs to offer. A squirrel, who seemed well acquainted with the visitors, waited his chance and leapt astride the cape. The feeding went on for a while: a scene of serenity, good will, and competence, each bird being known individually, the more timid ones being given special treatment. When the second lady arose and departed, she sent a little cry of farewell to her friend. "Goodbye for now!" she said, her voice rising. "Meantime, feed the birds!" This simple, bright warning, hurled against the terrible dark dome of the modern sky of anxiety and trouble, had a gentle, lunatic sound that has since echoed in our ear. It made us aware of our own need to send out at this season some general cry of good will to friends. We hope that another year will see the world of men and birds grow steadier, the free spirit stronger under its afflictive load; we hope the insane hatred of nation for nation will yield to the promise of a fertile world that is ready to be good to all when each is just to the other; we pray for the lifting of

*White's grandson Steven White.

curtains, so that the dimly discernible feeling of community among peoples may shine with a clearer light. We send best wishes for a bright Christmas and for the coming of man's humanity to man. Meantime, feed the birds!

REMEMBRANCE IS SUFFICIENT

12/25/54

IT IS NOT EASY to select the few words each year that shall serve as a Christmas greeting to our readers, wherever (like Mrs. Calabash) they are. While engaged in making the selection, we study the typewriter keys with the gravity you sometimes see in the faces of greeting-card buyers in stationery stores—faces taut with a special anguish (a sailor searching for a valentine message commensurate with his desire, a girl hunting for the right phrase to repair a broken friendship), as though all of life, all of love, must suddenly be captured on a small piece of decorative paper and consigned to the mails. This morning early, when we passed the angels in Rockefeller Center, we wished we could simply borrow a trumpet from one of them and blow our best wishes to the world in a single loud blast, instead of coming to the office and picking around among the confused shapes of a keyboard. But then, a few minutes later, gazing at the Dutch candy house in the window of KLM, we were reminded that everyone constructs a Christmas of his own, in his fashion, in sugar-candy form if need be, and that the quest for beauty, piety, simplicity, and merriment takes almost as many forms as there are celebrants, certainly too many to be covered by one note on a borrowed horn.

No one ever weeps for joy—we have this on good authority. We have it on the authority of a professor at the School of Medicine of the University of Rochester. (EXPERT DEEMS JOY NO CAUSE OF TEARS—*The Times.*) But it is true that at Christmas (season of joy, season of joy-to-the world), tears are not unknown, or even infrequent: many find themselves greatly moved by small events—by minor miracles of home or school or church, by a snatch of music, by a drift of paper snow across a TV screen. It is, of course, not joy but beauty that is responsible for this mild phenomenon: the unexpected gift of sadness—of some bright thing unresolved, of some formless wish unattained and unattainable. Since most of the common satisfactions of Christmas are available at the stores, and for a price, we wish our readers the pleasures that are unpurchasable, the satisfactions unpredictable, the nourishment of tears (if at all convenient).

There is one member of our household who never has to grope for words as we are groping now. She is our Aunt Caroline and she is ninety-two. She has observed all her ninety-two Christmases in good health and excellent spirits, and she is in good health and spirits now. Being so old, she goes back to a more leisurely period, and when she speaks, she speaks with a precision and a refinement rare in this undisciplined century. There is nothing stiff-backed about the furnishings of her mind, but it is her nature to sit erect, to stand erect, and to speak an upright kind of English that is always graceful and exact. A few weeks ago, she said something so close to the theme of Christmas that we shall quote it here. We were sitting with her at lunch in the country, and we apologized for not having taken her for a motor ride that morning to see once again the bright colors in the changing woods. "Why, my dear," she said without hesitating, "remembrance is sufficient of the beauty we have seen."

The sentence startled us—as though a bird had flown into the room. Perhaps her statement, so casually spoken yet so poetical, is a useful clue to the grownups' strange Christmas, the Christmas that often seems so baffling at first, and then so rewarding. At any rate, it suggests the beauty that surrounds the day, the sufficiency of remembrance, the nostalgia that is the source of tears. We are in perfect agreement with the professor at this joyous season; men weep for beauty, for things remembered, for the partridge in the pear tree—the one that their true love brought them and that somehow got mislaid. So we send our greetings to all who laugh or weep or dance or sing, our love to children, our cheers to their embattled parents. To any for whom by some mischance the magical moment fails in reenactment, we give Aunt Caroline's resolute words: Remembrance is sufficient of the beauty we have seen.

13

New York

INTERVIEW WITH A SPARROW

4/9/27

YOU HAVE NOTICED, if you go about much with your eyes on the ground, that English sparrows are resident here in great numbers; they are aperch beneath your bench in the Park, they are rather in the way when you are bringing up alongside the curb in crowded streets, they are in evidence generally. At this season the sparrows are particularly conspicuous because they are in love—and love addles any creature and makes him noisy.

As yet the onset of Spring is largely gossip among the sparrows. Any noon, in Madison Square, you may see one pick up a straw in his beak, put on an air of great business, twisting his head and glancing at the sky. Nothing comes of it. He hops three or four hops, and drops both the straw and the incident.

But it is a sign. Why these birds deliberately endure the hardships of life in town when the wide, fruitful country is theirs for the asking, is a matter of some moment. To content myself on this point I stopped a sparrow recently at the Seventy-second Street entrance of the Park and put the question bluntly.

"Take the matter of food alone," I suggested. "Certainly the rural districts offer inducements."

"That," he replied, "is a common misconception. New York is deceiving. Look at that bench—unpainted, shoddy—and beneath it a drab array of discarded sacks, candy wrappers, and gum labels. But do you (I suppose you don't) know that thirty-five per cent of all peanuts purchased go uneaten and fall to the ground? They are rich in proteins and carbohydrates.

"Crackerjack is also largely spilled. Every Runkel's chocolate wrapper contains important fragments. Only a small part of the oats fed horses at noon is eaten by the horses, because nosebags are difficult to manage and the horse ends by tossing the bag high in the air and spilling the contents. I merely mention these as typical."

The sparrow paused long enough to look into a refuse can.

"Why should I endure the rather stuffy existence in a farmyard," he continued, "when I can reside near a bear's den in a Zoo? Not only is the bear fed out of all proportions to his requirements, leaving me a full crop, but I am also in a position to meet the people, and see them, moreover, in a poor light.

"A man is at his worst when he is standing in front of a bear's den: he tries to appear contemplative and succeeds only in appearing silly, for he knows nothing about bears or he wouldn't be there." I nodded.

"Here in town I can get everything that the country offers, plus the drama, books, the museums, the stimulus of interesting contacts. I took space on a ledge of the Metropolitan two years ago; it afforded an extraordinary outlook on Greek statuary, and influenced my viewpoint. Do you see?"

"But isn't it crowded here in town?" I asked.

"Living conditions are bad, I admit," he replied. "The few trees extant are oversubscribed. But one gets along. There is a certain freedom from restraint. I can go any night to Bryant Park, for example, and slip in among the hundreds of birds which roost in the small tree overlooking the newsstand. It is a rowdy bunch (characteristic of Sixth Avenue) but no questions are asked and the next morning I tell my wife I was unavoidably locked in a loft where I had been looking for bits of plaster. Males need to get out of themselves once in a while. Am I making myself clear?" I nodded.

"Besides, people interest me. They are ingenuous to a pleasant degree. I would miss New York were I to make a change. The chimes in the Metropolitan tower—they are mildly amusing; in a way, they get under my feathers. I have even composed words to go with them. Let it go—I won't bore you with them.

"I go frequently to Gramercy Park, which, as you know, is privately owned. Do you see the humor of it? Sparrows, flying over the fence and perching on the statue of Booth. Merely a crotchet. Have I answered your questions?"

"Yes," I said, "thanks."

"One other thing," the sparrow said. "You may quote me on this, if you like. The upper cables of the Brooklyn Bridge—they are incomparable! I go there for spiritual release. The town hangs like a crystal drip across the west. It gets up from the sea, erect, on an idea. Very likely a spurious idea—I don't know. *Au revoir.*"

"Wait a minute," I cried. "What about love—I forgot to ask."

"Why, I'm in love. Why not? Possibly a good thing at this fresh season; they are mulching the soil around the perennials in Union Square. Why shouldn't I shout? Come around in late September, you'll find me more myself."

And the sparrow was off, flying low toward infinity.

ASCENSION

3/17/28

THE MEMORY OF old Madison Square Garden still haunts the Square, but a very tangible and very beautiful building has arisen on the spot to dispel it. One of the stirring adventures of this windy Spring is to approach the still unfinished New York Life Insurance Building across the park, with the blue sky of morning for a backdrop. At first the tower, still a dark web of steel, seems predominant, with the supporting structure gleaming white, rising tier by tier, majestically. Then as you get nearer, the tower becomes lost to view behind the vast ramparts, which swim dizzily forward out of white clouds, and put you in your place.

A mighty climber ourself, we got permission to make the ascent the other morning, and after wandering through tomblike depths peopled by a race of white and restless immortals who dwelt in a gloomy rain of plaster from above, we were inducted into an elevator made of a packing box, and hoisted twenty-three stories. The rest of the distance to the spidery tower was covered afoot, up dark stairs through interminable garrets that should have been full of old trunks and bats. To emerge, at last, on the hurricane deck, five hundred feet above reality, with no railing between us and the shimmering East River, with blocks of limestone pendulous about our head, with a whole new city of workmen trundling barrows of mortar, chipping stone, cutting tin, with blueprints aloft, with the canvas guards of the scaffolding bellying like sails in the breeze—this was a dream and a delight. "What time is it, buddy?" asked a red-headed bricklayer. "Ten of eleven," we replied, glancing down on the clock of the Metropolitan Tower.

Out of the strange confusion of dust and men was emerging, right under our feet, the modern pyramid—erect and without flaw and high. After five minutes, the sense of great altitude left us, and we discovered ourself peering inquisitively over the edge and poking around boldly on precipitous ledges. Workmen were nursing the great stone blocks into place, each dangling stone tended by a group of three men, while winch drivers sounded their rope signals and filled the air with bell-notes of progress. As the stones were eased down into seats of mortar and were levelled by eager-eyed constructionists, the whole thing grew, a perceptible upward thrust into the sky. It was magic of the most ethereal sort.

From the stone will rise a tall sloping tower of lead-coated copper, sparkling tourelles, and at the very peak (which an earthy little fellow in the engineer's office told us would be more than six hundred feet high) a bronze lantern.

It struck us, as we watched, that the workmen aloft there should find a mordant glee in rearing such a grand pile for the use of clerks who'll write policies for groundlings—to whom life, to be sweet, must be insured.

THE NEW YORK GARBAGEMAN

12/6/30

THERE IS NO ONE in all New York we envy more than the garbageman. Not even a fireman gets so much fun out of life. The jolly, jolly garbageman goes banging down the street without a thought for anyone. He clatters his cans as he listeth; he scatters ashes on the winds with never a thought that the wind-blown ash problem was settled in 1899 when the little old one-horse dump carts had covers put on them. He is shrewd in measuring his pace, and goes down the block bit by bit, innocently keeping just to windward of you. He drives like a ward boss through red lights and green, and backs his truck over the crossing with more privilege than a baby carriage on Fifth Avenue. He is as masterful as a pirate and chock-full of gusto. As we watch a garbage crew at work, we momentarily expect to see them burst into song and clink property beakers. Why shouldn't they? They have the town by the tail and they know it.

CROSSING THE STREET

7/16/32

POSSIBLY YOU HAVE NOTICED this about New Yorkers: instinctively, crossing a one-way street, they glance in the proper direction to detect approaching cars. They always know, without thinking, which way the traffic flows. They glance in the right direction as naturally as a deer sniffs upwind. Yet after that one glance in the direction from which the cars are coming, they always, just before stepping out into the street, also cast one small, quick, furtive look in the opposite direction— from which no cars could possibly come. That tiny glance (which we have noticed over and over again) is the last sacrifice on the altar of human fallibility; it is an indication that people can never quite trust the self-inflicted cosmos, and that they dimly suspect that some day, in the maze of well-regulated vehicles and strong, straight buildings, something will go completely crazy—something big and red and awful will come tearing through town going the wrong way on the one-ways, mowing down all the faithful and the meek. Even if it's only a fire engine.

VISITING MOTORISTS

12/2/33

FOR SIX DAYS of the week we find it no trouble at all to drive a car about town. New York's traffic, however furious, is predictable; and her taxis, even in moments of great verve, are accurate. For six days driving is a pleasure, but on Sundays all is changed: the town, we have discovered, fills up with visiting motorists who have come in from the Oranges and the Pelhams to see a movie. They make driving a hazard almost too great to take on. The minute a red light shows, they stop dead, imperiling everybody behind. The instant a taxi seems about to sideswipe them, they swerve desperately over and sideswipe somebody else, usually us. When they are confronted by a mass of pedestrians at the crossing, instead of charging boldly in and scattering them in the orthodox manner by sheer bluster (which is the only way), they creep timidly up blowing their horns, which lulls the pedestrians and ties up everything. They are easy to spot, these visiting motorists; and the only thing to do, we have found, is to nudge them frequently on the bumper, and chivy them about.

NEW YORK IN MARCH

3/2/35

THIS IS THE MOMENT in the year we are glad we're not on a tropical island, staring fatuously at a hibiscus flower or watching a lizard scale a white wall. The siren south is well enough, but New York, at the beginning of March, is a hoyden we would not care to miss—a drafty wench, her temperature up and down, full of bold promises and dust in the eye. There is a look in the clouds, a new power in the shafts of sun that tremble on the roofs of the "L" stations, a seductive whisper between snow flurries, an omen in the cold fire-escape shedding its skin. And when at five o'clock we emerge from the Library, where we are at work on a stark Northern proletarian novel called "So Rose the Red," we stand for a moment on the steps, looking through Forty-first Street to the chimneys in the east, and New York seems a wonderful brisk girl, whose arm we want to take on the way home.

Our deep affection for this galling and preposterous city is hard for some people to believe. Climatically New York amuses us; but an even stronger reason for the town's seeming habitable to us is that it is practically devoid of civic pride and wastes almost no time spreading its own gospel. At noon today the citizens of Mansfield, O., and Tacoma, Wash., will gather at luncheon clubs to bite the hard roll and taste the sweet *coupe municipale.* They will swat each other hopefully on the back and discover a mysterious significance in the latest realty report of freight-car loadings. Here, one doesn't hear the drumbeat at noontime. Our citizens have no notion of establishing, abetting, or recognizing any municipal puissance. When anybody brings up civic grandeur, New York bites its fingernails and gathers wool. Noons are given over to individual stomach disorders and private gain.

MOVING

10/5/35

GOADED BY restlessness and the delusion of greener pastures, we vacated an apartment where we had lived a long time. Four ape men, appearing in the steamy dawn, rolled up the mattresses, collapsed the beds, and with catlike tread removed all our effects, and our ineffects, to the inquisitive street and there wedged them into a red-devil horseless van. They stripped the place clean, to the eye. But as we sat on an empty fruit crate in the living-room, staring at the beloved walls with their unbleached rectangles where the pictures and mirrors had been, staring at the radiators whose first winter whisperings we will not hear this year, we knew that not even the stalwart movers could wrench loose something that was still there, invisible and ineradicable; we knew that people must inevitably leave something of themselves behind—something besides the mere residue of dust and bent paper clips and fallen coat hangers. We felt we should post a warning to the new tenants that there was something in the walls, musky and pervasive, as when a skunk vacates a nest under a summer cottage. There is sponginess about plaster, absorbing love. Not even a repaint job can quite rid a place of the people who once lived there.

There seems to be an uncommon amount of moving and shuffling about this October. Even old Mr. Eustace Tilley* has quit the pale-green diggings in West Forty-fifth Street where he lived in squalid terror for more than ten years, amid a rabble of importunate writers and artists. The old scamp was seen late one evening last week, his hat awry, his arms full of old wall mottoes, an andiron in his teeth and an unread poem tucked under his belt like a sword, sneaking through an arcade looking for new quarters. The load was too great: after a scant two blocks he gave up the search and took a year's lease near the top of a bleak redstone manse opposite the five-and-ten, where he can look out at the Harvard Club from the south, instead of from the north, and see directly into the mouths of patients in

*Fictional character representing *The New Yorker*; his portrait is reproduced each February on the cover of *The New Yorker* on the anniversary of its founding.

a dental school. Downstairs is the Life Extension Institute, and when they make too much noise down there, Tilley can be seen in one of his moods of magnificent irritation, drinking brandy neat and rapping on the floor with his cane.

Possessions breed like mice. A man forgets what a raft of irrelevant junk he has collected about him till he tries to move it. We found ourself one afternoon smothered at the bottom of a pile of ghastly miscellany: envelopes engraved with the wrong address, snapshots that had never been pasted up, a mahogany chip belonging to a broken chair, some high-school examination papers, a can of ski wax, several programs of the Millrose games,* a sneaker for the left foot, a build-it-yourself airplane that had never been built, some samples of curtain material, a catcher's mitt, and a red-and-silver ashtray made from the head of a piston. These objects suddenly seemed to be the possessor, ourself the possessed. An hour later we were wandering dully in the streets seeking lodging in a hotel and passed a little old fellow with all his worldly goods slung on his back in a burlap sack. In his face was written a strange peace.

THE LOOK OF A NATIVE

1/4/36

"HOW," writes a man from Atlanta (who perhaps has in mind coming to the Fair), "can a stranger in New York make himself *look* like a stranger, so that other strangers won't stop him on the street and ask a lot of questions about New York he can't answer?" That's an unusual question, and we doubt that it is an honest one. Actually, strangers ache to give the appearance of

*Indoor track competition at Madison Square Garden sponsored by the Millrose Athletic Association.

natives. The average New Yorker can spot a stranger in town easily. Strangers are extremely careful not to look up at tall buildings, for fear they will be spotted. They are unable to board a Fifth Avenue bus except after fearful experimentation. They overtip and are under the impression that the only places that sell theatre tickets are agencies.

Our own problem is to make ourself look like a New Yorker. Somehow, in spite of our fine clothes and worldly ways, nobody ever takes us for a native. Beggars, street photographers, men who have just located a nice fur piece, all spot us instantly as fair game. We are the perfect stranger. Probably it's because, although we have lived in New York all our life, the place never seems anything but slightly incredible, and we go along with our mouth open and our face unbuttoned.

WALKING TO WORK

2/13/37

FROM OUR HOME in the cinder belt to this Forty-third Street pent-up house where we work is a distance of some nine blocks—in a southwesterly direction. It has sometimes occurred to us that we take an unconscionably long time walking it, the time ranging from fifteen minutes to two hours and a half. Three-quarters of an hour is about par. This morning, arriving at work at eleven-thirty, after being on the road for more than an hour, we felt that perhaps we should attempt to reconstruct the journey to see what the hell went on when we were supposed to be covering ground. There were dim memories of many uninspired shop windows, including an imaginary decision involving a pair of madras pajamas, as between the gray with the narrow stripes and the deep blue. There was a pleasant ten minutes standing quietly with others of our ilk, watching a taxi that had hooked onto a limousine, watching the lady in the limousine pretending she had not been hooked onto by the middle classes.

There was the slow, steady perusal of a small bag of humus in front of a flower shop (ten cents) and the weighing of the question whether to buy it now—which would mean lugging it both to and from work—or to buy it on the way home, with the strong chance that we'd forget to. There was the pause in front of the art shop's nude-of-the-day, in company with the gray little group of men (art lovers all), each of us trying to look as though we were interested in gum erasers and T squares. There was the slowing of pace in front of Charles & Ernest's, to see who was getting his hair cut today. There was the pastry shop, with its fascinating handling of yet undigested material. There was Abercrombie's, effeteness blended with woodcraft; the side trip into the bookshop to examine new titles; the side trip to Radio City to see how the ice looked; the pause while two cats stared each other down in a parking lot. (And, incidentally, why will men stop and watch cats carrying on; women never? Is it because a tom is an unmistakable rake?)

Our reconstructed journey was not encouraging. The wonder is we arrived at all.

THE LURE OF NEW YORK

7/3/37

THE INQUIRING PHOTOGRAPHER of the *Daily News* stopped six people the other day and asked them why they loved New York. He got six different answers. One lady said she loved New York because it was vibrant. One man said he loved it because business was good here. These replies made us think of the fine, clear answer which a friend of ours, a Greek shoeblack, once gave to the same question. This gentleman had got sick of New York, had wearied of his little shoe-and-hat parlor with its smell of polish and gasoline, and had gone back to his native island of Keos, where, he told us, he would just swim and fish and lie in the grass while beautiful girls fed him fruit. He was back in town in about four months. We asked him what there was about this city, what mysterious property, that had lured him back from the heaven that was Keos. He thought for a minute. Then he said, "In New York you can buy things so late at night."

NEW YORK SOIL

9/30/50

AS WE GO TO PRESS we discover that the Friends of the Land are about to hold their harvest-home supper right here in town, in the Statler, across from the depot. Louis Bromfield, the dirt farmer, and Dr. Hugh Bennett, chief of the Soil Conservation Service, are scheduled to speak. We don't know what the soil is like down there near the Statler but it is probably a heavy clay with a lot of Consolidated Edison roots that haven't rotted up yet, and it undoubtedly needs top dressing to bring it back. This is a good month to top-dress, and there is no better man on a manure spreader than Bromfield.

If the Friends of the Land weren't so numerous, we would invite them to our apartment and take them to our bedroom, so they could look out the window by our desk and study a most inspiring example of Nature's soil-building. Just outside the window there is a stone coping that forms the top of a high wall. Three years ago an ailanthus seed came to rest on this bare ledge twenty feet above the ground. Encouraged by light rains and heavy sootfall, it germinated. Its root immediately struck solid rock, turned quickly, and found two dead vine leaves, a cigarette butt, and a paper clip. Here were perfect conditions for ailanthus growth. The little tree sprang toward heaven. Through a long, dry summer, watered by occasional fogs from the East River, nourished by mop dust and the slow drift of falling vine leaves, the sapling took hold. Today it stands a stalwart forest giant, as big around as our thumb, lively as a grig, covering its roots a living soil rich in those minerals and organic substances that only the fairest city in the world can scrape together to take care of its own.

NEW YORK'S COCKTAIL

1/30/54

THIS IS A DAY of fog and smoke in equal parts—a city cocktail familiar to all, the pure ingredient contributed by nature, the poisonous one contributed by Man, the mixture served slightly chilled, with a twist of irony. On our way to the office we heard complaints on every hand: the barber, the bus driver, the store-keeper, the elevator operator, all of them clearing their throats nervously, each indignant that pure air was denied him. One of them said, "Nobody does anything. Maybe you write a letter to the paper and it gets printed—so what happens? Nothing." The city has a debased feeling on its smog days, ill temper and foul air combining to form an unwholesomeness. Buildings fade out in their upper reaches, escarpments grow soft in the yellow haze. Chimneys discharge sable smoke in luscious folds, as when the rich intestines of an animal are exposed by the slaughterer's knife, and the sulphurous smoke, curling upward, quickly feels the control of the ceiling, turns, and drifts down instead, filling streets, alleys, areaways, parks, sifting through windows and doors, entering the rooms and the offices, even invading the oxygen tents where patients struggle for breath. Being in the city on such a day is like waiting, condemned, in a lethal chamber for the release that has not yet come. Certainly no other animal fouls its nest so cheerfully and persistently as Man, or acts so surprised and sore about it afterward. Everywhere common sense and general welfare await the indulgence of the special business and the particular chimney.

COPING WITH SOOTFALL

9/11/54

A PLAN TO BUILD an outdoor dining terrace at the headquarters of the United Nations, in Turtle Bay, has been abandoned because of "atmospheric conditions"—which is a diplomatic term for sootfall. We happen to be a student of atmospheric conditions in Turtle Bay, having dwelt there happily for many years, and we can testify that sootfall does not preclude terrace life if you have any guts. Our own terrace—a small, decadent structure a few blocks from the U. N.—is a howling success as far as we are concerned, and we are in a good position to give the U. N. a few helpful hints on terrace living under heavy sootfall. First of all, you have to get an awning. The awning is not to ward off soot but merely to give the terrace dweller a cozy feeling. It soon catches fire from cigarettes tossed out of upper windows, but the fire is a clubby affair and you get to know your neighbors (a valuable experience for the United Nations, if you ask us). Next, you've got to have a glass-top table and some iron chairs with little thin detachable cushions that fade. Every time you come indoors from the terrace, even if only for a moment, you pick up your cushion and heave it ahead of you through the open door into the living room. If you leave a drink standing on the table to go inside and answer the phone, you simply drape your handkerchief over the glass, and when you come back you dump the soot out of the handkerchief and resume drinking. If the drinks are properly mixed, the soot can lie roundabout, deep and crisp and even, and nobody will mind. Soot is the topsoil of New York, giving plants a foothold, or soothold, on ramparts far above street level. We have a five-year-old ailanthus, a lovely tree, rooted in soot, and we are shocked and discouraged at the capitulation of the United Nations in the face of this mild threat—an organization created to bring peace to the world yet scared to death that some tiny foreign particle is going to fall into its drink.

THE RAMBLE

JUST SOUTH OF the Seventy-ninth Street transverse in the Park, and lying between the East Drive and the West Drive, there is a tract of wild land called the Ramble. Like most urban jungles, it has a somewhat shabby appearance. It is thickly wooded and rocky, and in the middle of it there is a miniature swamp. Paths twist and turn back upon themselves and peter out in dirt trails leading down to the shores of the Seventy-second Street Lake. Except for one peculiarity, the Ramble is no different from dozens of fairly green mansions inside the city limits. What distinguishes it is the fact that, in the magical moments of migration, birds descend into the place in great numbers and in almost unbelievable variety. They ignore other attractive areas in the Park and drop straight into the Ramble. The reason is simple. The place offers good cover and it has water, the two requisites for the peace of mind of small songsters. Because of its phenomenal popularity among transient birds, the Ramble is known to ornithologists and nature students all over the world. They, too, dive straight into it when they come to New York.

On a hot, airless afternoon recently, we went up to the Park to take what may be our last look at the Ramble. The place has been marked for "improvement" by the Commissioner of Parks,* who plans to unscramble the Ramble, comb its hair, and build a recreation center there for old people—shuffleboard, croquet, television, lawns, umbrella tables, horse-shoe pitching, the works. This strikes us as an unnecessary blunder. Almost any place in Central Park would lend itself to shuffleboard, but the Ramble has lent itself to more than two hundred species of travelling birds. It is truly a fabulous little coppice. On a still summer's day, it is nothing to write home about; we found it populated by grackles, house sparrows, rats, gray squirrels, lovers, and one gnarled old editorial writer creeping sadly about. But on a morning in May the Ramble is alive with bright song and shy singers. (Soon it

---

*Robert Moses, New York City's Commissioner of Parks.

will ring with early TV commercials and the click of quoits.)

The conversion of the Ramble from a wild place to a civilized place, from an amazingly successful bird cover in the heart of the city to a gaming court, raises a fundamental question in Park administration. City parks are queer places at best; they must provide a green escape from stone and steel, and they must also provide amusement for the escapees—everything from zoos to swings, from ball fields to band shells. The original design of Central Park emphasized nature. The temptation has been to encroach more and more on the jungle. And the temptation grows stronger as more and more citizens die and leave money for memorial structures. It seems to us that if it's not too late, Mr. Moses should reconsider the matter of the Ramble and find another site for oldsters and their fun-making.

Robert Cushman Murphy, birdman emeritus of the American Museum of Natural History, wrote a letter to the *Times* not long ago on this subject. Mr. Murphy made the following statement: "There is probably no equal area of open countryside that can match the urban-bounded Ramble with respect to the concentration of birds that funnels down from the sky just before daybreaks of spring." Think of it! This minuscule Manhattan wildwood taking first place in the daybreaks of spring! It is no trick to outfit a public park for our winter mornings, our fall afternoons, our summer evenings. But the daybreaks of spring—what will substitute for the Ramble when that happy circumstance is tossed away?

TUMBLEWEED

2/23/57

IN A HALF-DESERTED STREET, on a day of high wind, a discarded Christmas tree came bearing down on us, rolling rapidly. "Tumbleweed!" we muttered, dodging to one side, and were suddenly transported to the Western plains and experienced again, after so many years, the excitement of our first meeting with the weed. New York seems able to reproduce almost any natural phenomenon if it's in the mood.

NEW YORK

6/11/55

THE TWO MOMENTS when New York seems most desirable, when the splendor falls all round about and the city looks like a girl with leaves in her hair, are just as you are leaving and must say goodbye, and just as you return and can say hello. We had one such moment of infatuation not long ago on a warm, airless evening in town, before taking leave of these shores to try another city and another country for a while. There seemed to be a green tree overhanging our head as we sat in exhaustion. All day the fans had sung in offices, the air-conditioners had blown their clammy breath into the rooms, and the brutal sounds of demolition had stung the ear—from buildings that were being knocked down by the destroyers who have no sense of the past. Above our tree, dimly visible in squares of light, the city rose in air. From an open window above us, a whiff of perfume or bath powder drifted down startlingly in the heavy night, somebody having taken a tub to escape the heat. On the tips of some of the branches, a few semiprecious stars settled themselves to rest. There was nothing about the occasion that distinguished it from many another city evening, nothing in particular that we can point to to corroborate our emotion. Yet we somehow tasted New York on our tongue in a great, overpowering draught, and felt that to sail away from so intoxicating a place would be unbearable, even for a brief spell.

14

Whims

CERTAINTIES

1/9/37

SEATED BETWEEN TWO INTELLECTUAL giants after dinner, we were borne lightly along on conversation's wave, from country to country, dipping into problems of empire, the rise and fall of dynasties, the loves and hates of kings, the warrings in Spain, the trends in Russia, strikes, revolutions, diplomacies, the dissolution of peoples; and without a pause heard everything under the sun made plain. We have the deepest envy for anyone who can feel at home with great matters, and who, armed cap-a-pie with information, can see into the motives of rulers and the hearts of subjects, and can answer Yes to this, No to that. Our envy was so strong that when we returned home at midnight and our wife asked us whether, in our opinion, our dog had worms, we answered with a bold Yes, in a moment of vainglory pretending that here was a thing on which we spoke knowingly—though such was far from the case, as we both secretly knew.

SEPARATIONS

6/13/31

IN THE SHORT SPACE of half a block, coming home from lunch, one encounters enough human dismay to keep one from getting any work done all the rest of the afternoon. In a building that had two entrances we happened to see, in one entrance, a girl waiting with apparent impatience and disappointment for somebody we suspected was a man, and in the other entrance a man waiting with just as great disappointment for somebody we didn't doubt was a girl. Whether to go up to one of them and whisper: "Go to the other entrance"—that was a problem for a noonday pedestrian who worries, as we do, about life's haphazards. Further along the block, another incident—this time we happened to encounter a kiss. Not a snippy, worn-out kiss, but an important emotional kiss of longing or promise. It was meant to be a kiss in parting, but the trouble was that in attempting to part, the two got held up by crosstown traffic, and had to stand right where they were in a silly fashion, waiting for the cars to pass before they could go their separate and significant ways. This spoiled the kiss and the occasion.

SALUTATIONS

9/19/31

STRANGE AS IT MAY SEEM, we continue to receive letters from people interested in the problem—broached by us last June—of the correct salutation to use in a letter to a girls' school. (Whether to begin "Dear Ladies," or "My Dears," or what.) First there is a communication from Thomas O. Mabbott, Ph.D., assistant professor at Hunter College, who says that the head of his department writes "Dear Colleagues." Appeals for contributions, he says, are likely to employ the feminine pronoun in the body of the text. An etiquette writer in the *World-Telegram,* propounding the same problem, by a funny coincidence, advises the use of the French "Mesdames," followed, the writer goes on, "by the customary dash." A man in Baltimore writes that the Governor of the Virgin Islands once wrote a letter to Goucher College beginning: "To the director of one group of virgins from another," which we neither believe nor think funny. A doctor's secretary writes that she was once faced with a similar problem answering a letter from a divine who had signed himself "Your brother in Christ." She saw no way out except to begin: "Dear Buddy." Our liveliest communication, however, was from a School and Camp Specialist—a lady who not only claimed that she could tell, by glancing at her files, the sex of every school principal, matron, dean, or trustee in the country, but that furthermore her office was situated right across the street from ours and that if ever we were really stuck for a salutation, we might write the name of the school on a large piece of cardboard, hold it at the window, and she would gladly flash back the sex of the principal. There, we felt, was help.

LINDBERGH'S GLORY

5/28/27

THE LONELY MR. LINDBERGH made the hop without a cup of coffee. This fact alone startled fifty million Americans who have never been able to get through a working day without one. Furthermore, the flyer came down in France without saying that he did it for the kiddies—un-American and unusual. We loved him immediately.

We noted that the *Spirit of St. Louis* had not left the ground ten minutes before it was joined by the Spirit of Me Too. A certain oil was lubricating the engine, a certain brand of tires was the cause of the safe take-off. When the flyer landed in Paris every newspaper was "first to have a correspondent at the plane." This was a heartening manifestation of that kinship that is among man's greatest exaltations. It was beautifully and tenderly expressed by the cable Ambassador Herrick sent the boy's patient mother: "Your incomparable son has done me the honor to be my guest." We liked that; and for twenty-four hours the world seemed pretty human. At the end of that time we were made uneasy by the volume of vaudeville contracts, testimonial writing and other offers, made by the alchemists who transmute glory into gold. We settled down to the hope that the youthful hero will capitalize himself for only as much money as he reasonably needs.

DISILLUSION

2/16/29

AS WE GROW OLDER, we find ourself groping toward things that give us a sense of security. Grimly we hang to anything firm, immutable. For that reason we've always set great store by clocks in telegraph offices—other clocks could say what they pleased; to us a clock in a telegraph office was in tune with the planets, was Time Itself. So when we happened to pass a Postal Telegraph office the other morning and saw a great palpable lie written across the face of its clock, life seemed to slip away treacherously from under our feet, and the Naval Observatory (to us a vast marble hall set in concrete on a mountain) slowly crumbled before our eyes, a wet and dripping ruin in a bog of quicksand.

HIPPODROME

THERE IS SOMETHING ineffably melancholy about the senescence of the Hippodrome—that once gorgeous place. Lately it has catered to the Sixth Avenue trade with such gray trifles as movies, sword swallowers, and pieces of the Wright Whirlwind motors on display in the lobby. Although we know by reading the papers that Sarah Bernhardt, Billy Sunday, and Captain George Fried have trod the Hippodrome's boards, we happen to belong to the generation to whom the Hippodrome means only one thing—the place where, in the long ago, marvellously beautiful maidens used to walk down a flight of stairs into the water, remain for several minutes, and later appear dripping and nymphlike from the unthinkable depths. Incidentally, it is the mansion where we lost, forever, our childlike faith in our father's all-embracing knowledge; for when we asked him point-blank what happened to the ladies while they were under the water, his answer was so vague, so evasive, so palpably out of accord with even the simplest laws of physics, that even our child mind sensed its imbecility, and we went our way thereafter alone in the world, seeking for truth.

OLD COAT

10/24/31

"IT IS NOT EVERY MAN," our tailor writes, "that can afford to wear a shabby coat." He hit home; for a shabby coat is our one extravagance, the one luxury we have been able to affect. Four winters, now, we have crept about the streets in the cold unkempt security of a battered Burberry—a thin, inadequate garment, pneumonia written in every seam, a disreputable coat, the despair of friends, the byword of enemies, a coat grown so gossamerlike in texture that merely to catch sight of it hanging in the closet is to feel the chill in one's marrows. What its peculiar charm is we don't quite know—whether it is a sop to inelegance, a faint bid for a lost virility, or the simple gesture of the compleat snob. Whatever its hold on us, it has gradually acquired the authentic gentility of an old lady's limousine, but without any of the limousine's protection against draughts. All we know is that every icy blast that grips our blue abdomen, every breeze that climbs the shin, feeds the dying fires of our once great spirit; and that as we shrink deeper into the shabbiness of this appalling garment, we find a certain contentment that no tailor could possibly afford us, for all his engraved announcements.

COLONIZATION

5/23/36

AMONG THE UNACCEPTED INVITATIONS that have been kicking around our desk for a couple of weeks is one asking us if we would like to become a member of an island colony—a place "where eugenic considerations would always be central." The letter seems to be from a Mr. Elmer Pendell, of DuBois, Pa., who points out that the typical community in America has now become atrophied and it is high time for us to colonize another land. He is not without his reasonable doubts as to the success of any such venture, for he candidly poses certain questions. "Would we," he asks us, "need to make arrangements to supply tobacco, coffee, tea, wine, beer, salt, pepper, other spices—or could these or some of them be left out?" It is the kind of challenge that keeps us pacing around our room when we should be at our work—pacing, pacing, wondering whether we could be eugenic without mace, whether we could pioneer sans paprika.

FRONTIER

8/26/39

A NOTE HAS ARRIVED from the Department of the Interior regarding the Great Smokies, last frontier of the East. Secretary Ickes,* it appears, has decided that the characteristics and habits of the mountain folk must be preserved, along with other natural features of the region—birds, trees, animals. A student of linguistics is at work collecting songs and ballads, and there is a definite movement afoot to encourage the Great Smoky people to continue speaking and acting in a distinctly Early American manner.

Our government, with its youthful hopes and fears, is sometimes hard to follow. Mr. Roosevelt has dwelt at length on the plight of the underprivileged third—ill-housed, ill-clad, ill-nourished. But this note from Ickes describes a toothless old grandmother who, though she sleeps on a cornhusk bed and wears no shoes, is apparently the Ideal Woman of the Interior Department. They want to preserve her just as she is—her speech, her homespun garments, her bare feet, her primitive customs, even her rebellious nature (she doesn't like the North). Well, who's right? If business is to revive, this old lady has got to buy our American products; she's got to spruce up her person and her home. She's got to have an electric orange-squeezer and a suitable tray for serving canapés. She's got to quit grinding her own meal and buy herself a bag of Gold Medal. She's got to trade the ox for a Pontiac, and she certainly must quit talking like a hick and get herself a radio, so that she can hear the pure accents of the American merchandiser. Yet if she does, the Great Smokies will be spoiled for Ickes and presumably for the rest of us. What quaint mountains will we drive to, in our restless sedans? What hillbilly program will we tune in on, with our insatiable radios? Truly, a nation in search of a frontier is in the devil of a fine fix.

*Harold L. Ickes, Secretary of the Interior 1933–46 and director of the Public Works Administration 1933–39.

BARRYMORE'S IDEAL

8/26/39

WE WERE GLAD TO LEARN in the *Mirror* that John Barrymore has never been in love in his life but is still in search of the Ideal Woman. This incurable romantic streak in Mr. Barrymore, which enables him to be both discourteous to the four women of his ex-choice and idealistic toward the yet unattained she, is a challenge to all males. Furthermore, Mr. Barrymore gave the reporter who interviewed him a description of his ideal, a description which enriches and enlarges the field of American love. He said her aura of glamour would trump the noonday sun, her oomph would be a symphony of tuba horns. With this definition from a member of the Royal Family, Love emerges from old moon-haunted glades and comes out into the broiling sun, where it belongs, among mad dogs and Englishmen. Hark, Chloë, is that the sound of distant tubas?

BOAT SHOWS

1/19/52

THE HEAVIEST CONCENTRATION of New York's dream life is almost certainly to be found under the roof at the annual Boat Show. Here is where more men can gaze at what they are never going to possess than in any other gathering. A man who is born boat-happy dies boat-happy, and the intervening years are a voyage that may never take him afloat but that keeps him alive. Much of the time, he is in exquisite torture from unfulfilled desire, and spends his hours reading books about the sea. The boating world contains, of course, tiny coracles that are cheap enough to be within the means of practically anybody. But it also contains, as many a man knows, the dream ship that is always just out of sight over the horizon. The second-hand market is not much help. A good boat, strongly built and well maintained, doesn't depreciate greatly in value, as a car does, and a man may wait thirty years to realize his dream, only to find that by the time he is wealthy enough to buy the boat, he has become too emaciated to hoist sail and get the anchor. A man feels about a boat entirely differently from the way he feels about a car: he falls in love with it, often from afar, and the affair is a secret one—comparable to that of a young girl who sleeps with an actor's photograph under her pillow. Many an otherwise normal man falls in love with a boat at the age of fourteen, guards his secret well, and dies with it; and the boat is just as beautiful, her profile as lovely, her sheer line as tantalizing, at the time of his death as at the beginning of the affair. When you encounter this poor fellow in Grand Central Palace, poking around among the booths and twiddling with the sheaves of blocks, you would never suspect him of being the Great Lover that he is. He looks just like the next man—which isn't surprising, for the next man is suffering too.

LEISURE CLASS

8/8/53

WE RAN ACROSS the phrase "leisure class" the other day and it stopped us cold, so quaint did it sound, so fragrant with the spice of yesteryear. You used to read a good deal about the leisure class, but something seems to have happened to it. One thing that may have happened to it is that too many people joined it and the point went out of it. In the big cities, everybody quits work now on Friday, climbs into a car, and beats it. That much is sure. Where these elusive people go we aren't quite sure, but they do go away, and presumably on the wings of leisure. A switchboard operator disappears from the switchboard on a Friday, and the next time you see her a lot of water has gone over the dam and she is unrecognizable because of leisure and exposure to the sun, which serves all classes equally. If your refrigerator quits making ice cubes on a Saturday afternoon (as ours did recently) or if you lose a gall bladder on Times Square after the Saturday-evening show, you might just as well walk over to the river, tie a rock to your foot, and jump in. Your repairman and your doctor are in the Catskills, probably fishing from the same boat. The few glimpses we have had lately of highways, beaches, and mountain-house porches have not been reassuring; these are the classic habitats of the leisure class, but the scenes have been confused and incredibly scrambled, like an infield during a bunt. Leisure used to have a direct relationship to wealth, but even that seems to have changed. A lot of people who are independently wealthy cannot properly claim to belong to the leisure class anymore: they are too nerved up to be leisurely and too heavily taxed to be completely relieved of the vulgar burden of finding a livelihood. They, too, swarm out of town on Friday, along with their switchboard operator, and they show up again a few days later, burned and exhausted, ready for another short, feverish period of steady gain, at desk, at dictaphone, at wit's end.

15

Endings and Farewells

IMMORTALITY

3/28/36

THE PUBLISHERS of a forthcoming volume of poetry have advised us that by subscribing to it we can have our name "incorporated into the front matter of the book" along with the names of the other subscribers. This, of course, would immortalize us as a person who once read a book—or at any rate as a person who once *intended* to read a book. It is not the sort of immortality we crave, our feeling being that deathlessness should be arrived at in a more haphazard fashion. Loving fame as much as any man, we shall carve our initials in the shell of a tortoise and turn him loose in a peat bog.

THE LIFE TRIUMPHANT

7/17/43

THERE IS A MAN in Indianapolis named William H. Fine, who writes me letters calling me a quitter. I have suffered under the sting of his lash for two or three years without saying anything in my own defense, but the time has come to reply. I am not a quitter and I feel that such a charge could be brought against me only by a person who is not in possession of the facts. Briefly, the facts are these:

I came to Fine's attention in the late nineteen-thirties, when I won a contest sponsored by a beer concern. I had to supply the last line of a poem and I did it satisfactorily. The prize was ten dollars. My success aroused Fine's interest, although he was clear out in Indianapolis, and he wrote congratulating me on my work and introducing himself as "America's Foremost Contest Counselor." Letter followed letter, and soon he had changed his tune and was upbraiding me for lying back on my oars after my early show of promise. Just this morning I heard from him again. His letter began, "A quitter never won anything but regrets" and then went on to describe the two distinct types of service Fine offers to contestants to enable them to win prize money. One type is for persons who enter contests regularly, persons for whom Fine has a real affection. The other type is for the flash-in-the-pan sort, the sort Fine thinks I am, the sort who wins one contest and then rests on his laurels. Fine prefers a plodder with guts and perseverance to a merely talented man who lacks staying quality.

The whole thing would be laughable if it were any charge but "quitting." Fine assumes, somewhat presumptuously, that he knows all about me. He has sized me up as a one-timer, a one-prize Johnny. The plain fact is, I am a prize-winning fool, victor of a score of contests. Fine just happened to run across me in the beer job, but he was thirty years late. I began winning prizes in 1909, have been at it steadily ever since, and expect to win many more in years to come. At the moment I am vacillating between the Alexander Smith & Sons Carpet Co.'s thousand-dollar award for the best letter on "How We Hope to Fix Up Our Home After the War" and the Harper ten-thousand-dollar prize for the best novel by a writer who had not been published prior to January 1, 1924. I shall enter one or the other. But that's in the future, of course, and has an element of uncertainty about it, whereas the past, my past, is something else again. My past is a kaleidoscope in which triumph follows triumph in intricate patterns of prodigious light. My past is an open book, which Fine obviously has not taken the trouble to read.

The first award I ever received for meritorious work was from the *Woman's Home Companion*. The year, as I say, was 1909, or "Oughty Nine" as it was then known. The prize was a copy of "Rab and His Friends," by John Brown, M.D. I can't seem to recall what I had to do to win it, but I think likely it was a literary contest. I was something of a writer in those days, as well as a dabbler in the other arts. I still have the postcard which brought me the tidings of that first victory. It is signed "Aunt Janet." "Assuring you of my constant interest in your work and hoping to see more of it from time to time, Very affectionately, Aunt Janet."

Well, what about that, Fine?

What about the silver badge I copped from the St. Nicholas League?* What about the gold badge? Let me see your badge, Fine! I have a feeling you never even won honorable mention in the puzzles division. Who are you, anyway, to be calling me a quitter?

My next smashing success in the contest world came in my high-school days. New York State (or it might have been Cornell University, I can't seem to remember which) was holding out a pretty plum to the winners of a special examination which had been trumped up out of the entire field of human knowledge. The prize was six hundred dollars' worth of tuition, or fun, at Ithaca. There were four of these prizes to be distributed, one to each assembly district. I took the exam and finished in fifth place, which would have left me out in the cold but for a most unusual and suspicious occurrence. It seems, Fine, that somebody had just divided one of the assembly districts in two, making five districts. A quick stroke of the pen on a wall map somewhere, and I drew the six hundred dollars. That's the kind of contestant I am, buddies with Lady Luck, my mouth bulging with silver spoons. I have never known who was responsible for cutting the district in two but have always assumed it was one of my relatives. We were a close bunch and pulled together. Still, it was none of my business and I never pried into it.

The prize money took me to college, where I would have gone anyway, as I was a well-heeled little customer who had gone after the scholarship from pure greed. At Cornell I promptly set to work entering other contests. I went out for track, and I am sorry to say, Fine, that in this particular field your accusation is justified: I quit track. I quit all right, but it wasn't because I couldn't run fast, it was on account of a pair of track shoes I had bought from a merchant named Dick Couch. They didn't fit, that's the long and short of it. Whenever

*The silver badge was for "A Winter Walk," published in *St. Nicholas*, June 1911: 757; the gold badge was for "A True Dog Story," *St. Nicholas*, Sept. 1914: 1045.

I wore them I was in torture, and I kept trying to persuade Couch to change them for another pair but he never would, so I spent all my time racing between Couch's store and my room in North Baker Hall and never had time to participate in any of the formal athletic contests. Of course, it is not for me to say that I would have won any of those races. Nevertheless, I was a swift thing on two legs and as light as a feather.

What about the way I came through with the winning sonnet in the Bowling Green contest in the old New York *Evening Post*? Surely you didn't miss that tourney, Fine? The track experience had been a hard blow but it didn't break my spirit and I did *not* quit. I was right in there pitching when Christopher Morley announced a sonnet contest. The prize was a book—one of his own, as a matter of fact. If you have never read that sonnet, Fine, get it and read it.* It will take your breath away. Meritorious as all hell. Fourteen big lines, every one of them a money-winner. Quitter, eh? Quitter my eye. Have you ever written a sonnet when your feet were killing you? A man who can go four years with a pair of track shoes that bind him across the toe and still turn out a workmanlike poem is no quitter. Not in my dull lexicon.

What about the first horse I ever bet on? That was in Lexington, Kentucky, where I had gone to seek my fortune in an atmosphere favorable to the competitive spirit. (I had held three or four jobs around New York that winter, but they were prosy things at best and I felt I was losing my fine edge so I got out.) My first horse was a female named Auntie May. She was an odd-looking animal and an eleven-to-one shot, but there was this to be said for her—she came in first. Perhaps you are the type of man, Fine, who doesn't recognize betting as a contest. You would if you had to run around the track twice, the way the horses did. Kentucky was lovely that spring. I got twenty-two dollars from the contest and would have let it go at that if I had not chanced to fall in with some insatiable people who were on their way to Louisville to enter other contests. Sport of kings, Fine. I went along with them. It seems I got hooked in Louisville. The Derby was a little too big for me, I guess. Easy come, easy go. But I didn't quit. I was temporarily without money but I still had a sonnet or two up my sleeve. After the

*"Bantam and I," *New York Evening Post* 17 Nov. 1923: 10.

race I returned to my hotel (I didn't say I was registered there, I said I returned to my hotel) and wrote a fourteen-line tribute to Morvich, the winning horse, and later that evening sold it to a surprised but accommodating city editor. If you will look in the Louisville *Herald* for Sunday, May 14, 1922, you will find my sonnet and will see how a young, inexperienced man can lose a horse race but still win enough money to get out of town. You needn't thumb all through the paper, Fine, it's right on the front page, in a two-column box.

Kentucky was indeed lovely that spring. Exhausted from my successes and my trials, I spent quite a while just wandering around the state and will always remember one little valley where the whippoorwills—but don't let me digress.

My next contest was in Minneapolis. True to form I blew into town just as a limerick contest was in full swing. I came through magnificently. The Minneapolis *Journal* was offering twenty-five dollars for a last line for a limerick, and I had that knack. A man has to live. The *Journal* was in search of a suitable conclusion for the following limerick:

> A young man who liked to rock boats
> In order to get people's goats
>   Gave just one more rock
>   Then suffered a shock

To thousands of residents of Minneapolis, this was a poser, but it was just my oyster. I sent in the surefire line "A bubble the spot now denotes." It rhymed, it was the right metre, and it was catchy. It had the mark on it of an experienced prize-winner. Apparently there was no question among the judges, once they came upon it. From among the thousands of other entries, it stood out as though etched in flame. The money was very welcome, when I received it, and as a matter of fact I could have used fifty rather than twenty-five, because I managed to dislocate my elbow about that time (no contest, just straight sailing) and was in the clutches of a medical man. I often think of those other Minneapolitans who got only honorable mention from all the effort they put into that contest—Stephen H. Brown, O. A. Glasow, Minnie R. Long, V. M. Arbogast, M. D. Rudolph. Talented people, all of them, but lacking that curious spark that touches off a genuine money-winner.

After my Minneapolis triumph there was a lapse of several years, a dull period, Fine, when I lay fallow and roused myself only long enough to produce a few listless pentameters in praise of coffee for some sort of promotion scheme cooked up by the caffeine interests. But once a contestant always a contestant. In 1929 I was again active in prize circles. I won the gold watch offered by Franklin P. Adams for the best "Conning Tower" poem of the year.* What if the watch doesn't keep time any more, I won it, didn't I? Who wants to know what time it is? It's no trick, in this world, to find out what time it is—you can glance into any barbershop—the trick is to win something. Then the beer concern came along and I ran away with that. The end is not in sight. About a year ago I spent a good deal of time working on the Ten Crown Activated Charcoal Gum gold-watch award for the best line to go with "Ten Crown Gum Helps Keep Teeth White" but got distracted by the Harper-125th-anniversary-twelve-thousand-dollar prize for the best piece of non-fiction. I hung fire so long I missed the bus in both contests. Chewing gum got scarce and the Ten Crown people either went off the air entirely or else my battery set got so run down I couldn't hear it any more, and the Harper offer expired.

This year, as I say, I am hesitating between the Alex Smith Dream Home contest and the Harper fiction thing. As I write this, I have only sixteen days to go on the Harper novel, but I have thought of a last line and I figure that if a man has a good last line he can build up the preliminary stuff in short order. I am also in line for an award from "Information Please"—they still have a question of mine. I asked them if they could tell the difference between a sow, a shoat, a boar, a pig, a hog, a gilt, and a barrow. So far they have not used the question and I can only assume that it is a little too hard for them. They're always shying away from things they don't know and getting back to Gilbert and Sullivan.

Well, I have spread my record before you, Fine. I'm not making any exorbitant claims for myself. In fact, I'm just an ordinary fellow in many ways, but I want to make it plain that

---

*"The Twentieth Century Gets Through," *New York World* 4 Dec. 1929: 13.

this is not the record of a quitter and I shall expect you to stop
using that word about me. When I decide to quit in the great
contest of life, I'll drop you a card. Maybe I'll sign it Aunt Janet.
Meantime, I'll thank you to mind your manners.

DOOMSDAY

11/17/45

THE WORLD, says Wells,* is at the end of its tether. "The end
of everything we call life is close at hand," he writes in his last
literary statement, distributed by International News Service.
We note, however, that Mr. Wells went to the trouble of taking
out a world copyright on his world's-end article. A prophet who
was firmly convinced that the jig was up wouldn't feel any need
of protecting his rights. We charge Mr. Wells with trying to
play doom both ways.

Wells has been a good prophet, as prophets go, and his crys-
tal-gazing is not to be sniffed at. And even lesser prophets,
these days, can feel that "frightful queerness" that he says has
come into life. At the risk, however, of seeming to suggest the
continuance of life on earth, we must admit that we found the
Wells article unconvincing in places. It is not clear yet, at any
rate, whether the world is at the end of its tether or whether
Wells is merely at the end of his. His description is not so much
of the end of life in the world as of the end of his ability to figure
life out. The two are not necessarily identical.

Wells is seventy-nine, and it is possible, of course, that he
confuses his own terminal sensations with universal twilight,
and that his doom is merely a case of mistaken identity. Most
writers find the world and themselves practically interchange-

*H. G. Wells, *Mind at the End of Its Tether* (London: Heinemann, 1945).

able, and in a sense the world dies every time a writer dies, because, if he is any good, he has been wet nurse to humanity during his entire existence and has held earth close around him, like the little obstetrical toad that goes about with a cluster of eggs attached to his legs. We hope Mr. Wells is wrong for once and that man is not the suicide he looks at the moment. Man is unpredictable, despite Mr. Wells' good record. On Monday, man may be hysterical with doom, and on Tuesday you will find him opening the Doomsday Bar & Grill and settling down for another thousand years of terrifying queerness.

H. W. ROSS

12/15/51

ROSS* DIED IN BOSTON, unexpectedly, on the night of December 6th, and we are writing this in New York (unexpectedly) on the morning of December 7th. This is known, in these offices that Ross was so fond of, as a jam. Ross always knew when we were in a jam, and usually got on the phone to offer advice and comfort and support. When our phone rang just now, and in that split second before the mind focusses, we thought, "Good! Here it comes!" But this old connection is broken beyond fixing. The phone has lost its power to explode at the right moment and in the right way.

Actually, things are not going as badly as they might; the sheet of copy paper in the machine is not as hard to face as we feared. Sometimes a love letter writes itself, and we love Ross so, and bear him such respect, that these quick notes, which purport to record the sorrow that runs through here and dis-

---

*Harold Ross founded *The New Yorker* in 1925 and was editor until his death. Katharine and E. B. White maintained a close personal friendship with Ross in addition to working with him at the magazine.

solves so many people, cannot possibly seem overstated or silly. Ross, even on this terrible day, is a hard man to keep quiet; he obtrudes—his face, his voice, his manner, even his amused interest in the critical proceedings. If he were accorded the questionable privilege of stopping by here for a few minutes, he would gorge himself on the minor technical problems that a magazine faces when it must do something in a hurry and against some sort of odds—in this case, emotional ones of almost overpowering weight. He would be far more interested in the grinding of the machinery than in what was being said about him.

All morning, people have wandered in and out of our cell, some tearfully, some guardedly, some boisterously, most of them long-time friends in various stages of repair. We have amused ourself thinking of Ross's reaction to this flow. "Never bother a writer" was one of his strongest principles. He used to love to drop in, himself, and sit around, but was uneasy the whole time because of the carking feeling that if only he would get up and go away, we might settle down to work and produce something. To him, a writer at work, whether in the office or anywhere in the outside world, was an extraordinarily interesting, valuable, but fragile object; and he half expected it to fall into a thousand pieces at any moment.

The report of Ross's death came over the telephone in a three-word sentence that somehow managed to embody all the faults that Ross devoted his life to correcting. A grief-stricken friend in Boston, charged with the task of spreading the news but too dazed to talk sensibly, said, "It's all over." He meant that Ross was dead, but the listener took it to mean that the operation was over. Here, in three easy words, were the ambiguity, the euphemistic softness, the verbal infirmity that Harold W. Ross spent his life thrusting at. Ross regarded every sentence as the enemy, and believed that if a man watched closely enough, he would discover the vulnerable spot, the essential weakness. He devoted his life to making the weak strong—a rather specialized form of blood transfusion, to be sure, but one that he believed in with such a consuming passion that his spirit infected others and inspired them, and lifted them. Whatever it was, this contagion, this vapor in these marshes, it spread. None escaped it. Nor is it likely to be dissipated in a hurry.

His ambition was to publish one good magazine, not a string

of successful ones, and he thought of *The New Yorker* as a sort of movement. He came equipped with not much knowledge and only two books—Webster's Dictionary and Fowler's "Modern English Usage." These books were his history, his geography, his literature, his art, his music, his everything. Some people found Ross's scholastic deficiencies quite appalling, and were not sure they had met the right man. But he was the right man, and the only question was whether the other fellow was capable of being tuned to Ross's vibrations. Ross had a thing that is at least as good as, and sometimes better than, knowledge: he had a sort of natural drive in the right direction, plus a complete respect for the work and ideas and opinions of others. It took a little while to get on to the fact that Ross, more violently than almost anybody, was proceeding in a good direction, and carrying others along with him, under torrential conditions. He was like a boat being driven at the mercy of some internal squall, a disturbance he himself only half understood, and of which he was at times suspicious.

In a way, he was a lucky man. For a monument he has the magazine to date—one thousand three hundred and ninety-nine issues, born in the toil and pain that can be appreciated only by those who helped in the delivery room. These are his. They stand, unchangeable and open for inspection. We are, of course, not in a position to estimate the monument, even if we were in the mood to. But we are able to state one thing unequivocally: Ross set up a great target and pounded himself to pieces trying to hit it square in the middle. His dream was a simple dream; it was pure and had no frills: he wanted the magazine to be good, to be funny, and to be fair.

We say he was lucky. Some people cordially disliked him. Some were amused but not impressed. And then, last, there are the ones we have been seeing today, the ones who loved him and had him for a friend—people he looked after, and who looked after him. These last are the ones who worked close enough to him, and long enough with him, to cross over the barrier reef of noisy shallows that ringed him, into the lagoon that was Ross himself—a rewarding, and even enchanting, and relatively quiet place, utterly trustworthy as an anchorage. Maybe these people had all the luck. The entrance wasn't always easy to find.

He left a note on our desk one day apropos of something that had pleased him in the magazine. The note simply said, "I am encouraged to go on." That is about the way we feel today, because of his contribution. We are encouraged to go on.

When you took leave of Ross, after a calm or stormy meeting, he always ended with the phrase that has become as much a part of the office as the paint on the walls. He would wave his limp hand, gesturing you away. "All right," he would say. "God bless you." Considering Ross's temperament and habits, this was a rather odd expression. He usually took God's name in vain if he took it at all. But when he sent you away with this benediction, which he uttered briskly and affectionately, and in which he and God seemed all scrambled together, it carried a warmth and sincerity that never failed to carry over. The words are so familiar to his helpers and friends here that they provide the only possible way to conclude this hasty notice and to take our leave. We cannot convey his manner. But with much love in our heart, we say, for everybody, "All right, Ross. God bless you!"

JAMES THURBER

11/11/61

I AM ONE OF THE LUCKY ONES: I knew him before blindness hit him, before fame hit him, and I tend always to think of him as a young artist in a small office in a big city, with all the world still ahead. It was a fine thing to be young and at work in New York for a new magazine when Thurber was young and at work, and I will always be glad that this happened to me.

It was fortunate that we got on well; the office we shared was the size of a hall bedroom. There was just room enough for two men, two typewriters, and a stack of copy paper. The copy paper disappeared at a scandalous rate—not because our production was high (although it was) but because Thurber used copy paper as the natural receptacle for discarded sorrows, immediate joys, stale dreams, golden prophecies, and messages

233

of good cheer to the outside world and to fellow-workers. His mind was never at rest, and his pencil was connected to his mind by the best conductive tissue I have ever seen in action. The whole world knows what a funny man he was, but you had to sit next to him day after day to understand the extravagance of his clowning, the wildness and subtlety of his thinking, and the intensity of his interest in others and his sympathy for their dilemmas—dilemmas that he instantly enlarged, put in focus, and made immortal, just as he enlarged and made immortal the strange goings on in the Ohio home of his boyhood. His waking dreams and his sleeping dreams commingled shamelessly and uproariously. Ohio was never far from his thoughts, and when he received a medal from his home state in 1953, he wrote, "The clocks that strike in my dreams are often the clocks of Columbus." It is a beautiful sentence and a revealing one.

He was both a practitioner of humor and a defender of it. The day he died, I came on a letter from him, dictated to a secretary and signed in pencil with his sightless and enormous "Jim." "Every time is a time for humor," he wrote. "I write humor the way a surgeon operates, because it is a livelihood, because I have a great urge to do it, because many interesting challenges are set up, and because I have the hope it may do some good." Once, I remember, he heard someone say that humor is a shield, not a sword, and it made him mad. He wasn't going to have anyone beating his sword into a shield. That "surgeon," incidentally, is pure Mitty. During his happiest years, Thurber did not write the way a surgeon operates, he wrote the way a child skips rope, the way a mouse waltzes.

Although he is best known for "Walter Mitty" and "The Male Animal," the book of his I like best is "The Last Flower." In it you will find his faith in the renewal of life, his feeling for the beauty and fragility of life on earth. Like all good writers, he fashioned his own best obituary notice. Nobody else can add to the record, much as he might like to. And of all the flowers, real and figurative, that will find their way to Thurber's last resting place, the one that will remain fresh and wiltproof is the little flower he himself drew, on the last page of that lovely book.

JOHN F. KENNEDY

11/30/63

WHEN WE THINK OF HIM, he is without a hat, standing in the wind and the weather. He was impatient of topcoats and hats, preferring to be exposed, and he was young enough and tough enough to confront and to enjoy the cold and the wind of these times, whether the winds of nature or the winds of political circumstance and national danger. He died of exposure, but in a way that he would have settled for—in the line of duty, and with his friends and enemies all around, supporting him and shooting at him. It can be said of him, as of few men in a like position, that he did not fear the weather, and did not trim his sails, but instead challenged the wind itself, to improve its direction and to cause it to blow more softly and more kindly over the world and its people.

SELECTIVE BIBLIOGRAPHY

I. PRIMARY SOURCES: E. B. WHITE

A. Books

Another Ho Hum: More Newsbreaks from The New Yorker. New York: Farrar, 1932.

Charlotte's Web. New York: Harper, 1952.

An E. B. White Reader. Ed. William W. Watt and Robert W. Bradford. New York: Harper, 1966.

The Elements of Style by William Strunk, Jr., and E. B. White. New York: Macmillan, 1959; 2nd rev., 1972; 3rd rev., 1979.

Essays of E. B. White. New York: Harper, 1977.

Every Day Is Saturday. New York: Harper, 1934. Ann Arbor: UMI, 1967.

Farewell to Model T by Lee Strout White [pseud.]. New York: Putnam's, 1936.

The Fox Of Peapack and Other Poems. New York: Harper, 1938. Ann Arbor: UMI, 1967.

Here Is New York. New York: Harper, 1949. New York: Warner, 1988.

Ho Hum: Newsbreaks from The New Yorker. New York: Farrar, 1931.

Is Sex Necessary? Or Why You Feel the Way You Do by James Thurber and E. B. White. New York: Harper, 1929. With new introduction by White, New York: Harper, 1950. White wrote the Foreword, Chapters 2, 4, 6, 8, "Answers to Hard Questions," and "A Note on the Drawings in this Book."

The Lady Is Cold: Poems by E. B. White. New York: Harper, 1929. Ann Arbor: UMI, 1967.

Letters of E. B. White. Ed. Dorothy Lobrano Guth. New York: Harper, 1976.

One Man's Meat. New York: Harper, 1942. *One Man's Meat: A New and Enlarged Edition.* New York: Harper, 1944. *One Man's Meat.* With Introduction by Morris Bishop, New York: Harper, 1950; with Introduction by Walter Blair, New York: Harper, 1964; with Introduction by E. B. White, New York: Harper, 1983.

Poems and Sketches of E. B. White. New York: Harper, 1981.

The Points of My Compass: Letters from the East, the West, the North, the South. New York: Harper, 1962.

Quo Vadimus? Or the Case for the Bicycle. New York: Harper, 1939. Freeport, NY: Books for Libraries, 1972.

The Second Tree from the Corner. New York: Harper, 1954; with "E. B. White: An Appreciation" by William W. Watt, New York: Harper, 1962; with new introduction by E. B. White, New York: Harper, 1984.

Stuart Little. New York: Harper, 1945. *Stuart Little* [first five chapters]. Chicago: Science Research Associates, 1963. *Stuart Little in the Schoolroom* [12th chapter of *Stuart Little*]. New York: Harper, 1962.

The Trumpet of the Swan. New York: Harper, 1970.

The Wild Flag: Editorials from The New Yorker *on Federal World Government and Other Matters.* Boston: Houghton, 1946. Ann Arbor: UMI, 1967.

B. Other Books Edited or with Contributions by White

"E. B. White." *More Junior Authors.* Ed. Muriel Fuller. New York: Wilson, 1963, pp. 225–26.

Foreword. The New Yorker *Album.* Garden City, NY: Doubleday, 1928.

Foreword. *The Second* New Yorker *Album.* Garden City, NY: Doubleday, 1929.

Foreword. *The Third* New Yorker *Album.* Garden City, NY: Doubleday, 1930.

Four Freedoms. Ed. E. B. White. Washington, DC: Office of War Information, 1942.

"I'd Send My Son to Cornell." *Our Cornell.* Comp. Raymond F. Howes. Ithaca, NY: Cayuga, 1939, pp. 11–18. Reprinted in *The College Years.* Ed. A. C. Spectorsky. New York: Hawthorn, 1958, pp. 464–67.

Introduction. *A Basic Chicken Guide for the Small Flock Owner* by Roy E. Jones. New York: Morrow, 1944, pp. v–viii.

Introduction. *The Lives and Times of Archy & Mehitabel* by Don Marquis. Garden City, NY: Doubleday, 1950, pp. xvii–xxiv.

Introduction. *Onward and Upward in the Garden* by Katharine S. White. New York: Farrar, 1979, pp. vii–xix.

Introduction. *The Owl in the Attic* by James Thurber. New York: Harper, 1931, pp. xi–xvi.

Introduction. *Spider, Egg, and Microcosm: Three Men and Three Worlds of Science* by Eugene Kinkead. New York: Knopf, 1955, pp. v–vii.

[Letter]. *The Pied Pipers: Interviews with the Influential Creators of Children's Literature* by Justin Wintle and Emma Fisher. New York: Paddington, 1974, pp. 126–31.

Preface. *E. B. White: A Bibliographic Catalogue of Printed Materials in the Department of Rare Books, Cornell University Library.* Comp. Katherine Romans Hall. New York: Garland, 1979, pp. ix–x.

"Ross, Harold Wallace." *Encyclopaedia Britannica*, 1964 ed.

A Subtreasury of American Humor. Ed. E. B. White and Katharine S. White. New York: Coward, 1941.

"A Teaching Trinity." *The Teacher.* Ed. Morris Ernst. Englewood Cliffs, NJ: Prentice, 1967, pp. 103–05.

"Walden—A Young Man in Search of Himself" and "Concerning Henry Thoreau/1817–1862." *Walden* by Henry David Thoreau. Boston: Houghton, 1964, pp. vii–xvi.

C. Articles

For a listing of 2,190 articles White contributed to periodicals, see *E. B. White: A Bibliographic Catalogue of Printed Material in the Department of Rare Books, Cornell University Library.* Comp. Katherine Romans Hall. New York: Garland, 1979. This is the definitive bibliography of E. B. White's books and articles.

D. Collections

E. B. White's papers are held by the Department of Rare Books and Manuscripts, Cornell University Library, Ithaca, New York. The collection contains approximately 2,350 printed items; 1,275 manuscripts; 3,491 letters by White; 23,384 letters to White; and 5,500 related items such as clippings, photographs, films, and tapes. Researchers must obtain permission from White's son Joel to study the correspondence (requests addressed to the Department of Rare Books will be forwarded for his consideration). Katharine S. White's papers are held by Special Collections, Bryn Mawr College Library, Bryn Mawr, Pennsylvania.

American Literary Manuscripts lists twenty-six other depositories together holding five manuscripts, 75 letters by White, and 19 letters to White: Wesleyan University, Yale University, the Library of Congress, Knox College, Boston University, Harvard University, Colby College, the University of Michigan, the University of Minnesota, the State University of New York at Buffalo, Hamilton and Kirkland College, American Academy of Arts and Letters (NY), Columbia University, Pierpont Morgan Library (NY), Dartmouth College, Princeton University, Ohio State University, State Library of Pennsylvania, Haverford College, Pennsylvania State University, the University of Pennsylvania, the University of Texas, Randolph–Macon Woman's College, Middlebury College, the University of Vermont, and the University of Wyoming.

The *National Union Catalog of Manuscript Collections* lists two additional depositories with letters either to or by White: the University of Illinois (Stanley White papers) and the Newberry Library in Chicago (Dale Kramer papers). Dorothy G. Lobrano in *Letters of E. B. White* indicates three more depositories with White letters: Stanford University, New York University, and the New York Public Library. A. J. Anderson in *E. B. White: A Bibliography* indicates that the New York Public Library at Lincoln Center has a typescript of a White play, "The Firebug's Homecoming." Library of Congress collections that should have letters to or by White include those of Henry F. Pringle, Irita Van Doren, James M.

Cain, Janet Flanner, and Frederick L. Allen. Three other collections at Cornell besides the White collection should contain letters to or by White: the papers of Bristow Adams, Romeyn Berry, and Morris G. Bishop.

II. SECONDARY SOURCES: E. B. WHITE

A. Bibliographies

Anderson, A. J. *E. B. White: A Bibliography*. Metuchen, NJ: Scarecrow, 1978. (This bibliography is particularly useful for its listings of secondary sources, such as book reviews of White's books.)

Hall, Katherine Romans, comp. *E. B. White: A Bibliographic Catalogue of Printed Materials in the Department of Rare Books, Cornell University Library*. New York: Garland, 1979. (This bibliography gives detailed information on each of White's books and identifies White's articles in periodicals, often by indicating from which words to which words are White's. No secondary sources are included.)

B. Biographical Items

Bacon, Leonard. "Humors and Careers." *Saturday Review of Literature* 29 Apr 1939: 3–4, 22.

Benet, Laura. *Famous English and American Essayists*. New York: Dodd, 1966, pp. 119–22.

Collins, David R. *To the Point: A Story about E. B. White*. Minneapolis: Carolrhoda, 1989. (Written for children.)

Elledge, Scott. *E. B. White: A Biography*. New York: Norton, 1985.

Thurber, James. "E. B. W." *Saturday Review of Literature* 15 Oct 1938: 8–9. Reprinted in *Saturday Review Gallery*. Ed. Jerome Beatty, Jr. New York: Simon, 1957, pp. 302–07.

Updike, John. "Remarks on the Occasion of E. B. White's Receiving the 1971 National Medal for Literature, 12/2/71." *Picked-Up Pieces*. New York: Knopf, 1975, pp. 434–47.

C. Interviews

[Lee, Bruce]. "Typewriter Man." *Newsweek* 22 Feb 1960: 72.

Mitgang, Herbert. "Down East with E. B. White." *New York Times* 17 Nov 1976: C19.

Nordell, Roderick. "The Writer as a Private Man." *Christian Science Monitor* 31 Oct 1962: 9.

Plimpton, George A., and Frank H. Crowther. "The Art of the Essay, I: E. B. White." *Paris Review* 48 (1969): 65–88.

Shenker, Israel. "E. B. White: Notes and Comment by Author." *New York Times* 11 Jul 1969: 37, 43.

van Gelder, Robert. "An Interview with Mr. E. B. White, Essayist." *New York Times Book Review* 2 Aug 1942: 2. Reprinted in *Writers and*

Writing by Robert Van Gelder. New York: Scribner's, 1946, pp. 308–10.

D. Critical Studies (Works for Adults)

Beck, Warren. "E. B. White." *English Journal* 35 (1946): 175–81.

Blair, Walter, and Hamlin Hill. "White and Thurber." *America's Humor: From Poor Richard to Doonesbury.* New York: Oxford University Press, 1978, pp. 437–47.

Core, George. "The Eloquence of Fact." *Virginia Quarterly Review* 54 (1978): 733–41.

Cox, Richard. "Nonfiction in the Classroom: E. B. White's 'Once More to the Lake.'" *Conference of College Teachers of English Studies* 52 (1987): 20–27.

Enright, D. J. "Laurel—or Brussels Sprouts?" *Encounter* Apr 1978: 70–75. Reprinted as "Lifting Up One's Life a Trifle: On E. B. White." *A Mania for Sentences.* London: Chatto, 1983, pp. 185–92.

Epstein, Joseph. "E. B. White, Dark and Lite." *Commentary* Apr 1986: 48–56. Reprinted in *Partial Payments: Essays on Writers and Their Lives*. New York: Norton, 1989, pp. 295–319.

Fadiman, Clifton. "In Praise of E. B. White, Realist." *New York Times Book Review* 10 June 1945: 1, 10, 12, 14–16. Reprinted in *Reading, Living and Thinking*. Eds. J. R. Chamberlain, W. B. Pressy, and R. E. Waters. New York: Scribner's, 1948, pp. 180–91. Reprinted in *Symposium*. Ed. G. W. Arms and L. G. Locke. New York: Rinehart, 1954, pp. 329–35.

Fuller, John Wesley. *Prose Styles in the Essays of E. B. White.* Dissertation, University of Washington, 1959. Ann Arbor: UMI, 1979.

Grant, Thomas. "The Sparrow on the Ledge: E. B. White in New York." *Studies in American Humor* ns 3 (1984): 24–33.

Haskell, Dale Everett. *The Rhetoric of the Familiar Essay: E. B. White and Personal Discourse.* Dissertation, Texas Christian University, 1983. Ann Arbor: UMI, 1983. DEQ-07824.

Hasley, Louis. "The Talk of the Town and the Country: E. B. White." *Connecticut Review* Oct 1971: 37–45.

Heldreth, Leonard G. "'Pattern of Life Indelible': E. B. White's 'Once More to the Lake.'" *CEA Critic* 45 (1982): 31–34.

Howarth, William. "E. B. White at *The New Yorker.*" *Sewanee Review* 93 (1985): 574–83.

Lang, Berel. "Strunk and White and Grammar as Morality." *Soundings* 65 (1982): 23–30.

Martin, Edward A. "Out of the World of Nonsense: Ring Lardner, Frank Sullivan, and E. B. White." *H. L. Mencken and the Debunkers.* Athens: University of Georgia Press, 1984, pp. 157–76.

Platizky, Roger S. "'Once More to the Lake': A Mythic Interpretation." *College Literature* 15 (1988): 171–79.

Rogers, Barbara. "E. B. White." *American Writers: A Collection of Literary Biographies,* Supplement I, Part 2. New York: Scribner's, 1979, pp. 651–81.

Sampson, Edward. *E. B. White.* New York: Twayne, 1974.

———. "E. B. White." *American Humorists, 1800–1950.* Ed. Stanley Trachtenberg. Dictionary of Literary Biography Vol. 11. Detroit: Gale, 1982, 2: 568–83.

Steinhoff, William R. " 'The Door,' 'The Professor,' 'My Friend the Poet (Deceased),' 'The Washable House,' and 'The Man Out in Jersey.' " *College English* 23 (1961): 229–32.

Warshow, Robert S. "E. B. White and *The New Yorker.*" *Movies, Comics, Theatre & Other Aspects of Popular Culture.* New York: Doubleday, 1962, pp. 105–08.

Yates, Norris. "E. B. White, 'Farmer/Other.' " *The American Humorist: Conscience of the Twentieth Century.* Ames: Iowa State University Press, 1964, pp. 299–320.

E. Critical Studies (Works for Children)

Apseloff, Marilyn. *"Charlotte's Web:* Flaws in the Weaving." *Children's Novels and the Movies.* Ed. Douglas Street. New York: Ungar, 1983, pp. 171–81.

Gagnon, Laurence. "Webs of Concern: *The Little Prince* and *Charlotte's Web.*" *Children's Literature: The Great Excluded.* Ed. Francelia Butler. Storrs, CT: Children's Literature Association, 1973, 2: 61–66.

Glastonbury, Marion. "E. B. White's Unexpected Items of Enchantment." *Children's Literature in Education* May 1973: 3–11.

Griffith, John. "Charlotte's Web: A Lonely Fantasy of Love." *Children's Literature* 8 (1980): 111–17.

Kinghorn, Norton D. "The Real Miracle of *Charlotte's Web.*" *Children's Literature Association Quarterly* 11 (1986): 4–9.

Landes, S. E. B. "White's *Charlotte's Web:* Caught in the Web." *Touchstones: Reflections on the Best in Children's Literature.* Ed. Perry Nodelman. West Lafayette, IN: Children's Literature Association, 1985, pp. 270–80.

Nodelman, Perry. "Text as Teacher: The Beginning of *Charlotte's Web.*" *Children's Literature* 13 (1985): 109–27.

Neumeyer, Peter F. "The Creation of *Charlotte's Web:* From Drafts to Book." *Horn Book* Oct 1982: 489–97; Dec 1982: 617–25.

———. "The Creation of E. B. White's *The Trumpet of the Swan:* The Manuscripts." *Horn Book* Jan/Feb 1985: 17. (Condensed from paper presented at University of North Carolina.)

———. "What Makes a Good Children's Book? The Texture of *Charlotte's Web.*" *South Atlantic Bulletin* May 1979: 66–75.

Rees, David. "Timor Mortis Conturbat Me: E. B. White and Doris Buchanan Smith." *The Marble in the Water: Essays on Contemporary*

Writers of Fiction for Children and Young Adults. Boston: Horn Book, 1980, pp. 68–77.

Sale, Roger. *Fairy Tales and After: From Snow White to E. B. White.* Cambridge, MA: Harvard University Press, 1978.

Shohet, Richard M. *Functions of Voice in Children's Literature.* Dissertation, Harvard University, 1971. Ann Arbor: UMI, 1971, 72-00297.

Solheim, Helene. "Magic in the Web: Time, Pigs, and E. B. White." *South Atlantic Quarterly* 80 (1981): 391–405.

Weales, Gerald. "The Designs of E. B. White." *Authors and Illustrators of Children's Books: Writings on Their Lives and Works.* Ed. Miriam Hoffman and Eva Samuels. New York: Bowker, 1972, pp. 409–10.

Welty, Eudora. "E. B. White's *Charlotte's Web.*" *The Eye of the Story: Selected Essays and Reviews.* New York: Random, 1978, pp. 203–06.

III. SECONDARY SOURCES: RELATED SUBJECTS

A. Katharine S. White

Davis, Linda H. *Onward and Upward: A Biography of Katharine S. White.* New York: Harper, 1987.

Nerney, Brian James. *Katharine S. White,* New Yorker *Editor: Her Influence on the* New Yorker *and on American Literature.* Dissertation, University of Minnesota, 1982. Ann Arbor, UMI, 1982, DEP 83-08103.

B. James Thurber

Burnstein, Burton. *Thurber: A Biography.* New York: Dodd, 1975.

Holmes, Charles S. *The Clocks of Columbus: The Literary Career of James Thurber.* New York: Atheneum, 1972.

Thurber, Helen, and Edward Weeks, eds. *Selected Letters of James Thurber.* Boston: Little, 1980.

Toombs, Sarah Eleanora. *James Thurber: An Annotated Bibliography of Criticism.* New York: Garland, 1987.

C. Harold Ross

Churchill, Allen. "Ross of the *New Yorker.*" *American Mercury* Aug 1948: 147–55.

Grant, Jane. *Ross,* The New Yorker, *and Me.* New York: Reynal, 1968.

Kramer, Dale. *Ross and* The New Yorker. New York: Doubleday, 1951.

Kramer, Dale, and George R. Clark. "Harold Ross and *The New Yorker.*" *Harper's* Apr 1943: 510–21.

Rovere, Richard H. "The Magnificent Fussbudget." *Harper's* Jun 1975: 97–100.

Thurber, James. *The Years with Ross.* Boston: Little, 1959.

D. Other Items on The New Yorker

Bone, Martha Denham. *Dorothy Parker and* New Yorker *Satire*. Dissertation, Middle Tennessee State University, 1985. Ann Arbor: UMI, 1985, DES 85-23970.

Gill, Brendan. *Here at* The New Yorker. New York: Random, 1975.

Houghton, Donald Eugene. The New Yorker: *Exponent of a Cosmopolitan Elite*. Dissertation, University of Minnesota, 1955. Ann Arbor: UMI, 1955, 00-13784.

[Ingersoll, Ralph.] *"The New Yorker." Fortune* Aug 1934: 72–86, 90, 92, 97, 150, 152.

Kahn, Ely Jacques. *About* The New Yorker *and Me: A Sentimental Journal*. New York: Putnam, 1979.

Kramer, Hilton. "Harold Ross's *New Yorker." Commentary* Aug 1959: 122–27.

Maloney, Russell. "Tilley the Toiler." *Saturday Review of Literature* Aug 1947: 7–10, 29–32.

Morton, Charles W. "A Try for *The New Yorker"* and "Brief Interlude at *The New Yorker." Atlantic Monthly* Apr 1963: 45–49; May 1963: 81–85.

Rouit, Earl. "Modernism and Three Magazines: An Editorial Revolution." *Sewanee Review* 93 (1985): 540–53.

Studies in American Humor ns 3 (1984): 7–97 (special issue: The New Yorker *From 1925 to 1950*).

Weales, Gerald. "Not for the Old Lady in Dubuque." *The Comic Imagination in American Literature*. Ed. Louis D. Rubin, Jr. New Brunswick: Rutgers University Press, 1973, pp. 231–46.